THE ERA
OF THE
JOY LINE
A Saga of Steamboating on Long Island Sound

EDWIN L. DUNBAUGH

Contributions in Economics and Economic History, Number 43

Greenwood Press
Westport, Connecticut • London, England

Library of Congress Cataloging in Publication Data

Dunbaugh, Edwin.
    The era of the Joy Line.

    (Contributions in economics and economic history,
ISSN 0084-9235 ; no. 43)
    Bibliography: p.
    Includes index.
    1. Joy Line (Firm)—History. 2. Steamboat lines—
Northeastern States—History. I. Title. II. Series.
HE945.J68D86   387.5′09747′21   81-6293
ISBN 0-313-22888-4 (lib. bdg.)   AACR2

Library of Congress Catalog Card Number: 81-6293
ISBN: 0-313-22888-4
ISSN: 0084-9235

First published in 1982

Greenwood Press
A division of Congressional Information Service, Inc.
88 Post Road West
Westport, Connecticut 06881

Printed in the United States of America

10 9 8 7 6 5 4 3 2 1

THE ERA
OF THE
JOY LINE

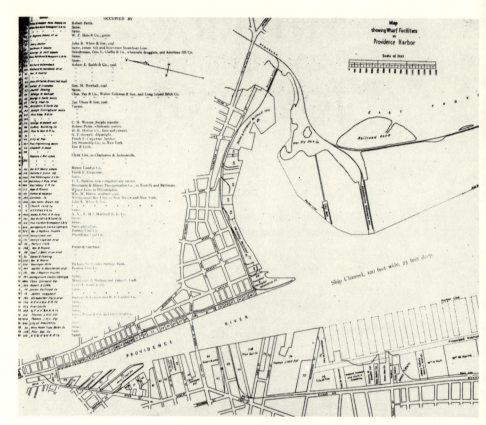

Map showing Wharf Facilities in Providence Harbor.

This book is dedicated to my brother
Frank M. Dunbaugh III
and to the memories
of my father and my grandfather for whom
he was named

CONTENTS

ILLUSTRATIONS

ACKNOWLEDGMENTS

Anyone who has worked in marine history will appreciate the debt I owe to Paul Hensley of the Mariners' Museum in Newport News, Virginia, to Laura Brown of the Steamship Historical Society's library at the University of Baltimore, to Kenneth Hall of the National Archives, and to Frederick Forrest of the library at Webb Institute in Glen Cove, New York, for their extensive knowledge of the materials and their unselfish help in leading me to them. I want especially to thank Nora Lester of the public library in Providence, Rhode Island, for many hours of patient and cheerful assistance.

Donald C. Ringwald, C. Bradford Mitchell, and William Ewen, Jr. were all kind enough to read the manuscript and to take the time to make many valuable suggestions.

INTRODUCTION

The Joy Line was a steamboat line which between March 1899 and October 1907 ran steamers on two routes through Long Island Sound: New York to Providence and New York to Boston. The name Joy Line was not intended to describe the trip: the line was named for J. Allan Joy, one of its three founders, although these men were quite conscious of the advantages of the name's connotation. While the Joy Line was popular during its short period of operation, it was by no means the only line on Long Island Sound or even a major one. Robert Fulton's steamship company had steamer service on Long Island Sound as early as 1815, soon after the first steamboat appeared on the Hudson, and from that time until the 1940s, a period of well over a century, Long Island Sound steamboats provided a convenient and popular means of transporting both passengers and freight between New York and New England. By the 1890s, there were at least at dozen steamer lines running between New York and various New England ports via Long Island Sound. Lines to Portland, Boston, New Bedford, Providence, Fall River, Stonington, Norwich, New London, Hartford, New Haven, and Bridgeport were only the major ones. Although their schedules varied according to the length of the routes, the typical pattern was for a line to operate two steamboats, one departing from New York and one from New England early each evening. Through the night, the two steamers would travel through Long Island Sound in opposite directions, passing each other at about one or two in the morning and arriving at the other port about dawn. The two steamers would remain at their docks through the day, unloading and reloading freight and taking on new passengers, and sail again in the early evening retracing the courses they had taken the night before.

Among the many steamers running on Long Island Sound in the late 1890s when the Joy Line first began operations, those of the famed Fall River Line were by far the largest and best appointed as well as the most popular. The steamers *Priscilla* and *Puritan*, then running between New York and Fall River, were as elegant as any hotel in this "Grand Epoch" and large enough to carry nightly as many passengers and as much freight as any steamship then afloat, including the largest ocean liners.

In 1899 when the Joy Line started, most of the steamer lines on Long Island Sound, including the prestigious Fall River Line, had recently come under the control of the New York, New Haven, and Hartford Railroad (hereafter referred to, for convenience, as the New Haven Railroad). At that time, the railroad was in the process of establishing a virtual monopoly over transportation between New York, America's largest port and distribution center, and the growing industrial areas of southern New England. On several occasions during a period of a little more than a decade following the completion of the railroad's acquisition of the major sound steamer lines in 1898, various small businessmen attempted to run independent opposition steamer lines on the sound, operating second-hand steamboats. The steamboats were usually purchased from the Maine coast or from Chesapeake Bay, where the typical overnight boats were much smaller and far more modest than the floating hotels of the railroad's Long Island Sound lines. Offering a simpler service, charging rates about half those on the monopoly's lines, and seeking customers among lower middle-class people who would not have been able to afford a trip on one of the established lines, these opposition boats were popular but never very profitable. One of the more successful of these was the Joy Line, whose short history is but one small chapter in the story of overnight steamboating on Long Island Sound.

This book is not essentially a business history, nor does it attempt to serve as one. Neither does it attempt to deal in detail with the people, the businessmen in the New York offices, or the officers and crewmembers on the steamers. This book is about the boats, their personalities and their operations. People and businesses are dealt with, of course, and as accurately as possible, but only to provide the necessary setting for the story of the steamers.

1b.

1. The (a) *Herman Winter* was one of three similar freight steamers running between New York and Boston for the Metropolitan Line. They were joined in 1900 by the slightly larger (b) *James S. Whitney.*

2b.

2c. *Courtesy of the Steamship Historical Society Collection, University of Baltimore Library*

2. The (a) *Connecticut*, the (b) *Massachusetts*, and the (c) *Rhode Island* operated on the summer service of the Providence Line until replaced toward the end of the decade by the winter boats of the Fall River Line.

3a. *Courtesy of the Peabody Museum, Salem, Mass.*

3. The (a) *Nashua* and the (b) *Pequot* (converted from the Providence Line's earlier passenger steamer *Thetis*) were the winter freight steamers of the Providence Line. After this line was acquired by the New Haven Railroad, the larger Fall River Line freighter, *City of Fall River*, replaced the *Pequot*.

4. The (a) *Priscilla* and the (b) *Puritan* were the summer steamers of the famed Fall River Line.

XIX

5a. *Courtesy of the Steamship Historical Society Collection, University of Baltimore Library*

5b.

5. The (a) *Plymouth* and the (b) *Pilgrim*, the winter boats of the Fall River Line, replaced the smaller steamers of the New York to Providence summer service in the late 1890s.

6. *Courtesy of the Steamship Historical Society Collection, University of Baltimore Library*

6. The *City of Brockton* was one of the three large sidewheel freighters of the Fall River Line.

7. Courtesy of the Mariners' Museum of Newport News, Va.

7. The twin steamers *City of Fitchburg* (pictured here) and *City of New Bedford* of the New Bedford Line were originally built to carry both passengers and freight, but by the 1880s and 1890s they carried only freight. When the *City of Fitchburg* burned, she was sold and rebuilt as the *Surprise*, under which name she ran frequently on the Joy Line under charter. In 1905 she became the *Warren* of the rival Enterprise Line.

8. When the *City of Fitchburg* burned, she was replaced on the New Bedford Line by the former Providence Line freighter *Pequot* (pictured here). The steamer in the background is the *City of Lawrence*.

9a. *Courtesy of the Steamship Historical Society Collection, University of Baltimore Library*

9b. *Courtesy of the Steamship Historical Society Collection, University of Baltimore Library*

9. The handsome twin steamers (a) *Maine* and (b) *New Hampshire* ran between New York and Stonington, Connecticut.

10a. *Courtesy of the Steamship Historical Society Collection, University of Baltimore Library*

10b. *Courtesy of the Steamship Historical Society Collection, University of Baltimore Library*

10. In the decade between 1894 and 1904 the (a) *City of Lowell* and the (b) *City of Worcester* ran on the so-called Norwich Line, which, in fact, operated between New York and New London, Connecticut.

11. The smaller *City of Lawrence* served as a spare steamer on the New London route after the New York to Norwich route, for which she had been built, was given up in the early 1890s.

12. The (a) *Middletown* and the (b) *Hartford* I were the Hartford Line steamers of the late 1890s.

13. After the first *Hartford* had been sold for service in the Spanish-American War, a new *Hartford* (pictured here) came on the line in 1900.

14a. *Courtesy of the Steamship Historical Society Collection, University of Baltimore Library*

14b. *Courtesy of the Steamship Historical Society Collection, University of Baltimore Library*

14c. *Courtesy of the Steamship Historical Society Collection, University of Baltimore Library*

14. The (a) *Continental* and the (b) *C. H. Northam*, the last steamers on the sound to carry their boilers on the guards, served on the New Haven Line with the fleet modern propellor steamer (c) *Richard Peck*.

15. Courtesy of the Peabody Museum, Salem, Mass.

15. The *Rhode Island* (left) of the Providence Line and the Fall River Line's winter steamer *Pilgrim* (right), which replaced the *Rhode Island* on the summer service to Providence, shown together at Fox Point wharf, Providence.

16. Courtesy of the Steamship Historical Society Collection, University of Baltimore Library

16. The little *Rosalie*, the first steamer of the Joy Line, shown at the line's Providence wharf.

THE ERA
OF THE
JOY LINE

PROLOGUE

Had you wandered down to the docks of lower Manhattan one chilly March day in 1899, all the way to Pier 1, North River, a city-owned pier from which many of the small excursion steamers departed in the summertime, you would have found the little freighter *Rosalie* tied up there taking on freight and preparing for a late afternoon sailing. The steamer would hardly have attracted your notice. She was a stubby little craft of 144 feet, about one-third the length of the Fall River Line steamers. She had a wooden hull, a Main Deck (completely devoted to freight) that looked as though it had been constructed of leftover garage doors, a short structure above that which included the pilot house and a few cabins, and one black smokestack, pathetically thin and placed a touch too far aft. Had you noticed this unprepossessing steamer at all, you might have assumed that she was loading freight for Newark or Poughkeepsie or perhaps even Bridgeport, the route for which she had been built thirteen years before. But this was not the case. The *Rosalie* was the first steamer of the new Joy Steamship Company, and that very night, March 19, 1899, she was to inaugurate the line's new low-rate freight service between New York and Providence, Rhode Island. If you were surprised to discover that this little steamer was about to travel all the way up Long Island Sound and around stormy Point Judith to Providence, you might have become incredulous if informed that in the course of the history of the Joy Line the *Rosalie* would later carry not only freight but also paying passengers on an ocean route around Cape Cod to Boston, often in midwinter. The *Rosalie* was in fact a far stauncher vessel than her appearance suggested, having been built with an exceptionally strong hull for carrying heavy loads of copper from manufacturers in Bridgeport to New York. In any event, the Boston route was still in the future; for the present only the line to Providence was envisioned.

Shortly after five that afternoon, such freight as the new enterprise had been able to solicit on short notice had been stowed aboard, and Captain David Wilcox, a veteran sound mariner who had come with the *Rosalie* from the Bridgeport Line, gave the order to cast off. The *Rosalie* gave an impertinent toot, poked her prow out into the river, made a sharp turn to port to head around the Battery, passed under the big Brooklyn Bridge (then the only bridge between Manhattan and Brooklyn), and, ducking the many ferries carrying commuters home from work, steamed cautiously up the East River.

It would be hard to convey what a courageous move it was to send this little steamer up the sound in March 1899 to compete with such established institutions as the Fall River Line or the Providence and Stonington Line. Only a few months earlier the directors of the New Haven Railroad, dominated in these years by J. Pierpont Morgan, had finished assembling a monopoly of all rail and steamship lines operating between New York and Boston. The elimination of competing railroads and the absorption of the sound steamer lines had required the kind of powerful financial influence that only Morgan could muster. Considering that it was a clearly stated policy of the New Haven Railroad to maintain its hard-won monopoly at any cost and to employ all means, fair or otherwise, to eliminate any form of competition, starting a new steamer line between New York and Providence at that time with one small steamer, with very little capital, with no financial backing, and without New York business connections was not so much courageous as foolhardy.

One reason why the little *Rosalie* dared buck such a formidable opponent as the New Haven Railroad's transportation monopoly was that her new owners, J. Allan Joy, Frank M. Dunbaugh, and Charles L. Dimon, had only recently arrived from the West, knew little if anything at all about Long Island Sound steamboating except that it looked lucrative, and were still innocent of much understanding of New York business practices. Frank Dunbaugh and Allen Joy were cousins who had started their careers in Pueblo, Colorado. By the mid-nineties they had relocated in Chicago. It was here that they encountered Charles L. Dimon, one of those men who always seemed to be able to put one hand on a good deal and the other on the shoulder of the right investor. Dimon's steamboating career had started in San Francisco where in 1893 he had built a small steamer (136 feet long and also named the *Rosalie*) to engage in the excursion business around the bay area. The following season, however, Dimon took his *Rosalie* to Seattle to operate her on commuter routes around Puget Sound. Then in 1897, when, with the discovery of gold in Alaska, people were apparently willing to board just about anything that would float to get up to the Yukon, Dimon sold the little *Rosalie* to Charles E. Peabody's newly formed Alaska Steamship Company (which in 1903 merged with another company to become the well-known Black Ball Line).[1]

Looking for ways to invest the gains from the sale of his steamer, Dimon discovered that meat was bringing high prices in Alaska, since the arrival there of the hordes of speculators had more than doubled the population of the area without increasing the food supply. It was in the process of organizing this venture that Dimon was introduced to Dunbaugh and Joy, who had contacts in the wholesale food business and were always interested in a lucrative venture. Somehow Dunbaugh, Joy, and Dimon procured a load of sheep and got them to Seattle, where they chartered a barge and a tugboat, loaded the poor sheep on the barge, and sent them off to Alaska. The voyage reportedly was a rough one, and the sheep arrived in Alaska in a decidedly disgruntled state of mind, but whatever their disposition on arrival, they sold at highly inflated prices.

Fly-by-night as this project may seem in retrospect, and undoubtedly was in reality, it proved very profitable. In company with Charlie Dimon, whom they always admired but never quite trusted, Dunbaugh and Joy now began to look for a new business in which to invest their gains. It was apparently Dimon's suggestion that a low-rate steamship line on Long Island Sound might be a profitable venture, so the three partners traveled east to New York to start the Joy Line. The Joy Steamship Company was incorporated in the state of New Jersey on February 25, 1899, with a capital stock of $100,000. Frank Dunbaugh was president, J. Allan Joy was secretary and treasurer, and Charles L. Dimon was general manager.

By the time these three western businessmen began operating the little *Rosalie* (II) to Providence, steamboats had been running on Long Island Sound for eighty-four years. The company formed by Robert Fulton and his associate Robert Livingston brought the first steamboat to Long Island Sound in 1815, soon after the conclusion of the war with England made sea travel safe again. The company's first line on the sound was between New York and New Haven. But when the state of New York granted the Fulton-Livingston company an exclusive right to operate steamboats in the waters of that state, Connecticut retaliated by refusing to allow the Fulton-Livingston steamers to enter its ports. In 1822, the company, undaunted, began sending its steamboats past New London, Connecticut, past Fisher's Island, beyond the protected waters of Long Island Sound into a dangerous stretch of several miles of open ocean, and then up Narragansett Bay to Providence, Rhode Island. It was thus forced into an early discovery that the fastest and most convenient route between New York and Boston, two of America's three leading ports, was by steamboat from New York to Providence and by stage from Providence to Boston. The direct route between New York and Boston by sea involved a rough ocean voyage around Cape Cod, which would have been a dangerous venture for the small experimental steamers of the time. A trip all the way from New York to Boston by stage occupied four long days of uncomfortable riding, interrupted by three short nights of uncomfortable sleeping in between. A steamboat ride of twenty-four hours from New York to Providence, however, followed by a stage ride of six hours between Providence and Boston, cut the traveling time in half and was far more congenial.

Thirteen years later, in 1835 (by which time the Fulton-Livingston monopoly had been broken by federal order, opening the trade to a variety of entrepreneurs), the completion of the Boston and Providence Railroad replaced the six-hour stage ride with a two-hour trip by train. By this time also, more modern steamboats had cut the time for the 185-mile run between New York and Providence to about twelve hours (a schedule that remained roughly the same right up to the last trip of a New York-Providence steamer in March 1942). Steamboat owners now advertised that they could take passengers from New York to Boston in a single day, an unheard of rate of speed in 1835. The "day" was a long one, however, and suggests that travelers of that era must have had hardy constitutions. The steamers usually left their piers in lower Manhattan at about 6:00 A.M., made their way up the sound by daylight, and arrived in Providence at about 6:00 P.M. or later. Passengers would then transfer to the waiting cars which would get them to Boston late that evening.

Providence was probably the most convenient port for transferring Boston passengers from the steamers to the trains, but it nevertheless declined in popularity after 1837, for in that year a new railroad was completed between Providence and Stonington, Connecticut. Although it ran only between these two cities, the railroad chose to bear the rather grandly optimistic name of the New York, Providence, and Boston Railroad (not to be confused with the Boston and Providence Railroad, previously mentioned, which actually did run between those two cities). Now passengers could take the much shorter steamboat ride of about eight hours to Stonington and transfer there for trains which would get them to Boston about two hours earlier. By taking the steamer to Stonington, travelers could also avoid the often terrifying passage around Point Judith, where the Providence-bound steamers left the protected waters of the sound for nearly an hour of ocean seas before turning into the calmer waters of Narragansett Bay.

The advantages of arriving in Boston at 6:30 A.M. rather than 8:30 A.M. must have been considerably mitigated by the inconvenience of the transfer at Stonington. A steamboat leaving New York at the usual hour of 6:00 P.M. would arrive in Stonington at 2:00 A.M. The passenger was then expected to leave his comfortable berth on the gently rolling steamer, dress, and board a train for the rest of the trip. Once seated on the train, however, he still could not close his eyes for long. In Providence, the terminal of the New York, Providence, and Boston was located on the west side of the river, whereas the Boston and Providence station was on the east side. Thus, the passenger who had already been obliged to transfer from a steamboat to a railroad train at 2:00 A.M. had to get off the train again at 4:00 A.M., take a ferry across the Providence River, and board another train for the last leg of his "fast" trip to Boston, where he arrived at about 6:30 A.M. in good time, but whether in good shape must remain a question.

Some steamers continued to run through to Providence, but after 1837 the majority of Boston passengers traveled by way of Stonington. A few years later, another steamer line was started between New York and Norwich, Connecticut. But the new Norwich Line did not seriously compete with the lines to Stonington or Providence for the through traffic between New York and Boston. Norwich was the southern terminus of the recently constructed Norwich and Worcester Railroad, which connected at Worcester with other lines leading to the newly developing manufacturing towns along the Merrimac River in Massachusetts and in southern New Hampshire. Thus, while Norwich and Stonington were only a few miles apart, the Stonington Line and the Norwich Line, because of their rail connections, served very different markets.

Stonington's primacy lasted only a decade. In 1847, a new railroad was completed between Boston and Fall River, Massachusetts, and in May of the same year, Colonel Richard Borden, in company with other Fall River businessmen, inaugurated the Fall River Line to run steamers from New York to Fall River and connect there with the new railroad to Boston. The steamers built for the Fall River Line were larger by far and had far more elegant passenger accommodations than any steamers then operating on the sound, and for the next ninety years the Fall River Line steamers continued to be the finest coastal steamers in the United States. From the first sailing of the *Bay State* from New York to Fall River in May 1847 to the final sailing of the *Commonwealth* in July 1937, with the exception of a brief period between 1867 and 1869, all other steamers on the sound were second rate compared with the big sidewheelers of the Fall River Line. On the *Bay State* of 1847, the *Empire State* of 1848 (the year the Mexican War ended), or the magnificent *Metropolis* of 1854 (the year the Kansas-Nebraska Act opened these two territories to settlement), passengers had no need to fear the high seas off Point Judith, for these large and well-constructed steamers were built to take them with ease. Given the opportunity of traveling to Boston on the luxurious new steamers of the Fall River Line, fewer passengers could now be persuaded of the virtue of arising at 2:00 A.M. at Stonington. On the Fall River steamers, passengers could indulge in the utter luxury of lying in bed in a comfortable stateroom as late as 5:30, the hour the steamer tied up at Fall River.

Once larger and more seaworthy steamers had been built for sound service, it would seem logical that Providence, which was after all closer to Boston by train than Fall River, should again become a popular port. But it did not. Aside from the fact that the enormous success of the Fall River Line would have been difficult to challenge, the Providence River tended to silt up so that the shallow channel could not really accommodate the larger steamers. Smaller steamers continued to run to Providence, the most successful of which was the fleet of freight propellors operated by the Commercial Line after 1851; but the bulk of the passenger traffic between New York and Boston tended to travel either on the Fall River Line or, to a lesser extent, on the Stonington Line.

The years during and after the Civil War brought many changes to the steamship services on Long Island Sound. New England's manufacturing was growing at an extraordinarily rapid rate, and the populations of its cities kept pace. While New England was becoming the American center for textile manufacturing, New York was becoming America's major distribution center. Thus, cotton coming up from the South (once the war was over), coal from Pennsylvania, and leather and other products from the new West, as well as the manufactured textiles moving from New England to the distribution centers in New York, tended to travel by steamboat. Many other New England products such as lumber from Maine, seafood from Boston, New Bedford, or Newport, shoes, boots, and other leather products from Providence or Pawtucket, to mention only a few, found the overnight steamboat the most convenient way of reaching the New York markets, so that by the 1850s, the cargoes carried on the steamers began to account for as much of the revenues as the passengers and, on some of the lines, a great deal more. William L. Taylor, in his book *Productive Monopoly*, points out that the peculiar geography of New York also helped to encourage shipping via the sound steamers. When the lower part of Manhattan became congested as a result of rapid and unplanned growth, it proved increasingly difficult and ultimately impossible to maintain large railroad freight yards within the city. Since Manhattan was an island, virtually all produce had to be transferred to barges or lighters, either in New Jersey or in the Bronx, to reach their destinations in New York. Thus, for freight coming down from New England, it proved more efficient in the long run, to load it near the points of origin onto overnight steamers which docked in the early morning right in lower Manhattan near the food and fish markets and near the garment district.[2]

Before the Civil War, most of the railroads of southern New England were small lines running from the inland manufacturing towns down the river valleys toward Narragansett Bay or Long Island Sound and were built largely as feeder lines for the steamboats. But in the era of growth during and after the war, a great deal of new capital went into the development of railroads, which now became one of America's largest and most prosperous businesses, and one on which all others were becoming increasingly dependent, so that by the 1860s the rail lines of southern New England were not so much feeders for the steamers as the steamers were extensions of the railroads. As the railroads became economically stronger and more closely associated with the manufacturing interests, the steamship lines tended to remain relatively small operations controlled by a handful of local businessmen and increasingly less able either to provide for the growing shipping requirements of the manufacturers and the railroads or to withstand the financial fluctuations of this era of rapid economic growth. As the railroads were dependent on the steamboats for their access to the New York markets, railroad management began to demand greater control over the connecting steamer lines. Therefore, during the 1860s almost all of the Long Island Sound steamboat lines were reorganized by interests close to the railroads they served. With railroad capital being fed into the new steamer lines, the 1860s became a period of very active construction as well as reorganization. During the decade, all of the new railroad-controlled steamship companies built new steamers for their fleets, not only larger and stronger than the earlier sound steamers, but also equipped with proportionately greater freight-carrying accommodations.

The first of the new lines was the Norwich and New York Transportation Company, better known as the Norwich Line, organized in 1860 by the management of the Norwich and Worcester Railroad. Dependent as it was on the steamer line from Norwich to New York, the railroad was somewhat surprised, not to say chagrined, when the existing steamboat line decided to go out of business in the wake of the Panic of 1857. To be certain of continued dependable steamer connections, the railroad decided to operate its own steamship line. In a pattern that was to become typical, the new steamship line was an independent corporation, but its controlling stock was owned by the railroad and the two boards of directors tended to have similar personnel.

For its connections with the New York steamboats, the railroad maintained three separate terminals along the Thames. Its main terminus, of course, was at Norwich, but this was too far up-river for the new larger steamers that were needed. An extension of the railroad, therefore, was built down to Allyn's Point, on the east bank of the Thames, where the river was deeper. The Norwich and Worcester Railroad also made an agreement with the New London and Northern (which ran northwest from Norwich toward Vermont) to run another boat train over its tracks between Norwich and New London, on the west bank of the river. To meet the trains at these points, the line ordered two new sets of steamers: a larger pair which ran only as far as Allyn's Point with a stop each way at New London and a smaller pair to run all the way to the railroad's main terminus at Norwich. The larger pair appeared first. The *City of Boston* (1861) and the *City of New York* (1862) were elegantly appointed passenger and freight steamers almost as large as the Fall River boats. They were also very fast, though since the New London steamers, like those running to Stonington, arrived in port at about two in the morning, it is hard to understand the line's preoccupation with speed. The *City of Norwich* (1862) and the *City of New London* (1863), smaller steamers carrying mostly freight, but with limited passenger accommodations, arrived soon after for the direct line to Norwich.

When still new, the *City of Norwich* was sunk in a collision off Eaton's Neck. Although she was later raised and rebuilt, the line decided to add a fifth steamer, the *City of Lawrence* ion 1867, which was similar to the *City of Norwich* and the *City of New London*, although somewhat larger, and was also the first iron-hulled steamer built for service on Long Island Sound. When the *City of New London* burned in the Thames in 1871, the *City of Lawrence* and the *City of Norwich* made up the Norwich Line for as long as it lasted. By the 1890s, however, New London became the only terminus of the line, and both the Norwich route and the stop at Allyn's Point were dropped. But to the confusion of all, the steamers running between New York and New London continued to use the name Norwich Line up to the time of World War I.

In 1863, a change of management also brought the Fall River Line more closely under railroad control. In that year, the railroad which operated the Boston-Fall River boat train extended its tracks from Fall River to Newport. At the same time, the directors of the railroad organized the Boston, Newport, and New York Steamboat Company, which bought the Fall River Line from its original owners. As was the case with the Norwich Line, the steamship line remained a separate corporation, but its controlling stock was owned by the railroad. In an effort to compete with the Stonington Line by shortening the steamboat part of the New York to Boston trip, the new company now made Newport rather than Fall River the eastern terminus of the steamers, and passengers now transferred here, in the darkness of the early morning, to the trains for Boston.

The Newport Line, as it must now be called, also contracted for new steamers, which were delivered in time to start the season of 1865, shortly after the war ended. Although most of the new liners in the 1860s were sisterships, the new steamers of the Newport Line, known as the *Newport* and the *Old Colony*, were not, although they were similar. The *Newport* was the larger of the two and at the time the largest steamer on the sound. Instead of the one stack on each of its guards that steamers of that time typically carried, the *Newport* had two boilers and two smokestacks on each side. These four tall stacks gave the powerful *Newport* an unusually impressive appearance and an equally impressive coal bill. The *Old Colony* was somewhat smaller, necessitated by the fact that she was built around the engine of the old *Bay State* which had recently been broken up, and carried the usual two-stack arrangement, making her not much larger than the rival Norwich Line's *City of Boston* and *City of New York* and similar to them in appearance. Both of the new steamers of the Newport Line were furnished in the new style of interior then just becoming popular which featured furniture made of dark, heavily carved woods upholstered in thick plush.

In 1864, a group of Providence capitalists, led by the directors of the firm of A. and W. Sprague and Company (mostly members of the Sprague family), decided that the small freighters of the Commercial Line were insufficient for the needs of their city and inaugurated a new steamer line between New York and Providence known as the Neptune Line. While they were at it, they decided to start a new service running from New York all the way to Boston as well, taking the longer route around Cape Cod. For their two new services, the Neptune Line outdid the Norwich Line by ordering three sets of three steamers: three passenger and freight steamers for their Providence Line, three freight steamers for their Providence Line, and three freight steamers for their new direct line to Boston. As the channel into Providence was still shallow, the new Neptune boats, all propellor steamers, were of necessity much smaller than the broad-beamed side-wheelers of the Fall River, Norwich, or Stonington lines, but they were still considerably larger and more commodious than the aging freighters of the Commercial Line, which soon thereafter went out of business.

The Neptune Line prospered and might have continued runnings its propellor steamers to Providence and Boston for many years had not their directors, taking their cue from the spirit of the age, embarked on a rather ambitious policy of expansion designed to kill the rival Newport Line. Since the directors of the Stonington Line were possessed of a similar ambition, the first step of each toward the destruction of their rival was to join forces. In 1866, therefore, the Neptune Line and the Stonington Line merged to create the Merchants Steamship Line, now operating to Stonington, Providence, and Boston. For their assault on the Newport Line, however, the directors of the new company elected to start still a fourth steamer line, this one between New York and Bristol, Rhode Island, connecting there with the trains of the Boston and Providence Railroad, which was also closely associated with the new company, for Boston. Bristol was only a short distance further by water than Newport, but much closer by rail to Boston. In addition, the channel at Bristol was deep enough to permit larger steamers than could navigate into Providence.

For its new line to Bristol, the Merchants Steamship Company placed orders for two sisterships which were to be far larger and far more elegant than anything then operating on the sound. These new steamers, which were later to be known as the *Bristol* and the *Providence*, were designed in a style previously known only on the Hudson River, with two full decks of staterooms above the Main Deck and with a large, open balustraded well between them. Whereas these high-decked steamers were well enough balanced for the placid waters of the Hudson, such a design seemed to border on the unsafe for steamers that would nightly face the ocean seas off Point Judith. But William Webb, their designer, was confident. The new steamers, built with exceptionally strong hulls and with large and well-braced hog frames, were strong enough, as their many years of service were to prove.

But the Merchants Steamship Company itself did not survive to see its steamers in operation. A series of accidents to the steamers of its Stonington Line forced the new company unexpectedly out of business in 1866. Actually, only the Stonington Line went under. The other two parts of the former Neptune Line, the Providence Line and the Boston Line, were quickly salvaged by local capitalists in these two cities. In Providence a group of businessmen, closely associated with the management of the former Neptune Line and again led largely by the directors of A. and W. Sprague and Company, which needed a steamer outlet to the New York markets, founded the Providence and New York Steamship Company later in 1866 and managed to rescue for it the six former steamers of the Neptune Line. Except for the two changes in corporate names during 1866, Providence citizens were probably not aware of any interruption in service; the same steamers kept sailing from Providence to New York for different companies.

In Boston, a group of local capitalists led by Henry Whitney of that city, in company with Thomas Clyde of Philadelphia, had organized the Metropolitan Line to run freighters between Boston and New York as early as 1863 and had begun operating a few small freight steamers on this line before the Neptune people began their Boston service. The Metropolitan Line, however, found it more profitable to lease its steamers to the government during the war rather than to run them to New York, and thus found itself with a promising business but no steamers just as the rival Neptune Line went under. Whitney, Clyde, and their backers found the capital and quickly purchased the Neptune's Boston freighters *Nereus, Glaucus,* and *Neptune.* With these larger steamers, their Metropolitan Line began its long and very prosperous history as a freight line between Boston and New York.

Even the unborn Bristol Line was saved in time to begin its operations not only alive but in financially sound condition. This time, unfortunately, the rescuers were not local businessmen with a personal interest in maintaining the service, but New York financial speculators led by the already notorious Wall Street manipulators Jay Gould and James Fisk, Jr. Their group organized a new and independent company, the Narragansett Steamship Company, with Fisk as president, which bought the unfinished steamers at a fraction of their value and had them completed. The *Bristol* and

Providence were finally launched in 1867, and the Narragansett Steamship Company began its new New York to Boston line via Bristol later that year.

That same year, another group organized a totally new steamer line to Stonington. As in the case of the Norwich Line and the Newport Line, the controlling interest of the new line was held by the railroad which it served. When the former Stonington Line failed in 1866, the New York, Providence, and Boston Railroad found itself with little function save to carry passengers and freight from Providence to a nonexistent steamer line from Stonington to New York. Taking their cue from the Norwich and Worcester Railroad and the Old Colony Railroad, the directors of the railroad realized that the best way to assure themselves of dependable steamer connections to New York was to start a steamship line of their own. Thus, in 1867, the new Stonington Steamship Company was formed, again an independent company, the majority of the stock of which was held by the New York, Providence, and Boston Railroad. A new line then being planned between New York and Philadelphia had failed to materialize, and the four steamers it was building for the route were offered for sale. The Stonington people bought two of these steamers, renamed them the *Stonington* and the *Narragansett*, and once again Stonington had a steamer line to New York. They were small steamers compared with the steamers of the neighboring Norwich Line, to say nothing of those of the Newport Line or the new Bristol Line. But the capital of the Stonington Line was limited, and the new company was fortunate in finding two such solidly built steamers at a relatively low price (though the bargain could hardly be compared with the one Gould and Fisk had swung the year before in acquiring the *Bristol* and the *Providence*). They proved sufficient for the needs of the line and ran for a quarter of a century.

The period from 1867 to 1869 was one of intense competition among the five major steamer lines on Long Island Sound: the Providence Line, the Bristol Line, the Newport Line, the Stonington Line, and the Norwich Line. By 1869, the Bristol Line had succeeded in its goal of forcing the prestigious Newport Line to its knees. In that year, the Boston, Newport, and New York Steamboat Company went out of business and sold its steamers *Newport* and *Old Colony* to Fisk's Narragansett Steamship Company. As part of the bargain, Fisk agreed to stop running the *Bristol* and the *Providence* into Bristol, where the channel had proved too narrow for the easy handling of these large steamers. Instead, the steamers would run to Fall River, connecting there with the trains of the Boston and Newport Railroad, which thus did not lose its steamer connection to New York by selling its steamship line to Fisk.

While the magnificent steamers *Bristol* and *Providence* now ran between New York and Fall River, reviving a route that had not been used for six years, the Narragansett Company continued to run the *Newport* and the

Old Colony between New York and Newport, the route for which they had been built, but as a summer service only. Through the rest of the year 1869, the Fall River steamers stopped at Newport en route in each direction, and the *Newport* and *Old Colony* served as spares on the Fall River Line.

Thus, by the end of the 1860s most of the major overnight steamer lines of the sound and their patterns of service had been established: the Metropolitan Line ran a freight service direct to Boston with the *Nereus, Glaucus,* and *Neptune.* The Providence Line ran the propellor passenger steamers *Electra, Galatea,* and *Metis* (a former freighter converted for passenger service to replace the *Oceanus* which burned in 1868) and the freight propellors *Thetis* and *Doris.* The Fall River Line operated the *Bristol* and *Providence* to Fall River and, in summer only, the *Newport* and *Old Colony* to Newport. The *Stonington* and *Narragansett* served the Stonington Line; the *City of Boston* and the *City of New York* ran to New London and Allyn's Point for the Norwich Line, while the *City of Lawrence* and the *City of New London* ran to Norwich (until the *City of New London* burned in 1871, when she was replaced first by the *Falmouth* under charter and later by the rebuilt *City of Norwich*).

In addition to the lines that ran large steamers between New York and the various New England ports at the eastern end of Long Island Sound or in Narragansett Bay, there were several smaller steamer lines. Three of them in particular were later to play important roles in the history of steamboating on the sound: the Hartford Line, the New Haven Line, and the Bridgeport Line. The Hartford and New York Steamboat Company, still an independent operation in the 1860s, operated the steamers *Granite State* and *City of Hartford.* The steamers left New York at 5:00 P.M. on a schedule similar to that of the Narragansett Bay night boats. They entered the Connecticut River at Saybrook at about two in the morning. The through passengers to Hartford were from this time on challenged to try to get a good night's sleep as the steamer made its several stops at the various waylandings up the river, blowing its whistle for each landing, trundling aboard a gangplank, unloading freight, its officers shouting orders to drop lines and cast off, and tooting into the stream for a quiet run up-river for perhaps another fifteen minutes or half an hour before reaching another landing.

This line added the *State of New York,* the largest steamer ever to run on the river, in 1867. She was similar in size and appearance to the Stonington Line steamers, with a half gallery deck topped by two tall stacks athwartship and close together.

The New Haven Line was the oldest of the sound steamer lines and was the only one of the lines founded in the early days of steamboating to maintain the same corporate existence past the 1860s—and, as it turned out, up to the end of the nineteenth century. Since New Haven was less than one hundred miles from New York, its steamers did not run overnight in each direction like the steamers running further up the sound. The New Haven Line boat left New York in the early evening, in company with the other overnight boats, but arrived in New Haven about midnight, where it reloaded and departed again at about two in the morning, the same steamer arriving in New York in the early morning at about the same time as the overnight steamers which had sailed the night before from ports on Narragansett Bay. The New Haven Line also ran a daylight round trip each day from New Haven. The two steamers of the New Haven Line, the *Elm City* of 1856 and the *Continental* of 1861, were similar in appearance to the *City of Boston*, the *City of New York*, or the *Old Colony*, though considerably smaller.

During the 1850s, the New Haven Line came under the control of three private investors: Chester W. Chapin, a banker in Springfield, Massachusetts, and Colonel C. H. Northam and Commodore Richard Peck of New Haven. These three names were later to be associated with popular Long Island Sound steamboats.

The history of the Bridgeport Line was more typical. This line served two railroads which converged at Bridgeport. One ran northward up the Housatonic Valley to Pittsfield, Massachusetts, where it connected with the Boston and Albany Railroad and thus with the industrial areas of Massachusetts in one direction and with trains for the west in the other. The other railroad ran up the Naugatuck River Valley to Ansonia, Waterbury, Torrington, and Winsted, Connecticut. In December 1865, these two railroads, maintaining their separate identities, took over the ailing steamer line to Bridgeport and created the new Bridgeport Steamboat Company, in which the two railroads jointly held the controlling stock.

While the 1860s had been an unusually active decade for the Long Island Sound steamer lines, the 1870s were relatively static by comparison, particularly after the national financial panic of 1873, brought on largely by overspeculation and mismanagement in American railroad expansion. The steamer lines established in the 1860s, however, continued to do a thriving business, and, since virtually all of the steamers were fairly new, relatively little new construction was needed.

Some new steamers appeared in this period, however, In 1873, the Metropolitan Line added the *General Whitney*, an iron freighter 227 feet in length and somewhat larger than the three steamers it had purchased from the Merchants (Neptune) Line. In the same year, the New Haven Line brought out the *C. H. Northam*, the last of the sound steamers with boilers on the guards. But the most interesting new steamer of the early 1870s, and also one of the most beautiful ever to run on the sound, was the *Rhode Island* which was built for the Stonington Line in 1873. At 312 feet, the *Rhode Island* was considerably larger than her running mates *Stonington* and *Narragansett*, but she was similar in general design with a gallery deck extending, as it did on the other two steamers, half way to the stern, ending near the tops of the paddleboxes, and two tall smokestacks, placed close together as they were on the *Stonington* and *Narragansett*.

In the wake of the Panic of 1873, the firm of A. and W. Sprague and Company, one of the major manufacturers of Providence, was unexpectedly forced out of business. Since the Spragues owned a large share of the Providence and New York Steamship Company, it was feared that the steamer line might also be force to close down, but once again Providence merchants combined to keep the steamers running. At a meeting in 1874, the directors took control of the company away from the Sprague family and voted to merge with the Stonington Line and to ask the management of the Stonington Line to assume full management of the combined services. The result was the formation of the Providence and Stonington Steamship Company in 1875, with much of the stock owned by the New York, Providence, and Boston Railroad, which had previously controlled the Stonington Line.

Under this new management the service to Providence was completely revised, a step made possible at that time by a major dredging operation in the Providence River, opening that port for the first time to larger steamships. The older Neptune Line passenger vessels, which had at best carried only a few passengers and not much freight, were sold off. Instead, the company planned to run two new passenger and freight steamers to Providence, in the summer only, which would be large enough and well-enough appointed to compete favorably with the *Bristol* and *Providence* of the Fall River Line. In the winter, however, the line would run the former Providence Line freighters *Thetis* and *Doris*.

As one of the steamers for the new Providence summer service, the line took over the *Rhode Island*, which had been built four years before for the Stonington Line. As a running mate, it ordered a brand new steamer, the *Massachusetts*, which was completed in time to start the new service, with the *Rhode Island*, in June 1877. The *Massachusetts* was of about the same length as the *Rhode Island* but had a much larger capacity, since, like the *Bristol* and *Providence*, she was equipped with two full stateroom decks, which, also like the Fall River boats, had a large balustraded well between them, giving the steamer's interior a look of luxurious spaciousness. The *Massachusetts* was also the first steamer on the sound to have her dining room located on the Main Deck aft of the Quarter Deck (an area generally occupied by staterooms) and surrounded by windows so that passengers could view the passing scenery while dining. Most of the sound steamers carried their dining rooms in the hold, with no windows at all, a hangover from the earliest days when steamers had nothing more than a sitting room on its upper decks, while one large cabin in the hold had served as a saloon, dining room, and dormitory all in one. Although several of the steamers which came to the sound from other areas in later times were to have their dining rooms located on the Quarter Deck, of the steamers built for service on the sound only two others, the *Connecticut*, a later addition to the Providence and Stonington Line, and the *Priscilla* of the Fall River Line, were to do so.

In 1874, the same year that the Sprague family lost control of the Providence Line to the Stonington Line, there was another change in the management of the Fall River Line, through which the connecting railroad again took control of the steamer line. Neither the flamboyant Fisk nor the cynical Gould had been very popular among the rest of the stockholders of the Narragansett Steamship Company, mostly New England businessmen who preferred to keep their unsavory business practices out of public notice. In 1872, when Fisk was shot, Gould became president of the steamship company for a time. But in the same year, the connecting rail line between Newport, Fall River, and Boston became part of the Old Colony Railroad then being organized with Boston capital, and, over the next two years, the directors of the Old Colony were able to buy out Gould's interest in the Narragansett Steamship Company. They then set up a system similar to that which the Norwich and Worcester Railroad had with the Norwich Line and the New York, Providence, and Boston had with the Providence and Stonington Line. In May 1874, the stockholders of the Old Colony Railroad formed a separate and independent steamboat company, known as the Old Colony Steamboat Company, in which the controlling stock was owned by the railroad. Then, in June, the directors of the new company (who were the same as the directors of the Old Colony Railroad) met with Gould and purchased from him the four steamers and the other assets of the Narragansett Steamship Company, which was thereupon dissolved.

The year 1874 also saw the beginning of a new steamship line on the sound between New York and New Bedford, which was later to become part of the Old Colony system. Steamship service between New York and New Bedford had started as early as 1853 and had continued intermittently but had never been a financial success. Here again, the connecting railroad, which was dependent on the steamship services, had to move in and create a steamer line of its own. The railroad concerned was the Boston, Clinton, Fitchburg, and New Bedford. In spite of its name, this railroad did not run into Boston, although it had obviously once had hopes of doing so. In a strange evolution which included a series of mergers of smaller lines, this road originated in Fitchburg, Massachusetts, and ran south on a line midway between Boston and Providence, well east of Fall River, and, after its merger with the small New Bedford Railroad in 1873, reached the sea at New Bedford. If it could be certain of regular steamer service from New Bedford, this railroad would be able to provide a link between New York and the industrial areas northeast of Boston, an area also served by the Norwich and Worcester Railroad and the Norwich Line. In 1874, therefore, parties associated with the railroad formed the New York and New Bedford Steamship Company and ordered two small wooden steamers, the *City of New Bedford* and the *City of Fitchburg*, to carry passengers and freight on an overnight route between New York and New Bedford. These steamers, at 190 feet overall, were about half the length of the *Bristol* or the *Providence* of the Fall River Line.

The economic decline that followed the period of postwar expansion and the Panic of 1873 was beginning to affect New England by that time, however, and neither the Boston, Clinton, and Fitchburg Railroad nor its steamer line out of New Bedford prospered. In 1879, the railroad was saved from bankruptcy only by being leased to the Old Colony Railroad, which was then gradually assuming control over most of the rail lines in the southeastern tongue of Massachusetts. When the Old Colony took over the Boston, Clinton, and Fitchburg, the question naturally arose whether the Old Colony Steamboat Company (the Fall River Line) should also acquire the ailing New Bedford Steamship Company. The directors decided in the affirmative, and in 1879 the New Bedford Line became part of the operation of the Old Colony Steamboat Company. But from the time it acquired the line until 1905, a period of twenty-six years, the Old Colony operated the New Bedford Line for freight only. Admittedly, the passenger business to New Bedford in this era before Cape Cod and the offshore islands of Martha's Vineyard and Nantucket became popular summer resorts was not prosperous, but the main reason for removing the passenger accommodations from the New Bedford boats was probably to divert such passenger business as there was to the Old Colony's Fall River Line.

During the 1880s, the country pulled out of its economic difficulties and began a thirty-year period of phenomenal growth and prosperity in which the steamer lines of Long Island Sound played a significant role. During this era, the small undercaptialized businesses which had appeared in such profusion in the wake of the Civil War and which had tended to go under in the Panic of 1873 gave way to larger corporations whose operations were national rather than local in scope. These corporations were financed neither by inexperienced entrepreneurs nor by Wall Street speculators more interested in quick profit than good business, but by established financiers who managed these businesses with an eye to long-term profits. The business practices of these new capitalists, among whom J. Pierpont Morgan, John D. Rockefeller, and Andrew Carnegie have emerged as national legends, were not always exactly altruistic. In their push for annexation and amalgamation, they often ran roughshod over the smaller local businessmen who had been better tuned to serving the needs of the localities in which they had operated. Both their customers and their laborers, especially the multitudes of newly-arrived immigrants, still too unfamiliar with their new surroundings to know how to protect their interests, were blatantly exploited. Exploiter and exploited alike justified and accepted such practices on the basis of the then pretty much generally accepted version of economic Darwinism: that the businesses which survived in this ruthless system were those best suited to serve the country.

However fallacious such concepts may sound to twentieth-century ears, the country grew very rapidly in the era in which they were popular. And no part of the country grew either in population or in prosperity so much as New England. As the nation doubled and tripled in size and its needs increased accordingly, most of the nation's fabrics (at least those not made at home) were still manufactured in New England and distributed in New York. Cotton from the South, leather from the West, and other raw materials all had to reach New England in ever-increasing amounts. Considering the difficulty, not to say impossibility, of carrying bulk freight through New York by train, one of the cheapest and most efficient ways of transporting it to the manufacturing centers of New England, particularly to the large cotton factories in or near Fall River, Massachusetts, was by Long Island Sound steamer.

The enormous increase in the population of New England, particularly the urban population, also brought new business to the steamers. Many more people on all levels of sales or management were now finding it necessary to travel between New England and New York. Many of these people found it both convenient and pleasant to board a steamer in New England at the end of a business day, enjoy a well-cooked meal while sailing peacefully down Narragansett Bay, sleep soundly in a private cabin, and find themselves docking early in the morning in lower Manhattan, within easy walking distance of the financial center or the managerial offices of the clothing distributors, or indeed of almost any establishment with which they needed to do business. Many such traveling businessmen did not even need to take a hotel room for the night but merely boarded the same steamer in New York at 5:30 or 6:00 that evening for a quiet overnight sail back through Long Island Sound to their home offices.

Concomitant with the growth of commerce and the growth of cities in America was the growth of a reasonably well-to-do middle class, a class of people, in short, who could afford summer holidays or travel for pleasure. Summer trips and summer holidays became immensely popular in the last two decades of the nineteenth century and opened up whole areas of New England to summer visits from the urban middle class: the craggy coasts of Maine, the mountains of New Hampshire, the sandy beaches of Cape Cod, Martha's Vineyard, and Nantucket, the rocky Connecticut shore of Long Island Sound itself, and, of course, for the very rich, Newport and the Hamptons.

In all of these areas, there appeared those great phenomena of the 1880s, which were so closely related to the overnight steamboats: the resort hotels, gigantic white wooden structures with miles of verandahs lined with wicker rockers. For those who could afford them, there were also private cottages. They ranged from the little boxes with two rooms and an outhouse to the copies of European palaces built at Newport, but most typical were the rambling Edwardian summer homes, coated with dark brown shingles and trimmed with white window frames. To all of these, summer vacationers, rich and poor, tended to travel via a Long Island Sound overnight steamboat. The usual pattern was for the wife and children of the family, plus whatever servants were available and a great many wardrobe trunks, hat boxes, and cartons of toys (one can quickly see why a steamboat, which was actually a large and gracious hotel afloat, was far better suited to this type of travel than a railroad train), to depart from the hot city—this was long, long before the days of air conditioning—late in June and remain in the "summer place" until Labor Day and the opening of school brought them home again. The man of the family would usually remain behind, retaining one servant or perhaps spending the summer in a hotel, visiting his brood whenever possible for short periods. These visits would not necessarily coincide with weekends as they would today, for in the 1880s most men worked a six-day week (although working a half-day Saturday was beginning to become popular) and would not have been able to travel far on Sunday alone. The lack of interest in weekending, which has become so basic an institution in American life today, is evidenced by the fact that most of the steamer lines, since there were no freight deliveries on Sundays, did not schedule a sailing from New England to New York on Sunday evenings, the night that most weekend vacationers would have wanted to return to the city. Some lines did have Sunday sailings, of course: the great Fall River Line scheduled Sunday sailings, but only in July and August, and even then it used only one steamer, whereas on other nights in the summer there were usually two steamers in each direction.

As a result of the growth and prosperity of New England in the last two decades of the nineteenth century and also of the increased use of summer resorts, steamboat travel also increased at the same prodigious rate, so that the period between 1880 and World War I became the great heyday of the overnight steamer. Almost every line experienced an era of expansion and construction. But however grand the scale of new steamers ordered, they seemed inadequate by the time they were in service, so that even larger steamers had to be considered almost immediately. The era of growth also brought such rapid advances in engineering that the steamers of this era became outdated rapidly, not only because they soon proved too small but also because technical innovations soon rendered each steamer obsolete.

At the start of the decade of the 1880s, the various pairs of sisterships and near-sisterships built in the 1860s and 1870s were still in operation and, for the most part, still in good condition. The *Bristol* and the *Providence*, the largest and most elegant of the sound steamers, even after more than a decade of service, ran on the Fall River Line, with the *Newport* and the *Old Colony* still running to Newport in summers and as spares to Fall River in winter. The same company also ran the two small freighters *City of New Bedford* and *City of Fitchburg* to New Bedford all year. The Providence and Stonington Line ran the big passenger liners *Massachusetts* and *Rhode Island* to Providence in the summer, the freighters *Doris* and *Thetis* to Providence in the winter, and the smaller passenger steamers *Stonington* and *Narragansett* to Stonington all year long, with the *Rhode Island* frequently coming on as a relief boat during the winter or early spring. The *City of Boston* and the *City of New York* still insisted on confusing the public by running to New London (the Allyn's Point landing was dropped during the 1880s) and calling themselves the Norwich Line, while their smaller sisters, the *City of Norwich* and the *City of Lawrence*, did in fact make the run all the way up to Norwich.

As the decade began, the four major overnight lines were engaged in a rate war. Before 1877, the Fall River Line had enjoyed a virtual monopoly of the passengers and freight moving between New York and Boston via Long Island Sound and Narragansett Bay with the short rail haul into Boston. Neither the Stonington nor the Providence boats were large enough to offer serious competition to such luxurious liners as the *Bristol* and *Providence*, while the Norwich Line tended to serve areas other than Boston. But when the newly organized Providence and Stonington Line placed the steamers *Rhode Island* and *Massachusetts* on its line to Providence in 1877, it was a direct challenge to the supremacy of the Fall River Line. The Old Colony countered with a tactic which was later to become a familiar one. It did not wish to damage the reputation of its own Fall River Line by reducing fares or curtailing services, but on its summer line to Newport, on which it operated smaller and slightly older steamers, it introduced a drastic reduction on through fares between New York and Boston. When passengers found that they could travel to Boston on even a second-rate Fall River Line boat at reduced rates, business on the other lines suffered. After three years in which none of the lines made much money, the three companies (Fall River Line, Providence and Stonington Line, and Norwich Line) met early in 1881 and agreed to fixed passenger rates between New York and Boston. A similar agreement, to which the Metropolitan Line was also a party, established fixed freight rates.[3]

One reason why an agreement had become possible in 1881 was that the Providence and Stonington Line, which had been attempting to challenge the supremacy of the Fall River Line, suffered two serious accidents during the season of 1880 and could no longer afford the expensive rate war. On the night of June 22, 1880, the twin steamers *Narragansett* and *Stonington* of the Stonington Line met in a head-on collision in a dense fog. The *Stonington* survived the accident with a badly broken bow, but the *Narragansett* took fire and sank with a large loss of life. The hull and engines were later raised and a new superstructure built over them, so that a more-or-less similar *Narragansett* rejoined the line toward the end of the season. Although many costly accidents occurred on the waters of the sound in spite of the officers' every effort to run the ships as safely as possible, and although the *Narragansett-Stonington* crash was probably as unavoidable as many others, this accident received a great deal of adverse publicity and did much to damage the Providence and Stonington's reputation as "Old Reliable." Hardly had the line recovered from this first tragedy than the *Rhode Island* ran on a rock near the entrance to Narragansett Bay in November of the same year. This time the line was more fortunate, for all passengers were taken off the steamer safely, but a storm came up the following day and the handsome *Rhode Island* broke up. A good part of the engine was salvaged, however, and was used in a new *Rhode Island* which was ready to run with the *Massachusetts* to Providence when the season of 1881 opened in May.

Early in the decade, both the Fall River Line and the Norwich Line added a fifth and larger steamer to its two pairs. Late in the season of 1881, the Norwich Line brought out the proud and very modern steamer *City of Worcester*, which now alternated on the New London route with either the *City of Boston* or the *City of New York*. The *City of Worcester* was similar in size and general appearance to the second *Rhode Island*, which had appeared earlier in the same season, but with two notable differences. The *Rhode Island*, designed to serve only in summer, had the usual wooden hull braced with heavy hog framing. But the *City of Worcester* was built, like the *City of Lawrence*, of the same line, with an iron hull and was thus the only large passenger vessel on the sound at the time not to carry hog frames. This gave her cleaner, longer lines than the other sound steamers and made her appear unusually fast and graceful underway, although she was, in fact, not as fast as her older sisters *City of Boston* and *City of New York*. Like the *Rhode Island*, the *City of Worcester* carried two smokestacks athwartship, but they were wide apart like those of the *Bristol* and *Providence* rather than close together like those of the *Rhode Island*, the *Stonington*, and the *Narragansett*. Since most steamers carried their engine housing in the center and had parallel corridors on either side of it and rows of staterooms outside the corridors, athwartship stacks either had to be quite close together and come up through the engine housing, or quite far apart to come up through the rows of staterooms; they could not come through the steamer where the corridors were without blocking them.

Two years later, the Fall River Line reaffirmed its supremacy beyond all doubt by bringing out the magnificent steamer *Pilgrim*, the first new steamer built for this line in seventeen years. It was designed by George Peirce who now became the marine superintendent for the Old Colony Steamboat Company and who was to design all of the steamers built in the future for the Fall River Line except its very last steamer, the *Commonwealth* of 1908. The new *Pilgrim*, measuring nearly 400 feet in overall length and more than one-fifth of that in width, was now by far the largest steamship on Long Island Sound. Like the *City of Worcester*, the *Pilgrim* had an iron hull—two in fact, one outside the other: the "double hull" was provided to reduce the chance of the steamer's sinking in a minor accident.

Soon after the appearance of the *Pilgrim*, the Fall River Line gave up its secondary line to Newport and instead began running two steamers each night between New York and Fall River during the summer months, with one of the steamers stopping in both directions at Newport. The arrival of the *Pilgrim* meant that the line no longer needed both the *Newport* and the *Old Colony*. Therefore, the proud four-stacker *Newport*, which had been so impressive when built in 1865 but whose period of supremacy had been cut short by the appearance of the much grander *Bristol* and *Providence* only two years later, was sent to the scrap yard in 1885, while her smaller sister, the *Old Colony*, which was both easier to handle and cheaper to operate, remained on the line for several more years. In the new four-boat summer schedule, one would expect the line to have kept a balance by running the big new *Pilgrim* and the smaller *Old Colony* from one end and the *Bristol* and *Providence* together from the other. But it did not work that way. Since the line ran only one steamer from each port on Sunday nights, it was not possible to keep any pair of steamers running on the same schedule more than six successive nights.

After the appearance of the *Pilgrim*, there was a brief hiatus in the construction of new passenger steamers for Long Island Sound. But with the enormous increase in the amount of cargo being moved to and from New England, the Fall River Line found a need to add a fleet of smaller steamers designed to carry freight alone. During the 1880s and early 1890s, three wooden-hulled sidewheel freighters were built for the line: the *City of Fall River* (1883), the *City of Brockton* (1888), and the *City of Taunton* (1893). In 1885, the Providence and Stonington Line also built a new freighter, the *Nashua*, also a wooden-hulled sidewheeler, to replace the old Neptune liner *Doris* on the winter run to Providence. The *Nashua* was similar in size and general appearance to the Fall River Line's freighters except that she carried a hog frame which they did not. At about the same time, the line rebuilt the older propellor-driven *Thetis* into a more modern freighter and renamed her the *Pequot*; from that time, the *Nashua* and the *Pequot* served as the winter freighters of the Providence Line.

In 1882, a new freight line appeared on the sound. In that year, the New London and Northern Railroad, which had by then been leased to the Central Vermont Railway and served as that line's route into New York, ended its freight contract with the Norwich Line and established a new freight line of its own, using older freighters which met the trains at New London and carried the Central Vermont's freight into New York.

The only other addition to the sound fleets during the earlier part of the decade of the 1880s was the Bridgeport Line's small steamer *City of Bridgeport* of 1886 which was essentially a freighter but which was equipped with minimal passenger accommodations. The term "minimal" used here describes not only their size but also the degree to which they were accommodating.

By the mid-1880s, the Metropolitan Line was also beginning to enjoy the swell of prosperity and to realize that it was time for it also to start replacing its older Neptune Line steamers with larger and more modern freighters better able to accommodate the increasing amounts of cargo moving between Boston and New York. As we have seen, the line had already added one new boat, the *General Whitney*, in 1873. But after the Whitneys bought out the Clyde interests in 1875, they began to replace their entire fleet with fast, new iron-hulled freighters, all characterized by one tall smokestack located just amidships. The *H. F. Dimock*, named for Whitney's brother-in-law, the New York agent for the line, appeared in 1884; the *Herman Winter*, named for the famous marine architect who designed many of the new coastal steamers then appearing, including the new Metropolitan Line steamers, followed in 1887; and the *H. M. Whitney*, named for the president of the line, came on in 1890.

With its unbalanced fleet proving inconvenient as well as inadequate, the Fall River Line asked George Peirce to design another large steamer to serve as a running mate to the big *Pilgrim*. Its plan was to run the larger steamers between New York and Fall River, with a stop at Newport, through most of the year, with the smaller *Bristol* and *Providence* augmenting the service by joining them in a four-boat schedule during July and August, and relieving them during the less busy months between January and May. When the new steamer, known as the *Puritan*, appeared in 1889, however, she was not at all a sistership of the *Pilgrim*. Technical advances had made it possible for Peirce to devise for this steamer a whole new concept in design which was to become the model for all sidewheel steamships to be built after this time. First, by improving a recently evolved system also used on the *Pilgrim*, known as "feathering," whereby the buckets of the side-wheels were equipped with a complicated set of synchronized hinges, which improved their pulling power while reducing their drag, Peirce was able to use much smaller sidewheels on the *Puritan* than were then common on the sound steamers. As a result, he decided to design a steamer on which all of the functional apparatus was camouflaged. By building a short third row of staterooms right along the outside railing amidships on each of the two passenger decks and enclosing the sidewheel housing within them, he was able to eliminate the big paddleboxes and to provide his new steamer with graceful uninterrupted lines extending the full 420 feet from the prow to the stern flagpole. And whereas the "daring" design of the *Bristol* and the *Providence* had called for a full-length Gallery Deck atop the Saloon Deck, a design still not attempted on any other sound steamers of the time except the *Massachusetts* of the Providence Line and, of course, the Fall River Line's other steamer, *Pilgrim*, the *Puritan* was built with still a third deck above the Main Deck, known as the Dome Deck, which carried the pilot house, sitting alone toward the bow. And then aft of the two smokestacks (located therefore much further forward than was customary) was another short row of staterooms in which was hidden the machinery of the walking beam. Since the introduction of the Bessemer process in 1878 had made the production of steel, which was both lighter and stronger than iron, practicable for general use, the *Puritan* also became the first steamer on the sound to be built with a steel hull.

Whether or not one approves of nonfunctional design in general, the effect in the case of the *Puritan* was unsurpassed. Although admirers of the Long Island Sound steamers are sometimes divided between the *Puritan* and her later near-sister, the *Priscilla*, most maintain that the *Puritan* of 1889 was the most beautiful Long Island Sound steamboat ever designed. (Readers are advised to treat themselves to a leisurely inspection of the excellent model of George Peirce's *Puritan* preserved at the Fall River Marine Museum.) Unfortunately, Peirce did not aim for one further innovation on the *Puritan*: namely, the abandonment of the traditional walking beam engine in favor of the recently developed inclined engine, which he was to install on the *Plymouth* of the following year and on all subsequent Fall River Line steamers with signal success. These engines were to prove more efficient, more reliable, and far more economical. The *Puritan*, for all her beauty, was never mechanically reliable. Both the *Pilgrim* and the *Puritan* were notoriously expensive to operate, particularly after the cost of coal began to escalate in the early years of the twentieth century. As a result, the beautiful *Puritan* was to have a relatively short life on the Fall River Line and was to be replaced by more modern steamers after only nineteen years of service.

In the same year, 1889, the Providence and Stonington Line also added a new steamer, the *Connecticut*, to run on the Providence route with the *Massachusetts*, in theory releasing the *Rhode Island* to provide increased service on the Stonington Line during the busier summer season. The new *Connecticut* (at 353 feet overall) was considerably larger than either the *Rhode Island* or the *Massachusetts* and was, like the *Puritan*, one of the handsomest steamers on the sound. But structurally the *Connecticut* was inexcusably out of date for 1889. On the assumption that she would be used only for summer service, the *Connecticut* was built with a wooden hull and hog framing and thus represented no structural improvement over the *Massachusetts* of twleve years earlier, at a time when the rival Fall River Line was abandoning iron hulls for steel. Whereas the Fall River Line might have profited by becoming more experimental with the *Puritan*'s engine, the Providence and Stonington Line would definitely have been ahead had it been less experimental with the engine of the *Connecticut*. For, beautiful as she was to behold, the *Connecticut* was a mechanical dud. The line attempted to use an oscillating engine, which was not generally employed in the United States and was not installed on any other passenger steamers on the sound, although a similar engine had been somewhat successful on the Providence and Stonington Line freighter *Nashua* of 1885. For some reason the *Connecticut*'s engine never worked properly, so that she was to spend a great deal of her short career either laid up and inactive or in the shops for repairs, while the older *Rhode Island*, theoretically reduced to a spare boat, continued to see a great deal of active service on the Providence run.

With the *Puritan* and *Pilgrim* expected to serve as summer boats and the *Bristol* and *Providence* to run in the winter, the Fall River Line no longer had any need for the *Old Colony*, which was slated for scrapping as soon as the *Puritan* appeared. But before the *Puritan* was completed, the Fall River Line's plans were unexpectedly upset when early on the morning of December 30, 1888, the *Bristol* caught fire at her dock in Newport soon after arriving from New York and was quickly consumed by the flames. Fortunately, this tragedy involved no loss of life, for all of the passengers and crew were alerted and were able to disembark before the fire began to spread. The *Pilgrim* was brought out of layup that same day to run through the winter season with the *Providence*, while the *Old Colony* was rescued from the scrappers temporarily to serve as the fourth boat of the line through the summer seasons of 1889 and 1890.

Meanwhile, the company ordered another new steamer to replace the *Bristol* and to run with the *Providence* as the winter boat of the line. Named the *Plymouth*, she was a smaller version of the *Puritan* in appearance and layout. However, she carried only a single stack, thus making her the only steamer in the history of the Fall River Line, except the *Katahdin*, which ran under charter one winter in the 1860s, to sport a single stack. The stack was placed somewhat further astern, above the Dome Deck housing rather than ahead of it. There was only one row of extra staterooms on each side on the Saloon Deck, but not the Gallery Deck, sufficient to hide the housing for her 35 foot sidewheels. In general, each new steamer of the Fall River Line was larger and more modern than her predecessors, and only as it was succeeded by newer and still larger vessels, was it relegated to the winter service of the line. The *Plymouth*, therefore, was the first steamer built especially for the winter service. At 366 feet overall, she was considerably shorter than either the *Pilgrim* or the *Puritan* and comparable in size to her much older running mate, the 370-foot *Providence*.

Only in size, however, was the *Plymouth* inferior to her older sisters. Functionally, her design turned out to be a significant improvement even over the *Puritan* of the year before, and in her forty-seven years of sailing on Long Island Sound, every winter to Fall River and most summers to Fall River or Providence, occasionally to New London, and, in her later years to New Bedford, she proved an exceptionally serviceable steamer. The *Plymouth* was the first of the sound steamers equipped with a triple-expansion inclined engine. As a result, the *Plymouth* burned just a little more than half as much coal per trip as the *Pilgrim* or the *Puritan*. In addition, the absence of the high walking beam placed a greater proportion of the weight of the machinery in the hull, making her far less topheavy than the older steamers—one reason why the *Plymouth* and the Fall River Line steamers built after her were all such excellent sea boats. Furthermore, with this more efficient engine, better utilization of space on the *Plymouth* gave her a freight capacity greater than that of the *Puritan* or the *Pilgrim*, and about as many staterooms as the *Pilgrim* as well. (The *Pilgrim* and the *Plymouth*, as originally built, each had about 240 staterooms and the *Puritan* about 320.) The interior decor of the *Plymouth* in general resembled that of the *Puritan*, although executed on a somewhat less impressive scale. In its effort to cram as many revenue-producing staterooms as possible onto its steamers, the Fall River Line elected not to adapt the plan of the Providence and Stonington Line steamer *Massachusetts*, used also on the *Connecticut* of the year before, of placing the dining room on the Main Deck with windows providing a view of the sea. Instead, the *Pilgrim*, the *Puritan*, and the *Plymouth*, like most of the older sound steamers, all hid their dining rooms in the darkness of the afterhold, below the Quarter Deck.

The new *Plymouth* arrived in November 1890, in time to take her place on the line's winter service. Although her interior was somewhat cramped and she appeared a touch bulky when viewed from certain angles underway, she emerged, in spite of her unusually large capacity, as a lovely steamer. The absence of paddleboxes gave her the same graceful unbroken lines that had made the *Puritan* such a handsome vessel, though, of course, she could never compare in beauty either to the regal *Puritan* or to the later *Priscilla*.

1890s

During the 1890s, the passenger and freight traffic on Long Island Sound began to reach that crescendo which was to peak in the first decade of the twentieth century before falling off precipitously soon after with the increasing popularity of gas-powered land transportation. The decade of the 1890s is also still remembered as the Gilded Era in America or as the Grand Epoch by Europeans—and with considerable justification, for the pictorial histories of the period which are preserved today tend, understandably, to dwell primarily on those opulent manifestations of new bourgeois wealth which were characteristic of the times. One must remember, however, that, while the 1890s were years of great prosperity for certain classes both in Europe and in America, they were years of poverty and misery for the majority. The 1890s witnessed crop failures that ruined many small farmers throughout the American Midwest and drove thousands of them to the growing industrial cities. There they joined the unskilled working classes who were then helping to create the opulence preserved for us in pictures but who themselves were forced into a standard of living that today would be hard to visualize.

Despite the rampant poverty, the overcrowded cities, and the crop failures that characterized the decade, the prosperous world of the urban upper classes, at once gracious and rapacious, was nevertheless very much in evidence, and it was this world, after all, that traveled on Long Island Sound steamboats. In fact, it would have been difficult to find more inspiring manifestations of the opulence of the era anywhere in America than aboard the *Puritan* or the *Pilgrim*, which were then the main steamers of the Fall River Line.

As mentioned earlier, these two steamers ran between New York and Fall River through most of the year, joined in July and August by the *Plymouth* and the *Providence*, while the latter two steamers ran alone on the route during the slack winter months. The *Massachusetts* and the *Connecticut* continued to provide service to Providence six months a year, with the *Rhode Island* filling in during the *Connecticut's* frequent breakdowns and otherwise assisting the *Narragansett* and *Stonington* on the Stonington Line. In the early 1890s, the Norwich Line dropped its service direct to Norwich, and the steamer *City of Norwich* was scrapped. The *City of Boston*, the *City of New York*, and the *City of Worcester* continued to alternate on the regular line, which now ran only from New York to New London, with the *City of Lawrence* remaining in service to carry extra freight when needed. In addition, at the start of the 1890s the older wooden sidewheelers *Elm City, Continental,* and *C. H. Northam* were still serving New Haven.

In 1890, the same year that the Fall River Line's *Plymouth* appeared, the Maine Steamship Company, which had been operating a small fleet of antiquated steamers carrying mostly freight between New York and Portland, Maine, added its first new steamer, the *Cottage City*. It was named for the town on Martha's Vineyard, now known as Oak Bluffs, where the Portland Line made a stop en route. Although she had a wooden hull, which by this time was outdated for a coastal steamer, and she was too small for the service even when she was built, the *Cottage City*, with her ocean-type hull painted black and her varnished-wood superstructure, had such beautifully proportioned lines that she seemed more like a private yacht than a passenger and freight steamer. The following year the line brought out the *Manhattan*, an exact sistership of the *Cottage City*, which was equally out of date, equally inadequate for the service, and equally beautiful.

For the season of 1892, the Providence and Stonington Line introduced the extraordinarily handsome steel-hulled twin steamers *Maine* and *New Hampshire* to replace the twenty-five-year-old *Stonington* and *Narragansett* on the Stonington Line. Although they were propellor steamers, and thus represented the first departure from the sidewheel by one of the major Long Island Sound steamer lines, in many ways the pair showed the influence, on a much smaller scale, of George Peirce's *Plymouth* of two years earlier, with their steel hulls, their pilot houses standing alone on the Dome Deck, their single tall stacks placed amidships, and the severe but exceptionally clean lines that made them so uniquely attractive. While their light Italianate interiors of ivory trimmed with gold leaf were also attractive, the *Maine* and *New Hampshire* should perhaps be thought of as essentially freight steamers with passenger accommodations, whereas the steamers of the Providence Line or the Fall River Line were essentially passenger steamers with accommodations for freight. While the *Maine* and the *New Hampshire* at 310 feet overall were only a few feet shorter than the same line's *Massachusetts*, they had only 106 staterooms, or somewhat more than half the number of the *Massachusetts* (184). On these two steamers, virtually all of the Main Deck was devoted to freight, whereas on the *Massachusetts* almost a third was used for the dining room, entrance hall, and so forth. Thus, the *Maine* and the *New Hampshire* had a freight-carrying capacity of 105,000 cubic feet, more than that of even the large Fall River Line passenger boats (the *Pilgrim* and the *Puritan* carried about 70,000 cubic feet each, while the *Plymouth* carried somewhat over 90,000 cubic feet), and even more than the two older Fall River Line freighters, *City of Fall River* and *City of Brockton*. The third Fall River Line freighter, *City of Taunton*, had 108,000 cubic feet of freight area, or just slightly more than the *Maine* and the *New Hampshire*.[1]

The fact that there was no necessity for cramming as many staterooms as possible onto these new Stonington Line steamers, as was the case on the Providence and Fall River boats, meant that the *Maine* and *New Hampshire* could afford the luxury of devoting most of their Gallery Decks (which extended, as they did on the *Rhode Island* or the *City of Worcester*, only slightly more than half the length of the Saloon Deck) to a charming dining room. There passengers could take their meals in comfort while watching the passing scenery from a vantage point three decks high.

With the arrival of the *Maine* and the *New Hampshire*, which were immensely popular, the older *Narragansett* and *Stonington* were laid up at Stonington. With the *Rhode Island* available as a relief steamer, there was no need for them at all. The *Stonington* was sold soon after and scrapped, but the *Narragansett*, whose upper works, after all, had been completely rebuilt only eleven years before, was chartered to the government later in the decade to serve as a barracks for immigrants during a three-year period when the facilities at Ellis Island were being renovated.

In 1892, Chester W. Chapin, Jr., president of the New Haven Line, decided that his line also needed a new steamer to replace the *Elm City* of 1856. Now that the *Old Colony* of the Fall River Line was gone, his three steamers, along with the *City of Boston* and the *City of New York*, both scheduled for retirement within a few years, were the only steamers on the sound that still carried their boilers on the guards. Chapin, an avid yachtsman, wanted his new steamer to be smart and fast, so he turned to A. Cary Smith, the famous marine architect of the yachting world, who was also a personal friend, and asked him to design the new steamer for the New Haven Line. Smith, who had never attempted a commercial vessel, demurred at first but ultimately accepted. The result was the *Richard Peck* of 1892, one of the fastest and most successful steamers on the sound.

The layout of the *Richard Peck* was similar to that of the *Maine* and the *New Hampshire*, with the Main Deck devoted mostly to freight, the Saloon Deck to staterooms, and the shortened Gallery Deck consisting only of a dining room and officer's quarters. In general appearance, however, she was quite different, and she was even more radical in design. Smith designed the *Richard Peck* to ride quite high in the water and gave her an exceptionally wide beam (one to five) for her length. And instead of broadening gradually and achieving her widest point amidships, as most of the sound steamers (generally sidewheelers) had been designed to do, the *Richard Peck*, like modern ocean steamers, broadened just aft of the bow, while her sides were relatively straight. As a result, the *Richard Peck* was not nearly as graceful as the *Maine* or the *New Hampshire*. Her two stacks, when she first appeared were also too short, too thin, and rather awkwardly raked, but these were replaced later with taller and more appropriate stacks. However, she had an unusually high tonnage for a steamer of her length and, like the *Maine* and *New Hampshire*, carried an immense load of cargo. Steamboat men who saw her plans when she was being built doubted if such a wide steamer could make much headway or if she could take any heavy seas. But once the *Richard Peck* was afloat, Smith's unusual plans were vindicated, for, with her twin screws and powerful triple-expansion engine, the *Richard Peck* proved one of the speediest steamers on the sound, and, while she did roll some in a heavy swell, she was also a good sea boat. During the course of her career, the *Richard Peck* ran on every one of the Long Island Sound steamer lines west of Cape Cod, including, for several short periods, the Fall River Line. When she was dismantled in 1954, she had served for sixty-two years, longer by several years than any other steamer built for Long Island Sound with the exception of the *Norwich* and the *Ansonia*, two much smaller vessels, both of which spent most of their active lives on the Hudson River.

Two smaller steamers also made their appearances on the sound in 1892, both propellor steamers designed primarily as freight carriers but with Saloon Decks devoted entirely to modest but comfortable passenger accommodations. The first was the *Nutmeg State*, a wooden-hulled steamer built for the Bridgeport Line's overnight passenger and freight round trip out of New York. The second was the iron-hulled *Hartford* for the Hartford Line.

Two years later, the Norwich Line, favorably impressed with the performance of the New Haven Line's *Richard Peck*, decided to build a new twin-screw steel-hulled propellor steamer to run with the *City of Worcester*, and they asked A. Cary Smith to design it. The new steamer, which began service to New London in 1894, was the *City of Lowell*, one of the most popular of the sound steamers and definitely one of the fastest, though once again one must ask why the Norwich Line, which dumped its passengers on the pier at New London at two in the morning, needed a steamer designed for speed. The *City of Lowell*, which was built at the Bath Iron Works in Bath, Maine, was similar to the *Richard Peck* in layout and general appearance, though her interior was somewhat heavier and darker than the *Richard Peck's* and therefore less attractive. At 336 feet overall, she was about twenty feet longer than the *Richard Peck*, and, unlike the *Peck* or the *Maine* and *New Hampshire*, the *City of Lowell* carried a full Gallery Deck. The Gallery Deck, however, was not a continuous row of staterooms as it was on the Providence or Fall River steamers, but consisted of two separate parts. The forward part was almost identical to the *Richard Peck's* and contained an upper deck dining room, galley, and officer's quarters. The after part, which could be reached only by a separate set of stairs and not from the dining room on the same deck, consisted of single rows of staterooms on either side and, like the other larger steamers, a balustraded well opening onto the Saloon Deck aft.

Soon after the *City of Lowell* came down from Maine and began her service on the line, the older *City of Boston* and *City of New York* were scrapped. For the next ten years, the fast steel propellor steamer *City of Lowell* and the iron sidewheeler *City of Worcester*, steamers similar in accommodations but very different in appearance and layout, ran on the Norwich Line's New York to New London service, with the much older and much smaller *City of Lawrence* serving as a spare.

June 24, 1894, marked the first trip of the Fall River Line's new steamer, *Priscilla*, the most loved of all of the sound liners and, her running mate *Puritan* excepted, the most beautiful. In creating the *Priscilla*, George Peirce virtually repeated the exterior design of his *Puritan* of five years earlier with modifications: the long unbroken lines, the short rows of staterooms amidships on both decks to hide the paddleboxes, the pilot house standing by itself on the Dome Deck forward, the two tall smokestacks placed close together and far forward, which was now becoming a trademark of the Fall River Line, and the small row of staterooms aft of them. The *Priscilla's* 440-foot overall length, which made her somewhat larger than the *Puritan*, gave her still longer lines than her running mate's and the different arrangement of windows and lifeboats made them appear even more graceful, with fewer interruptions to the eye, than the *Puritan's*. On the new *Priscilla* the Dome Deck staterooms no longer hid a walking beam, and they could therefore present a lower and more even line, for Peirce installed a large triple-expansion inclined engine in the *Priscilla*, like the one on the *Plymouth*. The *Priscilla's* engine was one of the most successful on the sound; it rarely gave any trouble, and it was far cheaper to operate than the walking beam engines on either the *Pilgrim* or the *Puritan*. As a result, the *Priscilla* often remained on the Fall River run well into January, long after the heavy traffic of the summer season had abated, and she was to survive as one of the regular summer boats of the line until the Fall River Line stopped running in 1937, a period of forty-three years.

The *Priscilla*'s interior was exquisite. It was heavier than that of the *Puritan*, for by the mid-1890s American taste was taking a romantic turn leaning toward Moorish or Baroque, both of which were represented in the *Priscilla*'s interior, although her basic design, like the *Puritan*'s, was Italian Renaissance. In working out the *Priscilla*'s deck plans, Peirce used the same magic he had employed on the *Puritan* and the *Plymouth*, and this time even more effectively. The *Priscilla* offered large, open, and luxurious public rooms; her two-storied grand saloon, lined with red plush chairs and potted palms and lit by an enormous tinted-glass chandelier, was the largest on any sound steamer and one of the most elegantly appointed public rooms to be found anywhere. With all this, she also had a tremendous passenger capacity, with about 360 staterooms packed into her interior, as well as large free dormitory rooms in the hold for men and for women. Even this large number of staterooms Peirce was able to fit onto the Saloon Deck, the Gallery Deck, or the Dome Deck, leaving the after part of the Main Deck free for public rooms, so that the *Priscilla* became the only Fall River Line steamer with her dining room located on the Main Deck. Decorated in the exotic Moorish style which then was very popular, it was located just aft of her unusually spacious entrance hall on the Quarter Deck, on the forward side of which were the Purser's Office, the bar, and the glass-enclosed stairway leading up the Saloon Deck. Although the *Priscilla*, like most of the sound steamers, had a large cargo area forward on the Main Deck, she carried somewhat less freight (92,500 cubic feet) than the smaller *Plymouth* (93,500 cubic feet). The freight traffic remained relatively stable throughout the year, so that the winter boats, which carried fewer passengers, tended to devote a proportionately larger amount of space to freight.

Many years later, during the last few weeks of her life, after the Fall River Line had stopped running, the *Priscilla* was tied up at the company's Fox Point wharf in Providence. The author, though then only a small boy, still well remembers standing in the pilot house of the Colonial Line steamer *Arrow* coming slowly up the Providence River at dawn one September morning, and, upon seeing ahead what he then thought, and still thinks, was the most beautiful steamboat he had ever seen, being informed in very solemn tones by Captain George Olweiler, whose brother had been her last commander, that she was the *Priscilla*.

With the large and modern steel-hulled *Priscilla* on the line, the *Pilgrim*, now sadly out of date after only eleven years of service, became a winter boat running with the *Plymouth*, with which she was fairly evenly matched in accommodations. The *Priscilla* and the *Puritan*, two of the largest and most beautiful steamships ever to sail on American waters, provided the main service of the Fall River Line, an arrangement that was to last for another ten years. The older *Providence*, which with her sistership the *Bristol* had been the pride of the sound in the late 1860s but which was now the only remaining steamer on the Fall River Line with a wooden hull and hog framing, was tied up at Newport to be brought back into service only in case of emergencies.

Having found their new propellor steamer *Hartford* more successful than the older and larger sidewheeler *City of Springfield*, the Hartford Line, which by now was deriving most of its revenues from freight, added a similar though somewhat larger steamer, named the *Middletown*, in 1895. As on the earlier *Hartford*, most of the Main Deck was devoted to cargo, the passenger accommodations being limited to the Saloon Deck, while only the pilot house and a few rooms for officers appeared on the Gallery Deck. Like the Maine coast steamers, the *Hartford* and *Middletown* did not carry dining saloons, but placed dining tables in the forward part of the Saloon Deck.

After the arrival of the *Priscilla* and the *City of Lowell* in 1894 and the *Middletown* the following year, most of the wooden steamers of the 1860s had been replaced by more modern boats. With the exception of the New Haven Line's *Chester W. Chapin* of 1899, of which we shall be reading a great deal more later, and another small propellor for the Hartford Line the same year, no new overnight steamers were built for any of the lines running to ports on the sound or on Narragansett Bay for another ten years. The Maine Steamship Company, however, finally realizing that the *Manhattan* and *Cottage City* were inadequate for a line running to the increasingly popular Maine coast, brought on two large and fast steel-hulled steamers: the *John Englis* in 1896, named for the shipbuilder who was also a shareholder in the line, and a near sistership, the *Horatio Hall*, in 1898, named for the line's New York manager. The line now took pride in the fact that their new steamers could reach Portland from New York in less than twenty-four hours and dropped the stop at Cottage City, which took too much time. With the newer steamers now on the line, the *Cottage City*, though still fairly new, found new owners on the West Coast and sailed around South America under her own steam, arriving in Seattle in time to participate in the Alaska Gold Rush. The slightly newer *Manhattan* stayed on and generally served as the winter boat of the line for another ten years.

In the following decade, when the Joy Line and other low-fare lines were attempting to undercut the elegant but expensive services offered by the Fall River Line or the Providence Line, most of their steamers were to come from lines operating along the coast of Maine. In the years following the Civil War, when the various Long Island Sound overnight steamer lines were taking shape, several steamer lines with similar overnight operations were also running out of Boston to the industrial towns and summer resorts then developing up the Maine coast. While the Maine steamers were similar in general design to the steamers of Long Island Sound, the traffic demands of these lines were considerably less and the steamers therefore much smaller. Most of them were about 250 feet overall, with only one passenger deck above the Main Deck, or roughly similar to the *Narragansett* and *Stonington* of the Stonington Line.

As a result of the different demands of the routes they served, however, the Maine coast steamers, which ran mainly to summer resorts or to cities with relatively smaller industries than those of southern New England, tended to devote a proportionately larger amount of space to passengers and less to cargo than the steamers of the sound. The *Governor Dingley* of the Boston and Portland Line, for instance, was built at the same time as the Long Island Sound steamer *Chester W. Chapin* and had roughly the same dimensions and tonnage. But, whereas the *Chapin*, which was considered a sizable passenger carrier in her home waters, had 138 staterooms, the *Governor Dingley* had well over 200. The *Chester W. Chapin*, on the other hand, had about twice the *Governor Dingley*'s cargo capacity. Moreover, since the routes between Boston and the ports of Maine were almost all on the open ocean, the hulls of the Maine coast steamers tended to be much more strongly built, with thicker timbers and more joiner-work, than those of the smaller steamers at least running in the semi-protected waters of Long Island Sound. Thus, since the Maine coast steamers were also relatively smaller, they did not need to carry the heavy hog framing to hold their hulls in shape that were typical of the wooden steamers on the sound. In later years, the Maine coast lines, like the Providence Line of the sound, tended to be unexplainably slow to adopt technological improvments. In spite of the often rough ocean route they covered, the Maine coast lines continued to build wooden-hulled sidewheel steamers with walking beam engines, not essentially different structurally, save for the lack of hog framing, from the *Bristol* and *Providence* of the 1860s, right through the 1890s, when most of the sound lines were running steel-hulled propellor steamers on far less dangerous waters.

Unlike the Long Island Sound steamers, the Maine boats, for some reason, did not carry dining rooms but instead, like the sound steamers before the Civil War, kept dining tables set up in the forward part of the Saloon Deck.

By the 1890s, there were four major overnight steamer lines running north from Boston to ports along the Maine coast and another line originating in Portland, Maine. The longest haul was that of the International Steamship Company, which ran between Boston and St. John, New Brunswick, a trip that took nearly twenty-four hours and was, therefore, like the New York to Portland Line, not strictly an overnight run. By 1890, this line was running three wooden sidewheelers, the *New Brunswick* of 1861 and two much newer steamers which were near-sisterships, the *State of Maine* of 1882 and the *Cumberland* of 1885, both of which later served on the Joy Line. This line generally had two of its steamers on a route which called for one or the other to sail from Boston three times a week at eight in the morning, put into Portland in the late afternoon, proceed from there on an overnight run to Lubec, Maine, and then, during the following day, after a stop at Eastport, Maine, sail on to St. John, arriving there in the mid-afternoon. The steamers would then depart from St. John the following morning and follow a similar route back to Boston, the round trip, including the overnight layovers in St. John and in Boston, occupying four full days. The third steamer of the line sailed between Boston and St. John without stopping and made two round trips per week.

In 1895, the old *New Brunswick* was replaced by a new steamer, the *St. Croix*, which was similar in size to her running mates *Cumberland* and *State of Maine* but of a totally different design. A wooden propellor steamer (steel hulls were still considered immoral in Maine), she was built with an ocean-type hull, far more sensible for this kind of route, rather than with the overhanging guards typical of the Maine sidewheelers and of most of the sound steamers. While her black ocean-type hull made the *St. Croix* much less vulnerable to the pounding ocean seas than the side-wheelers, it also made her much narrower, so that she carried only about 90 staterooms compared with about 110 each on the other two steamers. The *St. Croix*, which now took over the direct route to St. John, was also somewhat faster than the older sidewheelers of the line.

One of the most popular of the Maine routes was the overnight line between Boston and Bangor which, with its early morning stop at Rockland, where it was met by a fleet of smaller connecting steamers, served the numerous resort areas of lower Penobscot Bay as well as Bar Harbor on Mount Desert Island. After leaving Rockland, the steamers of this line proceeded up the Penobscot, stopping at various way landings until they reached Bangor at about 2:00 or 3:00 P.M. The trip from Boston to Bangor, however, was a little too long for a steamer to arrive in Bangor in time to start the return trip the same day. Thus, until the arrival of the *Camden* in 1907, the first Bangor Line steamer fast enough to make the round trip in two days, the line generally had two steamers on the run leaving each port two nights out of three, though often during the busy summer months it ran three steamers on a daily schedule. By 1890, the steamers running to Bangor were the *Penobscot* of 1882, an attractive little steamer but a bad roller, and the much older and somewhat smaller (but probably more popular) *Katahdin* of 1861. The *Lewiston*, an even older steamer, originally built for the Portland Line in the 1850s but still a beautiful boat, joined the other two in the summer to provide daily sailings.

In 1894, the same year that the *Priscilla* and the *City of Lowell* appeared on Long Island Sound, the Bangor Line also made local history by bringing on the *City of Bangor*, a steamer larger and grander by far than anything then seen on the Penobscot. She was 277 feet long and was the first of the smaller steamers to attempt to carry two full passenger decks, as well as the only wooden-hulled steamer to date without hog frame bracing to do so. An impressive steamer when underway, but much too crowded and top-heavy to be considered a beauty, the *City of Bangor*, like the *Rhode Island* of the Providence Line or the *City of Springfield* of the Hartford Line (which she somewhat resembled), carried two tall stacks athwartship placed far forward and close together. She was also equipped with the new style feathering paddle wheels which were much smaller than was customary and thus did not carry the large decorated paddleboxes which characterized the other Maine coast steamers. Her wheels were not entirely hidden, however, as they were on the Fall River Line steamers, but were enclosed in modest little paddleboxes that seemed out of proportion and thus added little to the steamer's beauty.

With the *City of Bangor* on the line, the *Katahdin*, for some reason, rather than the older *Lewiston*, was scrapped, and the *City of Bangor* and the *Penobscot* became the regular steamers of the Bangor Line, with the *Lewiston* continuing to provide three-boat daily service in the summer for another two seasons.

A third overnight steamer line ran from Boston to Bath, Maine, on the Kennebec River and from there to other landings up the Kennebec as far as Gardiner. The *Star of the East*, built for this line in 1866 and thus about the same age as the *Newport* and the *Old Colony*, covered the route alone, running alternate nights, until 1889. In that year, however, the line added a second steamer, the *Kennebec*, one of the best loved steamers on the Maine coast. At about the same time, it rebuilt the *Star of the East* and renamed her the *Sagadahoc*, and throughout the 1890s the *Kennebec* and the *Sagadahoc*, running summers only, made up the Kennebec Line. Later, as we shall see, both of these steamers were to serve for a time on Long Island Sound.

Later in the decade, the line thought that there might be some profit in offering winter service between Boston and the Kennebec ports. Therefore, in 1897 it built the small propellor steamer *Lincoln* for this service. But the winter service was not well patronized, and after two years the little *Lincoln*, after one summer on the Joy Line, was sold to run between Miami and Havana.

The shortest of the Maine coast routes, though one of the best patronized, was the Boston-Portland line of the Portland Steam Packet Company. This run was similar to those of the New London or Stonington Line on the sound in that the route was so short that steamers leaving Boston at 6:00 P.M. along with the other night boats would arrive at Portland at about

3:00 A.M., not exactly the favorite time for owners of summer homes to meet visiting relatives. Up to the 1880s, this line operated a fleet of relatively small steamers dating from the 1850s. But in 1883, the same year that the Fall River Line's *Pilgrim* appeared, it added a new boat, the *Tremont*, which, many years later, after she had been retired by the Portland Line, was to have the honor of being the first passenger steamer owned by the Joy Line. The *Tremont* had an unusually staunchly built wooden hull and, at 270 feet in length, was for a few years at least the largest of the Maine coast steamers. But one cannot find much to say about either her speed or her beauty. She rode quite low in the water, and this fact, plus her lack of sheer, gave her a box-like appearance which was not assisted by the one very thin unraked stack stuck squarely amidships. In addition, since the Boston-Portland route was so short, speed was not an issue, so that the *Tremont*, equipped with the usual walking beam engine, lumbered along at a cracking eleven or twelve knots at best, which still brought her into Portland well before dawn.

Beginning in about 1890, the summer traffic to Maine began to increase at such a pace that over the next twenty years the Maine coast lines were obliged to renew their fleets with steamers far larger than those that had been running in the 1880s. During the 1890s, the Portland Line added two new steamers, the *Portland* in 1890 and the *Bay State* in 1895, which were similar in size and appearance, though not exact sisterships, and both much larger than the *Tremont* or the other earlier steamers of the line. Both were wooden-hulled paddlers, of course, and, with an overall length slightly under 300 feet, they were roughly the same size as the *Maine*, the *New Hampshire*, or the *Richard Peck*, the steel-hulled propellor steamers built for sound service at about the same time.

With the arrival of the *Bay State*, the *Tremont* became a spare, although she generally replaced the larger boats during the winter when the traffic was lighter, often running with the *State of Maine* borrowed from the International Line. But the operation of the Portland Line with these two large and well-matched sisterships was to last only four seasons, for the steamer *Portland* met a tragic end toward the close of the season of 1898. On Saturday night, November 26, the *Portland* left her pier in Boston with an unusually large number of passengers aboard (many of them returning to Maine after spending Thanksgiving in Boston) and headed out to sea in spite of the fact that her captain had been warned of a severe storm then brewing on the ocean. What the *Portland* encountered once at sea, however, was a convergence of two storm systems, producing one of the most destructive blizzards in the history of the East Coast. In spite of the terrifying seas and the raging winds of nearly 100 miles per hour, the staunchly built *Portland* made most of her run intact before the storm reached its peak in the early morning hours. What happened next we can never know. But for some reason the steamer never entered Portland harbor. Whether some part of her engine became disabled or whether her captain decided that the seas were too rough to risk entering the tortuous passage into Portland harbor, no one survived to tell. Several hours later that same Sunday morning, during a short lull in the storm, distress signals from a steamer, more than likely the *Portland*, were heard at Provincetown on Cape Cod. Then that evening large pieces of wreckage from the *Portland* began washing ashore at Highland Light, south of Provincetown, and continued to come ashore, along with a number of bodies, for several days. Many years later, when the wreck of the *Portland* was finally located off the cape, the remains of a coal-laden schooner were also discovered nearby. Most probably, shortly before entering Portland harbor, the steamer became disabled, possibly by breaking a shaft, a common problem on sidewheelers, and, left helpless, drifted rapidly in the rampant winds to a point near Provincetown, well over 100 miles away, by the late morning. By then, it appears, the schooner, also left helpless by the storm, was floundering nearby. When the winds drove the schooner and the *Portland* together, sometime late on Sunday, it was all over. Not one person aboard either vessel survived.

After the loss of the *Portland*, the *Tremont* was brought back on the line to run with the *Bay State* until a new steamer could be completed. The new steamer, the *Governor Dingley*, which arrived from the builders late in the fall of 1899, was a complete departure from the wooden-hulled walking beam sidewheelers that were then characteristic of Maine coast night boats; she was a steel-hulled propellor steamer with a modified ocean-type hull (that is, with a guardrail but with very little overhang), adapted from the hull designs of the *John Englis* and the *Horatio Hall*. Although the *Governor Dingley* was only a few feet longer than the *Portland* or the *Bay State*, she rode very high in the water and appeared much larger. With her full Gallery Deck, virtually a repetition of her Saloon Deck rather than shorter and narrower as it had been on all previous steamers of her size, including all of those on Long Island Sound, the *Governor Dingley*, as mentioned earlier, carried 225 staterooms, which was probably at the time a larger number in proportion to her length than any steamer other than those of the Fall River Line. This unusual design made the new steamer a good revenue-producer for the Portland Line, but also made her topheavy, so that, in spite of her ocean-type hull, the *Governor Dingley* tended to roll in even a moderate sea.

A fifth Maine coast line ran from Portland, Maine, north to Rockland, Bar Harbor, and Machiasport. By 1890, the steamer which had been on this route for twenty-three years, the *City of Richmond*, a handsome little sidewheeler of 227 feet, was getting on in years, having been built in 1865, the same year as the *Newport* and *Old Colony* of the Fall River Line, though most of her superstructure had been rebuilt after an accident in 1881. In 1892, the Boston and Maine Railroad, by then the parent company of this line, replaced the *City of Richmond* with the new steamer *Frank Jones*, which by all odds was the most beautiful of the Maine coast sidewheelers. Like the *Plymouth* of the Fall River Line, she had an inclined engine, the first on the Maine coast, and, also like the new Fall River boats, she carried small feathering wheels enclosed in stateroom housing on the Saloon Deck. With her long parabolic sheer, her one slightly raked stack, and her lack of paddleboxes or a walking beam, her lovely clean lines quite belied the fact that in actuality the *Frank Jones* was a poor sea boat and hard to handle in the strong currents common among the islands of Penobscot Bay.

The *City of Richmond* remained in Maine waters for a few years longer, though rarely in use. Later, she went to Philadelphia under charter where she served for awhile as an excursion steamer and also occasionally carried large fishing parties out into the Atlantic. Then, in 1897, when Henry Flagler was looking for cheap tonnage to create a steamer connection from the terminus of his Florida East Coast Railway at Knight's Key to Key West and Havana, he bought the old *City of Richmond*, although she was patently unsuited for this service, to run her temporarily until he could find more suitable steamers and renamed her the *City of Key West*.

In line with the general trend in this era for larger financial interests to gather up smaller businesses, during the 1880s and 1890s the New York, New Haven, and Hartford Railroad completed its takeover of the various smaller railroad lines in southern New England. Thus it acquired along with them all of the various steamship lines running on Long Island Sound, which, although still nominally independent corporations, were all owned to a greater or lesser degree by the railroads with which they connected. As a result, by the end of the 1890s, all of the sound's major steamer lines came under a single management.

The New Haven's acquisition of the railroads of southern New England, like the creation of the British Empire in the same era, was at first accidental and then later, as the sport began to appeal, quite brutally deliberate. The original company, the New York and New Haven Railroad, running between those cities, was incorporated in 1844, three years before the founding of the Fall River Line. Its tracks were built during the years of the U.S. war with Mexico and were completed in 1848, the year the war ended. At the start, the railroad had trouble securing trackage rights into Manhattan but was ultimately able to arrange a deal with the New York and Harlem Railroad (later part of the New York Central System) to use its tracks into the city.

The New Haven was one of the first rail lines to parallel the route of the sound steamboats, since most of the other railroads of southern New England had originated as feeders for the steamer lines and thus followed north-south routes along the river valleys leading into the sound. But, while this railroad became immediately popular serving Westchester and lower Connecticut towns, it did not attract much long-haul business at first and thus offered little competition for the steamers.

The New Haven remained primarily a local line for a quarter of a century. Then in 1872 (the year before the panic in which many American companies failed), in a surprise move, it forced the financially ailing New Haven and Hartford Railroad (which actually ran from New Haven to Springfield, Massachusetts, connecting there with the Boston and Albany) into a merger, and, in the same year, managed to lease the Shore Line Railroad which ran from New Haven to New London. With these acquisitions, the New Haven now became a serious competitor of the steamer lines. The New Haven itself ran trains directly to the same cities as the Bridgeport Line, the New Haven Line, the Hartford Line, and the New London Line. More significantly, it now provided connections with other lines, making it relatively easy for the first time for a passenger to take a train all the way from New York to Boston on one of two routes. On one, he could take a New Haven train to Springfield and change there for the Boston and Albany to Boston. On the other he could take a New Haven train via the Shore Line to New London, ferry from there to Groton, where the New York, Providence, and Boston trains would take him to Providence, and there change easily (now that the two railroads serving Providence shared the same station and the ferry ride across the river was no longer necessary) to the cars of the Boston and Providence for Boston. Ten years later, in 1882, the New Haven leased still a third line running out of New Haven. This one, known as the Air Line, headed northeast to Middletown and Willamantic, where it connected with the New York and New England Railroad (like most railroads of the time, rather optimistically named, since it did not run anywhere near the city of New York) for Boston.

Although these two railroads cooperated with each other to the extent of running several through trains from New York to Boston over this route, which was the shortest of the three, there was considerable tension in the relationship between them. By that time the New York and New England Railroad and the New Haven Railroad were beginning what was to become a battle to the death for control of the rail system of southern New England. The New York and New England Railroad had originated with the former Boston and Erie Railroad, a line that had run west from Boston on tracks paralleling those of the Boston and Albany but south of them and designed to connect Boston with areas west of the Hudson via Poughkeepsie. When this railroad failed in the Panic of the 1870s, much of its trackage was taken over by the newly formed New York and New England. Soon afterward, the New York and New England also leased the ailing Norwich and Worcester Railroad, thus giving it control over the two steamer lines running to New London and to Norwich. (With this new rail association, the Norwich

Line now became, to a much greater degree than before, another competitor for the New York to Boston traffic.)

As the New Haven and the New York and New England competed for domination, each had one advantage over the other: the New Haven had access to New York but not to Boston; the New England had access to Boston but not to New York. The rest of the story reads like a fast game of chess in which the pawns were the small stockholders who had put their life savings into railroads. In its lust for a line into Boston, the New Haven naturally eyed with interest the two smaller roads, the New York, Providence, and Boston, and the Boston and Providence, the acquisition of which would extend its road from New London to Boston via the Shore Line route. This route became even more attractive after 1889 when the New York, Providence, and Boston completed a railroad bridge from its terminus in Groton over the Thames to New London, where passengers could now transfer directly to the New Haven's New York trains without having to take a ferry across the river.

The New Haven's ambitions were thwarted when the Old Colony Railroad unexpectedly leased the Boston and Providence Railroad in 1888, thus giving it control of the Boston rail connections of the Providence Line as well as of its own Fall River and New Bedford lines. But the New Haven was able to realize the other half of its objective by obtaining a lease on the New York, Providence, and Boston in 1892. With this railroad, the New Haven acquired two other assets which were to change the course of its history. One was the Providence and Stonington Steamship Company, with its overnight steamer lines between New York and these two ports, which for the first time brought the New Haven Railroad into the Long Island Sound steamship business. The other was J. Pierpont Morgan, who, as a member of the board of the New York, Providence, and Boston, had engineered the lease in order to get control of the New Haven, and who now became an influential member of the New Haven's board. From this time until his death in 1913, according to all witnesses, whether or not Morgan held an official position on the board, he ran the New Haven Railroad. And Morgan's policy was consistent; the best way to run a business, he professed, was to create a monopoly, for only by dominating all of the business in any given area could one effectively control prices and make profits, and to achieve this control, competition should be eliminated at any cost. Morgan's drive toward monopolies in the area of New England transportation as well as other fields sometimes emerges more as a psychological disorder than as a business tactic. Whatever his motivations, however, he was certainly financially successful, at least in his own time, although many have claimed that his policies, like those of his contemporary, Bismarck, in the field of diplomacy, were successful in his own day but destined to prove disastrous for those who came after.

One of Morgan's prime business antagonists at this time was Archibald McLeod, president of the Reading Railroad in Pennsylvania. Shortly before Morgan had engineered his way onto the board of the New Haven, McLeod had become president of the New York and New England and was then planning a new route between Boston and the west via the tracks of the New York and New England and across the Poughkeepsie railroad bridge, connecting on the west side of the Hudson with a planned northern extension of the Reading and thus bypassing both the New Haven Railroad and the port of New York. Meanwhile, McLeod also planned to extend his system into the lucrative industrial areas of eastern Massachusetts north and south of Boston by acquiring control of both the Boston and Maine and the Old Colony railroads. This Morgan could not possibly permit, and, as soon as he had gained his seat on the board of the New Haven in 1892, the full force of his extensive influence in the business and financial world was mustered for the battle with McLeod.

When, during the minor financial Panic of 1893, the Old Colony Railroad, unexpectedly embarrassed as a result of a serious accident, became available to anyone who could pick up its debts, McLeod began seeking the necessary backing to buy the road. But he found all doors closed to him, and he had to give up the project and watch helplessly while the New Haven, backed by the house of Morgan, grabbed the Old Colony and with it the much-desired trackage into Boston. In the process, of course, the New Haven also acquired control of the Old Colony Steamboat Company, which operated both the Fall River Line, then just building the *Priscilla*, and the freight line to New Bedford, bringing a total of four of the sound's steamer lines into the New Haven's spreading system.

During that same year, the value of the stocks of the Reading Railroad suddenly dropped sharply in value, probably as a result of some carefully directed manipulations on Wall Street, forcing the already troubled road to declare bankruptcy and the now totally defeated McLeod to resign. The New York and New England Railroad managed to pull out of the merger weakened but intact, and attempted to continue on its own. But its efforts to obtain a bond issue in 1895 to get back on its feet were also blocked by New York financiers, probably on Morgan's instructions. When the stocks of the railroad then began to decline rapidly as a result, they were bought up wholesale either by the New Haven Railroad or by its agents. By the fall of 1898, the New Haven controlled enough of the stock to add the New York and New England Railroad to its system. The game was over.

With the New York and New England the New Haven also acquired the Norwich Line, which by then had discontinued the direct line to Norwich and was running only the *City of Lowell* and the *City of Worcester* to New London, with the *City of Lawrence* as a spare. With the addition of the New London Line, the New Haven now controlled all of the major lines running between New York and ports at the eastern end of the sound or in Narragansett Bay: the Fall River Line, the New Bedford Line, the Providence and Stonington Line, and the Norwich Line to New London. Each of these lines maintained a separate corporate existence until the creation of the New England Navigation Company in 1904, but in essence the lines were operated after 1898 as a single unit. Only the Hartford, New Haven, and Bridgeport lines, among the larger companies, remained outside railroad control. Later, in 1898, the New Haven set up a special "marine district," which was merely an administrative unit, not a corporate entity, to manage the various steamship lines.

The amalgamation of the various sound steamer lines under the management of a railroad which was itself an amalgamation of the various railroads of southern New England had, needless to say, many advantages— and not a few disadvantages. The single unit eliminated competition, for the time anyway, and meant that the various lines could charge top dollar for travel and also use their profits to keep the quality of their service high. It certainly provided far more efficient service on all lines. Whenever an unexpected accident left one of the lines short of a steamer, for instance, one could always be brought over from another line on short notice. Crews could be shifted easily as well when need demanded. Freight, too, was more maneuverable; cargo destined for Boston via the Fall River Line could be shifted to the Providence Line or even the Stonington Line. Steamers in trouble on the sound could count on steamers of their own line in the neighborhood to tow them into port (although this service was generally provided by all sound steamers as a matter of courtesy, whether or not they were on the same line). Steamers could also find dock services available at any port along the route where they might seek shelter in case of a breakdown or a storm.

There were, of course, some disadvantages. Traditionally, American railroads have treated their paying customers with greater indifference than most other types of service. Unfortunately, this indifference was now often inherited by the steamer lines. Once actually on board a steamboat, passengers were almost without exception treated to exemplary courtesy on all of the steamer lines, but the administrators in New Haven were not known for designing their steamer services with much of an eye to the passengers' needs. There was also a new impersonality in the company's relationships with their crews and other employees that was sometimes reflected in the services they performed for passengers.

During the early years of the amalgamation, there was actually little noticeable change in either the management or the operation of the separate steamer lines. The railroad tended to let each of the lines continue its services much as before. The only significant operational change after the New Haven took over the steamer lines was on the Providence Line. This line actually provided the shortest rail and steamer route between New York and Boston, although the Fall River Line, which operated larger and more elegantly appointed steamers, was by far the most popular. Now that the New Haven controlled both lines, however, there was no need for them to compete, and, with traffic increasing continually through the 1890s, an effort was made to create a better balance by upgrading the summer service on the Providence Line. Some problem was encountered, however, by the fact that the mechanical difficulties of the Providence Line's newest and largest steamer, the *Connecticut*, had made her virtually inoperable, so that the older and smaller *Massachusetts* and *Rhode Island* had been covering the route for the most part, while the more luxurious *Connecticut* spent much of her time in the shops. The summer of 1896 was the last season that the seven-year-old *Connecticut* operated with any regularity, and even in this year she did not run at all after August 1.

For the season of 1897, the railroad decided that it could both improve the service on the Providence Line and save itself the expense of running two steamers by ending the four-boat summer service to Fall River, which the addition of the *Priscilla*, with her tremendous passenger capacity, had made less necessary, and run the Fall River Line's winter boats to Providence during the summer. In 1897, the regular Providence Line steamers *Massachusetts* and *Rhode Island* opened the season as usual, but during July, the *Massachusetts* was taken off and the Fall River Line steamer *Plymouth* placed on the Providence Line with the *Rhode Island*. By August, the *Rhode Island* was also off the line, and the big iron-hulled *Pilgrim* was running with the *Plymouth*.

By the time the season of 1898 opened, the New Haven's monopoly of Long Island Sound steamboat lines was virtually complete, for it was in that year that the railroad formally took over the New York and New England Railroad and with it control of the New London route. In that year, the Fall River Line's *Plymouth* ran again to Providence, but this time the *Rhode Island* stayed to run with her through the entire summer, while the *Pilgrim* was laid up for the season. In 1899, however, the *Plymouth* and the *Pilgrim* ran to Providence for the full season, and from this time until it was discontinued in 1917 the Providence Line was operated as a sort of second section of the Fall River Line. With some exceptions, the two winter boats of the Fall River Line now ran regularly on the Providence Line's summer service and were replaced, usually about the first of October, by the line's freight steamers, which ran to Providence through the winter. Before it came under the New Haven's control, the Providence and Stonington Line had been running the older propellor freighter *Pequot* (formerly the *Thetis* of the Neptune Line) with its newer sidewheel freighter *Nashua*. After 1897, however, two of the Fall River Line's sidewheel freighters ran to Fall River through the winter (usually the *City of Taunton* and the *City of*

Brockton), while the third (usually the *City of Fall River*) joined the *Nashua* on the Providence Line and the *Pequot* stood by as a spare.

Thus, by the last year of this gilded decade, the New Haven Railroad had created a monopoly of the rail and steamer lines of southern New England. On its overnight steamer lines on Long Island Sound, it operated the magnificent steamers *Priscilla* and *Puritan* to Fall River, *Plymouth* and *Pilgrim* to Providence, *City of New Bedford* and *City of Fitchburg* to New Bedford, *Maine* and *New Hampshire* to Stonington, and *City of Worcester* and *City of Lowell* to New London, with other large steamers such as the *Providence*, the *Connecticut*, the *Rhode Island*, and the *Massachusetts* all available for emergencies. It represented by far the finest steamship service anywhere in America.

1899

If one had been in a mood to take a walk across the Brooklyn Bridge on New Year's Day of 1899, he might have been surprised to see the little overnight steamer *Hartford* of the Hartford Line pull out of her East River pier during the morning and head down the harbor past Staten Island and into the cold Atlantic. She was on her way to Cuba to help bring American soldiers home at the end of the Spanish-American War. Her newer and slightly larger sister *Middletown* had proved such a success that the line had decided to order another steamer of the same dimensions. When the government made an attractive offer, therfore, for the *Hartford*, the line accepted it, even though its new steamer, also to be named *Hartford*, was not going to be ready in time for the 1899 season.

The Hartford Line did not operate through the winter, as the Connecticut River was usually frozen over until about mid-March. But in January 1899 most of the other lines were maintaining at least minimal service. Since not many vacationers wanted to go to Maine in January, the Portland Line's new steel-hulled *Horatio Hall* was laid up, but its older steamer, the wooden-hulled *Manhattan*, maintained a reduced schedule to Portland throughout the winter. The fast black-hulled freighters of the Metropolitan Line kept up their regular trips around the cape to Boston regardless of the weather. On the Fall River Line, the winter boats *Plymouth* and *Pilgrim* were already in service, though often they did not come on before mid-January. The sidewheel freighters *City of Brockton* and *City of Taunton* were also running to Fall River, while the *City of Fall River* and the *Nashua* served as the winter freight boats of the Providence Line. The small propellors *City of New Bedford* and *City of Fitchburg* ran freight all year to New Bedford; the *Maine* and the *New Hampshire* covered the Stonington

Line; and the *City of Lowell* and the *City of Worcester* ran to New London for the so-called Norwich Line. On the New Haven Line, which operated on a reduced schedule during the winter, the *Richard Peck* was running alone; the older sidewheelers *Continental* and *C. H. Northam* were both laid up. The *Nutmeg State* also ran alone to Bridgeport in January; the Bridgeport day boat *Rosedale* did not start her season until the middle of March.

The gracefully aging *Rhode Island*, which had been taken off the summer Providence Line when the railroad decided to use the winter boats of the Fall River Line on that route, was still kept at Stonington with steam up so that she could be used in case of emergencies. She also generally served as the relief boat on both the Stonington Line and the Norwich Line when the regular steamers of those lines were off for repairs or for their annual overhauls. Early in January 1899, the *City of Worcester* had to go to Fletcher's in Hoboken for some major repairs to her engines, and the *Rhode Island* took her place running to New London with the *City of Lowell*. On January 24, the *Rhode Island* had just passed through Hell Gate on her way to New London when her rudder chain broke. Left completely out of control, she ran aground at Sunken Meadows. The smaller *City of Lawrence* took her place for a few trips, but, fortunately, the *Rhode Island* was not seriously damaged and was soon repaired. When the *City of Worcester* came back on the line on March 18, the *Rhode Island* stayed to run with her for another month while the *City of Lowell* went for an extended overhaul.

Since the winter was a mild one, the Hartford Line was able to start service early in March that year. But as it had only one steamer, it had to begin by running the *Middletown* alone on alternate nights. Daily service was restored in April, however, when the Hartford Line chartered the *City of Lawrence* from the Norwich Line to run with the *Middletown* until its new steamer was ready. The *City of Lawrence* was no stranger to the run, having been chartered to the Hartford Line for several seasons before the first *Hartford* was built. The Montauk Line to Greenport and Shelter Island (another line that operated only in the warmer months) also began early in 1899, placing the *Montauk* in service on March 18. Its newer and larger steamer, the *Shinnecock*, however, did not come on the line until June. It was also during March 1899, as the various Hudson River steamers were preparing to start their summer seasons, that three of the Hudson River lines, the Homer Ramsdell Transportation Company between New York and Newburgh, the Poughkeepsie Transportation Company between New York and Poughkeepsie, and the Romer and Tremper Steamboat Company between New York and Kingston (and Kingston and Albany) announced their merger as the Central Hudson Steamboat Company.[1]

Wednesday, March 29, a typical windy March day, was the day one would have encountered the freighter *Rosalie* loading at Pier 1, North River, for the first trip of the Joy Steamship Company. There had been rumors earlier in the month, when it became known that the Bridgeport Line was selling the *City of Bridgeport*, that she had been purchased by a line recently established to carry freight between New York and Bangor, Maine, whose steamer *Pentagoet* had been lost with all hands in the same storm that had claimed the steamer *Portland* the previous November. But Dimon, Dunbaugh, and Joy had apparently outbid the Maine people, and now the *City of Bridgeport* appeared in fresh white paint and renamed the *Rosalie* (for Charlie Dimon's wife), the first steamer of the Joy Line.

Even the weather was unpropitious for the Joy Line's first sailing. When the little *Rosalie* swung into the East River shortly after five in the evening and headed slowly up toward the sound, she was bucking not only the New Haven Railroad' transportation monopoly but also a rapidly building northeaster. Her first run was to be a rough one. The winds roared up to gale force that night, and Captain Wilcox did not guide the *Rosalie* up the Providence River until nearly noon the following day. But she made it. She wasn't very fast and she certainly wasn't beautiful, but she was sturdy and seaworthy. On her first trip outside the protected waters of Long Island Sound for the Joy Line,* the *Rosalie* had encountered the full force of Point Judith's fury, and she had shown she could take it.

As she pulled proudly up to the wharf which the Joy Line had leased just south of the Point Street Bridge, the *Rosalie* probably did not attract much notice. The Providence waterfront was very busy in those days with schooners, barges, and large ocean-going steamers loading for various parts of the world,** while the white freighter *City of Fall River* of the railroad's Providence Line sat proudly at her berth just around the bend at Fox Point wharf. But once the merchants of Providence became aware that the Joy Steamship Company's little freighter carried cargo to New York at lower rates than those charged by the railroad-owned steamers, they began to give the new line their enthusiastic support, as is indicated by these encouraging remarks in the *Providence Board of Trade Journal*:

> As Providence manufacturers and merchants have for years advocated a freight line to New York independent of the railroad, they should bestow upon this enterprise such liberal patronage as will warrant the establishment

---

*In 1894 the *Rosalie*, then the *City of Bridgeport*, had been chartered by a short-lived freight line running between Boston and ports along the coast of Maine. Technically, then, this was not her first voyage outside of Long Island.

**Among the many steamship services operating out of Providence at that time were the Winsor Line whose steamers sailed from Providence on Wednesdays and Saturdays for Philadelphia, and the Merchants and Miners Line with sailings every Monday, Wednesday, and Friday for Norfolk and Baltimore.

of a daily service by the line in the near future. Such a line, supported by our businessmen, will aid materially in advancing the commercial interests of Providence.[2]

Throughout the year 1899, the Joy Line's *Rosalie* made two round trips per week between New York and Providence, leaving New York every Tuesday and Friday at 5:00 P.M. and Providence every Wednesday and Saturday at 6:00 P.M.

Not long after the *Rosalie* started running, the *Providence Board of Trade Journal* rejoiced at the news that the Joy Line was building a new steamer at the Newport News Shipbuilding Company in Virginia to join the *Rosalie* on the line.[3] Actually, they had been misinformed. The Joy Line did have another steamer, but she was not new. In fact, the Joy Line did not ever, in all its years of service, build a new steamer; every boat it operated was either chartered from another line or purchased second-hand. The steamer referred to in this case, however, was as nearly new as any steamer the Joy Line ever operated, having been built less than a year before. She was the *Cape Charles* which had been delivered new to the Norfolk-Cape Charles line in the spring of 1898. Although capable of making nearly eighteen knots, a good speed for a vessel of her class, she was not quite fast enough for the exceptional demands of this particular run, and the line had seriously considered not accepting her from the builders. In the end, they did accept her, but she ran on the line only one season. On December 16, 1898, while lying at her wharf in Norfolk, the *Cape Charles* caught fire and most of her superstructure was destroyed.

About the same time that the Joy Line people were negotiating for the *Rosalie*, Charles Dimon also went down to Norfolk to have a look at the remains of the *Cape Charles*. He found the hull and engine in excellent condition and was able to secure the steamer at a very good price. Since it was operating on limited capital, the Joy Line tended throughout its history to purchase steamers that could be acquired cheaply. The line was fortunate, in most instances, in having the services of Charlie Dimon, whose forte, it would appear, was finding exceptional bargains in used steamboats, *most* of them in good operating condition.

The Joy Line sent the *Cape Charles* over to Newport News where she was rebuilt as a freighter and renamed *Allan Joy*. At the time it was expected that, when completed, the *Allan Joy* would join the *Rosalie* on the freight run to Providence. By the time she was ready, however, a series of unexpected circumstances had forced the Joy Line to make drastic changes in its plans.

About the middle of May 1899, less than two months after the Joy Line began its operation, it became apparent that another steamship line was planning to run out of Providence. Some very serious-looking businessmen spent about a week in town inquiring about dock properties and finally arranged to lease the Lonsdale Corporation wharf, which lay at the foot of Hope Street a few hundred yards east of the Providence Line's Fox Point wharf toward the Seekonk River Bridge. Whoever these people were, they conducted their business in deep secrecy, for the New Haven Railroad controlled so much of the shipping in the area that, should it have known in advance that a competing steamship line was being planned, it could easily have used its considerable influence to prevent the new company from acquiring satisfactory wharfage. In any event, the new company obviously enjoyed the support of the city of Providence, for during the week these men spent in Providence, they had several secret meetings with Mayor Baker.[4]

Finally on Wednesday, May 24, the secret was out. Chester W. Chapin, the president of the New Haven Line, was planning to extend the route of his steamers to Providence. They would leave New York as usual in the early evening for New Haven, but then, instead of returning to New York, they would continue on to Providence, arriving there early in the morning. In the opposite direction, the steamer would stop at New Haven on its way to New York. The new service, to be known as the Narragansett Bay Line, or more generally the Bay Line, was to be a far more impressive operation than that of the Joy Line and would, in fact, constitute genuine competition for the railroad's regular Providence Line. Chapin planned to place his fast and popular steamer *Richard Peck* on the route and had ordered a sistership, which was then being built at Sparrow's Point, Maryland, to run with her. Until the new steamer was finished, however, the *Richard Peck* would be running with the much older *C. H. Northam*, a wooden sidewheeler with boilers on the guards, which was satisfactory for the New Haven route but not really suited for the longer run to Providence.[5]

Even with the planned new steamer, the Bay Line boats would still be much smaller than the big sidewheelers *Plymouth* and *Pilgrim* of the railroad's Providence Line. But they would be new, smart, and fast. A real challenge to the railroad was the Bay Line's announcement that its steamers would run between New York and Providence seven days a week and twelve months a year. This plan particularly pleased the people of Providence, who had always resented the fact that the railroad's major service, the line to Fall River, ran passenger steamers throughout the year and, in the summer months, seven nights a week, while the Providence Line ran only six nights a week and was served only by freighters in the winter. What appealed most to their civic pride, of course, was that the Bay Line's *only* operation was its line from New York to Providence, albeit via New Haven. So to the people of Providence, the Bay Line became *their* line. The railroad's steamers may have been larger and grander, but these steamers were the secondary boats of another line running to another city; the Bay Line boats were Providence boats. Providence was also pleased by the mere existence of competition. As long as the New Haven Railroad did not control all of the routes to New York, there was hope for competitive rates. And these hopes were soon fulfilled, for during the first week in June agents of the New Haven Steamboat Company came to Providence and met with local shippers to work out favorable freight rates.[6] (The new Bay Line had also worked out through freight rates between Providence and the West via the Baltimore and Ohio Railroad out of New York.) Another indication of official support came with the appointment of Daniel George, formerly Mayor Baker's personal secretary, as the Providence agent of the Narragansett Bay Line.[7] Apparently, in its forthcoming battle with the New Haven Railroad monopoly, the new line could at least count on close connections with city hall.

Eventually, the papers announced that the Bay Line would begin operating on Monday night, June 12, 1899, and that the *Richard Peck* would make the first trip of the new service *from Providence*. But these plans almost literally foundered when the two steamers of the line, then still running only to New Haven, met in a head-on collision less than a week before the new service to Providence was to begin. The *C. H. Northam* sailed from New York at midnight on Wednesday, June 7, and the *Richard Peck* from New Haven somewhat later. Once in the sound both steamers encountered a thick fog. By two-thirty in the morning when the two steamers were scheduled to pass off Greenwich, Connecticut, there was no visibility at all, even though the pilots on both steamers clearly heard the approaching whistle of the other. As it turned out, if both vessels had stayed on course, they could have passed easily starboard to starboard. But sound is often deflected in fog, and, as the whistles began to sound ominously close, the *C. H. Northam*, trying to avoid an accident, veered suddenly to port and the *Richard Peck* to starboard. In the process both steamers moved directly into the path of the other. By the time the pilot of the *Peck* saw the lights of the *Northam* emerging through the fog directly ahead of him, it was too late; the steel-hulled *Peck* sliced right through the bow of the *Northam*. The *Richard Peck* suffered only a blunted bow, but the *C. H. Northam* was in danger of sinking. Captain Aaron Hardy of the *Northam* therefore transferred his 250 passengers as quickly as possible to the decks of the *Richard Peck* and then headed for the shore, managing to beach his steamer at Greens Farm near Westport, Connecticut, before she went under.[8]

In a sense, the accident proved fortuitous for the Bay Line. The *C. H. Northam*, an older wooden steamer with big hog framing and boilers on the guards, appeared very old fashioned in 1899. Barely able to maintain a speed of thirteen knots compared with the sprightly *Richard Peck*'s easy twenty-knot speed, she was hardly a suitable advertisement for the "new" Bay Line. With only a few days to go before the line was scheduled to start running, Chapin had to work fast to find a suitable replacement. He was fortunate in being able to secure the *Shinnecock* of the Montauk Line, which had just come out of her annual overhaul but was not scheduled to start her own run for another week. The *Shinnecock* was smaller than the *C. H. Northam*, but she was modern, well appointed, and fairly fast, at least by comparision, and in every way a better advertisement for a new service.

The necessity of stopping at New Haven put the Bay Line at something of a disadvantage in scheduling compared with the Providence Line. In order to unload and reload freight in New Haven, the steamers had to put in there for about one and a half hours. Allowing at least another hour for the run into New Haven harbor and back into the sound again, the Bay Line needed almost three hours longer for its trip from Providence to New York than the Providence Line. In fact, while the *C. H. Northam* was on the line, it had to allow four hours more, and this time had to be found by advancing the departure time from Providence. Thus the Bay Line steamers sailed from Providence at 4:30 in the afternoon,* hardly a convenient hour, especially for passengers coming from Boston, who had to leave South Station before 3:00 P.M., whereas a passenger could leave Boston as late as 6:00 P.M. and still reach the Providence wharf in time to make the 7:45 sailing of the *Plymouth* or the *Pilgrim*.

The *Richard Peck* steamed into Providence to inaugurate the new line during the morning of Monday, June 12. She had been freshly painted, and she carried the long blue pennant, called the "whip," which a steamer was entitled to fly if she could honestly boast that no other steamer had ever passed her. All that day the *Richard Peck* was open to local visitors who cared to come aboard and look around. Just a short distance down the river, the Providence liner *Plymouth* was at her wharf and was also open for public inspection. The Providence Line was starting its summer passenger service on the same day, and for some reason, though it had never done so before, the line decided this year that it too, would open its vessel to the public before the first sailing.

*The New Haven Steamboat Company's schedule for the summer of 1899 called for the steamer to leave New York at 4:00 P.M., arrive in New Haven at 9:00 P.M., leave New Haven at 10:30 P.M., and arrive in Providence at 5:30 A.M. Returning, the steamers left Providence at 4:30 P.M., arrived in New Haven at 11:30 P.M., left New Haven at 12:45 A.M., and arrived in New York at 6:00 A.M. A third steamer (the *Continental*) left New York at midnight and arrived in New Haven at 7:00 A.M., left New Haven again at 11:00 A.M., and arrived in New York at 4:00 P.M.

At exactly 4:30 in the afternoon, a tugboat puffed up to the *Richard Peck*, ceremoniously threw her a line, and towed the white steamer out into the Providence River. Providence night boats of various sizes had managed for decades and in all kinds of weather to pull into the Providence River under their own steam, and the powerful *Richard Peck* was certainly capable of doing so as well. But that night the New Haven Steamboat management decided that the wind was so strong that the *Richard Peck* needed to be towed into the river in the manner of a large ocean liner. In any event, the crowds were impressed and watched while the fast and graceful steamer, once the tug had released her, sailed down the Providence River in the full sunshine of a June afternoon. Having watched the *Richard Peck* depart, however, many of them then wandered over to the *Plymouth* at the Providence Line wharf, where the party was to last another three hours. The Providence Line people had even asked the ship's orchestra to start early so that the visitors could enjoy some music with the evening breezes as they inspected the *Plymouth*'s ample saloons and long, carpeted corridors.

Very early the following morning, with relatively few observers to record the event, the handsome little *Shinnecock* paddled up Narragansett Bay for the new Bay Line's first arrival in Providence. The Providence Line steamer coming up behind her that morning was not the *Pilgrim*, as might have been expected, but the *City of Lowell* of the Norwich Line. The *Pilgrim* had developed engine trouble, as she frequently did, and had gone to Fletcher's for a few days for repairs. The *City of Lowell* at the time was just coming out of overhaul. By this time, the *Rhode Island* had been transferred to the Stonington Line to relieve the *Maine* and the *New Hampshire*, and the old *Massachusetts*, which had not seen service for nearly three years, had been put on the New London route with the *City of Worcester*. Since the *City of Lowell*, when she came from the yards, was not needed immediately on the Norwich Line, she went on the Providence Line for a few trips until the *Pilgrim* was ready. But was the "availability" of the *City of Lowell* merely fortuitous? The *City of Lowell* was similar to the *Richard Peck*, which was attracting so much attention in Providence. She had been designed by the same marine architect but was newer and larger. The *City of Lowell* was also the only steamer on the sound (with the probable exception of the *Priscilla*) that could claim to be faster than the *Richard Peck*. So perhaps the choice of the *City of Lowell* to start the summer service to Providence was not altogether coincidental.

As might have been expected, the new Bay Line was immediately popular with the people of Providence who supported it with the pride they might have felt for a local baseball team. Since the Bay Line had not been party to any previous agreements, it set its passenger fares at fifty cents below those of the regular Providence Line. The regular line's fare from New York to Providence was then $3.00 and to Boston, $4.00. The Bay Line charged $2.50 to Providence and $3.00 to Boston. The railroad line had one advantage in being able to sell through tickets between New York and any point in New England via steamship and rail. When the Bay Line applied to the New Haven Railroad for a through ticket arrangement, the request was, of course, refused. Instead, the Bay Line's New York agents had to go to Grand Central Station every morning and buy one hundred Providence-Boston railroad tickets to sell either at the New York pier or on board the steamer to passengers wishing to travel through to Boston. Passengers wishing to proceed from Providence to other cities simply had to purchase their own rail tickets at the Providence station.

For the season of 1899, the Providence Line made one change in response to the seven sailings a week of the Bay Line by scheduling sailings from Providence on Sunday nights instead of Saturdays. Since no freight was delivered on Sundays, most of the sound steamers did not sail on Sunday nights. Even the Fall River Line had Sunday sailings only in the summer season. The Providence Line, whose steamers were much more expensive to operate than the Bay Line boats, was not prepared to add one extra trip per week without freight revenue even to meet the competition. But since freight delivered in Providence on Saturdays was, for the most part, not needed in New York before Monday, the line decided to cancel its Saturday night sailing and run on Sundays instead as a concession to weekend travelers. It kept the Saturday night sailing out of New York, however, so that on Sundays both steamers of the Providence Line would be in Providence, one on either side of the Fox Point wharf. The Fall River Line now dropped its Sunday night stop at Newport, and on Sundays only the Providence Line steamer stopped to pick up Newport passengers instead.

In chartering the *Shinnecock*, the Bay Line had solved its problem only temporarily, for the charter lasted only ten days. Chapin had a hard time finding a substitute; the summer season was starting, and any line that had a suitable steamer was planning to use it. Almost at the last minute he was able to charter the *Lincoln*, the winter boat of the Kennebec Line, which took the *Shinnecock*'s place out of Providence on Thursday night, June 22. Although the little 200-foot *Lincoln* was the best Chapin could locate at the time, she was hardly suitable for his new service. Designed for the limited winter service between Boston and the Kennebec River, she was primarily a freight carrier and had only fifty staterooms. At least she was a new boat, having entered that service in 1897, and she was fast enough to cover the route on schedule.

It was fortunate that the *Lincoln*'s first sailing was from Providence, for the steamers coming up that night encountered one of the most severe electrical storms ever witnessed on the sound. The *Rhode Island*, bound for Stonington, was struck by lightning off City Island. Sparks danced over her Hurricane Deck for several seconds, her forward mast splintered and fell, and her pilot, standing at the front window, was knocked senseless, though he later revived.[9]

By June 25, the *Pilgrim* was ready to come on the Providence Line, so the *City of Lowell* returned to run to New London with the *City of Worcester*. By this time, the *New Hampshire* was back on the Stonington Line, but the *Rhode Island* stayed on to relieve the *Maine* for a few weeks. On April 11, the freighter *City of Fitchburg* had been badly damaged by fire while unloading at her pier in New Bedford. The marine district of the New Haven Railroad announced that, since she was too old to be worth repairing, she would be sold, and the *Pequot*, formerly the *Thetis* of the old Neptune Line, would run to New Bedford in her place. The *Pequot* was in fact even older than the *City of Fitchburg*, but she was in good shape and had a larger cargo capacity. Toward the end of June, the *City of Fitchburg* was sold to a group in Boston who wanted to use her for a new service between Boston and Portland, stopping at Portsmouth, New Hampshire, en route, which would compete with the established Portland Line much as the Joy Line and the Bay Line were competing with the established Providence Line.[10]

The embarrassment of the Bay Line at having to operate the diminutive *Lincoln* was somewhat mitigated by the publicity the line received when its new steamer, named the *Chester W. Chapin*, was launched on Tuesday, July 11, 1899. It was a fine, warm summer day, and, following the practice of the time, dignitaries from various parts of the transportation world traveled to Baltimore (by train) to participate in the festivities. Seven-year-old Cecelia Geraty, the daughter of the superintendent of the New Haven Steamboat Company, bravely swung a bottle of good New England rum (the nationalist fervor engendered by the recent Spanish-American War having prevented the use of "foreign" champagne).[11] With the *Chester W. Chapin* due for delivery in a few months, the Bay Line could promise Providence a line of modern steamers at moderate prices. Meanwhile, by mid-July, the *C. H. Northam*, newly repaired and painted, took her place on the line, and the *Lincoln*, after receiving due thanks for her efforts in the emergency, sailed back to Boston.

On Monday, June 19, just one week after the Narragansett Bay Line started running to Providence, the Joy Line's newly renovated steamer *Allan Joy* arrived in New York and tied up at Pier 1. Whereas the *Rosalie* was an odd-looking craft with awkward lines and a stack that was too thin and too far aft, the *Allan Joy* was one of the handsomest small steamers ever to appear on the sound. Her Main Deck was not very high, which made her a poor freight carrier, but also gave her unusually graceful lines and made her appear much longer than her 220 feet. Since the Joy Line had purchased the

Allan Joy to run with the *Rosalie* on its freight run to Providence, there was considerable surprise when, after her arrival, the line announced that she would not be used on this line but would inaugurate a new line from New York directly to Boston around the cape.

The unexpected appearance of the Narragansett Bay Line and its subsequent success had not been good omens for the Joy Line. When the *Rosalie* had first started running to Providence in March, the city and its merchants had greeted the new service with warmth and encouragement. But now the city's enthusiasm had been transferred, quite justifiably, to the new Narragansett Bay Line. With its two large passenger and freight steamers leaving Providence every day of the week, the Bay Line was a far more formidable champion of local interests against the New Haven Railroad than the Joy Line, with its one small freight boat, could hope to be. Throughout the spring and summer of 1899, the Providence papers joyfully chronicled every move in the gathering battle between the Bay Line and the monopoly, but barely referred to the Joy Line at all.

Encouraged no doubt by the success of the Bay Line, the Clyde Line, which ran steamers between Providence and various southern ports, announced early in June that it would place two of its smaller steamers, the *Cherokee* and the *Navahoe*, on a new freight service between Providence and New York. The Clyde Line's plans, which would have given Providence four steamer lines to New York, were not carried through, but the announcement was another factor in discouraging the Joy Line from expanding its service to Providence at that time.

On June 24, 1899, the Joy Line opened its new service direct to Boston with the steamer *Allan Joy* sailing from New York. In deciding to run to Boston, the Joy Line once again had chosen to challenge a formidable rival. For thirty-five years the New York to Boston route had been the exclusive domain of the Metropolitan Line which was known as one of the best run and most prosperous coastwise lines out of New York. Its three freighters were large ocean-type vessels, capable of sailing in virtually any weather and of taking the ocean route outside Long Island whenever ice or storms made travel through the sound difficult or dangerous. The Metropolitan also had a close working relationship with the New Haven Railroad, thus eliminating competition between them and keeping freight rates high. The Whitney family, which owned the Metropolitan Line as a private corporation, was quite prepared to join the New Haven in any moves to thwart unwanted competition. But, as it turned out, there were many merchants in Boston, as there were in Providence, who welcomed the lower rates offered by the Joy Line, and, after a slow start, the *Allan Joy* was soon loading all the freight she could carry.

In spite of early fears to the contrary, there was apparently enough business for everybody on the Providence route. Although the Narragansett Bay Line was very successful and the *Richard Peck* and the *C. H. Northam* sailed well booked every night throughout the summer season, the Providence Line does not seem to have suffered except perhaps in pride, for the *Plymouth* and *Pilgrim* carried about the same amount of traffic they had in past summers. And enough local shippers still favored the Joy Line for the *Rosalie* to carry a full load on most trips, particularly westbound. Thus, through the summer and fall of 1899, the Joy Line did a good business on both of its lines, with the *Allan Joy* leaving New York every Monday and Thursday for Boston and the *Rosalie* every Tuesday and Friday for Providence.

The season of 1899 concluded with two grand spectacles in New York: the three-day welcome for Admiral Dewey at the end of September and the America's Cup yacht races off Sandy Hook in the first week of October. Since several of the sound steamers participated in the big marine parade up the Hudson honoring Admiral Dewey and even more were chartered to carry spectators to the cup races, both events necessitated adjustments in the steamer schedules. The *Plymouth* of the Providence Line was involved in both events, so the *Rhode Island*, still serving as the general relief steamer for the railroad-owned lines, took the *Plymouth*'s place on the Providence Line out of New York on Wednesday night, September 27, and stayed on the line with the *Pilgrim* until passenger service to Providence was suspended for the year at the end of October. The *Plymouth* sailed in the naval parade that Friday, and then, since she was in New York with nothing else to do, she took a special excursion up the Hudson on Sunday.

Tuesday, October 3, was the day of the first cup race, and the *Plymouth*, the *City of Lowell*, and the *Richard Peck* were all chartered to carry spectators out to watch the event. Since the *Rhode Island* was then running to Providence and the *Massachusetts* was laid up for engine repairs, the old *Providence* of the Fall River Line was brought out of retirement to take the *City of Lowell*'s place on the New London route. At this time, the *Providence* had not turned her wheels in several years and had not been in active service since the arrival of the *Priscilla* in June 1894. The short stint on the Norwich Line in the fall of 1899 was to be the last for this grand old steamer whose appearance with her sister the *Bristol* in 1867 had set new standards for size and elegance in sound steamers. Since the *Providence* was considerably larger than the *Rhode Island*, it seems strange that she was not placed on the Providence Line with her old running mate the *Pilgrim* and the smaller *Rhode Island*, which was similar to the *City of Worcester* in size and design, on the Norwich Line. Quite possibly, the older steamer's engines had gotten out of condition and could not be counted on to make the Providence run on schedule.

The last week of September was apparently a time for farewell appearances. That same week the Metropolitan Line, finding itself short while its regular steamers were being readied for the winter season, reactivated the old *Glaucus*, which, like the *Providence*, dated from the 1860s and had also been out of service for many years. The Metropolitan Line's *General Whitney*, which had served as the line's relief steamer for the past several seasons, had recently been sunk in a collision off Cape Hattaras while en route to New Orleans under charter to the Morgan Line. The Metropolitan had a new replacement steamer under construction (to be known as the *James M. Whitney*), but until she was completed in 1900, the reactivated *Glaucus*, out of service since 1895, had to serve as the line's relief steamer. During her brief respite, the *Glaucus* was commanded by a former Metropolitan Line captain, A. B. Coleman, who, like the steamer, was brought out of retirement for the occasion.

When the *Richard Peck* was taken off the Narragansett Bay Line to take chartered trips to the yacht races, her place was taken by the *Kennebec*, one of the two summer steamers of the Kennebec Line (Boston to Kennebec River ports). The Bay Line had originally arranged to charter the *Kennebec* (for three months: 1 September to 1 December, later extended to 1 January 1900), now that her summer season was over, to replace the *C. H. Northam*, which had proved too old, too slow, and in general unsuitable for the Providence run. The *Kennebec* was much smaller (256 feet) than the *C. H. Northam*, and not much faster. But she was fast enough for the run, a better seaboat in winter weather, and much cheaper to operate. When the *Kennebec* was delivered on October 1, however, the *C. H. Northam* stayed on the line for another week, so that the *Richard Peck* could go to the races.

Bad weather through early October made the races of 1899 less than exciting for the spectators and less than profitable for the steamboat owners. On October 10, a thick fog lowered on New York and remained for several days, so that the last few races had to be postponed. On the morning of Tuesday, October 10, the *C. H. Northam*, the *Priscilla*, and the *Rhode Island* all had to wait at Whitestone until noon before the fog lifted enough for them to dare to pick their way through Hell Gate into the city. The following night the *Kennebec* ran aground at Throgs Neck and was caught there for about three hours before the rising tide lifted her off. The damage was slight and she proceeded to Providence, but, as the races had been called off because of the fog anyway, the *Richard Peck* made the next round trip for her so that the *Kennebec* could have her bottom examined.

The fog continued several days longer. On Friday, October 13, the big *Pilgrim* collided with a barge while feeling her way down the East River, and the following night the *Manhattan* of the Portland Line went aground at Hell Gate. But by far the worst tragedy of the week was the burning of the Bridgeport liner *Nutmeg State* early in the morning of Sunday, October 15.

By Saturday night, October 14, the fog was still thick. Although the *Nutmeg State* usually left Bridgeport at midnight and was due in New York at about five in the morning, the fog had made her late arriving in Bridgeport, and she was not able to load freight and get away again before three-thirty in the morning. For the first hour of the trip, she made her way slowly back down the sound through the mist. Then as dawn appeared, at about five, the fog finally began to lift and the *Nutmeg State* gradually picked up speed in an effort to regain lost time. By five-thirty, as the *Nutmeg State* was approaching Execution Light, hopelessly behind schedule, the air was again clear for the first time in a week. Just then the freight watchman appeared at the pilot house with the news that part of the cargo was on fire. Captain Charles M. Brooks, who had only recently retired to his stateroom after a strenuous night navigating through the fog, dressed quickly and ran down to the freight deck. Seeing that the fire was not a serious one, he decided not to disturb sleeping passengers with a general alarm just yet, but instructed several of the crew to extinguish the fire. After several minutes of playing the hoses on the freight deck, the men were apparently successful, but then suddenly new flames appeared behind them amidships that were already shooting up to the deck above. Summoned again, Captain Brooks now realized that his ship was in danger and ordered Pilot William Weatherwax to head toward Sands Point, which was only about a mile distant, and told the baggageman, Samuel Jaynes, to awaken all of the passengers and order them to stand by the boats.

By the time passengers began to arrive on deck, the flames, now out of control, had divided the steamer into two parts. Most of the officers found themselves in the bow with no way of reaching the passengers huddled in the stern with the flames moving toward them rapidly. Some of the passengers attempted to lower a boat themselves, but one of the ropes stuck, so that the boat went down one end first and dumped its occupants into the sound. Fortunately, someone on deck disengaged a raft and sent it into the water after them and no one drowned. Before any more boats could be lowered, the *Nutmeg State* suddenly struck the shore with a thud, sending many passengers crashing to the deck. But with the ship beached most of the passengers could now jump safely into the shallow water.

The first steamer to arrive at the scene was the *City of Lawrence*, then running on the Hartford Line. She, too, was running late as a result of the fog and was coming down the sound a few miles behind the *Nutmeg State*. Her pilot house crew had watched in horror as they saw flames suddenly shooting up from the *Nutmeg State* ahead of them, and they had pushed the old *City of Lawrence* as fast as she could move to go the rescue. By the time the *City of Lawrence* reached the burning vessel, her boats had already been swung out and were ready to be lowered to pick up survivors. The *City of Lawrence*, however, drew too much water to dare go too close to the beached steamer. But the tug *W. C. Reed* and the yacht *Kismet*, which were also close by and had seen the flames, came along a few minutes later and were able to take passengers directly from the deck of the *Nutmeg State*.

Samuel Jaynes, the baggageman whose courage in awakening all of the passengers had saved many lives, found himself trapped among the flames in the center of the steamer. He jumped overboard but hit his head on the guardrail and was knocked unconscious. He was fished out of the water and taken aboard the *City of Lawrence*, but he died soon after. Several of the *Nutmeg State's* engine room crew were trapped in the hold of the steamer and perished tragically in the flames. One woman and her small child were unaccounted for and were apparently killed in the fire, but otherwise all of the *Nutmeg State's* passengers were rescued safely.

Since the sidewheeler *Mount Hope* of the Providence-Block Island Line was in New York at the time taking excursionists to the yacht races, the Bridgeport Line arranged to charter her to fill in for the *Nutmeg State* until a more suitable steamer could be located.

Just over a week after her courageous service in rescuing passengers from the burning *Nutmeg State*, the *City of Lawrence* was relieved on the Hartford Line by the arrival of the new *Hartford* on Tuesday, October 24. There was talk of chartering her to the Bridgeport Line, for the *City of Lawrence*, essentially a freight carrier, would have been more suitable for that run than the *Mount Hope*, which was primarily a day boat. But the deal fell through at the last minute when her owners, the Norwich Line, decided they needed the boat themselves. The *City of Worcester* had developed mechanical problems and had to be off the run for several weeks. At first, the line planned to continue to run the old *Providence* with the *City of Lowell* but then decided that the *Providence* was too expensive to operate and that the *City of Lawrence*, though small, would be adequate for the fall traffic.

On November 1, as usual, the Providence Line discontinued its passenger service for the season. The big passenger steamers *Pilgrim* and *Plymouth* went to Newport to get ready for their winter service on the Fall River Line, while the freight steamers *Nashua* and *City of Fall River* took their places on the Providence Line. Now that the Bay Line was in operation, however, with the *Richard Peck* and the *Kennebec*, Providence was to have passenger service through the winter for the first time in about thirty years.

On Monday, December 4, the long-awaited new *Chester W. Chapin* of the Narragansett Bay Line finally arrived in New York from her builders in Maryland. On Thursday, December 7, she made a trial trip to New Haven with the usual load of dignitaries aboard. Then, after two weeks at her pier in New York receiving her furniture and final fittings, she made her first trip from New York to New Haven and Providence. As she was the first steamer since the *Connecticut* of a decade earlier built specifically to run to Providence, she was enthusiastically received in that city on her arrival the following morning. During the day, hundreds of visitors, flush with the mood of Christmas which was just three days away, came to visit the new steamer and wish her well.

The *Chester W. Chapin* was indeed a fine steamer and lived up to expectations. In general design, she was similar to her running mate, the *Richard Peck*. Her triple expansion engine was virtually a copy of the *Richard Peck*'s; her Saloon Deck stateroom arrangement was almost identical, and her interior decorations were in the same style. In profile, however, the *Chapin* more closely resembled the *City of Lowell*, which had also been designed by A. Cary Smith, than the *Richard Peck*. For while the *Peck*'s Gallery Deck extended only to midships, ending just aft of the smokestacks, the *Chapin*'s Gallery Deck, like the *Lowell*'s, extended all the way to the stern and contained a separate section of staterooms, giving her nearly thirty more staterooms (138) than the *Richard Peck*. In addition, the *Richard Peck* was unique in having a very marked sheer which the *Chester W. Chapin*, like the *City of Lowell*, did not have. Like both the *Richard Peck* and the *City of Lowell*, the *Chester W. Chapin* had an unusually wide beam (64 feet) for her length (323 feet). This width, plus exceptionally high Main Decks, gave all three of these steamers much larger cargo capacities than would normally be found on steamers of their size.

While it by no means approached the Renaissance grandeur of the Fall River Line steamers, the interior of the *Chester W. Chapin* was nevertheless exceptionally attractive, if one can accept as attractive the rather heavy Edwardian style that was then becoming popular.

> The main saloon aft, especially, is one of the most beautiful apartments of the kind on a sound steamer. The prevailing tone is one of old rose and gold, the painting of the paneling being done with light tints, relieved with gold leaf. The decks in the saloons are covered with a specially designed and extra heavy Axminster carpet, in the Persian style, the general tone being deep red, which is in harmony with the furniture.[12]

Like the *Richard Peck* (as well as the *City of Lowell*, the *Maine*, and the *New Hampshire*), the *Chester W. Chapin*'s dining area was located on the Gallery Deck forward. The *Chapin*'s upper deck dining room, painted a soft ivory trimmed in gold leaf, and with deep blue carpeting, evokes very special memories. With windows along both sides, from which passengers could watch the passing scene while dining, and a high clerestory dome, it always seemed bright and cheerful, especially in the summer when the sun did not set until after dinnertime.

With the arrival of the *Chester W. Chapin*, the Bay Line had two fast and modern steamers on the Providence route. It was possible, therefore, to tighten the line's schedule considerably, and the departure time from both ports was moved up to 5:00 P.M., although it could have been even later without putting a strain on either the *Richard Peck* or the *Chester W. Chapin*, both of which were exceptionally fast steamers. At the same time, the company announced that it had placed an order for still another steamer, this one to be an exact sistership of the *Chester W. Chapin*. When this new steamer was completed, the *Richard Peck* was to rejoin the *C. H. Northam* on the New Haven run, thus giving New Haven sufficient service so that the *Chester W. Chapin* and the new steamer could run directly to Providence without stopping at New Haven en route and could maintain a schedule similar to that of the regular Providence Line.

Early in December, the Joy Line indicated its intention of remaining a fixture on Long Island Sound by announcing that it was moving its New York terminus from the city pier (Pier 1, North River), where it had been renting space on a temporary basis, to Pier 35 (later renumbered Pier 27 for the sake of confusion), East River, on which the company had just signed a ten-year lease. A few days later, the line also announced that it had purchased an ocean-going steamer for its Boston route and had sold the *Allan Joy* to the Bridgeport Line as a replacement for the burned *Nutmeg State*. The *Allan Joy*, although fast and a good sea boat, as she would have to have been for the Norfolk-Cape Charles route for which she had been built, was still a sound-type steamer with overhanging guards and not really suitable for the heavy winter weather she would soon encounter on the outside run to Boston. On December 16, 1899, just six months after her first trip, the *Allan Joy* made her last run from Boston to New York for the Joy Line. The following day, she was turned over to the Bridgeport Line, on which she was to serve first as the *Allan Joy* and later as the *Naugatuck*, until passenger service to Bridgeport was discontinued more than twenty years later. The Joy Line had operated the *Allan Joy* as a freighter, but the Bridgeport Line, which needed her for an overnight passenger and freight service, left the Main Deck clear for freight, as it was on most of the sound steamers, but added staterooms the full length of the Saloon Deck. In either guise, she remained a very handsome little steamer.

Thus, by December 1899, the Joy Line was back where it started with the *Rosalie* running to Providence. But this was not to be the situation for long, for the larger steamer the line had purchased to replace the *Allan Joy* on the Boston route was already at Morse's yard being fitted out for the service.

1900

The beginning of January 1900 found the winter operation of the sound steamers about what it had been at the same time the year before with a few exceptions. The *Plymouth* of the Fall River Line had run aground in the East River on December 19 soon after she came on for the season and had damaged her hull, so that for most of January the *Priscilla* was back on the line running with the *Pilgrim*. The *Pequot*, of course, rather than the *City of Fitchburg*, was running to New Bedford with the *City of New Bedford*. The main difference from the year before was that Providence now had its first all-year passenger line with the *Richard Peck* and the brand new *Chester W. Chapin*, as well as low-rate freight service twice a week with the Joy Line's *Rosalie*.

The main event on the sound at the start of the new year was the appearance of the steamer *Old Dominion* on the Boston run of the Joy Line. Once again the Joy Line had found a bargain: a highly serviceable steamship which it was able to buy at a very low price. Built in 1872 for the Old Dominion Line to run between New York, Norfolk, and Richmond, and designed by Herman Winter, who had also designed the steamers of the competing Metropolitan Line, one of which bore his name, the *Old Dominion*, by 1900, was so old-fashioned as to be something of a curiosity along the New York waterfront. With her ocean-type hull, high freeboard, and large sidewheels protruding out from her hull, the *Old Dominion* belonged to a class that had been typical of ocean and coastal steamships between about 1850 and 1880, but that had tended to disappear rapidly after that time as propellor-driven vessels became more popular for ocean runs. By 1900, the *Old Dominion* was the only ocean-type sidewheel steamer on the Atlantic Coast and was definitely an anachronism.

For most of her long tenure on the New York to Richmond run, the *Old Dominion* ran opposite the *Wyanoke*, a similar though somewhat smaller steamer, which had been sunk in a collision in Hampton Roads in 1896. Although older, the *Wyanoke* was the faster of the two and was better able than the *Old Dominion* to make the run from New York to Richmond in the twenty-four hours their schedule called for. The *Old Dominion*'s speed was considerably improved, however, after the W. and A. Fletcher yards fitted her with new feathering sidewheels in 1890.

The Old Dominion Line had kept this steamer in service somewhat longer than it might have both because she was very economical to operate and because, as a relatively lightdrafted sidewheeler, she was better suited than its other steamers for its direct line between New York and Richmond with its final stretch up the winding James River. But in 1899 the Old Dominion Line had decided to discontinue its passenger service between New York and Richmond and to add a new overnight passenger line between Norfolk and Richmond which would connect at Norfolk with its New York-Norfolk passenger steamers. Two small night boats had been ordered for this new service which were to appear in 1902 as the *Berkeley* and the *Brandon*. When in 1899 the *Old Dominion*, which had been remarkably free from breakdowns for nearly thirty years, began to show signs of wear, the line decided it was time to retire her. It probably came to them as a surprise, however, when their old iron sidewheeler was purchased not by a scrap dealer but by a new steamship line that planned to use her on a new route between New York and Boston.

Mention of the *Old Dominion* in 1900 seemed to evoke two quite opposite reactions. One group revered the steamer as old but solid; the other regarded her as a slow and obsolete hulk. The management of the Old Dominion Line apparently had a high regard for their steamer. In a speech to his stockholders made shortly before she was sold, the president of the company gave her sincere praise.

> We regard the Old Dominion [to be] as safe and as comfortable as any ship this company owns. She has been steadily at work from the time she went into service and I do not think she has been idle during all those years more than one month at a time. I hold her up as a model of what can be done by taking proper care of a good ship. I believe her to be the best sidewheel ship ever built and the most successful. I wish to say to the underwriters that in looking over the records I cannot find that we ever made claim upon them for damage or loss of cargo upon this ship in one year of over $500.[1]

Although the *Old Dominion* was to serve the Joy Line with the same regularity and dependability for another seven years, she was not on the run for very long before the president's last statement had been rendered hopelessly out of date.

On the Joy Line's Boston run, the *Old Dominion* proved slow but steady. Her big wheels carried her along at about ten to twelve knots, hardly an ideal speed for a new line between New York and Boston. It took her just about twenty-four hours (when the weather and tides were favorable) to make the trip, about two hours longer than the *Allan Joy*. She left New York every Wednesday and Saturday at 5:00 P.M. and paddled into Boston harbor at about twilight on Thursdays and Sundays. In order to manage two round trips a week, the *Old Dominion* made a fast turnaround in Boston on Thursdays, slipping out of Boston harbor again either late Thursday evening or before dawn on Friday and arriving in New York either late Friday night or early Saturday morning, with a full day in New York to load before leaving again on Saturday evening at five. The other trips were much more leisurely. Arriving in Boston late Sunday afternoon, she lay over there a full twenty-four hours before sailing again on Monday at five; then arriving in New York late on Tuesday, she again had a twenty-four hour layover before her Wednesday sailing.

At ten knots, the *Old Dominion* often lacked the power to buck the heavy tides at Hell Gate, and unless the tides were particularly favorable, she usually hailed a tug to pull her through. Not infrequently, the Joy Line employed a tug to take the *Old Dominion* all the way from Pier 35 to Whitestone. Since she was essentially an ocean steamer, when the weather was bad, the *Old Dominion* simply avoided Hell Gate altogether and sailed out into the Atlantic and around Long Island, but it was difficult for her to maintain her schedule when she had to use this route too often.

Old and slow though she was, the Joy Line people loved the *Old Dominion*. Looking out their windows at Pier 35 late in the afternoon and watching the paddler backing into the pier and unloading freight, they felt for the first time that they were running a real steamship company. At 260 feet, she was not very large, but next to the *Rosalie* she seemed like a mammoth ocean liner. And, in spite of her limitations, the *Old Dominion* served the line very well on the practical level. She had a large cargo-carrying capacity, nearly twice that of the *Allan Joy*, and she was extraordinarily economical to operate.[2] She was also one of the best sea boats on the sound and handled well in any sea. One reporter described her as "steady as a church,"[3] while the *Marine Journal* claimed that the *Old Dominion* could paddle through the sound "as steadily as the Albany day boat."[4]

The *Old Dominion's* first trip for the Joy Line was on Saturday night, December 30, 1899, under Captain William S. Durkee, who was well known among coastal mariners for having served many years as grand captain of the National Association of Masters, Mates, and Pilots. Less than three weeks later, Captain Durkee had an opportunity to test his steamer's ocean-going qualities; from January 18 to 21, the sound was covered with such a dense fog that most of the steamers canceled their sailings, but the *Old Dominion* simply sailed out into the Atlantic, as did the steamers of the rival Metropolitan Line, and brought her freight into Boston only a few hours behind schedule.[5]

The *Rhode Island*, which usually served as the relief boat on the railroad lines, was at Fletcher's yard for most of the winter of 1900 having a new shaft installed. Fortunately, the weather remained fairly mild, for the only steamer available to take her place was the older *Massachusetts*, which was almost never used during the winter. That year, however, she ran on the Stonington Line through most of January and February, while the *Maine* and the *New Hampshire* had their winter overhauls and late in February relieved the *City of Worcester* on the Norwich Line. By mid-March, the *Rhode Island* was back relieving the *City of Lowell*, so that for a few weeks the old Providence liners *Massachusetts* and *Rhode Island* ran together again on the Norwich Line. The repairs to the *Plymouth*'s hull, meanwhile, took nearly two months, so that it was the middle of February before the *Priscilla* could go back to her winter layover.

During the last two weeks of March, the sound mariners got a brief look at the new steel-hulled steamer *Governor Dingley*, which had been completed for the Boston-Portland Line late in 1899 to replace the lost *Portland*. Since her season on her regular route had not yet started, the New York-Portland Line borrowed her for several trips while its own steamer *Horatio Hall* was out of commission. At about the same time, the little steamer *Lincoln* from the Boston-Kennebec Line, which had filled in for the *C. H. Northam* on the Narragansett Bay Line the previous summer, turned up in New York on her way to Florida. Now rather exotically renamed *Martinique*, she had been purchased for a new route between Miami, Key West, and Havana, recently established by the Florida East Coast Railway.[6]

Late in February 1900, Chester W. Chapin, Jr., of the New Haven Steamboat Company startled the marine world once again with the announcement that he was planning to start still another steamship line. With the *Chester W. Chapin* and the *Richard Peck* running to New Haven and Providence and the *C. H. Northam* running just to New Haven, he was now having the thirty-eight-year-old *Continental* completely reconditioned to start a new line on the Hudson River between New York and Rhinecliff as soon as the river opened up in the spring.[7]

Why a line to Rhinecliff, especially as this small town was already served by the Saugerties Evening Line? Chester W. Chapin, Jr., the president of the New Haven Steamboat Company, was a banker from Springfield, Massachusetts. As such he had also recently been elected president of the Central New England Railway, a line running from Rhinebeck, New York, to Canaan and Winsted, Connecticut, which posed so small a threat that it was the only railroad in southern New England which the New Haven Railroad had neglected to take over. Under Chapin's management, however, the railroad was soon extended at its eastern end to run northward to Springfield, Chapin's home town, where it could connect with the trains of the Boston and Albany Railroad for Boston. At the western end, a spur track extended the road from Rhinebeck south to Poughkeepsie, where, by crossing the Poughkeepsie railroad bridge, the Central New England could connect with the Erie Railroad to the West or with the Reading into the coal mining areas of Pennsylvania. In short, by adding a few miles of track at either end, Chapin had turned his small railroad into a link in a new route between Boston and the West, bypassing the New Haven Railroad. And by running a steamer line from Rhinecliff (the port for Rhinebeck), he was creating an alternate route between Boston and New York.

Meanwhile, Chapin continued to improve the Providence service of his Narragansett Bay Line. In March, he purchased the Providence wharf of the Lonsdale Corporation which until then he had only been leasing. The surest way to prevent the railroad from acquiring the wharf and blocking his entry into Providence, he reasoned, was to buy it himself. At the same time, the Bay Line also secured the rights to wharfage at Saunderstown, Rhode Island, a resort town on the west side of Narragansett Bay, where it proposed to make a landing during the summer season.[8]

During April, the *C. H. Northam* was back on the Providence route for several weeks with the *Chester W. Chapin*, so that the *Richard Peck* could have several staterooms added on her Main Deck. Chapin continued to solicit bids for the proposed sistership of the *Chester W. Chapin* and also announced plans for two new steamers for the Rhinecliff route, since operating the outdated *Continental* on this line was clearly only a temporary expedient.[9]

On March 28, Providence was surprised by the Joy Line's totally unexpected announcement that the *Rosalie's* sailing from Providence that evening would be her last in the Providence-New York freight service. "Henceforeward and until further notice,"[10] the Joy Line would run only to Boston. It was generally assumed at the time that "until further notice" was merely a euphemism meaning that competition from the Bay Line had forced the Joy Line to give up its Providence freight route altogether. But this was not the case. The fact was that business was so good the *Rosalie* could no longer handle it all, and the Joy Line was negotiating for a larger steamer to take her place. Before these negotiations could be concluded. however, the line had received an offer too attractive to refuse for chartering the *Rosalie*, and, rather than turn it down, it suspended freight service to Providence temporarily until the other boat became available.

The *Rosalie's* charter was to the Old Dominion Line. The line's new steamers for the proposed Norfolk-Richmond night line were still far from completion; but, anxious to start the line, if only with a freight service, it chartered the *Rosalie* from the Joy Line to run with its own steamer *Albemarle* on the route until the *Berkeley* and *Brandon* were completed.[11] On this run the *Albemarle* carried a few passengers, but the *Rosalie* did not, although she had carried some passengers both on the Bridgeport Line and on the Joy Line. It is hard to see why the Old Dominion Line brought the *Rosalie* all the way down from New York when it had several suitable steamers of its own which could probably have been diverted from other routes. Just possibly the Joy Line still owed them money for the *Old Dominion*, and this charter had been arranged by Dimon as part payment, or even to prevent the *Old Dominion*'s being reclaimed. Such an arrangement would have been consistent with some of the methods the Joy Line had resorted to in order to stay in business with its limited resources.

On Thursday, March 29, 1900, just one year to the day after her first trip to Providence, the *Rosalie* tied up at Pier 35, East River, unloaded her freight, and then sailed out again to Morse's yards in Brooklyn where she was to be readied for the ocean voyage down to Norfolk.

That night, the Joy Line, now down to one steamer, nearly found itself with no service at all when a fire broke out in the engine room of the *Old Dominion*, then laying over at her pier in New York. The fire raged for over an hour before it was finally brought under control. The next morning the *Old Dominion* was towed up to Roach's shipyard at the foot of East Ninth Street, where the damage was estimated at over $10,000 and the foreman predicted that the steamer would be out of service for at least a month.[12]

Without a steamer on either of its routes, the Joy Line was in bad shape for a while. For nearly two weeks, backlogged freight piled up on its piers, and the line faced the danger of losing valued customers to the established lines. Eventually, Charles Dimon was able to charter a steamer—for one round trip only—at a price the Joy Line could afford (which in this emergency must have been something close to credit). She was the *Santuit*, a 246.5-foot British-built collier, which happened to have a long layover in Boston at that time and was available. The *Santuit* sailed from Boston for the Joy Line on Tuesday evening, April 11, and from New York on Saturday, April 14, being returned to her owners on her arrival in Boston.

Actually, the repairs to the *Old Dominion* were completed sooner than expected. (While being repaired at Roach's the *Old Dominion* found herself berthed right next to the steamer she had replaced on the Boston route, the *Allan Joy*, which was there to have staterooms added.)[13] By Saturday, April 21, the *Old Dominion*, as sober and as solid as ever, was back carrying full loads of freight to Boston.

On April 18, 1900, all of Providence was shocked and genuinely infuriated to learn that Chester W. Chapin had sold his entire steamship operation— the New Haven Line and the Narragansett Bay Line—to the New Haven Railroad.[14] There had been no warning that such a sale was even contemplated.[15] Both the citizens of Providence and the employees of the line felt a deep sense of betrayal. They had given the line their full and whole-hearted support; they had cheered this small company's efforts to beat the monopoly and had done all they could to assure its success; they had taken sincere pride in this steamer line that ran two smart, fast steamships between their city and New York. Smaller than the grand Fall River liners, yes, but these boats were Providence boats and they were proud of them. Daniel George, who had been the Providence agent for the line during its one year of operation, was deeply disappointed.[16] He had been given no hint that his superiors were planning to sell. He had worked hard to make the line successful. The steamers were sailing nearly fully booked with both passengers and freight nearly every night. The line had been a success in every way. Why?

There was but one answer. Every man has his price, and apparently Morgan had found Chapin's. Morgan had chafed when Chapin started the Providence Line but was prepared to meet him with nothing more than stiff competition in the field. When Chapin began organizing alternate railroad routes between Boston and the West, however, Morgan's monopoly was in jeopardy. For such threats Morgan knew only one cure—buy.

Ironically, Commodore Richard Peck, the longtime officer of the New Haven Steamboat Company for whom the steamer had been named, died suddenly of a heart attack the same day that the line was sold.[17]

The railroad did not discontinue the Bay Line operation to Providence immediately as bookings had been made for some time ahead. Rather, the line was allowed to stagger on for a few more weeks until the Providence Line started its summer service and could absorb the Bay Line's business. The railroad did stop running its freighters, however, and sent all freight on the Bay Line steamers. The *Richard Peck* was still out having work done when the sale was made, and the new owners did not feel that the *C. H. Northam* was suitable for the run. Therefore, the *C. H. Northam* went back to making daily round trips to New Haven, and the *Rhode Island*, the old standby, was placed on the Providence run with the *Chester W. Chapin*. With the *C. H. Northam* now sufficient for the New Haven traffic, the Bay Line steamers, in the last two weeks of operation, no longer made the stop at New Haven.

At the time, the *Rhode Island* was still on the New London Line substituting for the *City of Lowell*, but the *Massachusetts* was brought out again to take over that route. On one of her last trips to New London, however, the *Rhode Island* had been called on to perform an errand of mercy. On Saturday, April 28, the big Fall River steamer *Puritan*, bound out of New York with a full load of passengers, broke her shaft off Eaton's Neck at about nine-thirty in the evening. About a half hour later, the *Rhode Island* bound for New London and the *New Hampshire* of the Stonington Line came up the sound, saw the disabled *Puritan*, and the two of them took her in tow across the sound, where her passengers found a train waiting to take them to Boston. The *Plymouth*, then at Newport getting ready for her summer service to Providence, took the *Puritan*'s place out of Fall River the following evening and ran on the line with the *Priscilla* for another two weeks until the *Puritan* had been repaired.

The accident to the *Puritan* apparently made the railroad aware that, although it had accumulated a large number of steamers through various acquisitions, it was still short of steamers large enough to fill in on either the Fall River Line or the Providence Line should one of the steamers of these lines become disabled during the summer. Until recently, the Fall River Line had always had extra boats available for emergencies. But now with its winter boats running to Providence during the summer it did not. When the *Puritan* broke down unexpectedly in April, the *Plymouth* had been able to take her place because she had not yet started her summer service to Providence. But what if such an accident had taken place at the height of the summer season, as it easily could? The old *Providence* had been officially retired after her brief service on the Norwich Line the previous fall,[18] the *Massachusetts* was getting too old to be used on one of the railroad's prestige lines during the season, and the *City of Lowell*'s passenger capacity was less than half that of the *Plymouth* or the *Pilgrim*.

There was one steamer that could serve in the event of an emergency— the *Connecticut*. She was not large enough for the Fall River Line, but she would be more than adequate on the Providence Line releasing the *Plymouth* or the *Pilgrim* to fill in on the Fall River Line. But there was one problem: she didn't run. Her oscillating engine, the only one ever installed on a Long Island Sound passenger steamer, had proved so cantankerous, so undependable, that, even though the *Connecticut* was by far the most modern and commodious of its three steamers, the Providence and Stonington Line had rarely used her after 1895 and had laid her up altogether after the season of 1896.

On several occasions after that, the railroad's marine department had sent the *Connecticut* to the shops to see if the engines could be made to turn with some degree of efficiency, but in each case the effort had proved unsuccessful. In 1900, however, the marine department determined to send the steamer to Fletcher's in Hoboken with instructions to do whatever was necessary to make her serviceable. So on Sunday, May 6, the *City of Taunton* ran from Fall River down to the docks at Stonington, took the beautiful but dormant *Connecticut* in tow to New York, and deposited her at Fletcher's yard in Hoboken for one more attempt to get her engines to function.[19]

That same week the Joy Line announced that it had finally been able to purchase the steamer it had wanted as a replacement for the *Rosalie* on the Providence run. She was the *Seaboard*, currently running on the Gulf of Mexico out of Tampa.[20] The *Seaboard* was older than the *Rosalie* by a decade, but she was forty feet longer (180 feet) and had a much larger cargo capacity. Built in 1874, the *Seaboard* was the last and largest of four similar freighters built for the Old Bay Line's service between Canton, Maryland, and Norfolk, Virginia. During the 1890s, the line had found that its new passenger steamers, the *Alabama* and the *Georgia*, plus one larger freighter, the *Gaston*, were sufficient to handle the traffic, so the three remaining small freighters (one had burned) were sold, two to carry coal between New York and various southern ports, and the *Seaboard* for freight service between New York and Philadelphia. After nearly foundering in a collision with a lumber schooner in New York harbor in February 1899, the *Seaboard* was rebuilt and sold again to a new company that was starting a line between Tampa and Mobile.

The *Seaboard*'s service on this line was considered temporary from the start as the line had plans for new steamers. As usual, Charles Dimon had an inside track on news of good steamers that were likely to be available at low prices. When he heard that the *Seaboard* might be for sale, he went down to negotiate the purchase. The line was willing to sell, but it took some time to find a suitable replacement, which was why the Joy Line got caught for over a month without a steamer to run to Providence.

Eventually, the Tampa-Mobile Line found another steamer (the *Josephine*) to replace the *Seaboard*, and the sale of the *Seaboard* to the Joy Line was consummated in late April. The *Seaboard* left Tampa on May 2, and arrived in New York on May 9, just one week later. Then, after a short visit to Morse's drydocks in Brooklyn to be checked out, she made her first sailing from Pier 35, reestablishing the Joy Line's Providence service, on Monday, May 14. The *Seaboard* was not only larger than the *Rosalie*, she was considerably faster and could easily make the overnight run to Providence on the same schedule as the larger passenger steamers. Thus, with the *Seaboard* the Joy Line could now schedule three rather than two round trips per week to Providence. With Captain Dave Wilcox again in command, the *Seaboard* left New York every Monday, Wednesday, and Friday evening, and Providence on Tuesdays, Thursdays, and Saturdays.

During May 1900, the Joy Steamship Company not only reestablished its freight line to Providence but also started a new passenger service between New York and Boston (for the summer season only: mid-May to mid-October). The *Old Dominion* had, after all, carried passengers as well as freight on the Old Dominion Line and had stateroom space for about one hundred passengers. She was not new (with the retirement of both the *Providence* and the *Continental* that year, the *Old Dominion* inherited the honor of being the oldest overnight passenger steamer operating on the sound), and the twenty-four-hour voyage could hardly be called an express service, but her passenger quarters had been considered quite elegant in their day and were still comfortable, if not stylish.

Since the rival Metropolitan Line did not carry passengers, the Joy Line was offering direct passenger service between New York and Boston for the first time since the Neptune Line of the 1860s. Boston businessmen with pressing affairs in New York would not, of course, have chosen to travel there aboard the slow-paced *Old Dominion*. If they preferred a steamer trip to the four-hour train ride, they would still have taken the cars to Fall River or Providence and boarded the overnight steamer there, which would have arrived in New York at 7:00 A.M. the following morning, a good ten hours and a full business day ahead of the Joy Line's *Old Dominion*. For those, however, who were prepared for a leisurely sea voyage at a price below that of any of the other steamer lines ($3.00 one way versus $4.00 via the Fall River Line), the *Old Dominion* apparently had considerable appeal, for the Joy Line did a good business to Boston. There were always a few passengers who did not know one steamboat from another from reading the ads in the papers and who boarded the *Old Dominion* in Boston expecting another version of the *Priscilla*. From such passengers the *Old Dominion*'s primitive accommodations, antidiluvian decor, and cheerful indifference to scheduled arrival times evoked more than a few outraged remarks. To others, however, the *Old Dominion*'s easy pace and old-fashioned simplicity seemed a virtue. Still, when one considers the fast and luxurious New York to Boston service to be offered aboard the *Harvard* and *Yale* only seven years later, the Joy Line's Boston operation of 1900 seems in retrospect an incredible anachronism.

The first trip of the Joy Line's new passenger service to Boston was out of New York on Wednesday, May 23. That same night the *Puritan* was back on the Fall River Line with a new shaft after crews had worked on her twenty-four hours a day to get her ready as soon as possible. The *Plymouth*, therefore, was now available to start the summer Providence service more or less on schedule. The *Pilgrim* came up from Newport first, sailing for the *Rhode Island* on Monday, June 4. Then, on Tuesday, the *Plymouth* arrived in Providence to take the place of the *Chester W. Chapin*. With the *Plymouth* and the *Pilgrim* on the Providence Line, all traces of the Bay Line were gone. The *Chester W. Chapin* and the *Richard Peck* were placed on the New Haven Line, now run by the railroad; the *C. H. Northam* was laid up as a spare; and the *Continental* was put up for sale as scrap. The Central New England Railway was absorbed into the New Haven system, and the proposed steamship line to Rhinecliff was simply never mentioned again.

With the Narragansett Bay Line now out of the picture and the return of freight service with the *Seaboard* so well received, the Joy Line, which still did not have any capital to speak of, decided to start a passenger line to Providence as well as to Boston. If the Bay Line had made a profit, why couldn't the Joy Line? For this new service the Joy Line chartered the little twin-screw steamer *Martinique,* which we encountered as the *Lincoln* when she served briefly on the Narragansett Bay Line just one year earlier. Her new run between Miami, Key West, and Havana was a service mainly for winter vacationers and did not operate in the summer. (The line's larger steamer, the *Miami,* was usually chartered for a route on the Great Lakes every summer.) Thus, the *Martinique* was available to inaugurate the Joy Line's passenger service to Providence. She arrived in New York from Florida during the morning of Sunday, June 10. Then on Tuesday, June 12, 1900, the *Martinique,* with David Wilcox again in command, made the first New York to Providence passenger trip of the Joy Line.

The *Martinique* looked like a tender running up Narragansett Bay behind the *Plymouth* or the *Pilgrim* of the Providence Line. She had only about fifty staterooms compared with well over two hundred on each of the Providence Line steamers. She did not even have a proper dining room as most of the sound liners did; instead, like most of the Maine coast steamers, she had tables set up on her Saloon Deck forward for dining. But at least she was still new; her interior was simple but clean, and, compared with the *Old Dominion,* she was fast.

At first, the *Martinique* ran opposite the *Seaboard,* giving Providence passenger service three times a week and freight service six times a week. (Actually, the *Seaboard* did have accommodations for a few passengers and did occasionally carry paying customers who especially needed to travel on the nights she was sailing. But these accommodations—three or four small staterooms opening onto the deck—were minimal, to say the least, and the Joy Line did not advertise the *Seaboard* as a passenger vessel.) The *Martinique* left New York on Tuesdays, Thursdays, and Saturdays at 5:00 P.M. from the Joy Line pier at the foot of Catherine Street, and on her way up the East River she paused briefly at a pier at the foot of East Thirty-first Street to pick up "uptown" passengers. On Mondays, Wednesdays, and Fridays she sailed from Providence at 6:30 P.M. The one-way passenger fare on the *Martinique* was $1.75, considerably less than the $2.50 the Bay Line had been charging. (The fare to Boston via Joy Line steamer and railroad was just $2.00, half the price of the Boston fare of either the Providence Line or the Fall River Line and a dollar less than the longer direct trip on the Joy Line's own *Old Dominion.*) With these fares, the *Martinique* had no trouble booking all fifty staterooms nearly every trip.

During the course of the summer, it appeared that Boston-bound cargo was getting to be more than the *Old Dominion* could handle alone. As a result, the *Seaboard* was taken off the Providence route and began running with the *Old Dominion* to Boston, although she continued to make an occasional round trip to Providence when too much freight got back-logged for the *Martinique* to take care of. The *Seaboard* was hardly suitable for the Boston run. She was now nearly thirty years old and had been built for a route on the protected waters of Chesapeake Bay. But she proved a staunch little craft and continued to run to Boston for the Joy Line, off and on, in winter as well as summer, for another seven years.

One reason for placing the *Martinique* on a Tuesday, Thursday, Saturday schedule out of New York was so that she would have her Sunday layover in Providence and thus be available for Sunday excursions down Narragansett Bay which were to be a new feature of the Joy Line's service. Her very first Sunday on the Joy Line, June 17, and every Sunday thereafter, the *Martinique* pulled away from her Providence wharf at 10:00 A.M. and sailed down Narragansett Bay to Cottage City (now Oak Bluffs) on Martha's Vineyard. She arrived there at 2:30 in the afternoon and waited at the pier for about two hours while the passengers inspected the picturesque village, and then departed again at 4:30 for a twilight sail back up the bay, depositing the passengers at the Point Street wharf at about 10:00 in the evening. This full day of cruising on Narragansett Bay and Buzzard's Bay cost the passenger only $1.00. Lunch and dinner were served on board for fifty cents each.

These Sunday excursions offered by the night boats were an established institution of the 1890s and early 1900s before the automobile became popular enough for the average family to have one of its own available for Sunday outings. By the late 1800s, many of America's eastern cities had grown into large crowded metropolises. But advances in local transportation systems had not yet made it feasible for the majority of the middle class to live outside the city. Instead, they lived in those miles on miles of row houses which, when the middle class later emigrated to the suburbs after about 1910, were to become the vast slums of our present-day cities. These middle-class quarters in the cities were comfortable enough, for the most part, but in the summer they tended to be hot. There was no air conditioning, of course, in those days, no radio or television for diversion, and very few automobiles. The only means of escape from the heat of the city on the one free day of the week was by trolley or by steamer.

The many day steamers operating out of the various ports of the Eastern Seaboard provided short trips on the open sea that were a welcome relief to the city-dweller during the heat of the summer. But as of 1900 most of these day steamers were designed for commuting services or for ferrying passengers on short routes to summer resorts near the city. Most were not equipped to handle the explosion of Sunday excursionists. The grandest of all the day steamers were those of the Hudson River Day Line between New York and Albany, which set the standards for day boats in the same way that the Fall River Line did for night boats, but in 1900 this line did not even deign to run on Sundays. The night boats on the other hand, with a few exceptions, tended not to sail on Sunday evenings, since freight was not delivered on Sundays. Therefore, in the 1890s, some of the night steamers began to experiment with Sunday excursions, particularly out of New York where the Hudson River excursion business was an open field on Sundays. Steamers arriving from an overnight run early Sunday morning would disembark their passengers and unload their freight and be ready to take on excursionists by 9:00 A.M. At about 10:00 the steamer would leave for a day trip up the Hudson, or perhaps south to Coney Island or Rockaway or up Long Island Sound to Rye, Bridgeport, or New Haven, returning to the New York pier late in the evening. In those days, crews were paid a regular salary, a small one at that, and were expected to perform their duties whenever the company chose to put the steamer to sea. Only because it was not yet necessary to think of paying crews double-time for Sunday work was it possible to offer these low-rate excursions.

The night lines that regularly scheduled excursions out of New York were the New Haven Line and the New London Line. The New Haven Line, which had a short day run as part of its regular operation in the summer, modified its schedule on Sundays (except during the year 1899 when both of its fast steamers were running on the daily service to Providence). Excursionists could therefore leave New York at about 10:00 A.M., arrive in New Haven around 2:00 P.M., spend two hours in New Haven (although a walk through the industrial areas of downtown New Haven on a Sunday afternoon could hardly compare with an afternoon in Martha's Vineyard, a swift-footed excursionist might find some verdant relief if directed to the New Haven Green or the campus of Yale University), and arrive back in New York at about 9:00 P.M., after a pleasant twilight sail down the sound. In addition, every Sunday the *City of Lowell* of the Norwich Line took passengers up the Hudson as far as Poughkeepsie (without landing) and back, or roughly the route of the present Hudson River *Dayliner*.

The *City of Lowell's* running mate, the big sidewheeler *City of Worcester*, had a complicated Sunday route out of New London. She left New London early on Sunday morning for Greenport, Long Island, where she picked up excursionists who had traveled the full length of Long Island via Long Island Railroad from New York. Here they boarded the *City of Worcester* which then speeded them across Block Island Sound for a day in Newport, Rhode Island. In the early evening, the *City of Worcester* picked up her passengers again and sailed them back to Greenport, where they were taken back to the city by train, while the *City of Worcester* made her way back to her dock in New London.

Neither the Fall River Line nor the Providence Line offered Sunday excursions, although both sent out a spare steamer on special occasions.

The Fall River Line steamers had to be ready for regular sailings on Sunday evenings and could not, but the Providence Line, which until recently had not run on Sundays, apparently had simply never thought of it.

The Joy Line thought of it, and the Sunday trips of the *Martinique* were well patronized. These excursions were not run by the regular management of the Joy Line, which was, of course, based in New York, but by an enthusiastic young man, Arthur S. Pitts, who had recently been hired as the Providence passenger agent for the Joy Line, now that the line had a steamer that carried passengers.

The Joy Line's experimental move into the passenger business was apparently a complete success, and the line's management now looked forward to expanding the passenger business to Providence by adding another steamer for a daily service and perhaps by acquiring larger boats. But their dreams were short-lived and the awakening came quickly. While the Joy Line still carried only freight twice a week on the aging *Old Dominion* to Boston or the tiny *Rosalie* to Providence, the New Haven Railroad had shown little concern. Chapin's Narragansett Bay Line was a far more serious challenge and had to be dealt with first. But with the Bay Line out of the way and the Joy Line planning to get into an all-year passenger business to Providence, the New Haven could now train all of its artillery on this small privately owned operation.

One might well ask why such a well-established institution as the New Haven Railroad, with its large and well-patronized overnight steamers, should even bother to notice a small operation like the Joy Line, when all of the passengers and freight on the *Martinique* fully loaded would probably not have been missed if taken directly from the decks of the *Pilgrim*. Besides, the Joy Line, for the most part, was *not* taking business from the Providence Line. The kind of passenger who might enjoy a trip down the sound on the *Martinique* could never afford to travel on the big *Plymouth* or *Pilgrim*. And the freight on the Providence Line steamers was generally through freight, destined for points further north on the trains of the New Haven Railroad which met the steamers at the dock, whereas the Joy Line, which, as it happened did not also own a railroad, carried mostly freight from small businesses in Providence.

The answer is to be found in Morgan's often declared policy that the best way to run a business was to control the field absolutely and not to have to deal with any competition. Morgan was also convinced that a small successful business could easily become a large successful business and that the time to eliminate competition was while it was still small.

For awhile the management of the New Haven Railroad considered lowering the freight rates on the Providence Line steamers.[21] But after some consideration the New Haven decided against a policy that might appear to debase the reputation of one of its prestige steamer lines. Once the Joy Line introduced its low-rate passenger service to Providence, however, the railroad turned to a different tactic: the New Haven would start its own low-rate steamer line between New York and Providence which could offer prices that would undercut those of the Joy Line, both for passengers and for freight, without tarnishing the reputation of its regular Providence Line.

Thus, early in July 1900 the management of the New Haven Railroad, in an atmosphere of cynical largesse, suddenly decided, only two months after putting the Narragansett Bay Line out of business, that the people of Providence deserved a low-rate steamship line to New York. Whereas the New Haven was experiencing a shortage of larger steamers now that the winter boats of the Fall River Line were employed on the Providence run in the summer, it had three smaller steamers lying idle: the *Massachusetts*, the *Rhode Island*, and the *C. H. Northam*. The *Connecticut*, too, might have become available if she could have been made to run. Even the brand new *Chester W. Chapin* was not really needed on the New Haven Line where she was then employed. But the *Connecticut* was still not running. As of late June, the *Marine Journal* reported that "the *Connecticut* is still at Fletcher's trying to get that big oscillating engine to work."[22] The *Rhode Island*, which, of the available steamers, was in the best condition, was therefore also the most valuable for use as a spare in the event of emergencies and so was kept aside. The *C. H. Northam*, as we have already seen, was much too slow to run regularly to Providence. But the *Massachusetts* would do nicely. With 184 staterooms she was smaller than the *Pilgrim* or the *Plymouth*, but still large enough to dwarf the *Martinique*. She was getting old, of course, for in those days twenty-three years was a long time for a wooden-hulled sidewheeler, but since the New Haven did not plan to keep the *Massachusetts* in operation much longer, her use or abuse by a class of passengers not accustomed to Fall River Line luxury would not prove a hardship. So the once-proud old Providence liner was brought from Stonington up to Newport for some minimal refurbishing and then on to Providence to start running on the railroad's new low-fare line to New York, which was to be known as the New Line.

The utter cynicism with which the railroad management entered into this new operation is apparent in a letter from John Hall, then vice-president of the New Haven Railroad, to Edward G. Buckland, the Providence lawyer in whose person the old Providence and Stonington Line maintained its legal entity:

You will note by tomorrow's paper that the steamer *Massachusetts* will begin a new excursion service between New York and Providence at one dollar fare each way. The week end *Journal* will probably say that this is done to crush out the business of the Joy Line. You know better than that and in putting this on we have only yielded to the urgent demand of the people of Providence for cheap rates during the summer season. If questioned, therefore, I can trust you to say that we are simply trying an experiment of cheap rates during the season to see if they are appreciated by the people or not and to give the people of Providence an opportunity to go to New York and back if they desire at a low rate. . . . Avoid any allusion to the Joy Steamship Company and of course any statement that may indicate that we are putting on this service to in any way interfere with their enterprise.[23]

The New Line, for some reason, found it convenient for the *Massachusetts* to sail from New York and Providence on the same nights as the Joy Line's *Martinique*. The fare was just $1.00, well below the Joy Line's $1.75 fare. The first sailing of the *Massachusetts* was from Providence on Monday, July 16. Her schedule called for her to leave Providence, from the Lonsdale wharf, which the railroad had acquired with its purchase of the Narragansett Bay Line, every Monday, Wednesday, and Friday at 7:30 P.M. (one hour later than the *Martinique*) and to arrive in New York at Pier 36, North River, recently leased for the New Line, at 7:30 the following mornings. Returning, she left New York at 5:45, later than the *Martinique* but just a quarter of an hour ahead of the *Plymouth*, and arrived in Providence at 6:00 A.M.

The New Line operation was immediately successful, or perhaps we should say popular, since, with its fare $1.00, it could hardly have been much of a financial success. Through the summer the *Massachusetts* regularly sailed fully booked, often with up to eight hundred passengers, many berthed in her free dormitories and many more with no berths booked at all, prepared to sit up all night or to sleep on the decks for the privilege of taking an overnight steamer to New York for a dollar.

It should probably not surprise the well-attuned reader to learn that, soon after the inauguration of the New Line, the railroad elected to treat the people of Providence to low-fare excursions on Sundays to—of all places— Cottage City on Martha's Vineyard. So for the rest of the summer of 1900, Sunday mornings would find both the grand old sidewheeler *Massachusetts* and the small twin-screw *Martinique* sailing down Narragansett Bay laden with excursionists.

Many Providence merchants were infuriated by the appearance of the New Line. It was obvious to them that the low freight rates promised on the *Massachusetts* would be withdrawn as soon as the Joy Line had been forced out of business, and that Providence people would again have a choice only between the railroad and the steamship line operated by the monopoly. In July 1900, the *Providence Board of Trade Journal*, which, now that the Narragansett Bay Line was gone, had again become a strong booster of the Joy Line, ran two large photographs on the same page. On the top was an illustration of the big sidewheelers *Pilgrim* and *Rhode Island* on either side of Fox Point wharf and under it was the caption: "The company operating this line is trying all ways to kill their little competitor, the Joy Line." The one beneath it showed the diminutive Joy Line steamer, which the *Journal* rather optimistically labeled, "The palatial steamer *Martinique*," with the further observation that "this company is making a gallant fight and our businessmen should help them."[24]

One might have expected that the Joy Line, with its limited resources and its one small chartered steamer, would have gone under soon after the *Massachusetts* started running. Not at all. The idea of cheap no-frills overnight trips to New York caught on rapidly, and there were apparently enough people anxious to patronize them to keep both lines well booked every night. In fact, the Joy Line probably profited from the publicity which the New Line brought to the concept. When the New Line introduced its $1.00 fare, the Joy Line fare also quickly dropped to $1.00. The New Line countered by offering the trip for seventy-five cents. But the Joy Line held, for a time, to the dollar fare, though it met the New Line to some extent by offering a round trip for $1.50.

Why would a passenger be willing to pay a dollar to travel on a small and sparsely furnished steamer like the *Martinique* when for only seventy-five cents he could go to New York on the *Massachusetts*, which, if getting on in years, was still one of the most luxurious and most beautifully appointed steamers on the sound? Apparently, many people who lacked the funds for a voyage on the big Providence Line steamers were still happy to pay an extra twenty-five cents to avoid the carnival-like atmosphere that prevailed aboard the *Massachusetts*. With up to eight hundred passengers crowding onto a steamer built to carry half that number, the air of quiet elegance which had always been associated with overnight trips on the Fall River Line or the Providence Line was lost on the New Line. According to one contemporary reporter, the *Massachusetts* would "arrive at and depart from the port every day with [her] decks black with people, the greater majority of which sleep on the floors of the saloons."[25] In their dealings with passengers, the agents and officers of the New Line made little attempt to maintain the dignity and courtesy for which the established steamer lines had been famous. Passengers were herded aboard the *Massachusetts* with very little ceremony as though she were an excursion boat to Coney Island. No one was allowed, for instance, to bring friends or relatives aboard for the usual farewell parties in the staterooms: the ticket-collection system was far too chaotic to prevent stowaways.[26] One could rarely find a seat in the saloons or even a pleasant spot to stand on a deck that was not already crowded. Many passengers brought their own food in baskets or paper bags, but those who attempted to use the steamer's dining room failed to find there the traditional service associated with steamboat travel; they usually had interminable waits and rather curt treatment once they were seated.[27]

The Joy Line's *Martinique*, on the other hand, lacked even the remnants of former elegance that were still visible on the *Massachusetts*. This small Maine coaster had a minimum of gold or plush to relieve the institutional ivory of her one passenger deck. With rarely more than a hundred people aboard, however, a passenger could at least find a chair to sit on in the saloon, could expect to be seated in the dining area and be properly waited on, and could stand on deck in the evening to enjoy the peaceful sounds of the sea at night. Moreover, Joy Line agents on shore and officers on the steamer were very particularly instructed to treat passengers with both respect and friendliness, a policy which, one likes to believe, helped keep the Joy Line in business against such overwhelming odds.

The line that suffered, of course, was the Providence Line. Through the summer of 1900, the *Massachusetts* and the *Martinique* each sailed regularly with full passenger lists while the *Plymouth* and the *Pilgrim*, both, but particularly the *Pilgrim*, expensive steamers to operate, sailed less than half booked. The $1.00 fare was not sufficient to run the *Massachusetts* at a profit, so with three large steamer running at a loss, the fight with the Joy Line was an expensive one for the railroad. The Joy Line's small steamer, on the other hand, was extraordinarily inexpensive to operate, so that, so long as she was full, as she usually was, the *Martinique* made some profit, even with the $1.00 fare. By the end of the 1900 season, the Joy Line, far from being forced under by the New Line, was still in excellent health.

Soon after the New Haven had attempted to get rid of the Joy Line in Providence by introducing a cheap line of its own, the Metropolitan tried a similar tactic on the Boston route. Like the New Haven's Providence Line, the Metropolitan was reluctant to meet the Joy Line competition by reducing its own rates, and thus not only cheapen its reputation but also risk becoming involved in contractual obligations which it could not afford to maintain. Rather than setting up a whole new line as the New Haven had done, the Metropolitan Line persuaded the Ocean Steamship Company (the Savannah Line) to place one of its older steamers—the *City of Macon*—on a regular run between New York and Boston, its losses secretly subsidized by the Metropolitan, with freight rates that were competitive with those of the Joy Line.[28]

The *City of Macon* (255 feet; built 1877) was about the same size and vintage as the *Old Dominion*, although its was propellor-driven, slightly newer, slightly larger, and probably slightly faster. At first, the *City of Macon* was scheduled to sail every fifth day from each port. The passage of $5.00 each way including berth and meals was probably roughly comparable to the Joy Line's $3.00 fare with berth and meals extra.[29]

Although the Savannah Line continued to operate the *City of Macon* between New York and Boston for almost two years, the operation was never successful and tended to lose money (for the Metropolitan Line). After the first summer season, sailings were reduced to one round trip every other week.

The Joy Line faced a short emergency toward the end of the summer when the *Martinique*, already fully booked in advance, developed engine trouble and had to miss two round trips (August 21-24). At this time of year, it was almost impossible to find a suitable steamer to fill in for her, particularly on short notice. But somehow Dimon was able to arrange to charter the Hudson River steamer *Newburgh*, which came around to Pier 35, East River, the very day the *Martinique* went to the shops, and ran to Providence for her until she returned four days later. The *Newburgh* was distinctly a river steamer in style, but she was about the same size as the *Martinique*, and she certainly sufficed to save face at the time.

During most of the summer of 1900, the *Old Dominion* was again alone on the Boston run while the *Seaboard* went to Morse's yards in Brooklyn for extensive renovations. In addition to having her engines repaired and her hull strengthened, the *Seaboard* had several staterooms added to her cabin deck, giving her accommodations for about twenty passengers. It was not the Joy Line's intention, of course, to convert the *Seaboard* into a passenger steamer. But with quarters for at least a few passengers she could be used in emergencies in off-season periods, should the line get caught without an available passenger steamer.

Freight from Providence was always heaviest in September when the New York clothing firms were placing their biggest orders, so when the *Seaboard* returned from her overhaul she went back on the Providence route running on opposite nights from the *Martinique*. This arrangement had lasted barely a fortnight, when the *Old Dominion* was involved in an accident and the *Seaboard* had to take her place on the Boston run. On the afternoon of Wednesday, October 3, the *Old Dominion* was making her way northward off Cape Cod with nothing visible in any direction except a dense fog when, with no warning whatever, the schooner *Jonathan Cone* materialized so close off her port bow that neither vessel had time to change course and avoid a collision. The impact was not great, however, as the two vessels merely struck each other along their port sides and then bounced apart again. But the *Old Dominion*'s wheel had been damaged and was out of commission. The steamer sat rolling helplessly in the fog for several hours while some of her crew rowed ashore to summon help. Eventually the tug *O. L. Halenbeck* came down from Boston, took the *Old Dominion* in tow back to Boston, waited there while she unloaded her cargo and reloaded again, then towed her back to New York, cargo and all, and over to Morse's to have her wheel repaired.[30] The *Old Dominion* was off the route for nearly two weeks just at the time of year when freight demands were heaviest. The *Porto Rico*, a small steamer of the Porto Rico Line (used locally around the island), was in New York at the time just finishing an overhaul, and the Joy Line arranged to charter her for one round trip (New York to Boston, October 9-10; Boston to New York, October 13-14) until the *Seaboard*'s schedule made it possible for her to take over the run.

As it turned out, the *Martinique* was not able to handle the Providence freight alone, so that for part of the time that the *Old Dominion* was out, the Joy Line had to charter a tugboat and barge to get all the freight moved.[31]

On October 15, the *Martinique*'s charter ran out, and it was time for her to sail back to Florida and get ready for her winter run. By now the Joy Line was committed, however, to staying in the passenger business, so Dimon had been looking around for a boat to charter over the winter. He talked first with the Atlantic Highlands Line about the possibility of using its steamer *St. Johns*. Built in 1874, she was as old as the *Seaboard*, although she was to continue in service for another forty years before she burned as the excursion boat *Tolchester* in Baltimore in 1942. On close inspection, Dimon decided that the *St. Johns* was unsuitable. She was in excellent condition, but, although she had originally served as an overnight steamer on a variety of lines, including the Hartford Line, she had recently had so many of her staterooms removed for her day service to Atlantic Highlands that she could no longer carry enough passengers to be profitable.[32]

Eventually, Dimon was able to arrange to charter the *Shinnecock* of the Montauk Line, which, since it served the summer resorts of eastern Long Island, did not operate in the winter. The *Shinnecock*, which made her first trip to Providence on Thursday, October 11, was not only a far more satisfactory boat than the *St. Johns*, but she was also one of the finest steamers the Joy Line ever operated. Like the *Martinique*, the *Shinnecock* was a relatively new boat, having come out in 1896, and at 226 feet was larger particularly as she was a sidewheel steamer and therefore considerably wider. Whereas the interior of the *Martinique* was a bit austere, the interior of the *Shinnecock* radiated much more of the warmth and elegance that the plush-covered chairs, Persian carpets, and cut-glass designs in the clerestory windows gave to the steamboats of that era.

Since the charter of the *Shinnecock* stipulated that she be commanded by her own captain, with the replacement of the *Martinique* by the *Shinnecock* on the Joy Line, David Wilcox returned to the command of the *Seaboard*.

In the same week that the *Shinnecock* came on the Joy Line to run in place of the *Martinique*, the Providence Line steamers finished their summer passenger season. There was some question as to whether or not the New Line passenger service should continue through the winter. No doubt the railroad was surprised to find the Joy Line still in business at the end of the summer season and even more surprised when the line chartered another passenger steamer to run through the winter. In the end, the railroad decided to keep the New Line running as well, but, as part of a general reshuffling of the railroad steamers at the end of the season, the *Rhode Island* came on the line to replace the *Massachusetts*. With the summer over, the railroad no longer needed two large passenger steamers on its recently acquired New Haven Line. By leaving the *Chester W. Chapin* on that route alone during the winter (with the *City of Lawrence* helping out with freight), the *Richard Peck* became available to be used that year rather than the older *Rhode Island* as the general relief boat on the Stonington and Norwich Lines. The *Rhode Island* had fewer staterooms than the *Massachusetts* but was a better sea boat and cheaper to operate and thus better suited as a winter boat on the New Line.

Once the passenger service on the Providence Line had been suspended for the winter, the New Line moved its operation from the Lonsdale wharf to Fox Point wharf until spring. Moreover, with the *Rhode Island* running to Providence three nights a week under railroad auspices, the Providence Line no longer found it necessary to run two freight boats through the winter. Therefore, the *Nashua* was alone on the line that year running on alternate nights with the *Rhode Island*, although the *City of Fall River* kept steam up in her layover in Newport and frequently made extra freight runs when needed.

During the fall of 1900, the Joy Line was apparently involved briefly in an abortive plan of the Pennsylvania Railroad to create its own access to southern New England and free itself of its dependece on the New Haven for through traffic. The Pennsylvania particularly chafed at the price which the New Haven charged for transporting coal to the New England factory areas and was apparently seeking an alternate way of getting it there. On Monday, October 22, several high officials of the Pennsylvania Railroad made a special overnight trip between New York and Providence aboard the steamer *Montauk*, the smaller running mate of the *Shinnecock* on the Montauk Line (which had recently become a subsidiary of the Pennsylvania Railroad), apparently for the purpose of examining the feasibility of establishing a line of its own on the route. Even more serious consideration, however, was given to a plan to subsidize the Joy Line so that it could serve as the Pennsylvania's route to New England. In particular, for reasons that are now not clear, the Pennsylvania wanted the Joy Line to establish a steamer line between New York and Newport.[33] Eventually, the Pennsylvania and the New Haven reached a mutually satisfactory agreement on through rates, for the Pennsylvania's plan was never carried out and its negotiations with the Joy Line were dropped.

During the first week of November 1900, the country was alive with anticipation of one of the most hotly contested presidential elections in American history between the Republican incumbent William McKinley and the Democratic candidate William Jennings Bryan. Much of the campaign was based on a largely manufactured argument between the two camps over the price of gold. Bryan maintained that the country should mint silver; McKinley insisted that we should keep a "sound" currency system by maintaining the gold standard. The Republican campaign climaxed on Saturday, November 3, with a grand "Sound Money" parade through the streets of New York. The *Rhode Island* of the New Line made a special excursion to New York taking a group down on Friday night and then postponing her return sailing from New York until 8:00 P.M. so that the passengers need not miss any of the great parade.[34] The Joy Line made no such promise; as westerners, both Dunbaugh and Joy fully supported Bryan's call for the minting of silver and therefore had little desire to treat their passengers to an extra hour or two of the "Sound Money" parade. No one was surprised that McKinley won the election, but there was surprise that he won it so overwhelmingly. Bryan did not even carry his home state of Nebraska.

While November 1900 did not bring about a change in the presidency of the nation, it did bring a change in the presidency of the New Haven Railroad. In that month, the elderly Charles P. Clark resigned as president of the railroad and was succeeded by Judge John Hall, the former vice-president who had expressed such antipathy to the Joy Line at the time of the inauguration of the New Line in July. As president of one of the nation's more prestigious railroad companies, one would have thought that Judge Hall would have had more lofty matters to deal with than the competition offered by one small struggling steamship line on Long Island Sound. But for the next two years Hall seems to have given a great deal of personal attention to the fight with the Joy Line. His correspondence abounds with references to it. As this struggle between the Joy Line and the New Haven Railroad continued and grew during Hall's two-year tenure as president of the New Haven, one cannot help noticing that the terms used to describe it are consistently those of a military campaign. Often the language seems to suggest that the struggle was motivated not by business or financial considerations alone but by the fight itself, the excitement of engaging in battle, or the satisfaction of defeating an opponent, for its own sake. One wonders how small businesses survived at all in this age of "free enterprise," which not only condoned such attitudes but actually viewed them as particularly American virtues.

During the late fall of 1900, the Joy Line apparently began to feel the bite of the New Line competition. The line had done well during the summer. But in the fall, as business began to decline, it became increasingly difficult to make a profit with a fare of $1.00. The company was seriously in debt, and the winter traffic was not bringing in enough revenue to let it catch up. The proposed deal with the Pennsylvania Railroad must have looked very attractive coming when it did, and, when it failed to materialize, the owners of the Joy Line were apparently not certain that they could afford to stay in business. At that time, they seem even to have given some thought to emulating Chapin and forcing the New Haven Railroad to buy them out. Someone connected with the Joy Line communicated to President Hall, through one of the directors of the New Haven, that another party (the Pennsylvania?) had made a bid for the Joy Line but that the Joy people would be willing to sell the line to the New Haven if it cared to match the bid. This blatant feeler had no effect on Hall except to give him another opportunity to make one of his acid blasts against the Joy Line:

> We certainly do not wish to buy out the Joy Line. . . . We cannot of course prevent other parties purchasing that property. . . . All we can do is assure whoever buys it that we will make it exceedingly warm while that opposition continues in Providence, and whoever buys it will buy a concern that is on its last legs in my judgment. . . . But they can rest assured that this company will not buy anything they have to sell for the reason that they have nothing to sell that is worth anything. One dilapidated steamer and the lease of a part of a dock in New York are the sole assets . . . of that company as I see the situation.[35]

Failing in this attempt, the Joy Line decided to stay in business, probably because, with so many debts, it could not afford to quit. For the next two years, the line continued to run on the brink of bankruptcy, though somehow always enough ahead to keep the steamers running.

The last weeks of the year 1900 also marked the end of an era in Long Island Sound steamboating, for in a short period the last three remaining steamers dating from the 1860s were consigned to the bone yard. Early in December, the federal government opened its new facilities at Ellis Island and returned the old Stonington Line steamer *Narragansett* which it had been chartering for housing. A few days later she was towed to Noank, Connecticut, to be scrapped. At about the same time, the former Fall River liner *Providence* was towed from Newport, where she had been laid up, to Providence and tied up at the now unused Lonsdale wharf to wait for a buyer to claim her for her metals. In the same week, the *Continental* of the New Haven Line, the oldest of the three, was sold to be dismantled and have her hull converted into a barge.

1901

The weather was still mild as the year 1901 began, so that the *Priscilla* and *Puritan* continued running to Fall River through the holiday season; the *Plymouth* and *Pilgrim* did not relieve them until the second week of January. Much to the surprise of the cynics, especially Judge Hall, these dark January mornings still found both the *Shinnecock* of the Joy Line and the *Rhode Island* of the New Line making their way up Narragansett Bay toward Providence. The *Rhode Island*, much the larger, looking somewhat old-fashioned these days with her big paddleboxes, hog frames, and single, tall, black smokestack, though stil regarded as one of the most beautiful of the sound steamers, was usually slightly in the lead, with the smarter but much smaller steel-hulled *Shinnecock*, her small sidewheels enclosed by deck-housing in the modern style, paddling along about half a mile astern.

The mild weather didn't last long. Late in January, it suddenly turned very cold, and by early February it was becoming apparent that this was to be a hard winter, too severe to keep the wooden-hulled *Rhode Island*, which had been built for summer service, on a nightly run through the often treacherous waters off Point Judith. The railroad people were not prepared for the problem, since it had not occurred to them that the Joy Line would still be running in February, but now it became necessary to make some changes. The *Rhode Island* was taken off the New Line late in January and again became the relief steamer on the less rigorous routes to New London and Stonington, going almost immediately on the Norwich Line in place of the *City of Worcester*. The *Richard Peck* went back on the New Haven run with the *City of Lawrence*, relieving the *Chester W. Chapin*, which now took the *Rhode Island*'s place on the New Line. Thus, through the winter and early spring of 1901, the railroad was running its newest and one of its finest steamers on its seventy-five cent line to Providence.

During the summer, there had been enough business to keep both steamers of the low-fare lines booked for nearly every passage. But in February and March there were pitifully few passengers choosing to board the *Shinnecock* (although she was the most modern steamer the Joy Line ever ran on the Providence route), rather than the new and much larger propellor steamer *Chester W. Chapin*, so that through the winter of 1901 the Joy Line survived almost entirely on its freight revenues.

On January 28, 1901, after a year of having her engines worked over, the *Connecticut* moved out of the W. and A. Fletcher yards in Hoboken under her own steam and made a highly successful trial trip up the Hudson.[1] With the *Connecticut* now at last in working order, the railroad planned to run her with the *Plymouth* on the regular Providence Line that summer, so that the more expensive and less fashionable *Pilgrim* could be kept at Newport with steam up in the event of an emergency on either the Fall River Line or the Providence Line. After another successful trial trip down New York Bay on Saturday, February 2, the proud and handsome *Connecticut*, her big wheels turning smoothly all the way, after five years of lying idle, sailed the full length of the sound to Newport, where she was to be fitted out for her summer service.[2]

Very soon afterward, a cold wave hit the Northeast. Beginning on Monday, February 4, the sound was subjected to three weeks of strong winds and extreme cold. On Friday, February 8, the recently delivered (December 1900) Metropolitan liner *James M. Whitney*, heading down the sound from Boston in a gale, performed the rescue of the half-frozen crew of a disabled fishing schooner off Faulkner's Island (so vividly described by Roger W. Macadam in *Salts of the Sound*, pp. 217-218). The following Wednesday morning, February 13, the *Seaboard*, coming in from Providence and trying desperately to fight her way to her New York pier, got trapped in the ice just after rounding Throgs Neck and had to stay there for three days before tugs were able to clear a channel for her. The *Seaboard* was carrying about twenty-five passengers that trip, and, as she was not really equipped as a passenger carrier, provisions began to give out by the end of the first day. But the emergency was resolved when distressed passengers discovered they could simply step off the steamer onto the ice, walk to the nearby Long Island Railroad station in Whitestone, and take a train into New York.[3]

The ice continued to plague the sound steamers through most of the month; some were forced to miss sailings several days at a time. One of the least perturbed by the weather was the sturdy *Old Dominion*, which continued running "regular as a clock, in spite of some pretty tough weather,"[4] frequently following the Metropolitan boats around Long Island whenever the sound became impassable. Late in the month, much to the relief of sound mariners, the weather improved and March turned out to be relatively mild.

Wednesday, March 20, was a proud day for the Joy Line. Most of the employees, including the owners, stopped work and ran out to the end of the pier to watch as Captain Wilcox proudly brought the steamer *Tremont* down the East River, having sailed her all the way from Portland, Maine. The Joy Line had just purchased the *Tremont* from the Boston-Portland Line, which had recently replaced her with the *Governor Dingley*. After two years, the Joy Line at last actually owned its own passenger steamer. On arrival, the *Tremont* sailed on past the Joy Line dock to Morse's yards in Brooklyn for fitting out. The following Tuesday, March 26, the *Shinnecock* developed a minor mechanical problem and had to miss a trip, so the *Tremont*, her aging timbers now freshly painted white, was brought around to make her first trip four days earlier than planned. She made one round trip on the *Shinnecock*'s schedule; then on Thursday night, she lay over in New York to finish fitting out. Then on Friday, March 29—just two years to the day after the *Rosalie*'s first sailing—the *Tremont* sailed in place of the *Seaboard*, thus inaugurating the Joy Line's first daily (six nights a week) passenger service between New York and Providence.

The *Tremont* had been built in 1883 (the same year as the *Pilgrim* and two years later than the *Rhode Island* and the *City of Worcester*) for the night line between Boston and Portland, Maine. At first, she had run with the much older *John Brooks* and *Forest City*, both dating from the 1850s. Later, however, when the Portland Line added two large new sidewheelers, the *Portland* (1890) and the *Bay State* (1895), the older steamers were withdrawn and the *Tremont* kept as a spare and as a winter boat. For a few months in 1895, the *Tremont* was chartered for the New York to Portland Line. This line normally operated three steamers during the summer months. When its steamer *Eleanora* developed mechanical problems early in 1895 and was sold, the line was caught short and chartered the *Tremont* to run for one season with its newer sisterships *Cottage City* and *Manhattan*, though it is difficult to see how the *Tremont*, hardly a speedy vessel, was able to maintain the Portland Line's schedule. By the summer of 1896, the Portland Line's new steel-hulled *John Englis* had been delivered, so the *Tremont* was no longer needed. After the loss of the *Portland* in 1898, the *Tremont* was back on the Boston to Portland line with the *Bay State* for one more season until the delivery of the big *Governor Dingley* relieved her in the late fall of 1899. After the arrival of the *Governor Dingley*, the Portland Line, for some reason, preferred to use one of the steamers of the International Line (usually the *State of Maine*), with which it was closely associated, as its winter boat, so that in the fall of 1900, the *Tremont* was laid up at the line's dock in Portland. Then in March 1901, she was sold to the Joy Line.

Like other steamers of her era, the *Tremont* had a walking beam engine and the large old-style wheels enclosed in big, colorfully designed paddle-boxes. Like the many small sidewheel steamers designed for all-year service on the rough waters of the Maine coast, her hull and Main Deck were solidly built, with very heavy timbers and extra braces, so that hog frames were not necessary to keep the hull tight. At 270 feet overall, the *Tremont* was slightly larger than the *Shinnecock* as well as most of the other steamers of her class, which tended to range between 240 feet and 265 feet overall. She was fairly commodious, too, with 104 staterooms, albeit all of them quite narrow and monastically furnished, compared to about 90 on the *Shinnecock* and only 138 on the much larger *Chester W. Chapin* of the rival New Line. The interior of the *Tremont*, in the style of the early 1880s, tended to be rather heavy with a great deal more dark-stained mahogany than the cramped saloons on smaller steamers could gracefully carry. Like the other Maine coast steamers, the *Tremont*'s Saloon Deck forward had tables and doubled as a dining room.

The Joy Line was proud of its first passenger steamer and began featuring a picture of the *Tremont* in its advertising. For the first time, the name "Joy Line" was painted on the prow of the steamer in large bold letters, with "Providence" and "Boston" in smaller letters on either side of it. However proud the Joy Line people may have been of their newly acquired passenger steamer, the *Tremont* had one unconquerable liability which Captain Wilcox undoubtedly discovered on the morning of March 27 when he found his steamer pounding up the Providence River well after daylight. There was no way around it; the *Tremont* was slow. On the short Boston to Portland run, speed was not a factor and the designers of the *Tremont* had obviously not considered it one. She could make about twelve knots when pushed, which was a bit better than the *Old Dominion*, but then the *Old Dominion* made no attempt to cover her route overnight or to compete with other steamers that did. With the arrival of the *Tremont*, the Joy Line was obliged to adjust its schedule drastically with the new departure time from Providence set at 5:30 P.M. (instead of 7:00 P.M.), so that the *Tremont* could have a fighting chance of arriving in New York by 7:00 A.M. with the other nightboats. The *Chester W. Chapin* of the New Line, which was probably the fastest steamer on the sound, left Providence a full two hours later. Arthur Pitts, the Joy Line's inventive Providence agent was hard put to account for the line's early departure time, but his ads in the local papers bravely announced that the Joy Line steamers would now leave Providence at 5:30, "affording a beautiful daylight sail down Narragansett Bay."

Why had the Joy Line bought the *Tremont*? For the same reason it had bought the museum piece it was running to Boston: she was cheap and she ran. The Joy Line was still fearfully undercapitalized. In its two years of operation, it had somehow managed to stay in business and avoid bankruptcy, but with the $1.00 fares and comparable freight rates forced on them by the New Line competition, it had not come close to accumulating the kind of capital that would have been necessary to build suitable boats of its own or even to buy used steamers of a class that could compare with the large and luxurious steamers run by any of the railroad lines, including the New Line. In short, the *Tremont* was simply the first steamer Dimon had found that the Joy Line could afford. And running its own steamer, at any speed, was, of course, considerably cheaper than chartering one on a permanent basis as the line had been doing for the past year.

Inexpensive as the *Tremont* may have been, she was not purchased out of the line's profits or from working capital, as the line had neither in amounts large enough to buy a steamboat. Using their other steamers, *Old Dominion*, *Seaboard*, and *Rosalie*, which they owned outright, as collateral, Dunbaugh and Joy had turned to old family friends, the Thatchers, who were bankers in Pueblo, for a loan. (Later, when New Haven officials learned through the financial grapevine that the Joy Line had been obliged to apply to a bank "out West" for funds, they concluded that the line was grasping for straws and must obviously be about to go under.)

About this time, for instance, the steamer *Terry*, formerly the first *Hartford* of the Hartford Line, had completed her transport duty and was back in New York and was advertised for sale. Of about the same size and specifications as the *Allan Joy* or the *Martinique*, she would have made a suitable addition to the Joy Line. But apparently the price was more than the Joy Line could afford, for she sat in New York for some time, without luring any satisfactory bids, before being purchased for service on Lake Michigan.

With the arrival of the *Tremont* and the start of six days a week passenger service to Providence with the *Tremont* and the *Shinnecock*, it was no longer necessary for the *Seaboard* to carry freight to Providence. After a lengthy overhaul, the *Seaboard* was placed on a regular schedule between New York and Boston with the *Old Dominion*, each steamer making two round trips per week. The *Old Dominion* kept to her former schedule, leaving New York on Wednesdays and Saturdays and Boston on Mondays and Thursdays. The *Seaboard* had a similar schedule, leaving from the opposite ports.

Within a few days after the arrival of the *Tremont* on the Joy Line, the New Line's *Chester W. Chapin* met with the only serious accident in her career of nearly half a century. The *Chester W. Chapin* sailed late on the evening of Wednesday, April 3, after taking on an unusually large load of freight. It was nearly 8:00 P.M. and already dark by the time Captain William Appleby guided her out of Fox Point wharf and down the river, by which time the Joy Line's *Shinnecock*, having left two and a half hours earlier, must have been about ready to round Point Judith. Near Cranston the *Chester W. Chapin* ran into fog, and Appleby slowed her speed while he listened for the whistle at Warwick Light which would give him his bearings for the entrance into the west passage. (The larger summer steamers always took the broader east passage down the bay, on the Newport side of Conanicut Island, but the smaller steamers of the New Line or the Joy Line generally preferred the west passage, which was shorter, though in fog or bad weather they, too, generally headed down the east side of the island. On this occasion, probably because the *Chapin* was already late, Appleby chose the west passage in spite of the fog.) Apparently, the fog whistle at Warwick Light was either blunted by the fog or deflected by the wind, because that night Appleby missed it. Staring out of the pilot house window into the white mist, he had no reason to suspect that he was off course until he heard the terrifying sound of his ship scraping over rocks. A few seconds later, the *Chester W. Chapin* came to an abrupt stop. Where were they? What had gone wrong? Some crewmembers jumped ashore and determined that the *Chapin* had struck on the northern tip of Patience Island at the entrance to the west channel. Since she was hard aground, at least there was no danger to the passengers. But the condition of the steamer was serious, for the rocks had pierced the forward part of the hull, and, to make matters worse, she had struck at high tide, so that receding waters would bring her down harder. The fog lifted, as it so often does, just minutes after the *Chapin* struck.[5]

Since the *Chapin* did not carry a wireless, which was then just in its experimental stages, two men were placed in a boat and were told to find help. There were no telephone booths at street corners in those days and certainly none perched on islands in Narragansett Bay. The nearest phone these men could find was at the Warwick railroad station which they did not reach until midnight, almost three hours after the accident.[6]

On the steamer the passengers were not alarmed. Some came on deck for awhile to watch the proceedings but soon tired of watching nothing and went back to bed. Finally, at about 2:00 A.M. the *Bay Queen*, a small excursion steamer, came down from Providence in response to the phone call and took the *Chapin*'s passengers back to Fox Point wharf, where the line's management helped them get to a train for New York.[7]

Early the following morning, both the *Tremont* and the *City of Fall River*, coming up from New York, saw the *Chapin*'s predicament and stopped, but on ascertaining that there was nothing they could do, especially as it was then low tide, they proceeded to Providence. Captain Wilcox, inter-viewed later that morning, praised his friend Appleby and took the opportunity to point out that the sound captains had long been complaining that the Warwick fog signal could not be heard under certain wind conditions and was thus more of a hazard than a help to navigation.[8]

At high tide that day, two tugs came and pulled hard to free the *Chapin* but succeeded only in churning up a great deal of foam. That afternoon Captain Henry O. Nickerson, the marine superintendent of the railroad's sound lines, arrived to look over the situation. The next day, Friday, April 5, no tugs appeared, and observers wondered why no further efforts were being made to pull the steamer loose. Their answer came before dawn on Saturday morning. When the *City of Fall River* came up the bay from New York, she came abreast of the *Chester W. Chapin* and anchored there until the tide was about to reach its peak. With the *City of Fall River* pulling and the *Chapin*'s pumps working hard, the steamer resisted awhile but then slowly glided off her rocky perch and floated into the bay. Nickerson had seen just where the power had to be applied to get the *Chapin* off, and, rather then tell someone else how to do it and then pay them for it, Nickerson simply waited until the line's own freighter came up the next morning and let her do it. With her wounds neatly patched, the *Chapin* was soon able to sail the short distance to the Newport shops under her own power.[9]

Meanwhile, the New Line needed a steamer in a hurry. The *Rhode Island* would have been the most logical replacement, since she was already scheduled to go back on the line in the spring, but she was then serving on the Norwich Line while the *City of Lowell* was out for her spring overhaul. The *Massachusetts* was laid up in Stonington, and it would take several days to get her ready. The only steamer actually available was the *Connecticut*, which was in Newport with steam up preparing for her summer service on the Providence Line. So on Friday, April 5, the *Connecticut*, which at that time had not made a passenger-carrying run in nearly five years, headed up to Providence and sailed that night on the *Chester W. Chapin*'s next regularly scheduled trip.[10] Since the *Chapin* was slated to return to the New Haven Line in June,* she was not brought back on the New Line after her repairs, and the *Connecticut* finished out her season on the New Line. Although her engines may not have been much of a success, above decks in the only sections known to passengers, the *Connecticut* was even larger and more beautifully appointed than the newer *Chester W. Chapin*. She was probably the finest steamer, other than those of the Fall

---

*On June 14, soon after she had returned to the New Haven Line, the *Chester W. Chapin* engaged in the only recorded race with her sistership, the *Richard Peck*. In a hotly contested sprint between Stratford Light and Throgs Neck, the *Chapin* beat the *Peck* by a good six minutes.

River Line, built for Long Island Sound service. By any standards, she so far outclassed the *Tremont* that it is safe to say that until the vacation crowds began to make an appearance, the Joy Line was probably dependent for its survival on its regular freight customers.

On Friday, April 5, the *Connecticut's* first night on the run, the New Line authorities quickly substituted her name for that of the *Chester W. Chapin* in the daily notice they ran in the *Providence Journal*, so that for one day the readers of the *Journal* were informed that they could travel to New York on the "new steel twin-screw steamer *Connecticut*."[11]

Soon after the Joy Line started running two passenger steamers to Providence, the reader will not be surprised to learn, the railroad management realized that the good people of Providence also deserved passenger service six nights a week on the New Line. On May 1, therefore, as soon as the *City of Lowell* was back from the yards, the *Rhode Island* sailed over to Pier 36 in New York and joined the *Connecticut* on the New Line. With the new daily service, which now employed two of the three steamers which, until a few years earlier, had made up the regular Providence Line, the New Line also announced a further drop in fare to fifty cents per passenger. Once the *Rhode Island* had joined the *Connecticut* on the New Line, the Providence Line's freighter *Nashua*, which had been running on alternate nights, was taken off and went into layup at Stonington.

When asked how the small and leisurely paced steamers of the Joy Line could compete with the *Connecticut* and the *Rhode Island* and whether the Joy Line planned to meet the new fifty-cent fare, Arthur Pitts, as usual, was ready with an answer:

> We do not think it would be fair to ourselves or to our passengers to drop below a dollar per trip . . . nor that we will be forced to do it if we can judge by the amount of business we have been doing. . . . We think we can carry a better class of passengers and as many as we want at the price we have established.[12]

As farfetched as it sounds, we have already seen from the experience of the summer of 1900 that there was a certain logic and justification in this announcement. The Joy Line did, in fact, hold to the $1.00 fare through the summer of 1901 with steamers far inferior to those on the New Line and somehow managed to keep its steamers well booked.

Barely three weeks after the start of its two-boat service, the New Line suffered a second accident. This time the *Rhode Island*, under Captain Walter R. Hazard, bound into Narragansett Bay, struck at the southern entrance to the west channel, not far from the spot where her predecessor, the first *Rhode Island*, had come to grief in 1880. The *Rhode Island* had a rough trip out of New York on the night of Wednesday, May 23. Heavy rains and winds kept the waters of the sound in a fury, tossing the aging wooden steamer high out of the water and then smashing her back down again with a resounding crash against the guards. Shortly after midnight, when the steamer was just past Faulkner's Island, the storm began to subside somewhat, but by the time she passed New London, the damp air had turned into a dense fog. Captain Hazard slowed the steamer's speed and proceeded cautiously through the Race. But, like the *Chester W. Chapin* a few weeks earlier, the *Rhode Island* had apparently gotten off course without his realizing it until she suddenly crashed onto the rocks at Point Judith breakwater. Hazard signaled to reverse the wheels, and, miraculously, the *Rhode Island* backed off. When an inspection revealed, still more miraculously, that the damage was not serious, she proceeded to Providence and even made her scheduled trip back to New York the following night. But in New York the authorities decided to take her off for a few trips for further inspection.[13]

For the next several days, the New Line played "Who's got the steamer?" The first trip missed by the *Rhode Island* (Friday, May 25) was not covered. The *Maine* of the Stonington Line took the second trip on Monday night while the *Richard Peck* took her trip to Stonington, and the *Chester W. Chapin*, just back from her repairs, returned to New Haven for the *Peck*. The following night, Tuesday, May 28, the *Connecticut* decided to stay in New York to finish refitting for the summer season. Thus, her place on the New Line was taken by the *Chester W. Chapin*, while the *City of Lawrence* went to New Haven. On Wednesday, the *Rhode Island* was back on the New Line (for the *Maine*) and on Thursday the *Connecticut* was back (for the *Chester W. Chapin*), but on Saturday, June 1, the *Connecticut* made the opening trip of the season out of Providence for the Providence Line, and her place on the New Line was filled by the *Massachusetts*, which had come up from Stonington that day. The reader may be pleased to learn that the *Rhode Island* and the *Massachusetts* then ran regularly for the New Line for the rest of that summer.

The *Massachusetts* sailed that night from Lonsdale wharf, to which the New Line returned now that the Providence Line had reoccupied its Fox Point wharf for the season. The old *Providence*, then still tied up at Lonsdale wharf, was towed over to the Providence River side of Fox Point wharf, where she sat until purchased by a Boston shipbreaker in September.

Now that her engines were apparently in working order, the *Connecticut* made a much more sensible running mate for the *Plymouth* on the Providence Line than the *Pilgrim*. With 200 staterooms, she could accommodate as many passengers as the *Pilgrim*, while, with her lighter coal consumption, she cost about half as much to operate. Though in her construction the *Connecticut* had been inexcusably old-fashioned even when built, her interior design, while less opulent, was much brighter and more modern than the

Pilgrim's. One feature that passengers particularly appreciated was the *Connecticut's* dining room, which, like the dining rooms of the *Priscilla* and the *Massachusetts*, was on the Main Deck and surrounded by windows, rather than in the hold as it was on both the *Plymouth* and the *Pilgrim*.

With the summer steamers now running on the Fall River Line and the *Connecticut* running in her place to Providence, the *Pilgrim* went off to Fletcher's in Hoboken for most of the summer of 1901 to have new boilers installed.

During the week that the New Line was juggling its steamers, the Joy Line was doing the same with such steamers as it had to juggle. The Joy Line's problems began on the morning of Saturday, May 25, when the *Shinnecock*, caught in a stiff wind while docking in New York, slammed against the pier and damaged her starboard wheel.[14] The Joy Line, with no available replacements, had to cancel its sailing out of New York that night. Since this was the night that the *Rhode Island's* sailing was also canceled, neither line had a steamer out of New York on May 25. Since, in any event, the *Shinnecock's* charter was to expire in a few more days (June 1), it was obvious that she would not be back on the line at all. The *Seaboard* (now commanded by Captain Frank Kirby), which was the best the Joy Line could produce just then, was brought out of overhaul to replace her. As it was necessary, however, to get the *Tremont* on the "primary" schedule (that is, Tuesdays, Thursdays, Saturdays, out of New York) until then observed by the *Shinnecock*, the *Tremont* laid over in New York on Monday night (the night the *Maine* went up for the New Line) and let the *Seaboard* take her place. By Tuesday night, the Joy Line was again synchronized, with the *Tremont* sailing from New York and the *Seaboard* from Providence. By the end of the week, all three New York to Providence lines had two steamers in regular service, with the *Connecticut*, the *Massachusetts*, and the *Tremont* usually running together from one port and the *Plymouth*, the *Rhode Island*, and the *Seaboard* from the other.

As the reader has by now already become aware, the Joy Line was in considerable difficulty by June 1, 1901, after the *Shinnecock* had been returned, slightly damaged, to the Montauk Line. The introduction of a two-boat service in March had only inspired the New Line to start running two rather than only one of the largest boats on the sound. Now the Joy Line had only the *Tremont*, which was barely adequate, and the *Seaboard*, which was not, to run to Providence. Furthermore, with the *Seaboard* on the Providence route, the Joy Line's Boston service was again reduced to only one boat.

The Joy Line had expected to charter the *Martinique* again in the summer of 1901 as it had in 1900. But in December 1900 the Florida East Coast Steamship Company, the owners of the *Martinique*, had merged with the Plant Line which operated from the west coast of Florida to Key West and

Havana. H. M. Flagler had been willing to let the Joy Line charter the *Martinique* in 1900, but Morton F. Plant was close to Morgan and the New Haven interests, who persuaded him to refuse to let the Joy Line charter the *Martinique* in 1901. The *Martinique* did come back to New England that season, however, arriving late in May to serve as the summer boat between Boston and Provincetown, replacing the *Cape Cod*, which had proved too small for the route and too undependable in heavy weather.

Plant's refusal turned out in the long run to be a blessing for the Joy Line. Had the *Martinique* been available in 1901, she would probably have run that year with the *Tremont*. Since she was not, Dimon had to scout around for another steamer, and in so doing he found one far better suited to the line's needs. She was the *Penobscot* of the Boston-Bangor Line, which had been running on that line for years with the *City of Bangor* but which became available with the arrival of the line's new *City of Rockland* on May 27, 1901.

The *Penobscot* was a good running mate for the *Tremont*. Also a Maine coaster, she was similar in size and layout, and, built in 1882, she was about the same age. On the Bangor run, the *Penobscot* had been described as cranky, unpopular, and slow,[15] which should have made her an ideal candidate for service on the Joy Line. But perhaps this judgment is unfair. The *Penobscot* underway was a nice-looking steamer and her interior, while not what one would call opulent, was less severe than the *Tremont*'s. She was also faster than the *Tremont*, but then most steamers were.

On Sunday, June 23, a beautiful day—in fact, New England was having an early heat wave—Captain Mark Pierce of the Boston-Bangor Line, who was to command the *Penobscot* that summer, brought her out of Boston harbor, around the cape, and up Narragansett Bay to Providence, arriving there in the late twilight. The following night she made her first trip to New York for the Joy Line (almost one month after the *Shinnecock* had been returned), taking the *Tremont*'s schedule, which meant that she sailed from each port on the same evenings as the *Connecticut* and the *Massachusetts*.

During the summer of 1901, the Joy Line made no attempt to run excursions to Cottage City as it had with the *Martinique* the previous year, since neither the *Tremont* nor the *Penobscot* could have made the run to Martha's Vineyard and back before midnight. When the Joy Line decided not to run Sunday excursions, the New Line ceased to feel the need to provide Providence citizens with Sunday outings either. So for the season of 1901, all four New York night boats (both Providence Line steamers were in Providence on Sundays) rested snugly at their piers on the Sabbath.

In June 1901, the Joy Line seems to have given serious consideration to starting a new freight service from New York to Fall River with a stop at Newport, in direct competition with the railroad's Fall River Line. Throughout its history, the Joy Line encountered difficulties in serving prospective customers outside the immediate areas of Providence or Boston, as the New Haven controlled virtually every mode of transportation beyond these points (rail or trolley) and was never exactly cooperative in establishing through freight arrangements with the Joy Line. To circumvent this problem, the Joy Line frequently attempted to start lines of its own to points where freight prospects seemed propitious, but invariably these attempts were frustrated by the railroad's countermoves. The plan in June 1901 seems to have been to run the *Seaboard* on the new route to Fall River and, now that the Joy Line was carrying passengers to Boston, to charter another steamer for that route with accommodations somewhat more suitable than those of the *Seaboard*.[16]

At one point, the line had wanted to charter both the *Martinique* and the *Penobscot*, running the *Penobscot* to Providence and the *Martinique*, temporarily at least, to Boston. But, as we have seen, Flagler chose not to make the *Martinique* available. A steamer which the Joy Line was even more anxious to obtain for its Boston route that summer was the *Manhattan* of the Maine Steamship Company's New York to Portland line. When its brand new steamer *North Star* had arrived from the builders in June to join the *Horatio Hall* on the Portland run, the line had taken off the older wooden-hulled *Manhattan* and had her tied up unoccupied in Hoboken for the summer. Captain Horatio Hall, the manager of the Portland Line, discussed the possibility of a charter with the Joy Line, but then, considering his close working arrangements with both the New Haven and the Metropolitan Line, he ultimately refused.[17]

Failing in every attempt to find a passenger-carrying steamer suitable for its Boston service, the Joy Line was resigned to running the *Seaboard* to Boston again, and, instead of the proposed line to Fall River with the *Seaboard*, the Joy Line made an arrangement with Captain Dyer, who ran a lighterage business in Providence. For $25.00 per day, Captain Dyer placed one of his lighters at the Joy Line's disposal to carry freight to Fall River after the arrival of the steamer in the morning and to bring freight up from Fall River in time for the evening sailing.

By the first week of July when the season of 1901 was getting underway, the Joy Line was in very good shape and its survival as a steamship line was no longer in question. The line was running two well-booked passenger and freight steamers to Providence. When the *Penobscot* arrived, the *Seaboard* had gone to the yards to complete the much-needed overhaul that had been interrupted as a result of the *Shinnecock*'s accident in June and to have her passenger quarters spruced up, but as soon as she was ready the line would also have two steamers carrying passengers and freight to Boston, with sailings four nights a week from each port. (The *Seaboard* did not have anything resembling the carpeted saloons, dining rooms, or grand stairways which characterized even the smaller Long Island Sound night boats. In the manner of many of the simpler coasters of that era, she merely offered twenty sparsely-furnished staterooms opening onto the deck and one small public room which served as both saloon and dining room.)

It would seem that at last the line could look forward to a peaceful and profitable summer. But such was not to be the case. During July, serious accidents to both the *Old Dominion* and the *Tremont* put the line's two main steamers out of commission through the peak of the season and pushed the company close to the point of bankruptcy once again.

The fourth of July holiday, which fell on a Thursday, had been marred by heavy fog along the Atlantic Coast. All of the sound steamers were running behind, especially the *Old Dominion*. Although she was scheduled to leave Boston at nine on Thursday evenings, on July 4 she was so late coming in from New York that she did not sail out of Boston again until 5:00 A.M. on Friday, July 5. All that day the fog persisted, and the *Old Dominion* could not make up the time lost. Throughout the day of July 5, Captain Durkee and the men with him in the pilot house saw nothing but fog in any direction as they guided the steamer around Cape Cod and through Nantucket Sound, first moving very slowly until they sighted a familiar buoy or heard a fog signal that gave them their bearings, then cautiously picking up speed until it was time to listen for another signal. It was grueling and frustrating work. By five in the evening, the time she was due in New York, the *Old Dominion* was just entering Long Island Sound. She would not be in New York before morning. Inside the sound the fog was thicker than ever, and the pilots continued to make judgments on the basis of the sounds that came to them through the misty atmosphere. By about nine they could hear Faulkner's, and by eleven they had safely passed Stratford Shoals. They continued slowly westward, and it was just past 1:00 A.M. on Saturday when they identified the fog whistle at Great Captain's Island; in another half hour, they should be able to spot Execution Light even through the fog. Just as Captain Durkee and his pilots were standing at the windows of the pilot house straining their senses for some hint of the beam from Execution, they were nearly knocked off their feet as the *Old Dominion* suddenly heeled over to port and then, after much screeching and thumping below, came to a stop. Following instinct, Captain Durkee ordered the engines reversed, but it was of no use. Like the *Chester W. Chapin* a few months before, the *Old Dominion* had run onto sharp rocks that had punctured her hull and held her fast.[18]

With the dawn on Saturday morning, the fog began to clear, and Durkee discovered that his ship had run aground near Rye Beach, which meant that, at the time, unaccountably, he must have been more than a mile off course. The *Old Dominion* was carrying over a hundred passengers that trip. Durkee managed to get them all safely ashore in boats, and then he arranged for the Merritt and Chapman tugs *John Nichols* and *Wallace B. Flint* to come out from New York and help him get the *Old Dominion* off. But it wasn't that easy. On viewing the situation, the Merritt and Chapman people were of the opinion that the *Old Dominion* was finished. The rocks had pierced the hull in several places, and some had penetrated as much as five or six feet.[19] Nevertheless, they continued their efforts to save the steamer. First, the freight was removed, and later a large part of the machinery as well to lighten the load, but still she stuck fast, just as the wrecking experts had predicted. It was nearly a month before they got the *Old Dominion* off the rocks, and this was accomplished in the end only by dynamiting the rocks from under her. Even then it was by no means certain that she would run again.

The owners of the Joy Line were still pondering whether they would be able to stay in business with their Boston steamer out of service, perhaps permanently, when a potentially more serious accident almost ended the career of the *Tremont* as well. On Tuesday, July 16, the *Tremont* left Providence as usual in broad daylight at 5:30 in the afternoon. As she sailed down the bay, the sea was calm and the air clear, though she encountered a few patches of fog when she entered the sound after dark. At about the same time, the sleek steam yacht *Wild Duck*, which belonged to Francis Greene but which had been chartered for the summer to Senator Nelson Aldrich, sailed out of New York for Rhode Island, the senator's home state. Senator Aldrich, whose daughter Abby had recently announced her engagement to John D. Rockefeller, Jr., was aboard at the time.

Shortly after midnight, the *Tremont*, cruising westward, was approaching Cornfield Reef, while the *Wild Duck* was nearing the same spot from the other direction. What happened next depends on which story the reader chooses to accept. According to Captain Wilcox, who was in the *Tremont's* pilot house at the time, it was a clear night, and he tried several times to signal to the *Wild Duck* but got no response. According to the captain of the yacht, the sound was shrouded in fog, and he neither saw the steamer approaching nor heard her whistle until it was too late to avoid an accident. In any event, the *Wild Duck* rammed right into the *Tremont* thirty feet aft of the bow, her sharp steel hull cutting almost clean through before she finally stopped. The yacht itself was not seriously damaged except that the crash caused her anchor to drop, or at least that was the explanation her captain gave for not coming to the *Tremont's* assistance after the passenger steamer drifted away from her.[20]

The *Tremont*, however, with three hundred passengers aboard, was sinking. Only good luck and good seamanship prevented the crash of the *Tremont* and the *Wild Duck* from becoming one of the tragedies of the sound. Fortunately, the accident took place in the section of the sound where the eastbound and westbound steamers crossed, so that virtually every steamer then operating on the sound was within hailing distance of the *Tremont* at the time. First to arrive was the *City of Worcester* bound from New York to New London, which loomed up next to the sinking *Tremont* only minutes after the accident. Shortly afterward, her running mate, the *City of Lowell*, just coming out of New London, also appeared on the scene. As the *City of Lowell* drew close, Captain T. Harvey MacDonald of the *City of Worcester* called on the megaphone to Captain J. Cleveland Geer that he should ease the *City of Lowell*, a propellor steamer, alongside the *Tremont* to take off passengers. With the *Tremont* in such a precarious condition, he was afraid that if the *City of Worcester* tried, the wash of her big sidewheels might swamp the smaller steamer and send her to the bottom.[21]

While the *City of Lowell* was taking off the *Tremont*'s passengers, the *Maine* and the *New Hampshire* of the Stonington Line, the *Plymouth* and the *Connecticut* of the Providence Line, the *Massachusetts* and the *Rhode Island* of the New Line, and even the *Priscilla* and the *Puritan* of the Fall River Line, all arrived at the scene and stood by at least long enough to determine whether their assistance was needed.[22]

After the *City of Lowell* pulled away taking the bulk of the *Tremont*'s passengers on to New York, the *Massachusetts* and the *Connecticut*, both bound for Providence, searched the surrounding waters and picked up the passengers in lifeboats, about fifty in all. Once the safety of the passengers had been assured, Captain William Appleby of the Stonington steamer *New Hampshire* took the *Tremont* in tow, stern first so as not to put too great a strain on the injured bow, and brought her into New London where she was beached.[23] Without the assistance of these other steamers, particularly the *City of Lowell* and the *New Hampshire*, the *Tremont* would undoubtedly have sunk and many lives might have been lost. As it was, the steamer and all aboard her survived, as well as all of her cargo.*

The Joy Line's other steamer, the *Penobscot*, having left New York before the other Providence-bound steamers, was still traveling well ahead of them when the accident to the *Tremont* occurred and was therefore about the only overnight steamer not in the vicinity. Her officers first heard about the accident when they arrived in Providence.

---

*The accepted practice among the steamship lines of Long Island Sound was never to claim salvage after assisting another steamer in distress. Thus, in spite of the intense rivalry that then existed between the Joy Line and the established lines, and the clearly stated determination of the railroad that summer to use all means to put the Joy Line out of business, the New Haven on this occasion made no claim against the Joy Line, even though every one of the steamers that came to the aid of the *Tremont* belonged to the railroad's lines.

Arthur Pitts met both the *Connecticut* and the *Massachusetts* as they arrived in Providence, both very late, to do what he could for the *Tremont* passengers brought in by these steamers. Many of them elected to accept free passage that night on the *Penobscot*. For the others, Pitts arranged either refunds or passage to New York by train. As it happened, Charles Dimon was aboard the *Tremont* the night of the accident. Since he wanted to stay aboard the vessel as long as possible to assist the crew in making sure the passengers all got off safely, he did not board the *City of Lowell* when she came alongside, but left the *Tremont* later in a boat which carried the last of the passengers to the *Connecticut*. On arrival, he did not stay to help Pitts but took the first possible train to New London to supervise the salvage of the *Tremont* and her cargo. Most of the crew stayed aboard the *Tremont*, while the *New Hampshire* stood ready to take them aboard should she start to go under.

In New London, the *Tremont* received temporary repairs, and then two days later, wearing an ugly patch over her port bow, she sailed under her own power, though accompanied for safety's sake by a tug appropriately named *Alert*, from New London to repair shops in the Erie Basin, Brooklyn.

As should be fairly obvious, by the middle of July 1901 the Joy Line was seriously short of steamers. It is hard to understand, in fact, how the Joy Line managed to stay in business at all after the accidents to both the *Old Dominion* and the *Tremont*. It was known that the line was already in debt. There is a good possibility, however, though one not easy to prove after all these years, that the line actually made a profit on the *Old Dominion*'s accident. When the amounts offered by the insurance companies failed to match the estimates for floating and repairing the *Old Dominion*, the Joy Line had no choice but to give up the old steamer by declaring her a total loss and letting the insurance company take title to her. They were taking a chance, but it worked. Later, when the *Old Dominion* had been repaired, and the insurance people offered her for sale, no one came along who was willing to bid more than her scrap value, so that the Joy Line's own relatively low bid turned out to be the high one. Rumor had it that the Joy Line bought the boat back for considerably less than it had received from the insurance companies in the first place.[24]

If this story is true, then it was about the only good luck the beleaguered line had that summer. They had plenty of business; their problem was that they had no boats. Although the *Tremont* was off the Providence route for over a month at the height of the summer season, Dimon was unable to find any suitable steamers to charter as replacements. The *Seaboard* had been in drydock at the time of the *Old Dominion*'s accident and had been pulled off once again with the work still not completed to take over the Boston route. Now that he needed the *Seaboard* to run with the *Penobscot* to Providence, Dimon again tried to find another steamer for the Boston route. Once again, however, every lead he followed was blocked by maneuvers of the New Haven Railroad or the Metropolitan Line which were now determined to take full advantage of the Joy Line's embarrassment to force them to quit. The first disappointment came when Dimon again went to Horatio Hall, this time, considering the emergency, probably willing to pay a considerably higher price to charter the *Manhattan*. The Portland Line was sympathetic, and charter arrangements were again under discussion when Captain Hall, this time subjected to pressure both from the New Haven and from the Metropolitan Line, abruptly ended the negotiations.[25] For his "manful" service to the cause, Hall was rewarded with a pass on the New Haven Railroad. "This will please him and will give us a hold on him," was how Robert Haskins, the Metropolitan's Boston agent, summed it up in requesting this favor from the New Haven.[26]

Finally, toward the end of July came the news that the P. and O. Line (the Plant-Flagler combination had taken the rather grand title of Peninsular and Occidental Steamship Company, lifted, without credits or apologies, from the famous British company of the same name) was willing to let the Joy Line charter its small steamer *Cocoa*. Formerly a Spanish vessel confiscated during the war, she was only 190 feet long, about the same size as the *Seaboard*. She was one of five steamers which, after the merger of the two lines, had been laid off by the P. and O. and offered for sale.[27] Since the line had not as yet had any acceptable offers for any of them, it was apparently glad to get at least a charter out of the *Cocoa* and so in this case overrode the objections of the New Haven to the deal. The *Cocoa* arrived from Florida on Thursday, July 24, and, so anxious was the line to move its backed-up freight, she was placed on the Boston run the following evening.[28]

Once the Joy Line people actually saw the *Cocoa*, they realized that she was no bargain. She had been stripped of her staterooms, so that the twenty-two Spartan cabins on the *Seaboard* (once she returned from her three weeks on the Providence route replacing the *Tremont*) now constituted the total accommodations of the Joy Line's new passenger service to Boston. Nor could the *Cocoa* carry anything but package freight (which, in any event, constituted the majority of the Joy Line's business), as her freight ports were not more than about four feet wide. Bulk freight had to be shipped down to Providence. The Metropolitan people sent "spies" over to have a look at her and were pleased to report that "with this boat they certainly can do little damage."[29]

Small as she was, and unsuited to the service, the *Cocoa*, during her brief tenure on the Joy Line, carried no less than three captains on her staff. Captain Daniels of the P. and O. Line remained with the steamer through the charter. Since he did not have a license for Long Island Sound, Captain Frank Burton, who had formerly commanded the Providence-

Block Island steamer *Mount Hope* but had recently come to the Joy Line to succeed Captain Durkee, was the *Cocoa*'s official commander. (Captain Durkee left the Joy Line after the accident to the *Old Dominion*, though whether the decision to leave was his or the Joy Line's is not recorded. He returned to his former job as captain of the tugboat *Honeybrook*.) Captain A. T. Coleman, a veteran New York-Boston captain, who had retired after having commanded the large freighters of the rival Metropolitan Line, decided that he missed the sea. So, in the summer of 1901 he had signed on with the Joy Line as pilot, although he frequently filled in as captain when the regular captains were on vacation.

Early in August, while the *Tremont* was still off the route, Long Island Sound was subjected to several days of gale winds and heavy rain. On August 8, the New Line steamer *Massachusetts* limped into New York so buffeted by the stormy seas of the previous evening off Point Judith that she had to come off for repairs. With all of the railroad's steamers then assigned to other routes, the only steamer that could be made available on such short notice was the much smaller *City of Lawrence*, which then made one round trip to Providence for the New Line.

By the summer of 1901, with the Joy Line having been in business for over two years and carrying passengers for over a year, in spite of the expensive opposition offered by the New Line in Providence and the Savannah Line in Boston, both the New Haven Railroad and the Metropolitan Line began to show their impatience with the unwanted intruder and to seek new methods for getting the Joy Line out of the way. With the Joy Line caught short of steamers after the accidents to the *Old Dominion* and the *Tremont* in July 1901, the time seemed propitious. Robert Haskins of the Metropolitan Line put the matter fairly directly: ". . . as they are in pretty bad shape now, . . . I thought it would be well to pound them harder while they are down."[30] Haskins, acting for the Metropolitan Line, made the first move by arranging with the Savannah Line to increase the New York to Boston sailings of the *City of Macon* from one round trip every other week to one round trip per week. His hope was that regular shippers, especially of perishable goods, might thus better be persuaded to use the *City of Macon* rather than the *Old Dominion* to reach the New York market. He also instructed the Savannah Line, which was still being subsidized by the Metropolitan Line, to quote freight rates at two cents lower than any rates quoted by the Joy Line.[31]

The *Tremont* finally came home from the shipyard on Monday, August 19, boasting a whole new bow and made her first trip to Providence that night. With the *Tremont* back on the Providence route, the *Seaboard* returned to the yards briefly to finish the overhaul from which she had twice been wrested and then went to join the *Cocoa* on the Boston run. A letter at this time from Robert Haskins to his friend Percy Todd, then second vice-president of the New Haven Railroad, gloated over the embarrassment of the Joy Line in not having a suitable steamer to run to Boston: "The *Seaboard* would not dare to run to Boston anyhow in the winter season; she can't."[32] But Haskins did not know the *Seaboard*. The little freighter ran to Boston all that winter, which turned out to be one of the most severe in New England history, and again for several winters thereafter.

Two days after the *Tremont* returned to the line, the *Cocoa* was badly damaged in a collision with the schooner *Charlie Buckie* off New Haven. She was not in sinking condition, however, and as the schooner was in somewhat worse shape, Captain Burton stood by her until daylight and then towed the *Buckie* into New Haven before proceeding to Boston. The *Cocoa* then made a regular run back to New York before going to the shops for repairs. By this time, marine reporters were becoming somewhat unsympathetic with the Joy Line's mishaps. The *Nautical Gazette* was kindest when it observed that "Since this is the third accident to the company's steamers this year, it is to be hoped that the hoodoo has passed."[33] The *Gazette* had its wish. The Joy Line managed to get through the rest of 1901 with nothing more than a minor brush to the *Seaboard* in Boston harbor—which is not to say the line had not had its share of troubles already.

As the season of 1901 was drawing to a close, the attention of the marine world was drawn once again to the America's Cup races held off Sandy Hook in late September and early October. Thomas Lipton, the British challenger, undaunted by his defeat in 1899, had a new boat designed for this race which was launched in Scotland on May 4 as the *Shamrock II*. A new American defender, the *Constitution*, slid into the water two days later at Herschoff's yard in Bristol. But in a series of runoff races near Newport during the summer, the *Constitution* was defeated by the *Columbia*, the winner of the previous race, so on September 6 the America's Cup Committee declared the *Columbia* once again the official defender. Local enthusiasm was dimmed only slightly by the news that same day that President McKinley had been shot, and it was held only briefly in check when the president died one week later on Friday, September 13.

The *Shamrock* arrived in New York in late August and attracted much attention. As a tender for the ship and as housing for his crew, Lipton chartered the little steamer *Porto Rico*, which, the reader may remember, made one trip to Boston for the Joy Line in 1900 when the *Old Dominion* caught fire.

The first race was held on Thursday, September 26. If the races were exciting for a yachting enthusiast, they would have been heaven for a steamboat buff. At least two dozen local steamers were chartered by various groups to attend the races. Among them were several of the sound steamers, the *Plymouth*, the *Chester W. Chapin*, the *Shinnecock*, the *City of Lowell*, and the Portland Line's new (delivered July 1) *North Star* among them. Some of the other steamers of interest chartered for the races were the *Gay Head* of the New Bedford, Martha's Vineyard, and Nantucket Line, the *Monmouth* and the *St. Johns* of the Atlantic Highlands Line, the *General Slocum* of the Knickerbocker Steamship Company, the *Mount Hope* from the Providence-Block Island run, and *La Grande Duchesse*, the beautiful white elephant of the P. and O. Line, which was damaged during the races in a brush with the Portland Line's brand new *North Star*. *La Grande Duchesse* had at that time already been sold to the Savannah Line and, in spite of the accident, was delivered to her new owners as soon as the races were over. The *Pilgrim*, laid up at Fletcher's in Hoboken to have her engines repaired, apparently had enough parts in place to run for the *Plymouth* to Providence before returning to the shops. The *C. H. Northam* filled in for the *Chester W. Chapin* on the New Haven Line, her last passenger run on record. And the *Manhattan* ran for the *North Star*, staying on the Portland Line for the winter. The Joy Line, with no steamers to spare from its regular runs, did not contribute a boat for the occasion. It is doubtful if any of them could have kept up with the races in any event.

The races, like those in 1899, were marred toward the end by a run of foul weather, so that many of the special excursions were called off and the steamers returned earlier than expected to their regular routes. By the time of the predictable announcement that the *Columbia* had successfully defended the cup for the second time, the public had generally lost interest.

During her recall to duty, the *C. H. Northam* managed to crash into a dock in New Haven in one of the squalls of that week and put herself out of commission. The *City of Lawrence*, always available in an emergency, went on the New Haven Line with the *Richard Peck* and, proving adequate for the traffic, stayed there for several weeks while the *Chester W. Chapin*, after the races, went first to relieve the *City of Lowell* on the New London Line and then later to run for a few weeks on the New Line.

Events were taking place in Boston during the fall of 1901 which caused little notice at the time but which were soon to send the marine world of New England into a monumental flap: namely, the acquisition of most of the Maine coast lines by Charles W. Morse. Morse was from Bath, Maine, where he had worked as a youth with his uncle on boats which collected ice in Maine rivers and brought it to New York to be stored and used for food refrigeration in the summer. In a remarkably short time, he built his business to a point that he was able to bribe a few New York municipal officials to help him corner the city's ice market. After milking this situation for what it was worth, he sold his shares in the ice company at a considerable profit and decided he would like to try the banking business and the steamship business. More specifically, he planned to place his recently gained capital in a few carefully chosen banks in such a way as to give himself considerable influence, if not actual control, over the investment policies of those banks. With the larger resources thus placed at his disposal, he aimed to gain control of as many of the steamship lines operating on the Atlantic seaboard as possible, a plan that was destined to bring him into conflict with J. P. Morgan and the New Haven Railroad's transportation monopoly in New England.

Morse began modestly enough by first acquiring control of the Kennebec Line which operated overnight steamers similar to the *Tremont* and the *Penobscot* on a route between Boston and points on the Kennebec River, including Bath, Morse's home town. He did not buy the line outright; he just quietly acquired available shares until in March 1901 he had the controlling interest. After this first step, Morse's moves became more deliberate, and in a few months he controlled all of the major lines operating out of Boston to the Maine coast. His methods were unique. Each of these lines was owned by a handful of small investors in Boston or Maine whose families, in many cases, had owned these steamship stocks for decades. Morse, using the assets of the banks he controlled, made offers for these stocks so far above their assessed values that the small investors would rarely refuse to sell. The steamer lines, Morse reasoned, once collected and amalgamated, would be so much more valuable than they had been singly, that by selling the stock of his amalgamated company, heavily watered, of course, the banks whose funds he had used would also make considerable profits.

In this fashion, Morse gained control of the Boston-Portland Line in May 1901. In September, when he bought the Boston and Bangor Line, Morse acquired not only a valuable piece of steamboat property but also the services of Calvin Austin, the line's Boston agent, who was to become Morse's right-hand man and the extraordinarily competent manager of all of his New England steamboat operations. In October, Morse purchased the International Steamship Line, then operating the *Cumberland* and the *State of Maine*, both later Joy Lines steamers, and the *St. Croix*, from Boston to Lubec, Eastport, and St. John, New Brunswick. Finally, late in October, Morse consolidated his acquisitions by uniting the four Maine coast steamer lines, along with some smaller Maine steamer lines, as the Eastern Steamship Company. Almost simultaneously, he announced a program of building new steamers, at a rate of approximately one a year, for the Maine coast lines.

While Morse was consolidating the night lines of the Maine coast, much as the New Haven Railroad had done on Long Island Sound, one small company which was somewhat analogous to the Joy Line on the sound continued to operate the old *City of Fitchburg* from Boston to Portland in competition with the Morse-owned lines on the Maine coast. It sailed from Boston every Monday, Wednesday, and Friday at 8:00 P.M. and from Portland every Tuesday, Thursday, and Saturday at the same hour. Again one cannot help noticing the absence of a sailing from a resort area on a

Sunday night. Like the Joy Line steamers on the sound, the *City of Fitchburg* was popular and did not lack business, either in passengers or freight. But her owners soon discovered what the Joy Line people could probably have told them already: that a line operating at reduced fares, even when fully booked, could not earn enough to pay for the frequent repairs required on an aging second-hand steamer. Late in October 1901, the *City of Fitchburg* developed engine trouble and was off her route for three weeks to have her boilers repaired. There were rumors that the *Martinique* would be chartered to take her place briefly before returning to Florida,[34] but it is unlikely that such a plan was seriously considered. On November 7, the *City of Fitchburg* was back on the run, but after only a week her engine was again giving trouble. This time the line simply lacked the resources for further repairs, and the *City of Fitchburg* was tied up at Lewis wharf to await better times.[35]

In the fall of 1901, the Joy Line again found itself checked in every direction in its efforts to charter a steamer to run with the *Tremont* to Providence. The frustrations began when Dimon encountered an unexpected problem over the *Penobscot*. When the Joy Line originally arranged the three-month charter of the *Penobscot* in June, it had been agreed that the charter could be renewed and that, should the Joy Line find the *Penobscot* satisfactory, it would have an option to buy her. But by the time the charter came up for renewal in September, the Boston and Bangor Line had changed hands and was now part of Morse's Eastern Steamship Company. This time the pressure came not so much from the New Haven as from the Metropolitan. Whereas Morse had no reason to bend to the demands of the railroad, he wanted very much to remain on good terms with both the Metropolitan Line and the Maine Steamship Line to Portland, on both of which his Maine lines were dependent for through freight arrangements. On this occasion, Robert Haskins of the Metropolitan used the good offices of Captain Horatio Hall, manager of the Portland Line, in approaching the Eastern. At Hall's request, Calvin Austin raised the cost of chartering the *Penobscot* by $2,000 a month, twice the original amount, and the asking price for the steamer by $20,000, thus effectively preventing the Joy Line either from keeping the steamer under charter or from purchasing her, without actually violating the renewal clause or the purchase option in the original agreement.[36]

Realizing rather late in the season that it would soon be losing the *Penobscot*, the Joy Line made another appeal to Flagler to let the line charter the *Martinique* between the time she finished her Providence season in September and her return to her Florida run in December. As Flagler, the president of the P. and O. (as well as of the Florida East Coast Railway), was also an associate in the Standard Oil Company, the New Haven persuaded

William Rockefeller, an active member of its board of directors, to approach him personally. At Rockefeller's request, Flagler refused not only to charter the *Martinique* to the Joy Line but even to extend the charter of the *Cocoa* past its expiration date on November 1.[37]

The Joy Line next began negotiations with the Long Island Railroad to charter the *Shinnecock* as it had the previous winter. She would be more expensive than the original cost of the *Penobscot*, but she was also a much newer boat and had been very popular on the Joy Line. This time Robert Haskins of the Metropolitan became almost apoplectic in pleading with his friend Percy Todd of the New Haven to try to prevent the charter. Haskins allowed that he had "been able to cut off nearly all the charters for Boston boats, [but] I have no influence whatever with the Long Island or the Pennsylvania Railroads and I think if I were you I would not wait until the charter has been signed."[38] Todd promptly acted on his friend's suggestion and began writing letters to various business acquaintances in the higher offices of the Pennsylvania Railroad, of which the Long Island Railroad, which now owned the *Shinnecock*, was a subsidiary.

Since it was then August, most of Todd's friends were away on vacation, and the answer he received eventually from a third or fourth vice-president, whom he did not know personally, contained only hard logic. This official reminded Todd that the railroad had to lease the *Shinnecock to somebody* and that the Joy Line would eventually end up leasing a boat *from somebody*, whatever the New Haven did to prevent it, in which case why should the New Haven care *what* boat, and therefore, why not the *Shinnecock*? The writer did, however, have one alternative to offer. If the New Haven really wanted to prevent the Pennsylvania from chartering the *Shinnecock* to the Joy Line, why did not the New Haven itself charter it?[39] Todd, apparently not tuned to the irony of the suggestion, answered flatly that the New Haven already had "eight or ten steamers tied up idle so the *Shinnecock* will be of no use to us."[40]

While Todd could not get the Pennsylvania to cooperate, at least while his friends were away, once again it was Flagler who obliged. He found that he needed another steamer for the Miami-Knight's Key-Key West route, so negotiations between the Long Island Railroad and the Joy Line were cut short, and the *Shinnecock* sailed off that season for Florida.

Frustrated perhaps but not undaunted, Dimon continued to shop for steamers, and, just weeks before the charter of the *Penobscot* was scheduled to expire, he managed to secure the former Old Bay Line steamer *Virginia* before either Haskins or Todd could find a way to prevent it. The *Virginia* was a good deal older than the *Shinnecock*, but then it was also a good deal cheaper to charter. Built in 1879, she even had a few years on the venerable *Tremont* (but not the *Old Dominion*!). In spite of her age, she was a beautiful steamer famous for her clean graceful lines, and she had an iron hull which made her especially serviceable for winter work on Long Island Sound.

The *Virginia* and her sistership the *Carolina* along with the *Florida*, which was similar, were all built in the late 1870s and had made up the fleet of the Old Bay Line on Chesapeake Bay for many years. In the spring of 1901 the *Virginia* was sold to J. W. Wainwright, who operated her for one season as a ferry between Cape May, New Jersey, and Lewes, Delaware, and from whom the Joy Line chartered her at the end of the season with an option to purchase her if she proved satisfactory. The *Virginia* sailed up to New York from Philadelphia, where she had been laid up, on Tuesday, October 15, and went directly to Morse's yards in Brooklyn for painting and fitting. Here she was berthed next to the *Old Dominion* whose repairs were by then nearly finished. The *Virginia* needed some major work to be really serviceable. But since the charter had been arranged so late and the *Penobscot* was soon due to come off, the line decided to settle for a few necessary repairs in order to keep two steamers on the route through the busy fall season. Later, when the traffic was less demanding and the *Old Dominion* back on the Boston run, thus releasing the *Seaboard* as a substitute, the *Virginia* could come off again for more complete overhauling.

On Friday, October 25, the *Virginia* made her first trip to Providence commanded by Captain Jacob Wise who had recently come to the Joy Line from the Iron Steamboat Company.

Just over one week later, on Sunday, November 2, the *Old Dominion* was finally welcomed back to the line after nearly four months out of service. It was estimated that the insurance companies had spent nearly $70,000 rebuilding her hull. Now that Captain Durkee had departed, Captain Burton of the *Cocoa* took over as master of the *Old Dominion* with the veteran Captain Coleman serving as first pilot. Since the *Cocoa's* charter ran to the end of November, she stayed on the route until then under Captain Frank Kirby (and Captain Daniels for the P. and O. Line). With the *Old Dominion* and the *Cocoa* handling the Boston traffic, the *Seaboard* was now free to go on the Providence route temporarily, so that the *Virginia* could go back to the yards for some very necessary overhauling.

Apparently, the Joy Line considered the steamer sufficiently successful after two weeks of service to invest in some extensive alterations. When she was built, the *Virginia* carried only about eighty staterooms, some on the Main Deck but most on the Saloon Deck. She had almost no Gallery Deck at all except for a few rooms reserved for officers just aft of the pilot house. Later, the Bay Line added about thirty staterooms by extending the Gallery Deck from the pilot house to a point just aft of the single tall smokestack. But when the *Virginia* later served as a day boat on the Cape May-Lewes run, the staterooms on the Gallery Deck as well as several on the Saloon Deck were removed to create additional open deck space, reducing her accommodations to sixty-nine staterooms. Now the Joy Line rebuilt the half Gallery Deck and also replaced the staterooms on the Saloon Deck aft, adding in all about forty staterooms and bringing the *Virginia*'s total to over a hundred, or roughly the same number as the *Tremont*'s.

At the same time, the Joy Line took the *Virginia*'s dining room out of the hold, where it had been, and set up dining tables on her Saloon Deck forward, like the dining arrangement on the *Tremont* and other Maine coast steamers. Where the *Virginia*'s dining area had been, in the afterhold directly beneath the Quarter Deck, the Joy Line installed free berth cabins for men and women. All of the sound steamers provided free berths for passengers who did not choose to pay for staterooms, but the free berths on the *Virginia*, which had been built to serve a segregated society, were in the bow and were not considered satisfactory by the Joy Line.

The New Line had enjoyed a good season in 1901, especially with the Joy Line able to run only one small passenger steamer through much of July and most of August, but by October the railroad could no longer justify running four of its largest sidewheelers to Providence. So this year the regular Providence Line ended its passenger service early, at the end of the first week of October. As a compromise, the line transferred its large steamer *Plymouth* to the New Line to run for two more weeks with the *Rhode Island*—probably the only time one could have taken an overnight voyage on one of the grand Fall River Line steamers for fifty cents. Toward the end of October, however, the *Plymouth* went down to Newport for rest and repair before starting her winter service on the Fall River Line, and the *Rhode Island* returned to her duties as a winter relief boat. For most of November and December, the *Connecticut* and the *Chester W. Chapin* ran on the New Line, providing pretty formidable competition for such venerable little sidewheelers as the *Virginia* and the *Tremont*. Then late in December the *Massachusetts* was back on the New Line for the *Chester W. Chapin*, which returned to the New Haven Line, while the *Connecticut* and the *Massachusetts* made up the New Line through December and January.

The year 1901 had been a hard one for the Joy Line. Two of the three steamers it actually owned had come close to foundering within ten days of each other right at the outset of the summer season. The *Old Dominion* certainly and probably also the *Tremont* would have been abandoned by any other steamship company that had not been desperately dependent on them for its survival. During this year, the New Haven Railroad not only operated its competing New Line with larger and newer steamers at lower fares, but also joined the Metropolitan Line in using all means available to prevent the Joy Line from chartering suitable steamers and in offering better deals in freight rates to lure away the Joy Line's customers. Of the four steamers operated by the Joy Line, all were too old and subject to frequent and expensive breakdowns; all were too slow for the service; and all were too small to be really profitable to operate. In spite of all these liabilities, the Joy Line actually made a profit in 1901 and showed every indication of intending to stay in business.

1902

The winter of 1902 turned out to be one of the coldest on record. Ice in the sound and severe winter storms plauged the sound steamers as they rarely had before. The dawn of New Year's Day found the *Old Dominion* paddling through heavy snow past Montauk Point, having taken the outside route to Boston that night.

As the year opened, the summer steamers *Priscilla* and *Puritan* were still in service to Fall River. As soon as the holiday season was officially over on Twelfthnight, however, the *Plymouth* came on the line to relieve the *Priscilla*. But Fletcher's had not quite finished repairing the *Pilgrim*'s engines, so the *Puritan* stayed on with the *Plymouth* until January 22. The Joy Line's *Tremont* was also having engine work done at Morgan's Iron Works at the foot of Ninth Street as the year began, so the *Seaboard* was running to Providence with the *Virginia*, leaving the *Old Dominion* alone on the Boston run.

The new year started in the usual style for the Joy Line when, early in the morning of January 2, the *Seaboard*, coming into the East River from the sound and changing course suddenly to avoid a sloop coming up-river, collided with a car float in Hell Gate and had to be out of service for several days. Fortunately, the *Tremont*'s repairs were then well enough along for her to return to the line for the *Seaboard* that night.

As winter storms continued to howl along the coast throughout January and February, the Joy Line fared somewhat better than the railroad lines. The *Old Dominion* continued her trips to Boston, unperturbed as ever by the elements, although on Wednesday, January 6, the seas raged so out of control that even the *Old Dominion*, soon after emerging from Boston harbor, turned about very cautiously and sailed back in again.[1] Throughout

January and February 1902, she tended to sail around Long Island for the most part, in the process losing all track of a regular schedule. She took this route largely because it was safer in the unusually heavy weather, and also because Captain Burton was on vacation and the *Old Dominion* was under the temporary command of Captain Coleman, who, after many years of guiding the Metropolitan liners through all sorts of weather, was more at ease with the outside route. The line was also fortunate in having chartered the *Virginia*, which, with her iron hull and large sidewheels, proved a good icebreaker. The *Tremont*, too, slow as she was, was staunchly constructed and was always a good sea boat.

The New Line, on the other hand, was running the *Massachusetts* and the *Connecticut*, both wooden-hulled steamers built for summer service. They had rarely been run around Point Judith in the wintertime at all, much less in such heavy seas as they were encountering with practically every sailing that season. Once again, the railroad, which had never expected the Joy Line to hold out this long, by continuing to operate the New Line after more than a year found itself seriously short of steamers suitable for the winter service. On the night of January 22, the *Massachusetts* was so damaged by the heavy seas that she had to be taken off the run and laid up at Lonsdale wharf for repairs. At that time, both the *Richard Peck* and the *City of Lawrence* were out for repairs so that the *Chester W. Chapin*, which had relieved the *Massachusetts* the previous winter, was needed on the New Haven Line and was not then available. The *New Hampshire* had been running to New Haven with her (in place of the *City of Lawrence*) and the *Rhode Island* with the *Maine* on the Stonington Line. Now the *Rhode Island* went on the New Line in place of the *Massachusetts*, and the railroad, for the first time that year but not the last, had to place a freight steamer (the *Nashua*) on the Stonington Line. Thus, Stonington was left with passenger service only three nights a week, which was probably enough to take care of the people who wanted to take an overnight steamer to Stonington in January. Later in the month, the situation became even more difficult when the *City of Worcester* was damaged and had to miss several trips. One of the freighters (*City of Fall River*) was assigned to the New Haven Line in place of the *New Hampshire*, which returned to the Stonington Line with the *Nashua*, while the *Maine* now joined the *City of Lowell* on the New London route. As though these were not problems enough, the heavy seas stove in the starboard paddlebox of the *Pilgrim* one night, less than a week after she had come back on the line, and the *Puritan* was back for several more trips.

By this time, the railroad was beginning to realize the impossibility of running the *Connecticut* and the *Massachusetts* through the winter, especially as it wanted to keep the *Connecticut* in shape to run on the regular Providence Line in the summer. Therefore, as soon as the *Richard Peck* and the *City of Lawrence* had completed their overhauls and were ready to resume service on the New Haven Line early in February, the *Chester W. Chapin* joined the *Rhode Island* on the New Line for the rest of the winter and the *Connecticut* and *Massachusetts* were laid up. With passenger service reduced on both the New Haven Line and the Stonington Line and no steamers at all available for emergencies or relief, except on the Fall River Line, maintaining the New Line through the winter was proving not only expensive for the railroad but also detrimental to its service.

In February the weather got even worse. On February 15, the Weather Bureau reported that, although more snow had fallen at one time in the blizzard of 1888, never within memory had so much snow been accompanied by such high winds over so long a period of time. Two days later, the coast had the worst storm of the season followed by another on Thursday and Friday, February 21-22. During the second storm, the *Rhode Island* limped into New London early one morning with part of her superstructure torn away by the winds. As there were no relief boats available, however, the railroad had to resort to the Joy Line's method of putting carpenters on board to make repairs while the steamer stayed in service.

Early in 1902, the New Haven was handed an opportunity to prevent the Joy Line from acquiring permanent ownership of the *Virginia*. On January 7, 1902, J. W. Wainwright, who had bought the *Virginia* from the Old Bay Line early in 1901 to run her from Cape May to Lewes, Delaware, sold her to the Champion Construction Company, a shipbroker in Philadelphia. Dimon immediately communicated to the new owners that the Joy Line was interested either in arranging a five-year charter of the *Virginia* at $18,500 per year or in purchasing the steamer outright for $100,000.[2] A Mr. Rosenbaum, representing the new owners, thereupon communicated this offer to A. H. Johnson and Company, his agents in New York, indicating to them that they were at liberty to sell the *Virginia* elsewhere if they could obtain a better price.[3] Max Strauss of the A. H. Johnson Company thought he knew where that price might be obtained and, in order to keep his moves secret, telephoned Percy Todd that night at his home offering to make the *Virginia* available to the railroad to prevent its sale to the Joy Line.[4] Todd was not interested and subsequently wrote to Strauss that he would "just as soon let the Joy Line have the *Virginia* as any other old tub," and told him to "go ahead and make the sale, if you can, but be sure and get a certified check."[5]

In any event, Rosenbaum did not sell the *Virginia* to the Joy Line. Instead, title was conveyed on March 11 to the Whidby Land and Development Company, which may well have been either an agent for the New Haven or acting under pressure from the New Haven, since Todd, after refusing to purchase the *Virginia* outright, wrote to Strauss the following day suggesting that there were other purchasers from whom he might "be able to get a little better price" than that offered by the Joy Line.[6] As the negotiations concerning the *Shinnecock* the previous summer indicated, although the New Haven was willing to use its influence or to employ almost any kind of business tactic to prevent the Joy Line from acquiring a steamer, the rules of the game did not permit the railroad to lay out actual cash. Direct acquisition of a steamer operating on a competing line could be interpreted as restraint of trade and thus too clear a violation of the Sherman Anti-Trust Act to be worth the risk.

The New Haven was still not above using other methods, however, to block the sale of steamers to the Joy Line. During the first week of February 1902, the Montauk Line announced that it sold its smaller sidewheel steamer *Montauk* to the Canadian-owned Algoma and Hudson Bay Railway Company to operate on Lake Huron (as the *King Edward*). By this time, it was apparent that the Pennsylvania Railroad, parent organization of the Montauk Line, had been persuaded to cooperate fully with the New Haven in its campaign to prevent the Joy Line from acquiring steamers, for the *Montauk*'s sale agreement included a clause stating that the steamer must never be used by the purchaser or by any successive owners "in the waters of Long Island Sound in competition with the boats of the New York, New Haven, and Hartford Railway Company for the term of two years from the date thereof."[7] There is no evidence that the Joy Line ever had its eye on the *Montauk*, a sidewheel steamer about the size of the *Seaboard*, but the insertion of such a specific clause by a company not even indirectly under the New Haven's control shows what difficulty the Joy Line encountered acquiring steamboats, even when it could afford them.

At the time it sold the *Montauk*, the line announced plans to replace her with a larger steamer similar to the *Shinnecock*. Since the new steamer would obviously not be ready by spring, the Montauk Line arranged to charter the old Norwich Line steamer *City of Lawrence* from the New Haven Railroad.[8] The *City of Lawrence*, however, as the Montauk Line was soon to discover, aside from being about the oldest steamer on the sound, was not really adapted to its needs. She was essentially a freighter with comfortable but very limited passenger accommodations, while the Montauk Line's operation catered mainly to passenger traffic.

Another sale of a small steamer at about the same time is also of interest. The owners of the former New Bedford Line steamer *City of Fitchburg* had apparently been unable to pay for the necessary engine repairs or even for those repairs that had already been made the week before she gave up her run in November, for on January 11, the steamer was sold at a marshall's sale in Boston. She was picked up by G. H. Whitcomb of Worcester for $8,200.[9] How did Charlie Dimon miss this one? With a few other investors from Worcester, mostly relatives, Whitcomb organized the Enterprise

Transportation Company (of which we shall be hearing a great deal more in a later chapter) and announced that he would continue to operate the *City of Fitchburg* on the Boston-Portland route in opposition to Morse's *Bay State* and *Governor Dingley*. Rather than waste any more cash on the *City of Fitchburg's* ailing engine, as her previous owners had done, Whitcomb had it removed altogether and replaced with a second-hand engine from the steamer *Dessoux*. This ship, once the private yacht of the khedive of Egypt, had brought the obelisk now standing in Central Park over to America and then, like Pheidippedes, had died on arrival. The new boilers for the *City of Fitchburg* came from the former Bridgeport steamer *Nutmeg State*, which, as we have seen, had burned in the sound two years before. Replete with a new engine, new boilers, new paint job, and a few new staterooms, the old *City of Fitchburg* emerged in the spring of 1902 with a new name as well, appropriately enough, *Surprise*.

Early in March, the *Seaboard* of the Joy Line was finally repaired after over two months in the shops following her accident in Hell Gate on January 2. Now it was her turn to take on the heavy rains and rough seas of the New York to Boston run (although the *Seaboard* always took the protected Long Island Sound route whenever possible), while the *Old Dominion* went for an overhaul. Finally, in April, almost for the first time since the *Old Dominion* went on the rocks in July 1901, the Joy Line was able to return to a regular two-boat schedule on the Boston Line.

Through March 1902, during which the storms, cold weather, heavy rains, and high seas continued almost without a break, the *Chester W. Chapin* and the *Rhode Island* were still running to Providence for the New Line and the *Tremont* and *Virginia* for the Joy Line. As long as the *Chester W. Chapin* was running to Providence, the *Richard Peck*, which had been the company's relief steamer the previous year, had to remain on the New Haven Line. Thus, the railroad had no relief steamers available for the spring overhauls, except the *Massachusetts* or the *C. H. Northam*, neither of which could be employed safely in the kind of weather New England was experiencing that season. As a consequence, the railroad again had to manage through most of the spring with only one passenger steamer, the *New Hampshire*, running on the Stonington Line with the freighter *Nashua*. Her sistership, the *Maine*, continued to provide relief service on the New London route, first for the *City of Worcester* and then, in April (by which time the weather turned positively balmy), for the *City of Lowell*.

During the spring of 1902, the New Haven Railroad and the Metropolitan Line stepped up their campaign to crush the Joy Line. Whereas a year earlier their emphasis had been on keeping the Joy Line from acquiring boats, the main thrust in 1902 was to cut off the Joy Line's freight revenues. The correspondence of both the railroad and the Metropolitan

Line in this period abounds with letters to the Joy Line's freight customers (or to each other regarding these customers), using every means at their disposal to persuade them not to ship via the Joy Line. In some cases they used pressure, reminding a company of favors the railroad was in a position to grant or to withdraw; in some cases they harassed, reminding shippers sharply of previous agreements or promises; most often, however, they began to show an unwonted willingness to meet the Joy Line's rates, although it would have been a naive merchant indeed who did not realize that, once the railroad had been successful in eliminating the Joy Line, the rates would go up again, and many of them, on those grounds, refused to take the bait.

Throughout the correspondence, it is clear that while the Metropolitan Line and the railroad had no written agreement of any kind, the two companies were willing to act totally in tandem on any matter relating to the campaign against the Joy Line. The railroad had no objections to a company's shipping via the Metropolitan Line rather than the railroad, and vice versa, as long as it did not ship via the Joy Line. It is also clear that it had become the Metropolitan Line's unwritten responsibility to bring pressure to bear on shippers in the Boston area to prevent their using the Joy Line, while the New Haven accepted the same responsibility in the Providence area.[10] Both companies used "spies" to see what firms were shipping via the Joy Line and in particular to check whether those with whom they had made agreements (low rates were often granted by the railroad's agents on condition that the shipper promise not to use the Joy Line at all) were living up to them.

A mere sampling of the vast correspondence of this period illustrates the methods employed. A report from New Haven "spies" that the American Sugar Refining Company had sent a shipment via the Joy Line contrary to a previous agreement elicited a sharp reminder by telegram from Percy Todd to W. B. Thomas of American Sugar: "Your people gave a large shipment of sugar to the Joy Line from New York to Boston last Saturday."[11] The following day, Thomas answered apologetically with another telegram: "Saturday's shipment was ordered before I saw you. . . . Instructions were given as promised."[12]

A few days later, Haskins of the Metropolitan complained to Todd of further infringements: "I would call your attention particularly to the lot of 350 barrels of sugar, 200 of which were delivered to the steamer *Seaboard*, and the balance to the steamer *Tremont*. . . . Mr. Thomas is evidently not controlling this in New York."[13] This intelligence set off another complaint from Todd to Thomas and another apologetic explanation from Thomas to Todd,[14] before the matter was cleared up. In other similar letters, Haskins whined over a shipment of hemp,[15] Todd thundered over a shipment of shoes,[16] and so on.

In another move, the New Haven deprived the Joy Line of its light-erage service to Fall River with the simple expedient of offering Captain Dyer $10.00 per day if he would promise not to carry Joy Line freight to Fall River. Since it cost Captain Dyer something in excess of $15.00 to run his lighter to Fall River and back each day, and the Joy Line had been paying him $25.00, he made a slight profit by accepting the $10.00 from the railroad and keeping the lighter idle.[17]

By this time, too, the New Haven had apparently persuaded the Pennsylvania not to accept any shipments in New York for points south or west that arrived via a Joy Line steamer. The Joy Line lost a great deal of freight in 1902 because it had no way of guaranteeing the shipper that his freight would get any further than the Joy Line's New York docks. Even more serious was the line's inability to take shipments of raw leather from the West or cotton from the South bound for New England.

The Joy Line did all it could to circumvent the problem. It apparently had no intention of allowing two of the country's largest and most powerful railroads to stop the line from getting its shipments through. If the New Haven was to be reduced to such tactics to prevent them from employing Captain Dyer's service, then the Joy Line would have to create its own lighterage service to get its freight to Fall River. One night Charlie Dimon took a berth on the *Tremont* for Providence, and once there scouted around the Narragansett Bay area for any available craft the line could use in this service. Before returning to New York, he had taken an option on the purchase of the lighter *Henry Sisson*. New Haven spies soon discovered the deal, but not soon enough to prevent it.[18] The railroad did, however, give Dimon considerable difficulty in his efforts to secure dock space in either Newport or Fall River for the new project. During the spring and summer of 1902, as the Joy Line waited for the city councils of these two cities to meet, the New Haven mustered its considerable influence (which was decisive as it turned out, in both places) to persuade them to vote against giving dockage to the Joy Line.[19]

While waiting for the city councils to reach a decision, the Joy Line still had freight to deliver. Therefore, later in June, Dunbaugh went up to Providence and purchased a whole stable, complete with horses and carts, which now became the Joy Express Company, and began carting freight directly to customers in Fall River or elsewhere in the Narragansett Bay area.

With deliveries now more or less provided for at the New England end of their run, the Joy Line began to consider the more difficult problem of getting freight to points south of New York now that the Pennsylvania had refused to carry it. Eventually it appeared that the only solution was to establish a steamer line of its own between New York and Philadelphia. Its first inclination was to run a line of small steamers through the Delaware and Raritan Canal. In the process of exploring the possibilities of starting such a service, Dunbaugh went down to Philadelphia to talk with the president of the Ericsson Line, which ran steamers between Philadelphia and Baltimore via the Chesapeake and Delaware Canal. Dunbaugh asked him first if he would be willing to sell the Joy Line any of his canal steamers. Since the Ericsson Line was then building two new steamers for its day route, it would soon have steamers available. Dunbaugh also asked whether, if the Joy Line did establish a new route between New York and Philadelphia, the Ericsson Line would be interested in cooperating with it in making through freight arrangements on goods going further south from Philadelphia to Baltimore. The president of the Ericsson Line, however, was suspicious of moves designed to circumvent the Pennsylvania Railroad, with which he preferred to stay on friendly terms, and of opposition steamship lines in general. He therefore refused either to sell the Joy Line any boats or to cooperate on through freight arrangements. Dunbaugh next went to the Clydes, who operated one of the canal boat lines on the Delaware and Raritan, and offered to buy it, but they did not wish to sell.[20]

Returning to New York, Dunbaugh conferred again with his associates and, accepting the unfeasibility of the canal boat project, decided to try to run a direct outside line from Providence to Philadelphia. Apparently undaunted by his earlier rebuff, Dunbaugh returned to the Ericsson Line in Philadelphia and offered to buy the two small steamers which that line had recently used between Philadelphia and New Haven. But the Ericsson people, unwilling to offend any of the existing coastal lines with which they had friendly relations, again refused to sell.[21]

There was a rumor at the time that the Joy Line was also negotiating with the Whitcombs to purchase the *Surprise* (ex-*City of Fitchburg*), which, while hardly new, might have been suitable for the service it had in mind and also as an extra when needed on the Joy Line's Boston route. It would have been an interesting irony had the Joy Line been able to outploy the New Haven with one of the railroad's own former steamers. But, if the rumor was true, the negotiations fell through, for the Whitcombs ran the *Surprise* that season as planned, on the Boston to Portland run.

Meanwhile, the Joy Line had also been dealing again with Henry Flagler in hopes of acquiring one of the five small boats that the P. and O. had put up for sale. The *Cocoa*, for instance, while not ideal, would suffice, at least to start the line to Philadelphia. But the *Cocoa* had been sold. However, Flagler informed the Joy Line that it could have the *City of Key West*, since this was the one boat on his roster that he had little hope of unloading. The Joy Line, apparently unable ever to resist a bargain, thereupon actually bought the *City of Key West* with half an idea of running her on an outside line between Providence and Philadelphia.

Built in 1865, the same year as the *Newport* and the *Old Colony*, the *City of Key West* had the honor of being one of the oldest steamers on the coast; she was even two years older than the *City of Lawrence*, which had survived longer than most on Long Island Sound because of her iron hull. The *City of Key West* had originally been built for service on the James River as the *City of Richmond*. But after one season there, she turned up on a new Maine coast route from Portland to Rockland and Bangor. Later, she ran from Portland to Rockland and then to Bar Harbor and points further north, a route she served (as noted in an earlier chapter) until replaced by the *Frank Jones* in 1892. In all fairness, we must point out that in this service the *City of Richmond* was described as "the most graceful in appearance of all the side-wheel steamers that once plied Penobscot waters," and "the fleetest of all the boats of her day, not excepting even the Boston and Bangor ships."[22] Unfortunately, this was 1902, and "her day" had been some time before. She was still a very lovely steamer, especially after she had been almost completely rebuilt in 1881 following an accident, but she could no longer be described as "fleet."

She had lain idle for some years after her replacement in 1892 when Henry Flagler, anxious to accumulate a fleet of steamers as quickly as possible to augment the routes of his Florida East Coast Railway, bought her in 1897 and took her down to Florida with every intention of replacing her with newer steamers as soon as possible. The purchase of the *Martinique* in 1899 and the merger with the Plant Line the following year rendered the *City of Key West* superfluous, and she was again laid up, this time in Jacksonville, until unloaded on the Joy Line in the spring of 1902.

By the early summer of 1902, the steamship operators were encountering a new problem which they had never had to face before—a shortage of coal. In this era, all steamships were fired by coal, and some of the larger steamers took on several hundred tons of it each day just for one overnight trip up the sound. Since, before 1902, coal had been a relatively inexpensive commodity, economy in coal consumption had never been a major consideration in the designing of steamers. But this situation was to change when, after a long and bitter dispute with the mine owners over wages and working conditions, the United Mine Workers of America called a general strike in the anthracite coal mines on May 12, 1902. With the mine owners unwilling to bend to the demands of the unions, the strike lasted all through the summer of 1902, creating a critical shortage in a commodity without which the sound steamers could not operate. By July, hot-burning coal of high quality was becoming difficult to obtain, and what was available was becoming increasingly expensive.

For a steamer line such as the Joy Line, operating with little, if any, reserve captial and charging fares that rendered it only a minimal profit, the unexpected sharp rise in the price of such a necessary commodity as coal proved almost the final strain on its already weak financial condition.

By the summer of 1902, as a result of many accumulated debts plus the sharp rise in the price of coal resulting from the strike, as well as a marked increase in the cost of steamer maintenance that all of the lines were experiencing at the time, the Joy Line became perilously short of working capital once again, even though its steamers, mercifully, managed to avoid any serious collisions that season. Since the line was experiencing difficulty in finding the cash to keep the steamers running to Providence or Boston from day to day, it was not able, for the time, to pursue its plan of buying new steamers to run to Philadelphia. By this time, the Joy Line also realized that the *City of Key West*, although she had served on ocean routes for most of her career, was not at all suited for the proposed Philadelphia service. But she had been obtained for a good price, and she could serve as a spare boat for the Providence route, a luxury which the Joy Line had never before been able to afford. Accordingly, Dimon arranged for her to go to a yard in Jacksonville to be prepared for the trip back north.

The policy of running large, expensive steamers on the New Line reached the ridiculous in April 1902 when the New Haven people put the *Pilgrim* on the New Line for several weeks. The *Massachusetts* and *Connecticut* were still laid up, and the *Chester W. Chapin* needed overhauling before starting her summer service to New Haven. So when the *Priscilla* and the *Puritan* came back to the Fall River Line on April 20 (somewhat early this year), the *Pilgrim* went up to Providence to relieve the *Chester W. Chapin*. The one month the *Pilgrim* spent on the New Line was anything but a success. Her troubles began early in the morning of Thursday, April 24. Steaming into New York at dawn, the tiller rope jammed and the big Fall River Line steamer went out of control, coming to rest, fortunately, on the mud flats at Sunken Meadows. Later in the day, two New Haven tugs went out there and brought her back to Fletcher's for repairs, where she remained for two days. Obviously, the New Line had no passenger steamers to put on the line in her place, but the *Block Island*, a small excursion steamer recently acquired by the railroad, came down to New York the next night with a load of freight.

By May 1, the *Massachusetts* and the *Connecticut* were ready for their summer runs. The *Massachusetts* went on the New Line with the *Pilgrim* so that the *Rhode Island* could go for an overdue overhaul, and the *Connecticut*, while waiting for the summer Providence Line to start in June, joined the *New Hampshire* to reestablish daily passenger service to Stonington. With these two large passenger steamers back in service, the railroad's lines were again in good shape—for about ten days. Then, at about one in the morning of Friday, May 8, the *Pilgrim*, headed toward Providence (still on the New Line), was steaming along peacefully in the dark somewhere off of Saybrook. Suddenly there was a fearful crack, followed by ominous crashing sounds from deep within the steamer. The *Pilgrim* had broken the cylinder head of her engine, and, as a result, her whole engine room was a wreck. Luckily, no one was injured. The freighters *City of Brockton* bound for Fall River and the *Pequot* for New Bedford, both following along not far astern, came up and towed the disabled *Pilgrim* into New London.

The next day the *Rhode Island*'s overhaul was postponed indefinitely, and she went up to Providence to take her place on the New Line with the *Massachusetts* for the rest of the summer.

The damage to the *Pilgrim* was devastating. When she was towed down to Fletcher's a few days later, the repairs were estimated at over $100,000.[23] The steamer, which had just returned to service after being out nearly a year for engine repairs, would now be out again for several months more. It was fortunate that the railroad had decided to have the *Connecticut* repaired, or it would have been caught in 1902 without a suitable steamer to run with the *Plymouth* on the Providence Line.

The *Pilgrim*'s mechanical breakdown was only the first of a series of disabling accidents suffered by the steamers of the railroad's lines during 1902, which turned out to be as disastrous a season for them, if that was possible, as 1901 had been for the Joy Line. The next incident occurred on one of the Fall River Line's freighters. Early in June, less than a month after towing the *Pilgrim* to safety, the *City of Brockton*, when steaming along in almost the same place, had an almost identical accident. Towed into Newport by her consort the *City of Taunton*, the *City of Brockton*, too, was out of service for several months in 1902. There was no shortage of freight steamers, however, particularly now that none was needed on the Providence Line, so her near-sister, the *City of Fall River*, was available to take her place.

A few weeks earlier (on May 6), the freight steamer *Mohawk* (one of two sisterships operated by the New Haven between New York and New London under contract to the Central Vermont Railroad) burned down to the Main Deck. The Providence Line freighter *Nashua* ran to New London that summer while the *Mohawk* was being rebuilt.

The railroad's summer service to Providence started as usual on the first Monday night in June, once again with the *Plymouth* and the *Connecticut*. The one-way fares to Providence in 1902 remained the same as the year before: $3.00 on the *Plymouth* or *Connecticut* of the Providence Line, $1.00 on the *Tremont* or the *Virginia* of the Joy Line, and fifty cents on the *Massachusetts* or the *Rhode Island* of the New Line.

That same week the brand new day steamer *William G. Payne*, a side-wheeler, made her first trip on the Bridgeport Line replacing the *Rosedale*. From this time the *William G. Payne*, which ranked as one of the fastest steamers on the sound, made the daylight round trip from Bridgeport to New York and back, while the *Allan Joy*, the former Joy Line steamer, made the night-time round trip to Bridgeport out of New York.

Although the summer season of 1902 did not launch the avalanche of disasters on the Joy Line that the 1901 season had, the line was not without its share of troubles that year. At about six in the morning of May 19, as the *Virginia* was cautiously feeling her way through the fog toward Hell Gate, the excursion steamer *Glen Island*, then substituting as a freighter on the Starin Line's New Haven freight line, suddenly materialized to starboard too close to avoid a collision. The crash smashed the *Virginia's* beautifully decorated paddlebox and left a long open hole along her freight deck. But in typical Joy Line fashion, with no other steamers to run in her place, carpenters were placed aboard the steamer to continue the repairs at both ends of the route, and the wounded *Virginia* did not miss a single trip.[24]

No sooner was the *Virginia* more-or-less patched up than more serious problems arose. On Friday, June 13, government inspectors announced that the *Virginia* could not be licensed to carry passengers unless she had what promised to be long and expensive repairs.[25] Once again, as in the previous season, the Joy Line was caught with only one steamer on the Providence route just at the time of year when it needed as much passenger space as it could provide. This time not even the *Seaboard* was available. The *Old Dominion* was also at Morse's for emergency engine work (one feels that Morse's could have been doing a thriving business if it had no other customers than the Joy Line), so that the *Seaboard* was then running alone to Boston.

On Friday, June 13, the day of the inspection, there was no Joy Line sailing out of New York. Then on Monday, June 16, the line put the *Virginia* back on the run carrying freight only, so that for the last two weeks of June, just as the seasonal passenger traffic was becoming lucrative, the Joy Line could offer passenger service only on alternate nights with the *Tremont*. After about a week, the *Virginia* was taken off altogether, and the *Rosalie*, which had arrived back in New York a few days before, took her place carrying freight to Providence on alternate nights. (The *Berkeley* and the *Brandon* had been delivered to the Old Dominion Line that spring and were now in operation on the new passenger service between Norfolk and Richmond, thus releasing the *Rosalie* from her charter.)

Meanwhile, Dimon telephoned Jacksonville to send up the recently purchased *City of Key West*, which now paddled up the coast from Florida as fast as she could. She arrived in New York on Friday, June 27, going directly to Morse's to be fitted out for service and making her first trip to Providence for the Joy Line on Monday evening, June 30.

The night before the *City of Key West* arrived in New York to allow the Joy Line some semblance of daily passenger service, the line, apparently determined to start the season in the usual fashion with a new cliffhanger every week, almost lost the *Tremont*, the only passenger steamer it had operating at the time, to another yacht. The *Tremont* was paddling along through the darkness of the open sound on her way to New York in the very early morning of Friday, June 27, with the steam yacht *Alcedo* sailing in the same direction slightly ahead of her to starboard. The *Tremont*, according to Captain Wilcox, was just about to overtake her, when the yacht suddenly veered to port and attempted to cross the *Tremont's* bow. Wilcox swung his steamer to starboard to avoid a collision, but he was too late and the inconsiderate yacht rammed right into the *Tremont's* brand new bow. The impact was not severe, however: only the bowsprit of the *Alcedo* pierced the *Tremont's* timbers above the guards. Once the two vessels pulled apart, both were able to proceed without danger. The *Tremont* could not afford to miss a trip, so once again the line's carpenters sailed with the steamer for several days to complete their repairs while the *Tremont* was underway.[26]

Two nights later, the *City of Key West* made her first trip out of New York for the Joy Line under Captain Jacob Wise. The simple entry, "The Joy Line's newly purchased *City of Key West* arrived here at 11:30 yesterday," in the next day's *Providence Journal* tells at least part of the story well enough without much further comment. We must take into consideration that the *City of Key West* had just made the long trip up the coast from Florida after two years of lying idle and had then been pressed into service on the Joy Line without taking the time she should have for a thorough overhaul of her machinery. In addition, given the high price of coal during the strike, Dimon had been obliged to purchase inferior coal. With all of these problems, the *City of Key West* had apparently broken down en route, with the result that she arrived in Providence on her first trip over five hours late.[27]

When the *City of Key West* finally tied up at the Point Street Bridge at mid-day, the line had an ambulance waiting. While the *City of Key West* had been paddling leisurely up Narragansett Bay in the early morning, occasionally stopping altogether to make repairs to the machinery, a young woman on board had begun to go into labor and there were some anxious hours before the steamer finally reached Providence. But the ambulance got the woman to the Providence General Hospital in time for a comfortable delivery.[28]

Captain Wise had apparently had a full night of it. Not only had his steamer refused to run properly and a woman on board started labor, but one of the crew had also managed to stage a case of the "D.T.'s" on this trip. After a hard fight, the man was finally secured and tied up for the night. On arrival in Providence he was turned over to the police.[29]

Early in July, after receiving a report on the condition of the *Virginia* from Morse's shipyard, the Joy Line decided against making the necessary repairs and instead opted to return the steamer to her owners and to operate that summer with the *Tremont* and the *City of Key West*. Why would the Joy Line drop its option to buy a beautiful steamer like the *Virginia*, on which it had already spent a great deal of money for improvements, and run a bona fide antique like the *City of Key West*, which was patently too small for the service? Apparently, several factors were involved in the decision. One was that the *Virginia*'s new owners, whether or not they were responding to control or influence from the New Haven (as seems most likely), had decided not to sell the *Virginia* to the Joy Line, at least not at a price the line was then able to pay. Since the estimate for repairs was high, the line was not inclined (or was perhaps unable) to spend so much on a steamer it did not own. A second factor, which may have been the deciding one, was that by the time Dimon received the report on the *Virginia* from Morse's, he had heard of the possible availability, at a very reasonable price, of a far more valuable steamer. He therefore wanted to keep whatever assets or credit the Joy Line still had intact in the event that he could purchase this steamer, as indeed he eventually did (of which more later). Dimon and the other Joy Line officers undoubtedly reckoned that it was worth the gamble to let the old *Virginia* go and to try to hobble through the summer season with the *City of Key West* and the *Tremont* rather than spend money repairing the *Virginia*, which probably would not have made it back to the line during the summer season in any event. Thus, on July 11, 1902, the *Virginia* returned to Philadelphia at the end of a towrope.[30]

Whatever the reason, the Joy Line lost a good boat, for after some reconditioning, she was to run for another quarter century as the *Tadousac* on the St. Lawrence River, where she was later purchased to run with the *Murray Bay*, ex-*Carolina*, her sistership and former running mate on Chesapeake Bay.

Once the *City of Key West* worked out her initial mechanical difficulties, she ran through the rest of the summer season without incident, except for a brush with the *New Hampshire* in the East River one foggy morning (July 13) soon after she began her service, carrying as many passengers and as much freight as her limited capacity would allow. In fact, all four of the line's steamers, the *City of Key West* and the *Tremont* to Providence, and the *Seaboard* and the *Old Dominion* to Boston, managed to stay on their runs throughout the season without missing a trip as a result of accident or mechanical failure—quite a record for the Joy Line. But the jinx that had followed the Joy Line boats in 1901 apparently decided to move to the railroad's lines in 1902. The burning of the *Mohawk* and breakdowns on the *Pilgrim* and the *City of Brockton* in the spring turned out to be only the first in a series of accidents involving the railroad's steamers which, before the summer was over, severely crippled their services.

Through the early evening of Thursday, July 3, the usual hordes of vacationers arrived at Lonsdale wharf by train or by trolley and boarded the New Line steamer *Massachusetts* for an overnight trip to New York. It was still daylight at 7:30 P.M. when the big white sidewheeler, still proud and still elegant in spite of her twenty-five years and her demotion to a cut-rate line, blew one long blast of her whistle to announce her departure and then, her big wheels slowly churning up the waters, pulled slowly away from her dock and turned sharply to port into the narrow channel down the Providence River. No one on board suspected that this would be the *Massachusetts'* last trip. The *Tremont*, of course, had sailed two hours earlier and was no longer visible. But the *Connecticut*, the former running mate of the *Massachusetts*, was still on the more prestigious Providence Line and pulled away from Fox Point only minutes later, so that the two former Providence and Stonington Line sidewheelers sailed together down Narragansett Bay.

It was about 10:30 P.M. when the bright lights of the two steamers, both still alive with the revels of expectant vacationers in spite of the hour, were seen emerging from Narragansett Bay and turning past Point Judith, mercifully calm on this summer's evening, toward Long Island Sound. One hour later, as it was nearing midnight and some of the six hundred passengers on the *Massachusetts* were at last thinking of retiring to their staterooms or staking out quiet spots for sleeping on the after deck, the calm was suddenly shattered by a banging and clattering of iron. After several minutes of this unexpected racket, the big sidewheels stopped turning altogether; the *Massachusetts* coasted awhile and then stopped. The frame of her walking beam had broken, leaving the old steamer in the middle of the sound with her engine rendered useless. The *Massachusetts* was just off New London, within a few miles of the place where both the *Pilgrim* and the *City of Brockton* had broken down a few months earlier.[31]

Fortunately, the *City of Lowell* was just sailing out of New London and the *New Hampshire* out of Stonington. These two steamers together towed the disabled *Massachusetts* as far as the entrance to New London harbor. At that point, the freighter *City of Fall River* came along to tow the *Massachusetts* on into New London, so that the two passenger steamers could proceed to New York.[32]

The railroad's marine division had some tough decisions to make in a hurry. The next night's sailing out of New York was not only the first Friday of the summer season, but also the fourth of July, and the *Massachusetts* was already heavily booked. But there were no steamers available to replace her except the *C. H. Northam*, which at that time was not in condition to operate on such short notice. The railroad's only other spare steamer, the *City of Lawrence*, had just started her charter to the Montauk Line and would not have been much help in any event with the New Line's fourth of July crowd. In the emergency, the *Chester W. Chapin* was transferred to the New Line for a few trips, leaving the *Richard Peck* to handle the holiday traffic to New Haven alone. Then during the weekend the railroad's marine division, realizing that the *Massachusetts* would not be repaired soon, if ever, decided to curtail the passenger service on its Stonington Line for the rest of the season to make an additional passenger steamer available for the New Line. While the freighter *Nashua* (back from her charter to the Central Vermont) again went on the Stonington Line with the *Maine*, the *New Hampshire* took the place of the *Massachusetts* on the New Line. Although this arrangement was probably the best one possible at the time, the *New Hampshire* was hardly a satisfactory steamer for the New Line. She was a good cargo carrier, but with barely more than a hundred staterooms, not much more than half the number on the *Massachusetts* (184), she was ill-equipped to handle the human stampedes that often characterized the New Line's summer night sailings.

But the worst was still to come. Just four days after the *Massachusetts* broke down, the railroad's largest steamer, the *Priscilla*, was rammed and nearly sunk between Newport and Point Judith, and was out of service for nearly a month right in the middle of the summer season. Soon after the last trip of the *Massachusetts*, a heavy fog had moved in, so that, like the year before, the sound was covered by fog through the fourth of July weekend. By Tuesday, July 8, it still had not lifted. That night, as the big *Priscilla* was moving cautiously toward the open sea after leaving Newport, the black-hulled *Powhatan* of the Merchants and Miners Line, bound into Providence, appeared suddenly out of the fog and rammed into her bow, cutting through to the keel. Since the Fall River Line steamer was generally the last to leave the bay each night, there were no other steamers coming down that might have been able to render aid. The badly wounded *Priscilla* had to wait until the eastbound *Puritan* and *City of Fall River* appeared at dawn to tow her back to Newport. Only her double hull and watertight compartments kept the *Priscilla* afloat for so long. Had such an accident occurred to one of the Joy Line boats, she would have gone down in minutes.

Not to be outdone, the *Tremont*, coming up the bay on the morning of the ninth and passing by the *Puritan* and the *City of Fall River* towing the *Priscilla* to safety, managed to run aground at Warwick Point, where it was her turn to sit unassisted for several hours. This time, however, she was fortunate and floated off about noon with the rising tide.

Already seriously short of steamers, the railroad faced a severe problem when its largest steamer was unexpectedly put out of commission at the height of the summer season. The only possible replacement for the *Priscilla* was the *Plymouth* of the Providence Line, which was transferred from the Providence Line to the Fall River Line in New York the next evening. Even so, the *Plymouth* had only about 250 staterooms compared with about 340 on the *Priscilla*. Replacing the *Plymouth* was even more difficult. The most logical substitutes, the only other steamers with more than 150 staterooms, were the *Pilgrim* (240) and the *Massachusetts* (184), both of which had recently decided to wreck their machinery. The largest steamer then available was the *City of Lowell* of the Norwich Line with only 138 staterooms, which was now assigned to the Providence Line with the *Connecticut*, while the *Maine* took the *Lowell's* place on the Norwich Line, leaving Stonington, for the first time since the 1860s, with no service at all for several weeks.

Thus, for most of July 1902, the *Puritan* and the *Plymouth* ran to Fall River; the *Connecticut* and the *City of Lowell* ran to Providence for the regular line, and the *Rhode Island* and the *New Hampshire* for the New Line; the *Nashua* every other night* to Stonington with freight only; the *City of Worcester* and the *Maine* made up the Norwich Line; while the *Chester W. Chapin* ran alone to New Haven, because the *Richard Peck* had also chosen this month to develop engine troubles.

For the rest of July, the *Priscilla* joined the *Pilgrim* and the *City of Brockton* at the Fletcher works in Hoboken. The yard was given instructions to work on her night and day to get her back on the line as soon as possible.[33] The big *Priscilla* was, therefore, ready to sail again early in August. When the *Plymouth* then returned to run on the Providence Line, the *City of Lowell*, for some reason, was placed on the New Line for several trips, while the *New Hampshire* returned to restore some semblance of service to Stonington. With a steamer of the quality of the *City of Lowell* running on the New Line for a fare of fifty cents, one again wonders why anyone but an incurable steamboat antiquarian would want to pay $1.00 to go to New York on the *City of Key West*.

While running on the New Line in 1902, the *City of Lowell* was placed on the Monday, Wednesday, Friday schedule out of New York (which she shared with the *Plymouth* and the *City of Key West*), so that she could continue her Sunday trips up the Hudson. This meant that the *Rhode Island* was the New Line steamer laying over in Providence on Sundays, and, beginning July 13, the line decided to use her to revive the Sunday excursions from Providence to Cottage City, originated in 1900 by the Joy Line with the *Martinique*. The fare was still a dollar for a whole day's outing down Narragansett Bay and out to Martha's Vineyard, returning by twilight. Meals again were fifty cents extra.

---

*With the *City of Brockton* out of commission, the *Pequot* now running to New Bedford, and the *City of Lawrence* out on charter, the railroad did not even have a second freight steamer available to run with the *Nashua* to Stonington.

During early August, there were heavy rains along the Eastern Seaboard. Passenger traffic was down on all of the steamer lines, and, although the *Rhode Island* made her run to Cottage City on August 3, with so much rain and so few passengers, it had hardly been worth making the trip. The following Sunday, August 10, there was enough sun, in spite of some clouds, to encourage 625 men, women, and a great many children to spend their one free day on the decks of the *Rhode Island*. Shortly after leaving Lonsdale wharf at 10:00 A.M., the excursionists were surprised to see the *Connecticut* wallowing unattended in the bay off Crescent Park. Given the coal shortages resulting from the strike, they assumed that she had simply run out of coal coming up the bay. Actually, the *Connecticut's* engines had once again decided not to function. The steamer had stopped several times that night coming up from New York and by 11:00 A.M. on Sunday had made it only as far as Crescent Park where she had stopped again. As it was difficult to find assistance on Sundays, especially in July, the steamer's engineers had to make the best of it. Eventually, they had her underway again, and the *Connecticut* got her passengers into Providence shortly after noon.

Meanwhile, the *Rhode Island* continued down the bay and out toward Martha's Vineyard. With the poor coal they were forced to use, most of the steamers tended to run somewhat behind schedule during this summer, and the *Rhode Island* did not get to Cottage City until 3:45, rather than 3:00 as advertised. As she slowed down to approach her landing, there was a sudden jar, which knocked several passengers to the decks. The steamer lurched over to port but then righted herself again in time to make a normal landing. Apparently, Captain John S. Bibber, in making a sweep large enough for such a big steamer to approach the dock properly, had swung outside the narrow channel and run over a sand bar. After the passengers had disembarked, an inspection showed that the *Rhode Island* had sprung several planks and was taking water. When her passengers returned at 5:45 as instructed, they were told to come back again at 6:30. But by that time Captain Bibber had determined that the *Rhode Island* was not in condition to sail. So the 625 disgruntled passengers were ferried to Woods Hole and returned to Providence rather unglamorously on a New Haven railroad train, arriving there about midnight.

The *Rhode Island* made it to the protected waters of Vineyard Haven harbor that night, and, with her pumps working, managed to stay afloat until morning when temporary repairs made it safe for her to sail across to the company shops at Newport.

With the *Rhode Island* now the fifth of its steamers to be put out of commission in less than three months, the shortage of steamers on the railroad lines became critical. By the time of the grounding of the *Rhode Island*, the railroad had already decided to let the *Massachusetts* go for scrap rather than spend the money to repair her engine. The railroad had also gotten steam up again on the *C. H. Northam*, old and outdated as she was, since she was the only steamer it had available in the event of an emergency; with the *Rhode Island* now likely to be off the run for several days, that occasion had arrived. The *New Hampshire* was ordered back on the New Line to run with the *City of Lowell* after only a week on her regular run to Stonington, and the *C. H. Northam* took her place on the Stonington Line alternating with the freighter *Nashua*. When the *Rhode Island* returned to the New Line on August 24, the *New Hampshire* stayed on to run with her, and the *City of Lowell* returned to the Norwich Line. Since the *City of Worcester* now needed time off for repairs, however, the *Maine* did not go back to the Stonington Line until September.

Rather than run the risk of getting caught again without a first-class steamer on the Fall River Line through the full summer season, the railroad announced late in August that it was planning a sistership for the *Priscilla* to replace the *Puritan* which would thereafter be maintained as a spare. One of the most beautiful steamers ever to run on the sound, the thirteen-year-old *Puritan* was an ideal running mate for the *Priscilla*, as the two were similar in appearance and in accommodations. But the *Puritan* had never been an engineering success. Her oversized walking beam engine, while more dependable than the oscillating engine of the *Connecticut* and less coal-hungry than the walking beam engine of the *Pilgrim*, was nevertheless both cranky and expensive, whereas the inclined engines of the *Plymouth* and the *Priscilla* had proved both dependable and economical. So the Fall River Line had decided that the *Puritan* should be replaced.[34] Actually, however, this plan was later postponed. When, by the end of the summer, the *Connecticut*'s engines were again giving frequent trouble and the increasing cost of coal as a result of the strike made the return of the *Pilgrim* to the run unpopular, the railroad realized that its first priority should be a steamer specially designed to serve with the *Plymouth* both as a summer boat to Providence and as a winter boat on the Fall River Line. Thus, the plans George Peirce was then drawing up were modified to materialize in 1905 as the *Providence* (II), while the building of a running mate for the *Priscilla* was put off for a few more years.

During the summer of 1902, the small steamer *Chelsea*, running on a small independent line between New York and Norwich, Connecticut, had to come off for some major repairs. During this time, the line chartered the Joy Line's *Rosalie*, which was about the same size as the *Chelsea* and similar, giving rise to rumors that the ubiquitous Joy Line had started a new service to Norwich.[35]

By this time, the Joy Line had announced plans to use the *Rosalie* to carry freight from the Joy Line dock in Providence to Fall River, replacing the Dyer Line lighterage service that the railroad had successfully blocked a year earlier.[36]

In August 1902, Charles Dimon consummated one of his most successful deals in buying for the Joy Line a first-rate steamer at a bargain price. On August 20, the Joy Line announced that it had purchased the International Line's steamer *Cumberland*, which had recently sunk after an accident in Boston harbor, from the underwriters for $60,000 and that as soon as she had been repaired, she would join the *Tremont* on its Providence route as the *Larchmont*.

The *Cumberland*, like the *Tremont*, was a typical Maine coast wooden-hulled sidewheeler. Roughly the same size and vintage as the *Tremont* (built in 1885, two years later than the *Tremont*, she was 255 feet in length, or about fifteen feet shorter), she was even more strongly built, had far more graceful lines and better passenger accommodations, and was faster. Averaging about fifteen knots, she was not what would be labeled a flyer, but, unlike the *Tremont*, she could make the New York to Providence run in the twelve hours that the usual schedule called for, with even some time to spare in the event of unexpected delays. Or at least she could have done so had her own scheduled times of arrival and departure at first not been determined by the limited speed of her consort.

Built in 1885 for the International Line, the *Cumberland* was similar in most respects to her running mate, the *State of Maine* of 1882. Both had a more sweeping sheer than the *Tremont*, their guards rising sharply in either direction from the low point at the paddlebox, though this was more pronounced on the *State of Maine* than on the *Cumberland*. They had walking beam engines, of course, but unlike most of the Maine coast paddlers, such as the *Tremont* or the *Penobscot*, which were one-stackers, the *Cumberland* and the *State of Maine* had two tall stacks, placed athwartship and wide enough apart that their housing did not come through the center of the steamer but (as on the *City of Worcester*) between staterooms on either side.

As noted in an earlier chapter, on the International Line the *Cumberland* and the *State of Maine* had covered the route from Boston to St. John, New Brunswick, stopping at Portland, Eastport, and Lubec along the way, while a third steamer, the *St. Croix*, made the run from Boston to St. John without stopping. With the phenomenal increase in the popularity of the Maine coast as a summer resort area, by 1900 these three steamers were becoming woefully inadequate for the service. When Morse's new Eastern Steamship Company absorbed the International Line in 1901, therefore, this company decided to replace the older wooden-hulled vessels as soon as feasible with much larger steel-hulled steamers similar to the

Portland Line's new *Governor Dingley*. By 1902, the first of the new steamers, the *Calvin Austin*, was already being built and was expected to come on the line in the spring of 1903, at which time the *St. Croix* was to be retired.

But things were not to work out quite that way. On the morning of Monday, July 7, 1902, the *Cumberland* left her Boston pier at 8:00 A.M. on her regular run to Portland, Eastport, Lubec, and St. John with three hundred passengers aboard, an unusually heavy passenger list, though many were taking only the day trip to Portland. As the *Cumberland* pulled out of her pier into the crowded Boston harbor, Captain Allen could see nothing in any direction but the persistent white mist, for the harbor was shrouded in fog that July morning, the same fog that was to be responsible for the *Priscilla-Powhatan* crash the following evening. Since the *Cumberland* operated on a fairly tight schedule, however, Captain Allen, who knew the harbor intimately, apparently pushed the steamer through the fog at nearly normal speed, blowing his whistle at very short intervals and listening carefully for echoes. Under his guidance the *Cumberland* navigated the harbor safely, as she had often done before, and by 9:00 A.M. she was winding her way deftly among the islands that guard the entrance to Boston harbor. She was just passing Deer Island when Captain Allen heard a loud whistle to starboard that seemed to be just outside the pilot house window. Then, with no further warning, the towering prow of the new United Fruit liner, *Admiral Farragut*, inbound, came crashing into the starboard bow of the *Cumberland*, lifting the wooden sidewheeler practically out of the water. As the *Admiral Farragut* pulled out and stood by to offer assistance, and the *Cumberland* again rolled back on a fairly even keel, Captain Allen decided to take what in retrospect might be considered a culpably dangerous risk. When in the course of the muted megaphone calls that succeeded the crash, the *Admiral Farragut* and other smaller craft in the vicinity offered to take the *Cumberland*'s passengers, Captain Allen refused any assistance but instead immediately turned his sinking steamer about and headed back to Boston through the fog at a fairly high speed. The *Cumberland* was taking water but slowly. Apparently, Captain Allen reasoned that if he waited there in the outer harbor to discharge passengers, his steamer would undoubtedly go down in the deep water and become a total loss, whereas if he could make it back into Boston, he could beach the steamer and save her.

Miraculously, the *Cumberland* made it all the way back to Commercial wharf, though by that time she was taking water rapidly and was down at the bow above the guards. By the time the last passenger had safely disembarked, tugs were waiting to tow the sinking steamer to McKie's yards in East Boston. But before they reached the yard, it became apparent, with the *Cumberland*'s whole bow now dipping under the water, that they would not make it, so the tugs nosed the steamer onto the mud flats in East Boston where she rested safely.

Meanwhile, the *Cumberland*'s Portland passengers were sent on by train, but most of the through passengers simply boarded the *St. Croix* which was scheduled to sail at noon the same day for St. John.

One year earlier, the International Line would not have had a spare steamer to run in the *Cumberland*'s place. But now that the line was part of Morse's Eastern Steamship Line, steamers from any of the Maine coast routes were available. Therefore, by the time of the *Cumberland*'s next scheduled sailing, the *Penobscot* of the Boston-Bangor Line had been secured to take her place. After her charter to the Joy Line the year before, the *Penobscot* had been assigned to the Kennebec Line with the steamer *Kennebec*, replacing the older *Sagadahoc*. Meanwhile, the *Sagadahoc*, which was faster, was frequently used to supplement the *City of Bangor* and the *City of Rockland* on the Bangor Line during the busy summer season. When the *Penobscot* was taken for the International Line, where she was to run until the *Governor Cobb* came on the line late in 1906, the *Sagadahoc* came back to the Kennebec Line, but only for a short time, as the new *Ransom B. Fuller* was then nearly finished and was soon ready to replace her.

Within a few days the *Cumberland* was raised and patched and towed at last to McKie's shipyard where she had originally been headed. The estimate for repairs was set at between $65,000 and $70,000.[37] With the new *Calvin Austin* ready to go on the line the following season and the *Penobscot* proving a suitable substitute, Eastern decided that it was wisest simply to retire the *Cumberland* (rather than the *St. Croix*) and turn her over to the insurance company. This decision was reached on August 13. Charlie Dimon must have moved fast, for the *Cumberland* was sold "as is" to the Joy Line exactly one week later,[38] though Dimon had made preliminary arrangements with the insurance company several days before that.[39] Captain A. B. Coleman, first officer of the *Old Dominion*, took a crew over to McKie's that day (August 20) and brought the patched up *Cumberland* under her own steam down to Morse's shipyards in Brooklyn for repairs.

This time the Joy Line had made a wise choice. The *Cumberland*, now renamed the *Larchmont* (for a town in Westchester County, New York, which was located on Long Island Sound) to match the *Tremont*, was by far the best ship operated on the Providence route that was actually owned by the Joy Line. Designed for use on the rough coast of Maine, she was a superb sea boat. Her walking beam engine had been thoroughly overhauled and many parts replaced by Eastern only a few months before her accident.[40]

Once the hole in her bow had been patched, which was merely a matter of carpentry and a job at which Morse's shipyards must by now have been becoming quite adept, the *Larchmont* was a fine steamer in excellent shape.

Morse's had the new steamer ready in ten days, and she was delivered to the Joy Line pier in New York on August 30, 1902. It was a Saturday night at the end of the season, and bookings were heavy. The *Tremont* was already scheduled to make the run from New York that night, but, since the *Larchmont* was there and ready, the Joy Line ran both steamers to Providence, the *Tremont* leaving on schedule at 5:00 P.M. and the *Larchmont* with the overflow at 8:30. (As a result, there were no less than five steamboats berthed in Providence on Sunday, August 31, 1902. In addition to the *Larchmont* and the *Tremont* of the Joy Line, the *Connecticut* of the Providence Line and the *Rhode Island* of the New Line also arrived that morning. Since the Providence Line steamers lay over in Providence on Saturday nights, the *Plymouth* was also at Fox Point wharf that Sunday.) The *Larchmont* managed to make her maiden voyage in good Joy Line tradition; her engines, though recently rebuilt, broke down en route, and the *Larchmont* had to heave to for over an hour before her engineers had them turning again.

With two fairly evenly matched steamers now on the run, the Joy Line announced that it would thenceforward schedule sailings between Providence and New York every night of the week, Sundays included. The *Larchmont* inaugurated the new Sunday sailings by taking the run out of Providence the night she arrived, Sunday, August 31. The *City of Key West* also sailed from New York that night and then had a double sailing with the *Tremont* from Providence on Monday. Afterwards, the *City of Key West* sailed over to Morse's yard in Brooklyn where she was maintained as a spare passenger steamer, a luxury (if the *City of Key West* in any capacity could be called a luxury) the Joy Line had not until then been able to enjoy.

Although Captain Wilcox, in every sense the senior captain of the line, eventually transferred to the *Larchmont*, while Captain Wise of the *City of Key West* was given command of the *Tremont*, Captain Coleman stayed with the *Larchmont* for her first several trips.

The Joy Line had enjoyed owning a new steamer for less than a week before it nearly lost her. Only fast and efficient action on the part of Captain Coleman and his crew prevented a serious disaster. On Wednesday, September 3, the *Larchmont* left her New York pier at 5:00 P.M. on her third trip to Providence. At 5:45 she had just passed through Hell Gate and was paddling past North Brother's Island when a fire broke out in a pile of mattresses being stored in the men's free berth cabin located in the hold at the very aft end of the steamer. Captain Coleman immediately ordered the steamer stopped, then rushed down to the scene of the fire where he personally assisted the crew in manning the hoses. The fire generated a great deal of smoke, which, needless to say, alarmed the passengers, but, as the crew seemed to have the matter under control, there was no panic. After about half an hour, the fire had been extinguished, and the *Larchmont* was again underway. Although three of the crew passed out from smoke inhalation, no one was seriously injured, and while the mattresses, which should not have been there in the first place, were in pretty bad shape, the steamer itself was undamaged.

Just two years later, in about the same location, a fire on the *General Slocum* was to take over a thousands lives. The *Larchmont* was saved from a similar fate by Captain Coleman's judgment in stopping the steamer and by the fact that her hoses, unlike the *General Slocum*'s, had been kept in good working order.

On October 1, just a month after the arrival of the *Larchmont* on the Joy Line, the *Chester W. Chapin*, no longer needed on the New Haven Line now that the busy summer season was over, came on the New Line to run with the *Rhode Island*, replacing the *City of Lowell*, which returned to the New London run. But the *Chester W. Chapin* was not to run to Providence for long. On October 11, the railroad made the totally unexpected announcement that the New Line would be discontinued the following day. In an ultimately unsuccessful attempt to keep the public from suspecting a deal between the New Haven and the Joy Line, the railroad accompanied the announcement with a statement that the New Line had been forced to suspend operations as a result of the coal shortage.[41]

What had happened was that both the railroad's marine division and the Joy Line had been suffering badly that summer and had decided to come to an agreement whereby the Joy Line could continue to run its lines to Providence and to Boston but only under terms dictated by the railroad, while the New Haven on its part would discontinue the New Line.

Apparently, the Joy Line management had come to the realization during the summer of 1902 that it was no longer possible to keep the line in operation. Business was excellent, and the steamers were sailing regularly both to Providence and to Boston nearly fully booked. But the line was still losing money. The competition from the New Line had not taken business away from the Joy Line, but it had forced the Joy Line people to set their fares so low that they could not run their steamers at a profit. Moreover, the maintenance of their outdated steamers entailed frequent unexpected expenses that were draining the company's already strained resources, while the coal strikes of that summer were driving the operating costs of the steamers higher by the day.

Meanwhile, as we have seen, the railroad lines were also in trouble that summer. In order to run the New Line, the New Haven had kept older steamers such as the *Rhode Island* and the *Massachusetts* in commission, which, like the Joy Line steamers, were subject to frequent and expensive breakdowns. With so many steamers unexpectedly out of commission in the summer of 1902 and the necessity of discontinuing passenger service to Stonington in order to keep the New Line in operation, the railroad had begun to realize that maintaining the New Line no longer made much sense financially.

In addition, the operation of the New Line had not only been expensive for the railroad, but had also taken more business away from its own Providence Line than from the Joy Line. Merely by helping to advertise the concept of cheap steamboat travel, the existence of the New Line had probably done the Joy Line as much good as harm. The Joy Line boats, in comparison with those of the Providence Line or the New Line, were small. The number of passengers or the amount of freight the Joy Line could take from the railroad's lines was limited. But literally hundreds of passengers were traveling to New York every night on the New Line steamers. More significantly, the New Line steamers, even those with relatively small passenger accommodations such as the *New Hampshire* or the *City of Lowell*, carried an enormous amount of freight at cut rates, several times the amount any Joy Line steamer could have carried. Thus, the railroad's own New Line was taking far more business from the Providence Line than the smaller Joy Line steamers could possibly have done. In short, in order to compete with the Joy Line, the railroad was operating two large and expensive steamers in each direction every night and making far less profit for doing so than if it had operated only one. Clearly, a different policy was called for.

In the discussions leading up to the decision to discontinue the New Line, the railroad's management had concluded that the original purpose of the line, to force the Joy Line out of business, was now no longer desirable. The popularity of both the Joy Line and the railroad's own New Line had made it clear to the New Haven that the people of southern New England were prepared to patronize a low-fare line to New York, and, if both the New Line and the Joy Line were unceremoniously discontinued, they reasoned, another successful line would soon appear. Such a line might well have sufficient capital behind it to operate much larger and more modern steamers, as Chester Chapin's Bay Line had done, for instance, at rates lower than the railroad's and thus provide far more formidable competition for the Providence Line than the Joy Line did. If, on the other hand, the New Haven were to allow the relatively innocuous Joy Line to continue operating, with certain restrictions, it would thus not only discourage other potential competitors from entering the field but also please the people of Providence by allowing them to believe that competition still existed.[42]

Cautious feelers first initiated by the Joy Line were thus received with unexpected warmth. One day in late June, Frank Dunbaugh and Allan Joy wandered across town to the offices of the New Haven's marine division at Pier 18, North River, where they had arranged an interview with J. M. Hall, the president of the railroad. When the cousins rather hesitatingly suggested that the Joy Line and the railroad try to work out some mutually satisfactory arrangements dividing the passenger and freight business to Providence between them in some equitable fashion, Judge Hall, instead of responding with the scorn and mockery his earlier statements might have led them to expect, seemed actually to welcome the suggestion, and assured them he would give it careful consideration.[43]

Hall then passed the idea on to Percy Todd, the New Haven's vice-president actually concerned with marine matters, who was less enthusiastic and inclined to let the matter ride without taking any positive action. A few weeks later, however, Todd received a note from John Rowland, the traffic manager of the Joy Line, asking for an appointment. When Rowland subsequently appeared in his office, Todd was surprised to discover that he was a young man he had known well and liked very much when both had been working in Cincinnati a few years before. Thus, from this point, talks progressed more rapidly and on a fairly friendly basis.[44]

By the time of Rowland's next interview with Todd on Wednesday, August 6, the railroad had been informed of the Joy Line's application for wharfage in Fall River and had therefore begun to see some urgency in getting negotiations underway. When Rowland turned up in his office that morning, Todd took him completely by surprise by announcing that the railroad was willing to discontinue the New Line and to allow the Joy Line to operate with lower passenger and freight rates, mutually determined, than the Providence Line, without further harassment or interference. In return, the Joy Line had to agree not to solicit passenger or freight business for its Providence route anywhere outside the city of Providence itself and its immediate environs. More specifically, the Joy Line would have to agree to stop carrying through passengers between New York and Boston via its Providence boats or between New York and any other city serviced by the New Haven except Providence; to give up any freight business outside the city of Providence; and to abandon any plan to run steamers to Fall River, Newport, or any other port except Providence or Boston. Were the Joy Line to agree to these conditions, Todd assured Rowland, the New Haven would recognized that "there would in all probability always be a competitive line from Providence to New York and that we would rather have the Joy Line fill that space, they having had several years experience in the business, than to have a new line attempt it."[45]

Rowland, somewhat nonplussed, confessed his inability to negotiate on this level and returned the next day with Frank Dunbaugh. Todd found he did not like Dunbaugh very much, and the discussions that day proceeded somewhat coolly. He also noticed that Dunbaugh "did not seem to understand traffic matters at all and apparently leaned on Mr. Rowland's opinion." Nevertheless, by the end of the interview, Dunbaugh and Todd had agreed in principle to continue negotiations along the lines suggested by the New Haven. Dunbaugh asked, however, that some preliminary arrangements be concluded within a week, before the Fall River City Council's committee on wharves met to decide whether to accept the Joy Line's bid for dockage there.[46]

In what must be regarded as either a classic of understatement or an example of Percy Todd's poker-faced business manner, Todd later remarked that "Dunbaugh seemed to be very much impressed with the possibility of our withdrawing our New Line. . . ." One would think he would be![47]

Todd apparently found the matter important enough to send a wire to President Hall, who was then vacationing in the Adirondacks, immediately following the conference. Hall wired back, "Go ahead." In a subsequent letter to Hall, Todd emphasized that "it is to our interest from every standpoint to make some such agreement, and I do not hesitate to recommend it."[48]

In his response, Hall indicated that he had given the matter a great deal of thought, even on his vacation, and he urged Todd to complete the negotiations with all possible dispatch. The present situation, he admitted, "is costing us too much money to continue if we can avoid it. . . . Anything, however, that will let us out of the present situation with honor I think will put us in a better situation for the future." Realizing, of course, the importance to the public relations of both companies of preserving the fiction of the Joy Line's complete independence from the railroad, Hall reminded Todd "to keep the whole matter of any arrangement a secret from the public if possible." He added, however, that Henry Dimock of the Metropolitan Line should be informed.[49]

Todd was in a good position to comply with this last request, for that weekend he took a trip up to Mount Washington in New Hampshire in company with his friend, Robert Haskins, the Metropolitan's traffic manager. 'Haskins was empowered to make decisions for the line, since Dimock was vacationing in Bar Harbor through the month of August. In the course of the journey, Todd told Haskins about the proposed agreements between the New Haven and the Joy Line, and asked him whether the Metropolitan Line would care to become a party to them. As Todd had pretty much predicted, Haskins categorically refused, making it very clear that "the Metropolitan Line would enter into no agreement with the Joy Line, would answer no communications from them, . . . would not meet them," but would "fight them until the Metropolitan Line or the Joy Line was killed."[50]

The following Monday, August 11, Todd was back at his office in New York, where he met again with his old acquaintance, John Rowland, to work out the details of the proposed agreement in regard to passengers.[51] Then the following Thursday, August 14, Rowland met at length with

J. M. Williams, the New Haven's freight traffic manager, to work out a double schedule for freight rates. This meeting, according to Williams, went very smoothly:

> I want to say right here that I think Mr. Rowland has been very fair in his way of meeting differentials, and I have tried to be equally fair on our part. He has conceded some things to me which I presume he feels he ought to have a little more on, and I know I have granted some differentials to him which I think are liberal and will give him the business.[52]

Since the Metropolitan Line did not choose to participate, the Joy Line's Boston service was not affected by the agreements, except for the stipulation that it not carry passengers or freight bound for destinations beyond the city of Boston. The many and complicated arrangements regarding passenger fares and freight rates applied only to the Joy Line's Providence route. In regard to passenger fares, the agreement stated that the railroad's Providence Line one-way fare would remain at $3.00 and that the Joy Line would be required to raise its fare to $2.00 during the summer months when the Providence Line was in operation, but could reduce it to $1.50 during the winter months. This "requirement," of course, seemed to Dunbaugh, Dimon, and Joy much as a "requirement" to eat a hearty meal would to a starving man. With rates so close to those on the more luxurious Providence Line steamers, the Joy Line's passenger business fell off considerably—by about one-third in 1903—but with its rates doubled the line was still able to make a better profit.

The specification that the Joy Line not accept freight for points beyond Providence also did not create much of a hardship in the long run. Since the Providence Line was owned by the railroad and the tracks ran right onto the line's Fox Point wharf, while the railroad had steadfastly refused to carry any freight arriving in Providence on Joy Line steamers, most of the through freight had been carried by the Providence Line or the New Line anyway, with the Joy Line pretty much limited by circumstances to local shippers. Such revenues as the Joy Line lost by these restrictions were more than made up by its being able to charge higher rates according to the new schedules, which were still enough lower than the Providence Line's to assure continued local patronage, and by its being relieved of the necessity of granting rebates and special reductions to lure customers away from the New Line.

In the course of further discussions, the New Haven also required the Joy Line to give up its newly instituted Sunday sailings, which would compete with those of the Fall River Line and the Providence Line, hitherto the only lines sailing out of New England on Sunday nights, and to abandon plans for a line to Philadelphia. Since, under the new agreement, there was now no need to prevent the Joy Line from sending southbound freight from Providence via the Pennsylvania, a separate line to Philadelphia, for which the line did not have the capital in any event, was no longer necessary.

With the negotiations between the New Haven and the Joy Line progressing rapidly through the month of August 1902,[53] it is somewhat easier to understand why the Joy Line, which in June had elected to operate the *City of Key West* through the summer rather than risk spending money to keep the much larger *Virginia* in operation, now in August found the financial confidence to invest $60,000 to purchase the *Larchmont*.

The arduous task of working out a complicated dual schedule of freight rates, left to John Rowland for the Joy Line and J. M. Williams, the railroad's freight agent, lasted through most of September. To the credit of these two competent men, it was finally completed in a spirit of friendliness and mutual cooperation. The agreements were signed on October 3 and were to go into effect on October 12 for a trial period of one year, at which time they would be subject to annual revision and renewal. Since the Providence and Stonington Steamship Company, although totally owned and managed by the railroad, was still in October 1902 a separate legal entity, it had to be a party to the agreements. Mr. Edward Buckland, therefore, as the president and only member of the board of directors, read, debated, and duly approved the rate agreement with the Joy Line.[54]

A question that has often arisen is whether the Joy Line, in signing this agreement, did not in practice, if not in fact, become just another subsidiary of the New Haven Railroad. The question is quite valid but has no specific answer. Certainly after October 1902, the Joy Line could no longer be considered a truly independent operation. In the course of an Interstate Commerce Commission investigation many years later, one high railroad official admitted that after 1902 one could have said that the Joy Line had come under railroad "control."[55] On the other hand, as long as the Joy Line held to certain specific terms dictated by the railroad, terms that were by no means unpalatable to the line, it was allowed to continue under its own management without any interference from the New Haven. In any event, it survived.

During the course of an investigation in 1916 into the New Haven's management of its marine properties, railroad representatives produced figures showing that the New Haven had been forced to close down the New Line with its cheaper rates because the operation was costing the company money.[56] But a closer look at these same figures seems to show quite the opposite: that in spite of the fifty-cent fare, the New Line made a great deal of money for the railroad in its two years of operation. What the astute railroad statistician managed to do was to take the increase in business on all of the railroad's other sound lines and parallel rail lines over the succeeding two years, arbitrarily call this figure the equivalent of the amount of business that the New Line was taking *away* from the company's other operations—an incredible lapse of logic—and subtract this figure from the profits of the New Line, coming up therefore with a figure well in the red.

Of course, these figures fail to take into account any number of factors that are difficult to measure: the wear and tear on the steamers, the general increase in travel in the years 1902-1904, which was considerable, and, most important, the number of people who would not have traveled at all between New York and Providence had the fare been more than fifty cents. What the figures really show is that the Providence Line was losing money, while the New Line was running at a profit. The message that the railroad refused to read was that it might well have made more money continuing its cheap line and discontinuing the Providence Line.

In this report, the railroad economists produced figures showing the number of passengers carried on each of the three lines running to Providence in one particular month, which was intended as a typical sample. Since that time, many studies have used these figures to show the relative number of passengers carried by the Providence Line, the New Line, and the Joy Line. But, unfortunately, the month the railroad chose for its sampling was July 1902, the one month when all three lines were running steamers with significantly smaller passenger-carrying capacities than the steamers which normally ran on these lines. In July 1902, the *City of Lowell* with 138 staterooms had replaced the *Plymouth*, which had twice that many; the *New Hampshire* with 110 staterooms was running on the New Line for the *Massachusetts* which had 184; and the *City of Key West* on the Joy Line had about 70 staterooms compared with over 100 on the *Virginia*. Considering the number of passengers that must have been turned away with these smaller steamers operating in midsummer, and the number that must have moved from one line to another as space allowed, any passenger figures for July 1902 cannot have much validity.

News of the agreement between the New Haven and the Joy Line leaked to the press and set off a wave of legitimate anger and resentment from the people of Providence.[57] They were particularly disillusioned with the Joy Line for "selling out" to the railroad after the city had given it so much patronage and support. They were even more angry with the railroad for dropping the New Line, which for two years had made it possible for a great many people who would never have been able to pay Providence Line prices to enjoy the pleasure of traveling by steamer to New York.

In the wake of these complaints, the railroad, partly to placate the people of Providence but also in anticipation of increased traffic on the regular line now that the New Line was gone, decided that the time had come for improving the service on the Providence Line. The Fall River steamer *Plymouth*, with her efficient inclined engine and her extraordinary capacity for both passengers and freight, was ideal for the summer service to Providence. But neither the *Pilgrim* nor the *Connecticut*, the two steamers that had been running with her in recent years, was proving satisfactory. Both were mechanically undependable and expensive to operate, and the *Connecticut* was now also going to be too small to carry the increased traffic, especially in freight, now that the New Line was no longer operating. It was at this time, therefore, that the company decided not to build a running mate for the *Priscilla* as announced a few months earlier. Instead, it decided to build a new steamer similar to the *Plymouth*, which would be specifically designed to run on the Providence Line in the summer and to Fall River in the winter, and to let the beautiful *Puritan* run on the Fall River Line a few years longer.

George Peirce, the company's marine architect, who was then working on designs for the new steamer, modified his plans and produced a steamer similar to the *Plymouth* in many ways but thirty feet longer and with two tall stacks placed far forward like those on the *Priscilla* and the *Puritan* (though above the Dome Deck, as on the *Plymouth*, rather than forward of it). In an effort to win back the affection of the city she was designed to serve, the new steamer was to be named *Providence*. In December 1902, just a few days after the plans for the steamer had been completed and the contract awarded to the Fore River Iron Works in Quincy, Massachusetts, Peirce, the designer of all of the Fall River Line steamers then in operation, the three freight steamers, as well as the *Pilgrim*, the *Puritan*, the *Plymouth*, and the *Priscilla*, died at his home in Newport.

Satisfactory as the new arrangements may have been for the New Haven and for the Joy Line, the immediate result was several days of chaos on the Providence waterfront. The agreement called for the New Line, then operating the *Chester W. Chapin* and the *Rhode Island*, to cease operations abruptly on October 12, which by sheer coincidence was the very day that the Providence Line was to end its service for the season. This left the Joy Line in the happy position of operating the only passenger steamers between Providence and New York for the winter season and of being able to charge each passenger an astronomical $1.50 for the trip. It also left a great deal of New Line freight, which the railroad was committed to carrying at the old low rate until its contracts expired, piled up on the docks in Providence and New York. With the *City of Brockton* still out of service, however, and the *City of Fall River* still running to Fall River in her place (with the *City of Taunton*), now that the railroad was again obliged to run freight steamers to Providence through the winter, it found that it did not have enough to go around. As soon as the New Line was discontinued, the *Nashua*, which was now available, returned to the Providence route. But even with help from her former running mate, the *Pequot*, borrowed occasionally from the

New Bedford Line, the *Nashua* could not handle the fall freight rush. So, late in October, the big *Connecticut* made several trips to Providence carrying freight as did the *Richard Peck*, once she was relieved on the New Haven Line by the *Chester W. Chapin*. Occasionally, excess Providence freight had to be placed aboard the Fall River Line freighters, which would make an extra trip up to Providence after unloading at Fall River.

The situation was further aggravated when the *City of Fall River* was struck by a coal schooner in the fog while passing Stratford Shoals in the early morning of November 15. Towed into New York by the *Richard Peck* then inbound from New Haven, she joined the *Pilgrim* and the *City of Brockton* at Fletcher's.

By the end of November, freight traffic was beginning to resume a fairly stable pattern. By this time, both freighters had been repaired. The *City of Brockton* was again running to Fall River with the *City of Taunton*, and for the rest of the winter the *Nashua* and the *City of Fall River* ran freight to Providence as they had in the days before there was a New Line; the *Pequot* returned to the New Bedford route; and the *Connecticut*, resuming her dignity as a passenger steamer, went to lay up for the winter in Stonington.

As soon as the New Line was discontinued, the *Rhode Island* went on the New London line with the *City of Lowell*, so that the *City of Worcester* could be taken off for the winter to have new boilers installed. The *Chester W. Chapin* went back to the New Haven Line. With the *Richard Peck* thus available during the winter of 1902-1903 as the general relief boat, both the *Maine* and the *New Hampshire* could now return to reestablish daily passenger and freight service on the Stonington Line.

In the same week that the New Haven and the Joy Line had signed their agreement, President Roosevelt decided that the coal shortage had become a national emergency and that it was necessary for the government to intervene. On October 16, he appointed a commissioner to mediate the strike, and by October 21, the miners were back at work. Had Roosevelt not taken action, it is doubtful that the sound steamers could have continued operating much longer. After a few weeks, coal was again available. But in March 1903 the commission appointed by the president awarded the coal miners a much-deserved and overdue wage increase of 10 percent. The consequent rise in the price of coal was but one of many increases in this era in the general cost of operating steamships.

After the agreements of October 1902, the Joy Line lost some of its independence, but it also finally moved away from its apparently perman-ent position on a financial precipice. From this time it became a moderately profitable and even reasonably respectable business. It was also relieved from the necessity of operating steamers that were patently unsuited to the service. The *Old Dominion*, old and lumbering as she was, continued her runs between New York and Boston around the cape, still steady and dependable in all kinds of weather. After her month at Rye on the rocks, she rarely gave the line any trouble. And she always carried a good load of freight. The *Seaboard*, neither quite so commodious nor so dependable, nevertheless continued to augment the *Old Dominion* on the Boston run. On the Providence route, the Joy Line at last had two passenger liners that it actually owned. The *Larchmont* and the *Tremont*, sailing six nights a week from Providence and New York, gave the Joy Line a new appearance of dependability and dignity. To be sure, the *Tremont* had still not been persuaded to run any faster, so that the Joy Line's scheduled departures were still embarrassingly early. But even the *Tremont* was a comfortable and respectable steamer. With the *City of Key West* and the *Rosalie*, such as they were, both also owned outright, the Joy Line now had two spare steamers, one passenger steamer and one freighter, as well. The *City of Key West* had very limited accommodations, but at least, when the *Larchmont* or the *Tremont* was taken off the run for repairs or for an overhaul, the Joy Line could offer a passenger steamer of sorts rather than the *Seaboard* in its place. As business continued to pick up, even the little *Rosalie* was not often idle, for she was used frequently to carry extra freight for either Providence or Boston.

As the year 1902 ended, therefore, the Joy Line was for the first time a viable operation.

17a. Courtesy of the Steamship Historical Society Collection, University of Baltimore Library

17b. Courtesy of the Steamship Historical Society Collection, University of Baltimore Library

17. In 1899 the New Haven Line began running their fast and modern steamers (a) *Richard Peck* and (b) *Chester W. Chapin* between New York and Providence, with a stop at New Haven in each direction.

18. The small Maine coast steamer *Lincoln* (pictured here) was chartered by the Narragansett Bay Line to run with the *Richard Peck* while the *C. H. Northam* was being repaired.

19. Courtesy of the Peabody Museum, Salem, Mass.

19. The *Allan Joy*, the Joy Line's second steamer, inaugurated the line's new freight service between New York and Boston. This photo shows the *Allan Joy* in later years after the Bridgeport Line, which purchased her, had added a row of staterooms on the Saloon Deck.

20. Courtesy of the Steamship Historical Society Collection, University of Baltimore Library

20. The Joy Line steamer *Old Dominion* (pictured here), which replaced the *Allan Joy* on the line's New York to Boston route, formerly ran from New York to Norfolk and Richmond, Virginia, for the Old Dominion Line.

21. Courtesy of William B. Taylor

21. Deck view of the steamer *Old Dominion*.

22. Courtesy of Mrs. William Gatewood

22. The freighter *Seaboard* (pictured here), formerly of the Old Bay Line on Chesapeake Bay, replaced the *Rosalie* on the Joy Line's Providence route in the spring of 1900.

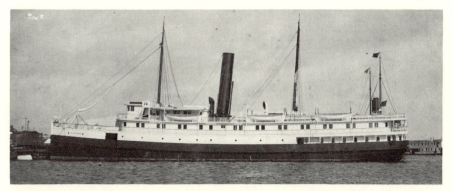

23. The *Martinique* (pictured here), formerly the *Lincoln* of the Boston-Kennebec River Line, chartered for the summer of 1900 from the Florida East Coast Railway, was the Joy Line's first passenger steamer.

24. A busy scene at the Joy Line's New York pier in the summer of 1900. In the background the *Old Dominion* (pictured here) takes on freight for Boston; in the foreground Providence freight is being loaded aboard the *Martinique*.

25. During the summer of 1900, when the Joy Line steamer *Martinique* developed engine trouble, the Hudson River steamer *Newburgh* (pictured here) made two round trips to Providence in her place.

26. When the *Martinique* returned to her Florida run, the Joy Line chartered the sidewheeler *Shinnecock* (pictured here) from the Montauk Line to run to Providence during the winter of 1900-1901.

27. The first passenger steamer owned outright by the Joy Line was the former Boston to Portland steamer *Tremont*, purchased by the Joy Line for its New York to Providence route in the spring of 1901.

28. The Steamer *Tremont* at the Joy Line wharf in Providence.

29. The Joy Line began six-day-a-week passenger service to Providence by chartering the Boston to Bangor steamer *Penobscot* (pictured here) to run with the *Tremont* in the summer of 1901.

30. The *Penobscot* at the Joy Line wharf in Providence, summer 1901.

31. The yacht *Wild Duck* (pictured here) after collision with the Joy Line steamer *Tremont*, July 1901.

32. The *Old Dominion* on the rocks at Rye, New York, July 1901.

33. The small freighter *Cocoa* (pictured here) ran to Boston for the Joy Line through the summer of 1901 while the *Old Dominion* was being repaired.

34. The steamer *Seaboard* after several staterooms had been added aft of the pilot house, thus allowing her to qualify as a passenger steamer of sorts.

35. Courtesy of the Steamship Historical Society Collection, University of Baltimore Library

35. The Joy Line's efforts to purchase the handsome *Manhattan* from the Portland Line in the fall of 1901 were blocked by the officers of the Metropolitan Line.

36. Courtesy of the Peale Museum, Baltimore, Md.

36. The beautifully proportioned *Virginia* (pictured here), formerly of the Old Bay Line, was chartered by the Joy Line through the winter of 1901-1902 to run to Providence with the *Tremont*.

37. Courtesy of the Mariners' Museum of Newport News, Va.

37. This touched-up photograph shows the *Virginia* as she appeared when running on the St. Lawrence River.

38. Courtesy of the Mariners' Museum of Newport News, Va.

38. Caught short of suitable steamers, the Joy Line had to run the small and aging *City of Key West* on its Providence route through much of the summer of 1902. On the Joy Line, the forward freight deck was enclosed.

39. Courtesy of the Mariners' Museum of Newport News, Va.

39. During the summer of 1902 the Joy Line was fortunate in being able to purchase the steamer *Cumberland* (pictured here) from the International Line (Boston to St. John, New Brunswick). Renamed the *Larchmont*, this steamer joined the *Tremont* late in August of that year on the Joy Line's New York to Providence route.

40. During the years 1903 and 1904, the *Longfellow*, a former Boston to Providence boat, carried freight between New York and Providence for the Clyde Line.

41. The steamer *Aransas* (pictured here), which had previously served the Morgan Line on various routes in the Gulf of Mexico, was purchased by the Joy Line early in 1904 to join the *Old Dominion* on the line's New York to Boston run.

42. On February 8, 1904, the Joy Line steamer *Tremont* burned and sank at the pier in New York.

43a. *Courtesy of the Steamship Historical Society Collection, University of Baltimore Library*

43b. *Courtesy of Frank E. Claes*

43. Soon after the *Tremont* burned the Joy Line was able to purchase the *State of Maine* (pictured here), the former running mate of its steamer *Larchmont* on the Maine coast. Renamed *Edgemont* by the Joy Line, this steamer was similar to the *Larchmont* but not an exact sistership.

44. Between 1904 and 1907 the (a) *Edgemont* and the (b) *Larchmont* ran between New York and Providence for the Joy Line.

45. Stern view of the *Old Dominion* leaving the East River pier.

46. Backed-up freight in front of the Joy Line's East River pier in New York.

47. Freight being delivered to the Joy Line dock in Providence.

48. In the summer of 1904, the *Pilgrim* (pictured here) was back on the Providence Line with the *Plymouth*, replacing the smaller *Connecticut*.

49. The new steamer *Providence* (pictured here), the largest steamer ever to run regularly to Providence, came out in time to replace the *Pilgrim* on the Providence Line for the season of 1905.

1903

The years 1903 and 1904 mark the highpoint of the history of the Joy Line.
Relieved from the harassment of the powerful New Haven Railroad and
from the nearly overwhelming competition of the New Line, the Joy Line
was now no longer a struggling enterprise whose daily decisions were
directed toward survival rather than service. The agreement with the New
Haven severely limited the Joy Line's sphere of activity, but this very
limitation liberated the line in many ways. For example, it freed the line
from the necessity of sending its agents to all parts of New England to
solicit business at rates that yielded merely marginal profits, or of stretching
its already overextended credit still further by creating its own circuitous
routes to points south of New York. The agreement restricted the Joy Line
to carrying passengers and freight between Providence and New York or
between Boston and New York, and as a result the company could now
concentrate its limited resources and limited personnel on doing this job
more efficiently.

With the higher rates and restricted market imposed by the agreement,
the Joy Line's passenger and freight business was down by about one-third
in 1903; but with rates on both nearly doubled and many extraneous
expenses nullified, revenues were up by more than one-third. Operating at
last on a sound financial footing, the Joy Line could now offer the kind of
service it had intended from the start—a first-rate second-class steamboat line.
Compared with the "mammoth palace steamers" of the Fall River Line, the
Joy Line steamers were not very large; they were certainly not very fast,
and their accommodations were modest at best. But they were clean, they
were comfortable, and they were attractively maintained. And while the

service made no pretense to the elegance for which the Fall River and Providence lines were famous, it was always both courteous and friendly.

The main reason for the Joy Line's success, however, in the short period of its relative independence was that it catered to a new class of passenger which the railroad lines had largely overlooked. Steamboat travel on Long Island Sound had matured during the nineteenth century and had therefore geared its services to the needs of that era. In the nineteenth century, travel had been limited pretty much to people of some means. The steamers of the railroad's lines, particularly the Fall River and the Providence lines, like many of the large, sprawling resort hotels of the era, had been designed to provide this class with the kind of accommodations and services they had come to expect.

The world of the well-to-do in the late nineteenth century produced a degree of richness and elegance of style, typified in the steamers of the Fall River and Providence lines, which is sorely missed in the modern world of neon and plastic. But those who enjoy paging through the abundant books of photographic nostalgia recording this era and who lament its passing should remember that the elegance there depicted, and the elegance of the sound steamers as well, was maintained by a vast army of human beings, the crews of the steamers, captains, mates, deckhands and stewards, as well as carpenters, stevedores, ticket-sellers, and dockhands on shore, all of whom were quite literally overworked and underpaid. One must add, too, workers in shipyards, coalminers, steelworkers, and joiners, without whom the steamers could not have been built or maintained, none of whom could ever have afforded to travel on one of the "palace steamers" themselves.

As the twentieth century began, America was changing. Some of the best and admittedly some of the worst that America has since produced have resulted from our ability to extend the privileges and pleasures once reserved for the leisure classes to the majority. In the process, a great deal has been lost, and America's overnight steamer lines have been among the casualties. At first, the changes were slow, although the coal strikes, the writings of the muckrakers, and the new trustbusting tendencies of the federal government were harbingers of greater changes to come.

The Joy Line was able to provide modest but comfortable accommodations to people of the urban middle class who could afford to travel but who could not afford the luxury of traveling first class. This function was limited to the brief era in which it flourished between the time when travel was limited to the rich and the age of mass transportation.

The winter of 1903 was a relatively mild one, especially compared with the hard winter of 1902 or the two unusually bitter winters that were to come. With the supply of coal still short after the prolonged strike of the previous summer, and the prices high and still rising, the mild winter was a blessing. But while the winter of 1903 was not as cold as some of the others of this period, it brought an unusual amount of fog. By the time the sound mariners had guided their steamers through heavy fogs several nights a week throughout January, February, and March, many of them undoubtedly would have preferred another winter of ice and winds where the strain was on the steamer rather than on their nerves.

For the second year in a row, the Fall River Line's *Pilgrim* was laid up for engine repairs well into the winter season. In 1902, the *Puritan* had run with the *Plymouth* through most of January. In 1903, however, the *Priscilla*, which was larger than the *Puritan* but a better sea boat and cheaper to operate, stayed with the *Plymouth* until the *Pilgrim* finally returned on January 24. The *City of Worcester* also spent most of the winter at Tietjen and Lange's getting new boilers, so the *Rhode Island* stayed on the Norwich Line that winter with the *City of Lowell*. The *Chester W. Chapin* ran alone on the New Haven Line, and the *Richard Peck* did the rounds as the general relief boat.

Throughout the year 1903, the *Larchmont* and the *Tremont* managed to run between New York and Providence six nights a week without incident, allowing the *City of Key West* to run in their places occasionally when they went off for regular overhauls. That winter, for the first time since the Joy Line began operating passenger service, its steamers were the only passenger liners operating between Providence and New York. With the fare held to $1.50 by its agreement with the New Haven, however, there was no appreciable increase in the number of passengers carried over previous years, in spite of the removal of the New Line steamers from the scene. For the most part, the *Tremont*, then under Captain Jacob Wise, arrived on the same mornings as George Rowland's *Nashua* on alternate days, while Dave Wilcox on the *Larchmont* regularly followed Captain Walter Hazard's *City of Fall River* up the Narragansett Bay.

Although the Joy Line was to have the winter passenger business to itself for another three years, the New Line had barely withdrawn before another line had a freight steamer serving Providence. In the fall of 1902, the Clyde Line began running the small freighter *John B. Collins* between New York and Providence. The *John B. Collins* left New York every Monday and Thursday and sailed from Providence on Tuesdays and Saturdays (the same schedule the *Rosalie* had in 1899), tying up at the Clyde Line dock, later occupied by the Colonial Line, just ahead of the Joy Line boat. Actually, the Clyde Line's freighter, which was even smaller than the *Rosalie*, was intended primarily as a feeder for the line's larger steamers running south from New York and did not compete seriously with the Joy Line's established business.[1]

Unfortunately, the Joy Line's Boston steamers were not as free of troubles that winter as its Providence boats. During January 1903, both of the line's

Boston steamers managed to get into serious difficulty in the same week. The sturdy *Old Dominion*, whose operation since she fetched on the rocks in 1901 had been so dependable that we have hardly had need to mention her, led off early in January by colliding with a schooner off Cape Cod. Through the night of Sunday, January 19, 1903, the *Old Dominion* had sailed through fog all the way up the sound. As she paddled through Nantucket Sound at daybreak, the fog persisted, and as she moved her slow and deliberate way out into the ocean around Cape Cod, the fog steadily thickened. Standing on the decks of a steamer moving through fog, one gets a very eerie feeling of isolation. No world exists except the small vessel itself and the rhythmic splashing of its wheels. Beyond its dampened decks in all directions is nothing but a misty void. Should the steamer next emerge on the surface of another dimension, one would not be surprised. The steamer itself, continuously seeking to establish contact with reality, or more accurately to ward it off, screeches regular blasts from its whistle, to which, though they are timed, the passenger never quite becomes accustomed, but these are quickly absorbed into the thickness of the atmosphere. Then, just as one is being lulled into passivity by the monotony of it all, one blast unexpectedly bounces back with a resounding echo, meaning that it has reflected off another vessel or perhaps a large land mass close by. As a rule, by the time the men in the pilot house hear such an echo, the other ship is too near to avoid a crash if there is to be one. Most often, however, the two vessels pass without touching, and the passenger experiences a moment of shock as some large steamer suddenly materializes very close, sliding past in shrouded silence like the Flying Dutchman and then, just as quickly, disappearing again into unreality.

On this occasion Captain Burton was not so lucky. The unnamed schooner was already directly in his steamer's path when he first sighted her. Fortunately, the two vessels did not crash head-on but bounced together along their starboard sides, their timbers cracking noisily, and then separated. The schooner could not easily stop and so continued on her way after her skipper had assured Captain Burton by megaphone that his vessel was not sinking. Rather than take unnecessary risks by continuing to Boston, Captain Burton turned about and sought the safety of Vineyard Haven harbor to make a closer examination. There he found that the exposed wooden paddlebox was a wreck and the starboard wheel badly bent, but that the *Old Dominion*'s iron hull was hardly scratched. Assured that there was no danger to passengers or cargo, Burton struck out again through the fog toward Boston. Back in New York after her next trip, she went over to Morse's for several days to have her injured wheel repaired.

The next New York to Boston sailing of the Joy Line was that of the *Seaboard* due to leave New York two days later, on Tuesday, January 20, at 5:00 P.M. As a result of the fog, however, which by then had lasted several days, the *Seaboard*, like the *Old Dominion*, was running considerably behind schedule and had arrived in New York so late that day that she was not reloaded and ready to sail again until nearly 8:00 P.M. Faced with fog once again, Captain Frank Kirby prepared to spend yet another night without leaving the pilot house. Through the night he guided the *Seaboard* from one fog horn or whistling buoy to the next, listening carefully for each sound that would tell him the location of his steamer before moving ahead. As the *Seaboard* reached the Race early in the morning, a stiff wind began to blow and by the time she was passing Block Island it had risen to a raging gale. Fog and heavy seas at the same time were more than Kirby cared to risk, so he swung the little *Seaboard* to port to seek temporary shelter in Narragansett Bay. Heading northward into the west channel at about four in the morning, he heard the fog horn at Beaver Tail on the end of Conanicut Island guarding the entrance to Narragansett Bay and even perceived the light vaguely through the mist. Moving on slowly, he waited for the next light at Dutch Island (a small rocky island tucked into the west side of Conanicut Island). After running the prescribed time, he saw nothing and slowed the steamer. By this time, the fog had become so thick that he could barely see the bow of the steamer a few feet away. Suddenly, the bow watchman called back that there was a black buoy off the port bow. The port bow! Kirby knew immediately that he was off course; the buoy had to be the marker for a rocky reef extending about fifty feet westward from Dutch Island. He knew that the *Seaboard* was about to pass on the inside of it. Unfortunately, a steamboat does not have brakes. Stopping or even reversing the screws will not slow a steamer, let alone stop it for several hundred feet. At high tide, the *Seaboard* would be able to clear the rocks, and for several seconds she seemed to be passing safely over them. Then she stopped. Since she was moving slowly, there was no jar as she struck; but she hit the rock somewhere aft of midships where her draft was deepest, and she stuck fast. The engines were reversed, but the *Seaboard* did not budge.

Had the tide been rising, the *Seaboard* might have come off without a scratch. But the tide was going down, and, as it did, it brought the *Seaboard* down so hard that the rocks punctured her hull in several places. Kirby meanwhile rowed ashore and telephoned Arthur Pitts to get lighters down to Dutch Harbor to unload the cargo, much of which was produce, mostly beans, before it was spoiled.

When the fog lifted the next morning, viewers from Sanderstown across the bay saw the *Seaboard* sitting on the rocks, at low tide her stern held high out of the water and her bow now submerged up the guards. She sat right at the edge of the ledge jutting out partly submerged from Dutch Island; had she been as much as ten feet further into the channel, she would have passed by safely.

Arthur Pitts arrived at about noon aboard the lighter *Sagamore*, chartered from the Dyer Line to help unload the *Seaboard*'s freight, and with two tugs to assist in pulling her off. But by this time the *Seaboard* had filled with water so that even relieved of her freight, she could not be floated off. As with the *Old Dominion* two years earlier, moving a steamer impaled on rocks proved a difficult job. Charlie Dimon came up from New York to supervise the operation, and a Scott wrecking crew was brought in, but it was nearly two weeks later, on February 2, before they got her off. Fortunately, the weather remained fairly calm throughout the period, or the staunch old *Seaboard* might have been pounded to bits, much as the old *Rhode Island* had been when she got caught on the rocks only a few hundred yards away on the other side of the channel twenty years before. Scott towed the *Seaboard* up to a drydock in East Providence, but the job was greater than they could tackle, so Dimon invited New York yards to come up and make bids. The low bid was not from Morse's this time, but from Townshend and Downey, who had recently opened a new yard at Shooter's Island in Newark Bay, where the *Seaboard* was next towed to have her hull rebuilt at a cost of $30,000.

With the *Seaboard* now out of service for several weeks and the *Old Dominion* at Morse's having her starboard wheel straightened, the Joy Line had no boats at all running to Boston. Almost immediately, however, Dimon was able to charter the old *Surprise*. Since her Portland run was a summer service, not only was she now available, but the Whitcombs were glad to have her earning some money. The *Surprise* got steam up in time to take the *Seaboard*'s next scheduled trip out of Boston and stayed on the line until the *Seaboard* returned in April. The *Rosalie* filled in for the *Old Dominion* as well as she could, and when the *Old Dominion* was back, the *Rosalie* continued to make unscheduled trips for the next several weeks to help with backed-up freight.

Captain Kirby commanded the *Surprise* for her first several trips and then decided to leave the employ of the Joy Line as Captain Durkee had done after landing the *Old Dominion* on the rocks in a similar fashion two years earlier. Once again, there are no records to indicate whether the decision was voluntary, but in light of the fact that it happened twice under similar circumstances, one is led to conclude that the decision probably came from the offices at Pier 35. Dismissing a captain after one accidental grounding, when he had spent years guiding the company's steamers through the sound day after day in safety under all kinds of conditions, does seem uncommonly ungrateful. Possibly, the decision may have been a response to some requirement from whatever insurance companies were willing to underwrite these antique steamers and the cargoes they carried.

Early in February 1903, the New Haven Railroad added one more sound steamer line to its collection by purchasing the Bridgeport Line.² With this acquisition the railroad could now count among its floating stock a steamer named the *Allan Joy!* The *Allan Joy*, it will be remembered, had been purchased by the Bridgeport Line, late in 1899. Since then, she had been taking the line's overnight round trips in the summer months, while the newer sidewheeler *William G. Payne* ran the daytime round trips. In the winter, however, the *Allan Joy* ran alone, leaving New York at 11:00 A.M. and Bridgeport at 1:00 A.M.

The *Rhode Island* remained on the Norwich Line relieving the *City of Worcester*, as mentioned earlier, through February; at the same time, the *Richard Peck* was relieving the *Maine* on the Stonington Line. When the *Maine*'s overhaul was completed, instead of returning to her own run, she joined the *Rhode Island* on the Norwich Line while the *City of Lowell* went for an overhaul. During another dense fog on Sunday morning, March 5, the *Rhode Island*, coming down from New London, crashed into the railway transfer ferry *Express* in the East River and had to go over to Fletcher's for some carpentry. Since there were not many passengers traveling to New London in early March, the railroad did not drag the *Connecticut*, the only available steamer, out of her winter quarters at Stonington but settled for the services of the smaller *City of Lawrence*.

Long Island Sound continued to be buried in fog through much of February and March 1903. Throughout this arduous winter, the steamers of ten different sound lines coursed through the sound, as they did every night, operated by officers who knew their routes so well that they could, and indeed virtually often did, run their steamers blindfolded. But it was during this month of March 1903, after several weeks of almost continuous fog, that the staid Fall River Line, which had remained so remarkably free of accidents until the almost fatal *Priscilla-Powhatan* crash a few months before, experienced the most serious accident in its long history, one involving two of its steamers. On the night of March 19-20, the Fall River steamer *Plymouth*, sailing eastward out of New York through the unrelenting fog, was just passing through the Race at the eastern end of the sound when she was struck on her port side near the pilot house by the Fall River Line freighter *City of Taunton*, westbound. Seven people aboard the *Plymouth*, one passenger and six crewmembers, were killed instantly. As with the *Priscilla* a few months earlier, the *Plymouth*'s steel double-hull withstood the impact. Although her wooden superstructure was smashed to bits where the *City of Taunton* had struck, the steamer was not taking water and was able to proceed slowly into New London under her own power. The wooden-hulled *City of Taunton*, on the other hand, was in greater danger, so the *Nashua* of the Providence Line, which had stood by to offer assistance, towed her stern first, also into New London.

The *Priscilla* had practically no layover at all in the winter of 1903. The

Pilgrim had not come back from having her engine repaired until the end of January, and now, barely seven weeks later, with the *Plymouth* out of commission for several weeks, the *Priscilla* was back on the line for the rest of the season. It had been a strange year for the Fall River Line with the *Plymouth* running for the *Priscilla* in July and now the *Priscilla* running for the *Plymouth* in March. The need for another steamer roughly the size of the *Plymouth* or the *Pilgrim* was becoming more apparent, and the line looked forward to the completion of the *Providence*.

About the time of the *Plymouth-City of Taunton* crash, the Montauk Line announced the purchase of the old Kennebec steamer *Sagadahoc*, which it renamed *Greenport*, as a running mate for the *Shinnecock*.[3] The Kennebec Line's new sidewheel steamer *Ransom B. Fuller*, the second new entry (after the *City of Rockland*) in Morse's major replacement program, had finished her trial trips late in 1902 and would be ready for the coming season to run with the *Kennebec*, thus releasing the *Sagadahoc* for sale. The Montauk Line had been announcing plans for a new sistership for the *Shinnecock* since the sale of the *Montauk* in 1901, but as yet no contract had been awarded and no keel laid. Once again, with the announcement of the purchase of the *Sagadahoc*, the line promised that the new acquisition would be used only temporarily and that the promised new steamer would be ready for the season of 1904. But no new steamer ever appeared. With the rising costs of shipbuilding, of coal, and of the general maintenance and operation of the steamers, plus a marked decline in passenger traffic, the Pennsylvania Railroad, which owned the line, elected not to expand a service which, after all, competed with its other subsidiary, the Long Island Railroad. The Montauk Line's decision not to add another steamer, coming as it did five years before the Fall River Line built the largest—and last—steamer to run on Long Island Sound, was probably the first harbinger of the rapid decline in sound steamer traffic, which was to become fully apparent in the years following World War I.

Early in May the *Seaboard*, now commanded by Captain C. E. Rood, was back on the Boston run after four months and $30,000, just in time to let the *Surprise* get ready for her own summer service. This year, Whitcomb had recently announced, he planned to run the *Surprise* all the way up to Eastport, Maine, in competition with Morse's International Line, rather than to Portland as previously.[4] Also in May, both the *City of Lowell* and the *City of Worcester* returned to the Norwich Line, which meant that the *Maine* and the *Richard Peck* could go back to their regular routes for the summer. The *Rhode Island*, now no longer needed on the New Line, went to lay up in Stonington. Since the *Priscilla* had not been given time for an overhaul that season, the *Puritan* came on in May to relieve her (one of the few times after 1894 that the *Pilgrim* and the *Puritan* had run together). By the second week in June, both the *Priscilla* and the *Puritan* were on the

Fall River Line again and the *Pilgrim* also laid up for the summer. By this time, the *Plymouth* had been repaired, and, on the first Monday in June, as usual, the *Plymouth* and the *Connecticut*, for the third season now, made up the summer Providence Line. This was the first time in three years, however, that the Providence Line would not be facing the competition of its own company's New Line steamers, and there was some question whether the *Connecticut* would be large enough for the expected increased traffic. The fears were unfounded. The fifty-cent passengers who had thronged the decks of the *Massachusetts* and the *Rhode Island* in previous years simply stopped traveling when the fares went up to two and three dollars, for the Joy Line fares, as per the agreement with the railroad, rose to an unprecedented $2.00 as soon as the railroad's passenger line started its season. While both the Providence Line and the Joy Line enjoyed a good season in 1903, neither experienced an unmanageable increase in traffic and the *Connecticut* not only proved adequate, but she also kept running.

By June 1903, Morse's replacement plans were progressing so rapidly that three fine new steamers appeared that month, all named, like the *Ransom B. Fuller* of a few months earlier, for men who served on one or more of Morse's boards of directors. The largest of them, of course, was named the *C. W. Morse*. This steamer, a magnificent new sidewheeler the size of the *Priscilla* for the Hudson River Night Line, was launched that month but was not ready for service until the following season. Also in June, the small but beautifully proportioned sidewheeler *J. T. Morse*, named for the magnate's uncle and business associate, took her place on the Rockland-Bar Harbor run replacing the much beloved old *Mt. Desert*. Then on July 3, the new propellor steamer *Calvin Austin*, named for the president of Morse's Eastern Steamship Company, turned up briefly in New York on her way from her builders on the Delaware to Boston. Two weeks later, the *Calvin Austin* which many consider the handsomest of all the Maine coast steamers, took her place on the International Line. She replaced the old *Penobscot* (which had gone on the line for the *Cumberland* the year before), but only temporarily, for, as we shall soon see, she was back on the run in 1904 for another three seasons.

This same week, the graceful and speedy *Asbury Park* made her trial runs in New York harbor prior to joining the Jersey Central's Atlantic Highlands service.

Still another steamer appeared in New York harbor that week, one that attracted little notice at the time but that was to play a more direct role in the story of the Joy Line: the little *Longfellow* which had just sailed back to New York after several years in Puerto Rico. The *Longfellow* had been built back in 1883, the same year as the *Pilgrim* and the *Tremont*, for the summer Boston to Provincetown run which she covered successfully for another seventeen years. When she was superseded in 1900 by the new *Cape Cod*, which did not prove to be much of a success, the *Longfellow* was sold to the Porto Rico Line and assigned to meet large liners arriving in San Juan and carry passengers and freight from there to the other smaller ports around the island. When replaced there by a larger steamer (the *Porto Rico*, which had made one round trip for the Joy Line in 1900), the *Longfellow* was chartered by the Clyde Line to run from New York to Providence in place of the *John M. Collins*. She made her first trip out of New York on Thursday, July 2, making her way to Providence on the same night as the *Connecticut* and the *Tremont*.

The Joy Line did not have any special steamers to run in the summer, but the faithful *Tremont* and *Larchmont* were both freshly painted in the late spring to begin the season. When the *Tremont* went off for her overhaul, her captain, Jacob Wise, took this opportunity to announce his retirement. On her return, the *Tremont* was commanded by George Olweiler, then thirty-five years of age. He was to command various New York to Providence steamboats for another thirty-five years, serving at the time of his retirement in 1938 as the deeply respected captain of the Colonial Line's *Arrow*.

The summer of 1903 in Providence was known as the summer of the heat wave when temperatures through the first week in July soared close to a hundred and stayed there. It was also when Thomas Lipton made his third try for the America's Cup. The fourth of July fell on a Saturday that year, and many escaped the heat by boarding the Providence Line steamer *Plymouth*, which, since she did not sail on Saturday nights, took a crowd of spectators down to Newport and around Block Island to watch the three American ships *Columbia, Constitution*, and *Reliance* in their first runoff heat to see which would defend the America's cup. Among the spectators was Thomas Lipton himself who had come over on his yacht *Erin* to watch the event.

That weekend the Joy Line brought the *City of Key West* up from New York for another attempt to get into the lucrative excursion business out of Providence. On this occasion, for some reason, the name Joy Line was not used. Instead, the excursions for the holiday weekend were advertised under the name of Arthur Pitts, the enterprising Providence agent of the line, who dared describe the steamer in his ads as the "large and commodious steamer *City of Key West!*" The Joy Line's fifty-cent excursions were obviously designed to appeal to a different sort of passenger from those who followed yacht races, for the *City of Key West* offered only a moonlight cruise that day leaving at 7:30 P.M. (thus accommodating passengers who worked a full day Saturday) and attempting no more of a trip than around Prudence Island and back. It is possible, on the other hand, that the *City of Key West*'s schedule that day was imposed by the railroad, which may not have permitted the Joy Line to run an excursion in competition with the *Plymouth's*. Whatever the reason, the Joy Line's public certainly did not work on Sundays, and the *Plymouth*, since she sailed every Sunday evening, could not make Sunday excursions. Thus, on Sunday, July 5, the *City of Key West* left Providence at 9:30 in the morning, ran down the bay and out as far as Watch Hill, and, without docking anywhere along the way, returned her passengers to the heat of Providence late in the evening.

The Sunday cruise of the *City of Key West* on July 5 was obviously a stalking horse for the cruises the Joy Line was planning to run with the *Larchmont* the following Sunday and each Sunday thereafter for the rest of the season to Cottage City and back for $1.00. As described earlier, the line had run these cruises with great success with the *Martinique* back in 1900. But the *Larchmont* was the first steamer the Joy Line had operated since 1900 that was capable of making it all the way to Martha's Vineyard and back in one day, so that in 1901 and 1902 the *Tremont* had sat in her pier in Providence while the *Massachusetts* or the *Rhode Island* had sailed down the bay loaded with Sunday excursionists. At the time, however, the *Larchmont* was on the wrong schedule for laying over Sundays in Providence, so during that week, the Joy Line had to execute some schedule-juggling. On the night of July 5, at the end of the holiday weekend, the *Tremont* made a special Sunday trip to New York, contrary to the agreement with the railroad, while the *Larchmont* remained, as usual, at the pier in New York. Since the *City of Key West* was already in Providence, she made the Monday trip down that the *Tremont* would normally have made, while the *Tremont* sailed from New York and the *Larchmont* again stayed at her pier. Now the *Larchmont* was on the Tuesday, Thursday, Saturday schedule out of New York, and would thus be in Providence on Sundays to make the excursions to Cottage City.

The *Larchmont's* first cruise was well timed. A heat wave hit Providence on Saturday, July 11, with temperatures well into the mid-nineties, and when the *Larchmont* sailed the following morning, she was loaded to capacity. The Joy Line had just begun to bask in the success of its return to the excursion business when Dunbaugh received a call from Percy Todd of the New Haven pointing out that the *Larchmont's* Sunday trips were in violation of the line's agreement with the railroad which stipulated that it would not run steamers to any port except Providence or Boston. Dunbaugh's response is not recorded, but it is obvious from subsequent correspondence that the Joy Line's president was not pleased. For the time, however, a compromise was reached, and the *Larchmont* continued her cruises that summer but circumvented Todd's complaint by not making any stops during the day. A second trip scheduled for Cottage City for July 19 was canceled anyway because of rain. On July 26, the *Larchmont* experimented with a new route, running down Narragansett Bay and then westward as far as

Race Rock at the far end of Fisher's Island and returning without a stop. The restrictions imposed by the railroad at least had the advantage that the passengers had to buy all their refreshments aboard the steamer. On August 2, it was Cottage City again but apparently without docking. That week the Clyde Line decided to cash in on the excursion business, and the *Longfellow*, which, although now a freighter, had, after all, been built as an excursion boat, was advertised for a Sunday trip down Narragansett Bay and around Fisher's Island and return, also for a dollar. But the Clyde people apparently did not make enough profit to warrant disrupting their schedule, for the *Longfellow* made no subsequent Sunday trips.

Now that the *Larchmont* was not docking anywhere for her passengers to disembark, the line planned some more ambitious itineraries for her. On August 9 and again on August 16, the *Larchmont* paddled all the way to Montauk and back. As usual, no mention was made of a scheduled time for returning, but after such a long trip, it must have been close to midnight before she returned to her pier in Providence. On August 23, apparently anxious to give its regular customers some variety, the line sent the *Larchmont* out to Martha's Vineyard again, not to Cottage City this time, however, but merely to have a look at the island from the sea. To give some purpose to the trip, the line's ad promised that passengers would have an opportunity to view the famous Gay Head Indians but neglected to mention that this view would be from the decks of the steamer at sea and then only if the weather were particularly clear. The trip to Gay Head was apparently not altogether successful, for on August 30 the line was again advertising that the *Larchmont* would head across to Montauk. This trip had to be canceled on account of a storm that day, but the *Larchmont* made it to Montauk on September 6 and again on September 13, her last for the season.

The excursions out of Providence that summer were so successful that the line decided to put the *Tremont* to work in New York as well. On August 2, the *Tremont*, crowded with passengers, headed up the Hudson as far as she could made it in one day, which was roughly Newburgh. The *Tremont's* Hudson trips were repeated on August 9 and 16, but then, as we shall see, she developed engine troubles late in the month and was off the route for several weeks. Her Hudson River excursions were, therefore, canceled for the rest of that summer and were never repeated.

During August, there was a minor shakeup in the New York office of the Joy Line which may have been a reflection of deeper internal cleavages. George Brady, sometimes known as "Captain" Brady, though he seems never to have served in any capacity aboard a steamer, was summarily dismissed as the general passenger agent of the Joy Line, and the position returned to W. Arnold, the man who had held it before Brady had been hired the year before. Brady had come to the Joy Line in 1902 soon after being fired by the New Haven Railroad's marine district for practices which, while perhaps not exactly illegal, even the Joy Line could not have condoned. The specific reasons for Brady's dismissal by the railroad in 1902 were not disclosed, but one story circulated at the time was probably illustrative: Brady had come to the New Haven's marine department with its purchase of the Norwich Line, and, while working for that line in the 1890s, according to the story, Brady had made more money in kickbacks from cartage companies for whom he arranged Norwich Line contracts than the cartage companies themselves.[5] In all probability, Brady, or "Captain" Brady, had been hired by the Joy Line early in 1902 at the time when the railroad was blocking the line's every effort to transport either passengers or cargo to points west and south of New York or north and east of Providence. At that time, the Joy Line would have welcomed a man with connections and with innovative imagination in this area, as well as one familiar with the inner workings of the railroad's carting operations. Whether he turned out to be ineffective in the job, or his personality grated on other officers at Pier 35, or his presence there, after the agreement with the railroad, proved either unnecessary or embarrassing, or whether he continued his dubious practices and his dismissal was requested by the railroad, is not recorded. But neither the railroad nor the Joy Line had seen the last of Captain Brady.

This seemed to be the year for the *Seaboard* to find herself fetched up on islands at the eastern end of the sound. She had been back in service barely a few months after her near-fatal grounding at Dutch Island before she struck again on July 22, this time hitting a dock at Great Gull Island, near the spot where the *Priscilla* was to do the same thing twenty-three years later. With her bow badly smashed in, but with apparently little damage to her hull this time, the *Seaboard* pulled herself out of her predicament and made her own way over to New London for temporary repairs before heading back to Shooter's Island for a new bow. The *Surprise*, of course, was not available to replace her in July, but freight was fairly light in midsummer, so the *Rosalie* was brought out of layup to run to Boston for the *Seaboard*. Captain Coleman, according to one marine reporter, was "promoted" to captain of the *Rosalie* for this period.[6] Considering that Coleman had commanded the big Metropolitan Line freighters for many years, it is hard to conceive of his summer stint on the *Rosalie* as a promotion, but undoubtedly he thoroughly enjoyed the suggestion. This time the *Seaboard* was back in about three weeks, but again the *Rosalie* was kept on the run for several more trips to take care of backed-up freight.

On one of her trips down from Boston, the *Rosalie* passed by the former Providence liner *Massachusetts* headed slowly northward at the end of a tow-rope. Just one year after part of her walking beam had dropped unexpectedly into the Gallery Deck, the railroad authorities decided to sell her for scrap. On July 30, therefore, though still a beautiful steamer and barely more than twenty-five years old. the *Massachusetts* was pulled out of her layup at Stonington by a towboat and taken up to Quincy, Massachusetts, not far from where her successor was then being built, to be dismantled.

The America's Cup races were held early in 1903, probably because the bad September weather had nearly ruined the races both in 1899 and in 1901. This time, therefore, the races were scheduled for the last week in August. So too, although the racing authorities were never informed, was the bad weather. Once again many of the steamer lines placed their spare boats on the regular runs, though this was not as convenient in August as it would have been in September, so that their larger steamers could carry spectators to the races. The *Pilgrim* came back on the Providence Line (with the *Connecticut*) on Sunday, August 16, for the first time in three years, to relieve the *Plymouth*, and the *City of Lawrence* went on the New Haven Line with the *Chester W. Chapin* in place of the *Richard Peck*. For once the Joy Line had enough steamers on hand so that it, too, could send a boat to the races. Unlike the other lines, however, it did not send one of its regular steamers out; the *Larchmont* had to stay on her schedule to be available for her Sunday excursions out of Providence, while the *Tremont* would probably not have gotten as far as Sandy Hook before the races were over. So the line's spare steamer, the *City of Key West*, took spectators out to the races for a dollar.

The event failed to generate much excitement this time, for the American entry, the *Reliance*, easily outreached the *Shamrock III* in every race. His *Shamrocks* three having brought him precious little luck, Lipton sadly announced at the end of the races that he would make no further attempts to win back the cup.

The races, which again had been conducted in cloudy, damp weather, ended on Thursday, August 27—and just in time, for on Friday, Saturday, and Sunday, the last weekend of the season, the whole East Coast was drenched in torrential rains driven by gale-force winds. The Joy Line steamer *Tremont* sailed from New York on Friday, the night the storm was gathering, but she was only a few hours out of the city when she developed engine problems (the steam pipe connecting the boiler with the steam chest broke open) and was forced to seek shelter from the storm in Huntington harbor. Early the following morning, Captain Wilcox on the westbound *Larchmont* somehow heard the frantic whistles of the *Tremont* through the rain and turned into Huntington harbor to see what was the matter. In spite of the increasing wind and rain, the *Larchmont* managed to tow her consort across the sound to Bridgeport, where the passengers could at least get trains to their destinations and, leaving the *Tremont* there temporarily, proceeded to New York.

By that evening, Saturday, August 29, the wind and rain were so strong that neither the *Larchmont* nor the *Old Dominion* sailed from New York, and the *Seaboard* in Boston also remained in port. The *Larchmont*, as we have seen, was scheduled to take an excursion out of Providence the following day, but it was canceled. By Monday, the seas were calm again and sailings were normal. That night the *City of Key West* sailed for the *Tremont* and stayed on the line several weeks while the *Tremont* was repaired at the North River Iron Works.

After the races, the *Plymouth* went to lay up at Newport, and the *Pilgrim* stayed on the Providence Line with the *Connecticut* until the season ended on October 12.

During the fall of 1903, the competition which had posed some threat to the Joy Line both in Boston and in Providence unexpectedly ceased to exist. The Savannah Line had a steamer (the *City of Macon* had been sold in 1902 and replaced on the route by the *Chattahoochee*) running two round trips a week between New York and Boston carrying cargo at low rates. Its losses for some time had been underwritten by the Metropolitan Line, which used the Savannah Line operation, much as the railroad had used the New Line, to undercut the Joy Line without committing its own line to low-rate contracts that might be embarrassing later. But with the Joy Line, now buttressed by its agreement with the New Haven in Providence, showing no signs of giving up and the Savannah Line, as some statistics seemed to show, taking more business from the Metropolitan Line itself than from the Joy Line, the Metropolitan decided to withdraw its support, and the Savannah Line discontinued its New York to Boston freight service late in September.

The Metropolitan Line was also instrumental, though quite unintentionally, in removing the Clyde Line competition from Providence. The *Longfellow* was passing through Hell Gate in a fog on her way to Providence on October 31, when she was rammed from the rear by the fast-stepping *Herman Winter* of Metropolitan Line, tearing away the whole starboard quarter of her stern. She was subsequently towed to Crane's in Brooklyn and repaired, but the Clyde Line had meanwhile decided to give up the run and simply turned the steamer over to the underwriters.[7]

In October 1903, the agreement between the Joy Line and the New Haven Railroad was due for renewal. A year earlier, when the agreements had been signed, President Hall of the New Haven had pleaded with Percy Todd to arrive at some accommodation with the Joy Line as quickly as possible, assuring him that any arrangement which would permit the immediate suspension of the New Line would save the railroad a great deal of money. Now, Todd, who had never been enthusiastic about the agreement, treated it as a great concession on the railroad's part and responded to all requests for minor modifications with haughty disdain.[8]

When the date for renewal approached, Dunbaugh wrote to Todd that, "There are some matters in the agreement which we would like to take up with you, and would be pleased if you would kindly set a date, at your convenience, when they may be discussed."⁹ Todd arranged a meeting for Friday, October 30, at 3:30 in the afternoon in the New Haven's offices in the old Grand Central building. (The present structure was not built until 1910.) Facing each other across a table were Todd and F. S. Holbrook (who had replaced J. M. Williams as freight agent) representing the railroad and Dunbaugh and Rowland, the Joy Line. At this meeting, Dunbaugh outlined several requests for modifications in the original agreement. First, he wanted to reduce the winter passenger fares to Providence from $1.50 to $1.25 and the fare to Boston from $2.50 to $2.25. In seeking some relief from the restrictions on through freight, he asked that the Joy Line be allowed some permanent working agreement with the Union Railway (an electric trolley company with freight facilities which delivered Joy Line freight locally in Providence) rather than having to pay them by the piece as the original agreement stipulated. He also asked that the line be allowed to make through freight arrangements with some of the smaller railroads running west out of New York. In response to requests from his customers, he asked if the line might charge somewhat lower rates on certain kinds of cotton goods. Finally, Dunbaugh requested in particular that the Joy Line be permitted to run its excursions to Cottage City in 1904.¹⁰

Nothing was decided at this meeting, but later, after many exchanges of memos among Todd, Holbrook, and George Conner, the railroad's passenger agent, Todd refused every one of Dunbaugh's requests except the reduced passenger fare to Boston, which had not been covered formally in the first agreement anyway. As far as the Sunday excursions were concerned, Todd insisted that any excursions run by the Joy Line at all, with or without stops, would be contrary to the agreement with the New Haven. One accommodation only was granted after several subsequent meetings and plaintive letters. After writing once that the Joy Line had not given the $1.50 winter fare a reasonable trial, Todd finally conceded that, if the line maintained the $1.50 fare through most of the winter season, it might drop to $1.25 for the months of January, February, and March.¹¹

An accident on the *City of Worcester* in the fall of 1903, although not serious in itself, seems to have had a considerable effect in determining the future of some of the railroad's steamers. The series of heavy rainstorms which had begun the last week of August let up in September, but began again early in October with such force that all of the sound steamers were again obliged to miss several sailings rather than risk a terrifying trip up the sound in a heavy sea. On Saturday, October 10, however, the *City of Worcester*, which rarely missed a trip since her whole run lay within the semi-protected waters of the sound, set out from New York on schedule followed by the *New Hampshire* bound for Stonington. The *City of Worcester* was just entering the open part of the sound and beginning to pitch in the heavy seas when the pin at the forward end of her walking beam snapped, leaving her powerless just between Hart's Island and Execution. The *New Hampshire* pulled up alongside, but the seas were too rough to risk a transfer of passengers. The *New Hampshire* turned about to report the problem and summon assistance. Soon tugs arrived and towed the *City of Worcester* back to New York.

Although the accident was a minor one and the *City of Worcester* was back on her run in a few days, it apparently led to some serious reconsiderations on the part of the railroad's marine division. It was becoming clear that the newer steel-hulled steamers with their more compact inclined engines located mostly in the hold were operating efficiently and almost without incident, whereas the older beam-engined steamers, however sound their hulls or elegant their furnishings, were breaking down frequently and costing the company a considerable amount of money to maintain. The *Pilgrim,* the *Connecticut* (although not a beam-engined steamer, she certainly had her share of problems), and the *City of Worcester,* in particular, had all spent a great deal of time in the shops having their engines overhauled, only to be put out of service time and again, at great expense to the company, to say nothing of inconvenience to the passengers, simply because some relatively small part had worn out with age.

With the discontinuance of the New Line, the company no longer needed to maintain such a large fleet. Moreover, the shifting about of steamers during the summer of 1902 had shown that dropping passenger service to Stonington had not proved a particular hardship, since Stonington passengers needed to ride only a few more miles on a train to reach the New London passenger steamers, which were rarely overbooked. On December 12, 1903, therefore, passenger service on the Stonington Line, one of Connecticut's oldest institutions, was simply discontinued with very little fanfare. The *New Hampshire* was placed on the New Haven Line to run with the *Richard Peck,* while the *Maine* was kept at Stonington with steam up to replace the *Rhode Island* as the company's regular relief boat. Meanwhile, freight service to Stonington was maintained by the *City of Lawrence* and the *Pequot* temporarily, pending the completion of new freighters that the company intended to add.[12]

With the *New Hampshire* on the New Haven Line, the *Chester W. Chapin* now moved to the New London Line to run with the *City of Lowell* in place of the *City of Worcester,* which was taken off after having run on the Norwich Line continuously, summer and winter, for twenty-two years without a break except for repairs or overhauls. (Except for a brief period in the 1880s when the first *Providence* was out of commission for several weeks and the *City of Worcester* was chartered by the Fall River Line to take her place, there is no record that the *City of Worcester* ever ran regularly on any other overnight run than between New York and New London, in spite of the fact that the New Haven system tended to transfer steamers from one line to another with almost perverse abandon.) Actually, the *Chester W. Chapin*, in appearance at least, seemed a better running mate for the *City of Lowell* than the *City of Worcester* had been. The *City of Lowell* and the *City of Worcester*, although they ran together for nearly a decade, were very different in appearance, whereas the *Chester W. Chapin*, although built for a different line, was a product of the same marine architect as the *City of Lowell* and had been designed quite specifically to resemble her. These two fast steamers, quite indistinguishable except to a practiced eye (the *City of Lowell*'s stacks were noticeably thicker), were to run together, with one brief break in the early 1920s, first on the New London route, then to New Bedford, and finally to Providence, for the next thirty-three years until the spring of 1937.

With the New Line gone, the increasing business on the Providence Line, and the price of coal returning to normal, the company decided at the same time to retire the undependable wooden-hulled *Connecticut* and bring the *Pilgrim* back to the Providence Line again to run with the *Plymouth* in 1904, but only for one more season, as the new *Providence* would be ready to go on the line in 1905.

The reassignment of steamers in December 1903 was intended to effect the retirement of the older steamers *Connecticut*, *City of Worcester*, and *Rhode Island*, with the *Pilgrim* slated to come off as soon as the *Providence* was ready and the *Puritan* soon after that, since plans for still another new Fall River Line steamer were then already being considered. None of the three steamers retired at this time, however, followed the *Masschusetts* to the scrap yard. Instead, they were laid up at the railroad's now unused wharves at Stonington. Perhaps the railroad rememberd the summer of 1902 when it had unexpectedly found itself so perilously short of steamers. In any event, as a result of circumstances unforeseen at that time, all three survived to see further service, and even the staunch *Pilgrim* was to run for another year after the arrival of the *Providence*.

Far more significant to the later operation of the railroad's sound lines as well as to their relationship with the Joy Line—and ultimately also to the Joy Line itself—was the appointment in October 1903 (effective January 1904) of Charles S. Mellen as successor to John M. Hall as president of the New Haven Railroad. John Hall, a Boston lawyer, had been a competent administrator in the era when the New Haven was attempting to absorb its many recent acquisitions. On Hall's retirement, J. P. Morgan, always the railroad's dominant board member, favored a more aggressive president and one with a railroad background. Mellen was Morgan's choice and remained, for the most part, willing to carry out Morgan's policies throughout his ten years in the office.[13] On his own, Mellen was also to embark on a gradual reorganization of the railroad's marine properties which was to have its effect on the operation of the Joy Line was well.

The appointment of a new president in October 1903 undoubtedly accounted for Percy Todd's refusal to accept any changes in the railroad's agreement with the Joy Line when it came up for its first renewal that month. When it later became apparent that Mellen would not decree any changes, for the moment, in the relationship between the railroad and the Joy Line, Todd became considerably more malleable.

The year 1903 ended with good news for the Joy Line. Early in December, the line was able to purchase another ship to run with the *Old Dominion* to Boston in place of the *Seaboard*, which had never really been suited to this run. The steamer it acquired was the *Aransas* of the Morgan Line which operated in the Gulf of Mexico. Also designed by Herman Winter, the *Aransas*, like the *Old Dominion*, was an ocean-going ship; she was about the same size with a similarly large freight-carrying capacity. As a propellor steamer, however, she was quite different in appearance from the *Old Dominion*, though very typical of a whole generation of coastal steamers of that era. She was a good-looking ship, too, with a long black iron hull in which were located the engines and almost a full deck of cargo space, one deck of white wooden superstructure with accommodations for crew and for a few passengers, and the pilot house above that with one very tall black stack, jauntily raked, just amidships. Captain Coleman volunteered to travel down to New Orleans to take possession of the *Aransas* and bring her up to New York, sailing from New York on a Mallory Line steamer shortly after Christmas.

1904

Americans were horrified on January 1, 1904, to read about the fire the night before on New Year's Eve in the Iroquois Theater in Chicago in which almost a thousand people were trapped and burned to death. Several other fires during the year 1904 began to awaken Americans, now more than ever before inclined to crowd into large public places, to the necessity of planning and even legislating adequate fire protection methods, both on land and at sea.

On the East Coast the new year began with a blizzard, the first intimation that the mild weather of 1903 was not to be repeated. By Saturday, January 2, the storm began to intensify early in the morning as huge quantities of snow were blasted across southern New England by winds up to fifty miles per hour. In Providence, trains and trolleys were brought to a standstill, businesses closed early, and by mid-afternoon the streets of the city were deserted. Providence had been abandoned to the snow.

Down at Fox Point wharf, Captain Edward Geer held a consultation with the railroad's Providence agents and decided that he would hold the *Nashua* in port until the storm subsided. But at exactly 5:25 that afternoon, George Olweiler stood in the pilot house of the *Tremont* and pulled the whistle cord for three long blasts to announce to anyone who could hear them that the *Tremont* was preparing to sail. Five minutes later he blew the whistle again, the *Tremont*'s big wheels began thrashing the icy waters, and the steamer moved slowly down the river, disappearing very quickly into the falling snow. This, perhaps somewhat unfortunately, was the way the Joy Line tended to operate. Sailing into raging blizzards as it often did was not simply an act of bravado; it was a necessary part of the kind of business the Joy Line did. The railroad lines dealt mainly with large manufacturers, their arrangements were made through form letters and published rate schedules, and the cargo itself arrived by the carload. But the Joy Line dealt entirely with small local shippers, as we have seen, and their freight was largely package freight, much of it perishable produce. The arrangements with its customers were often very personal, and it often received shipments only on condition of their early and safe delivery. For the Joy Line to keep the kind of customers it particularly depended on, therefore, it was necessary for its steamers to sail if they possibly could.

Not surprisingly, the *Larchmont* also sailed from New York that night with two hundred passengers aboard in spite of the fact that the western end of the sound was becoming clogged with ice and all of the steamers coming east had difficulty getting through. Eventually, orders came from the railroad that its steamers should also prepare to sail as soon as they could, taking perishable freight, since the railroad trains were no longer getting through to New York. Geer finally got the *Nashua* out several hours late, and the *Priscilla* sailed from Fall River just before midnight. The *City of Taunton* also sailed from New York, but after several hours of battling ice floes in the sound, thick snow, and driving winds, Captain George Rowland guided her into New Haven harbor to wait for the dawn. Wilcox's *Larchmont*, however, continued on to Providence, although her progress was slow. That night, as the temperature dropped to several degrees below zero, one of the lowest ever recorded on the sound, icy waves kept breaking over the *Larchmont*'s bow, the spray freezing as it fell. When the *Larchmont* finally appeared in Providence after 10:00 on Sunday morning, she looked more like an iceberg with sidewheels than a steamer.

The ice and the heavy winds lasted all through January and February of 1904, which turned out to be one of the coldest winters on record, colder even than 1902. Throughout this period, the sailings of the Joy Line boats, as well as all of the the Long Island Sound steamers, became hopelessly erratic. With regular sailings frequently canceled, with the twelve-hour trip sometimes taking fifteen or twenty hours through heavy seas or ice-clogged channels, with steamers often putting in at New Haven or New London to sit out a storm, and with cargoes, as a result, backlogging on the piers, the steamers were often obliged to sail whenever conditions allowed, or as soon as they had taken on a load (passenger traffic, needless to say, was minimal), in order to keep up with their contracts as well as they could.

It was into this bitter weather that the Joy Line's latest acquisition, the *Aransas*, which had spent the first thirty years of her life in the warm waters of the Gulf of Mexico, made her first voyage northward guided by Captain Coleman. Coming up from New Orleans, parting from the Gulf Stream undoubtedly with great reluctance, the *Aransas* did not go into New York but sailed directly to Boston, where she arrived one day later than expected because of the heavy weather encountered en route. She made her first voyage for the Joy Line from there on Saturday night, January 16. Although Captain E. R. Rood was to be her regular master (Burton, the senior captain on the Boston run, apparently preferred to stay with the slow but steady-handling *Old Dominion*), Captain Coleman again agreed to keep command until the ship and her new crew became accustomed to each other.[1]

With the arrival of the *Aransas*, the Joy Line for the first time had a complete fleet of steamers suited to its services, with two fairly well-matched ocean-going steamers, the *Old Dominion* and the *Aransas*, on the Boston run and two fairly well-matched sound-type steamers, the *Larchmont* and the *Tremont*, on the Providence run. The reliable *Seaboard*, which had never been satisfactory for the outside route to Boston, was quite adequate as a relief steamer on this run, as was the *City of Key West* for the Providence route. In addition to its four steamers and two spares, the Joy Line even had a back-up steamer in the *Rosalie*, which also stood by for use in case of emergency.

When the *Aransas* first arrived on the line, she took over the *Seaboard's* schedule, but on the same day that the *Aransas* made her maiden sailing for the line out of Boston, the *Seaboard* also sailed from Boston to New York, under Captain Richard Holmes, on the first of several special sailings taking Clyde Line freight to New York.[2] On Christmas Eve of 1903, the Clyde Line steamer *Kiowa*, bound into Boston in a blinding snowstorm, had just dropped anchor off Boston light in an effort to get her bearings when she was struck amidships by the United Fruit Line steamer *Admiral Dewey* (a sistership of the *Admiral Farragut* which had sunk the *Cumberland* the year before) and sank immediately. The crew was taken off safely and most of the freight was later salvaged, but the steamer was abandoned. By January, with the Clyde Line short of steamers and both the New Haven trains and the Metropolitan freighters running irregularly because of the weather, Clyde Line freight had begun to pile up in Boston. So the Joy Line arranged to let them use the *Seaboard* as soon as the *Aransas* arrived to replace her.

When this special job had been accomplished, the *Seaboard* was back on her regular run, with the *Rosalie* making frequent extra trips to Boston to assist her, while the *Old Dominion* went to the Morgan Iron Works at the end of Ninth Street for new boilers. The old paddler thus missed the worst of the tough winter, for she did not get back on the line until late in March.

Once on the line, the *Aransas* proved almost as serviceable as the *Old Dominion* in some ways. She was of unusually light draft for an ocean-type vessel, since many of the gulf ports she had been designed to serve had exceptionally shallow harbors. Thus, she was not nearly as good a sea boat as the *Old Dominion* and less likely, therefore, to take the outside route when the ice was thick in the sound. On the other hand, she was somewhat more powerful and could push her own way through the currents at Hell Gate without the aid of tugs, thus making her operation considerably cheaper than her running mate's. The *Aransas* might have made the run in somewhat better time than the twenty-four hours scheduled for the *Old Dominion*, but the Joy Line did not change its schedules for the *Aransas*, partly because, as was also the case on the Providence route, it was more convenient to keep both boats on the same schedule, and this, by necessity, had to be the schedule of the slower one. In addition, the agreement with the New Haven had specifically stated that, in return for allowing the Joy Line lower freight rates than charged on the New Haven's New York to Boston trains or for Boston freight via the railroad's steamer lines, the Joy Line must not attempt to run steamers direct to Boston in less than twenty-four hours.[3]

During 1904, the *Larchmont* developed a penchant for going ashore in Narragansett Bay. While coming out of New York on the night of Saturday, January 23, the ice so slowed her progress that it was nearly 6:00 on Sunday morning before she passed Point Judith. Encountering fog as well as ice at the approach to the bay, and perhaps remembering Kirby's experience with the *Seabord* just a year, almost to the day, before, Wilcox decided to run up the longer but safer east passage, even though he was running late. Moving very slowly, the *Larchmont* passed Newport at about seven and continued pushing through the grey mist. At about seven-thirty, however, the *Larchmont* suddenly halted with a slight jar. She had gone ashore at the northeastern tip of Prudence Island, which, fortunately, unlike Dutch Island on the other side, was bordered by sand rather than rocks. Given the hour of the day and the fact that they couldn't see anything, the passengers were unperturbed. They thought they had arrived in Providence and prepared to disembark. Meanwhile, the *Larchmont*'s wheels reversed furiously but failed to pull the steamer free. Eventually the tug *Solicitor*, taking the Sunday papers from Providence down to Newport, heard the steamer's whistles, and, with the assistance of the tug *Roger Williams*, which also came along, helped the *Larchmont* slide off unharmed at high tide just about noon. The *Larchmont* sailed unconcernedly into Providence at about two in the afternoon, by which time the fog had lifted; after all, she didn't have to sail that night anyway.

One week later, the last day of January, New England was struck by another blizzard, this one even more furious than the one at the first of the year. This time Block Island reported winds up to eighty miles an hour. As it was a Sunday night, most of the steamers were not scheduled to sail. But the *Aransas* (having left New York late Saturday night) was caught in the storm eastbound and arrived in Boston Monday morning leaking badly, the ice floes in the heaving seas having ripped open her plates in several places. With the *Old Dominion* already out of service for repairs and now the line's recently acquired iron-hulled *Aransas* off the route for several days, already worn down by the elements, the reliable old wooden-hulled *Rosalie* went on the Boston run again with the *Seaboard*, both running regularly through Nantucket Sound and around Cape Cod through some of the roughest weather in New England's history.

On the morning of Sunday, February 7, just two weeks after her first grounding and the day when the whole downtown area of Baltimore was destroyed by fire, the second major conflagration of that year to shock the country, the *Larchmont* again ran aground in Narragansett Bay. The day before she had spent in drydock in New York having extra copper sheathing placed on her hull against the ice she had been encountering on almost every trip for the past month, and that night she did not get away from her pier before 10:00. Coming up the west passage by daylight on Sunday morning, Wilcox again ran into thick fog, and at Warwick Neck, where the steamers had to execute a sharp starboard turn at the narrowest part of the passage, she struck sand once again. This time Wilcox was lucky, however, for she floated off a few hours later with the rising tide and proceeded on to Providence.

That same Sunday morning found Captain Olweiler guiding the *Tremont* cautiously down the East River after an unusually difficult night navigating through the sound in the dense fog. On this trip the *Tremont* was carrying a unique cargo. A man who made his living with a circus act involving two trained lions wanted to take his act from New England to New York and had inquired in several places to find the safest and cheapest way of transporting his lions. Needless to say he did not find all cargo carriers enthusiastically seeking the assignment. The Joy Line, however, made a specialty of soliciting cargo that required special handling and persuaded the man that the line would get his lions to New York safely.

By 8:00 A.M. the *Tremont* was backing into her pier near the Manhattan Bridge. As a rule, when the steamers arrived in New York on Sundays, only perishable freight was removed that morning, while most of the bulk freight simply remained on board until the regular dock crew arrived to unload it on Monday morning, since the steamers did not sail on Sunday nights. On this occasion, arrangements had been made for the two lions to be removed from the freight deck sometime Sunday morning.

For some reason, however, no one arrived to remove the lions. So on Sunday night, the lions were still tethered to their posts on the *Tremont's* freight deck. Shortly before dawn on Monday morning, a fire broke out in the *Tremont's* galley, where the cook was preparing a small breakfast for the skeleton crew that had remained on board. With only a few of the crew aboard at the time and many of them still asleep, the fire was soon out of control, and within minutes the entire superstructure was in flames. Of the forty-three people still aboard at the time, all got off the steamer safely, thanks largely to the efforts of First Pilot George McVay, who risked his life to run through the already burning steamer knocking on every door. But one member of the crew, a fireman, was trapped below decks and lost his life. The entire cargo was lost, including, lamentably, the two lions. Newspapers covering the story carried reports of firemen threatened on the burning decks by huge snarling beasts. In actual fact, the lions perished early in the conflagration, probably from the smoke, or they would have been led off, and the firemen never even knew they were there.

Once it became apparent that the reliable old *Tremont* was doomed, the two New York fire boats that arrived on the scene began pouring tons of water into the burning steamer. When the line's owners appeared at the pier at about eight o'clock, all that was left of the *Tremont*, now not much more than a mass of charred and smoking timbers, was sitting at the bottom of the water by her pier. The following day the Chapman and Scott Wrecking Company, using two large cranes, partially raised the burned-out hull and dragged it over to Shewman's Docks* in Brooklyn. Two weeks later, on February 22, once it had been positively determined that the *Tremont* was unsalvageable, Chapman and Scott's cranes appeared again to pull the remains of the Joy Line's first passenger steamer over to Gregory's graveyard in Perth Amboy, New Jersey.

Between the fire in Baltimore the day before and the Japanese bombardment of Port Arthur (signaling the opening of the Russo-Japanese War) on January 8, the same day as the burning of the *Tremont*, the Joy Line escaped some of the adverse publicity it might have had to face had the papers been less sated with more sensational news that week.

For once the Joy Line used some judgment and apparently realized that Long Island Sound in this weather was no place for the *City of Key West*. So, although she was laid up only a few miles away at Morse's in Brooklyn, Dimon quickly arranged to charter the *Surprise* which was faster and had a hull far better adapted to icy winter seas. The *Tremont's* crew was sent on to Boston by train, and, on Tuesday, February 9, the day after the *Tremont* burned, Captain Coleman brought the *Surprise* around from Boston to Providence where he turned her over to Captain Olweiler. That night she took *Tremont's* run out of Providence. The line had missed only one trip.

The weather continued to batter the sound steamers throughout February. The following Tuesday, February 16, Captain Olweiler, arriving late in Providence with the *Surprise*, explained that he had encountered unusual

*Morse's yards, which generally took care of the many problems of the Joy Line boats, had been temporarily forced out of business in late 1903. The line's spare steamer, the *City of Key West*, was allowed to board at Morse's docks until the yards reopened later in 1904.

difficulty plowing through the ice coming up Narragansett Bay.[4] That Saturday found the *Rosalie* anchored in Vineyard Sound sitting out a gale. Captains of ocean steamers arriving in New York and Boston reported harrowing voyages; more than one claimed to have had the worst crossing of their careers. The *City of Taunton* became damaged in the ice and was briefly replaced on the Fall River run by the *City of Fall River* and the latter on the Providence Line by the *Pequot*. Thus, for a few weeks in February the original Providence Line freighters, *Pequot* and *Nashua*, again made up the line.

Dimon lost no time finding a permanent replacement for the *Tremont*. For once the Joy Line was in a strong enough position to bid for a boat it actually wanted instead of limping along with an unsatisfactory charter until some old tub turned up at a bargain price. The Joy Line knew exactly the boat it wanted. The *Larchmont* had proved ideal for the service; she was not speedy, but, unlike the *Tremont*, she was fast enough for the run, she was solidly built, and she held up in any weather. She had even survived having Captain Wilcox ram her hull onto the shores of Narragansett Bay at fairly regular intervals. Her engine was simple but very dependable. The *Larchmont* had a near-sistership, the *State of Maine*, which, while slightly older and somewhat shorter than the *Larchmont*, had an almost identical layout and therefore about the same capacity. What's more, those who handled her rated her performance higher than the *Larchmont's*. This was obviously the steamer the Joy Line wanted.

The only hitch was that the *State of Maine* was not then for sale. The replacement of the *Cumberland* with the *Penobscot* and the arrival of the new *Calvin Austin* in 1903 had given the line an extra steamer. But by February 1904, Eastern had started negotiations to sell the *St. Croix* to parties on the West Coast, which meant that it would need both the *Penobscot* and the *State of Maine* to run with the *Calvin Austin* on the International Line that season.

Apparently, Dimon found Morse and Austin in an unusually negotiable frame of mind, for Austin immediately canceled plans for selling the *St. Croix* and agreed to sell the *State of Maine* to the Joy Line. Just a few years earlier, when Morse was starting to build his steamship empire, the Eastern had refused even to charter the *Penobscot* to the Joy Line. But at that time Morse, and more particularly Austin, had been anxious to remain on friendly terms with both the New Haven Railroad and the Metropolitan Line. Now the New Haven made no objections, and Morse no longer saw any advantage in deferring to the Metropolitan. For once the Joy Line was in a position to make a decent offer for a steamer it actually wanted, an offer apparently attractive enough to persuade the Eastern to change its plans.

The more immediate problem was that the *State of Maine* was then in service on the Boston to Portland line. As usual, the line's new steel-hulled *Governor Dingley* was laid up for the winter, while the line was served on alternate nights by the older wooden sidewheeler *Bay State* running alone. But on Wednesday evening, January 20, a defect had been discovered in the *Bay State's* shaft just as she was about to sail for Boston. Her trip that night was canceled, and the next day the *State of Maine* came over to take her place and was still running on the line when Dimon came up asking to buy her. As a measure of willingness to do business, Austin had the big *Governor Dingley* brought out of her winter layup almost immediately so he could turn the *State of Maine* over to the Joy Line. Times had certainly changed.

By March 11, the *State of Maine* was in New York fitting out for her new service, and a few days later, with her name now changed to *Edgemont*,* she was ready to make her first trip to Providence. Now, with the *Larchmont* and the *Edgemont*, which were to run together between New York and Providence for the next three years, the Joy Line had two genuinely well-matched vessels. While they differed in some minor respects, they were very similar and could be operated as sisterships. In addition, for the first time since the arrival of the *Tremont* three years before, the Joy Line had two steamers that could make the run between New York and Providence, under normal conditions, in twelve hours. The Providence Line steamer could make the trip easily in ten hours and often did when departures were held up, though the normal schedules called for a run of between eleven and eleven and a half hours. The *Tremont*, on the other hand, had taken fourteen hours for the trip, and the *City of Key West* was not much faster. But the *Larchmont* and the *Edgemont* could paddle along at about thirteen or fourteen knots. This was not spectacular, but enough to maintain a reasonable schedule, although the Joy Line does not seem to have advanced its departure times until several months later.

Soon after the Joy Line returned the *Surprise* to the Enterprise Line in April 1904, the Whitcombs decided to give up their line on the coast of Maine. It had simply not proved profitable. During the spring, the Whitcombs negotiated with a company that wanted to charter the *Surprise* for a run between Lewes, Delaware, and New York, bringing fruit and other produce from the Delaware peninsula to the New York market.[5] At the last minute the venture failed to materialize, and the *Surprise* spent a full year laid up at her dock in Boston, by which time, as we shall see, the Whitcombs themselves had new plans for their aging steamer.

---

*The *Edgemont* does not seem to have been named for any place in particular. It was a name chosen arbitrarily to match that of the *Larchmont*, her running mate.

Early in March, the weather at last began to break and the ice in the sound to disappear. It had been an unusually hard winter, but now the Northeast was rewarded with an early and pleasant spring. The weather remained balmy through most of March and April, and overnight trips through the sound were again a pleasure, the officers relaxed, and the steamers alive with passengers.

During March, the Fall River Line installed the new Marconi wireless invention aboard its steamer *Plymouth* as an experiment. The experiment was considered an unqualified success, and the railroad soon announced that it would install the invention on all of the steamers of the Fall River and Providence lines and set up a series of receiving stations along the route as well.[6] The Joy Line was still thinking in terms of operating its steamers as economically as possible and therefore did not consider such modern devices as necessities.

With the ice breaking up on the sound and, more particularly, on the Hudson, and spring weather coming somewhat earlier than usual, the various steamers that operated only during the warmer season began to come out of hibernation. On the Hudson the Troy Line started first, chartering the steamer *Onteora* from the Catskill Evening Line for several trips before bringing on its own *Saratoga* and *City of Troy* later in April. The Albany night line started the season with the *Adirondack* and the old *Dean Richmond*, but some weeks later the *Dean Richmond* was replaced by the new *C. W. Morse*. Generally, the summer schedule of the Bridgeport Line also began early in April. Between 1904 and 1907, the *City of Lawrence*, no longer needed as a winter boat to New Haven now that the *New Hampshire* was running on that line with the *Richard Peck*, took over the Bridgeport route from the *Allan Joy* for several weeks in the early spring, as she was a good freight carrier, and, with the freight for Bridgeport increasing rapidly, the *Allan Joy*, running alone, did not have the capacity to take care of it. Once the *William G. Payne*, a day boat with a large cargo space on her Main Deck, came on in April, however, the *Allan Joy* was back on the night route and the *City of Lawrence* returned to her layup in Stonington.

That spring the Bridgeport Line sold its older steamer *Rosedale* to Captain Anning J. Smith of Bridgeport, who planned to use her as an excursion steamer in New York harbor that year. By April, most of the other New York excursion boats were in the yards for paint and fitting out, getting ready for the usual series of preseason charters to clubs, schools, or churches that preceded their regular summer season. On April 21, one journal carried the cheerful announcement that the *General Slocum* was then fitting out and looking forward to a particularly successful season.[7]

Also by April, the *Old Dominion* at last had her new boilers and was ready to return to the route. Since this was the first time the two larger steamers were together on the Boston run, the Joy Line now worked out an entirely different schedule. Instead of two boats each making two round trips a week, the line was able to step up its sailings so that one of its two steamers left each port every other day. The trip still took about twenty-four hours, and the steamers laid over at each port for about twenty four hours; thus, each round trip occupied two full days. This way no two steamers needed to be in the same port at the same time, an important consideration since the Joy Line's space at both ends was limited. In New York the line leased only the north side of Pier 35, East River, for both the Providence and Boston boats, while in Boston it rented only enough space at the Atlas docks to accommodate one steamer. Thus, if the *Old Dominion* sailed from either port on a Monday night, the *Aransas* would arrive at that port on Tuesday night, lay over twenty-four hours, and sail again on Wednesday night. Then Thursday evening the *Old Dominion* would arrive again and so forth. The steamers sailed from both ports at 5:00 P.M. Dawn would thus find the Boston-bound Joy steamer somewhere off Point Judith headed toward Nantucket Sound. The rest of the trip around Cape Cod and into Boston would be made by daylight. Returning, the *Old Dominion* or the *Aransas* would sail around Cape Cod and through Nantucket Sound during the night, passing through the Race in the early morning, and travel down the sound by daylight arriving in New York at about 5:00 P.M., about the time that the Providence boat was getting ready to sail.

On Sunday, May 7, just as the Joy Line was beginning to enjoy the luxury of having two good steamers on each of its runs, the *Edgemont* had an engine breakdown when off Eaton's Neck at about 4:00 A.M. In a way, it was her turn. Most of the other Joy Line steamers had broken down on their first or second trip; the *Edgemont* had merely waited a few weeks. Soon after her wheels stopped turning, however, the Providence Line freighter *Nashua*, which had been following her down the sound, came up and towed her all the way into New York. The *Edgemont*'s problems, as it turned out, were fairly serious, and she had to be off the run for over two months having her engines repaired. Once again the Joy Line was caught short of steamers at the outset of the season and had to manage with the much smaller *City of Key West* until the *Edgemont* returned in mid-July.

In the spring of 1904, Charles S. Mellen, the new president of the New Haven Railroad, decided it was time to reorganize the corporate structure of the railroad's marine holdings. The year 1904 was an election year, and the Republican incumbent, Theodore Roosevelt, who had succeeded the assassinated McKinley, now planned to stand for the office on his own. Picking up on the exposes of exploitation and financial mismanagement on the part of America's large corporations then very popular in the press, Roosevelt based his campaign partly on an active program of preventing big business from becoming bigger, to which he gave the typically vigorous-sounding name of "trust-busting." Looking at the jerry-built relationships that then existed betweeen the railroad and its steamer lines, Mellen concluded that, in the event of federal investigations such as Roosevelt was promising, the New Haven might be in an embarrassingly vulnerable position. As things then stood, the steamer lines were not subsidiaries of the railroad; the New Haven did not even own them. Each of the steamship companies was still, in theory, an independent corporate entity in which the New Haven Railroad happened to own a majority of stock and whose boards of directors included so many of the directors of the railroad that at some of their meetings these men probably had difficulty remembering which company they were sitting for. As a first step toward reorganization, Mellen persuaded his friend, Stevenson Taylor, then a vice-president and senior engineer with the W. and A. Fletcher Works in Hoboken, to resign his post and accept a position with the New Haven.[8] Taylor's first assignment was to make a careful appraisal of all of the properties, both the steamers themselves and the wharves, owned by the various steamer lines under the railroad's control. Once these appraisals had been made, it was Mellen's plan that the railroad should "buy" each of these companies outright and create one large company, which would be independent legally but also a subsidiary owned by the railroad, to operate all of the steamer lines.[9] This plan was not completed until later in the year.

Another part of the railroad's reorganization of its steamer properties in the spring of 1904 was the decision to discontinue the Stonington Line altogether as soon as the corporate reorganization gave the railroad the clear right to do so.[10] An examination of the railroad's steamer operations had indicated to Mellen that the system then in use for shipping freight was inefficient. The various steamer routes had, after all, been created to meet the needs of an earlier era, and not all of them were now geared to the changing demands of the times. The Stonington Line had been founded originally so that Boston-bound passengers would not have to face the dangers of rounding Point Judith in a small wooden steamboat. But with the large iron and steel passenger vessels now running to Fall River and Providence, few passengers were so concerned about the perils of Point Judith, which most of them slept through, that they were willing to be awakened at 2:00 A.M. at Stonington.

Also by 1904 the Stonington Line was carrying relatively little freight, whereas the New London Line had more freight than it could manage. The only railroad feeder line into Stonington was one which ran from Providence to New York via New London. Thus, whatever freight did travel via the Stonington route could as easily be unloaded in Providence or continue on to New London. On the other hand, the feeder roads for the New London Line, whose terminus was only a few miles away, originated in the rapidly growing industrial areas in southern New Hampshire and along the Merrimac River. This area could also be served, however, by another railroad which branched off at Fitchburg and ran southeast to New Bedford. Thus, in 1904 the railroad reasoned that a more efficient operation could be effected by discontinuing the Stonington Line and rerouting its freight via either the Providence Line or the New London Line. Meanwhile, the railroad could relieve the added pressure on the New London boats by significantly increasing its freight service to New Bedford, which at that time was served only by the aging *Pequot* running alone on alternate nights, as the *City of New Bedford* had been retired about a year before and had not been replaced.[11]

At the time, the New Haven was expecting the delivery of the large, new propellor freighter *Boston* for its Fall River freight service. The plan then was for the *Boston* to run to Fall River with the *City of Taunton*, the newest and largest of the older sidewheel freighters, while the line's other two sidewheel freighters, the *City of Brockton* and the *City of Fall River*, would now run to New Bedford. The *City of Fall River* had, of course, been running winters to Providence with the *Nashua*. But the new plan called for retiring the *Nashua* and running the *Maine* and the *New Hampshire* as freight boats to Providence in the winter, with the *Pequot* assisting occasionally so that one of them could also serve as a relief steamer on the New London Line. In the summer, the *New Hampshire* would run to New Haven and the *Maine* would stand by as a spare.[12]

The last trip of the Stonington Line was scheduled for May 28, 1904, and the new daily freight service to New Bedford was scheduled to start the following day. A few days earlier Vice-President Todd wrote to J. W. Miller, the manager of the railroad's marine district, pleading with him to place two bona fide freighters on the new service to New Bedford and not to use either the *Maine* or the *New Hampshire* for this route. The people of New Bedford, he argued, had been clamoring for years for the railroad to reinstitute passenger service between their city and New York, which the railroad was reluctant to do as such a line would take too much business from its Fall River Line. If the railroad were now to place either the *Maine* or the *New Hampshire* on the New Bedford run, it would have a hard time explaining why the steamer could not be equipped to carry passengers.[13] Miller responded that at that time he did not have enough freight steamers available to run two of them to New Bedford. The new *Boston* had not yet arrived from the builders. The *City of Fall River* and the *City of Brockton* were running to Fall River; the *Pequot* and the *City of Lawrence* were both too small for the proposed increased traffic from New Bedford; and the *Nashua* was in bad shape and needed an immediate overhaul. This meant that the *City of Taunton* was the only freight steamer he could place in the new service until the *Boston* arrived. Meanwhile, he would therefore have to use the *Maine* (the *New Hampshire* ran on the New Haven Line with the *Richard Peck* again that summer), and Todd would have to explain the situation to the people of New Bedford as well as he could.[14]

One week later, on June 6, the Providence Line began its summer season, so that the Joy Line no longer had the Providence passenger business to itself. As in 1904, the agreement between the Joy Line and the railroad stipulated that the one-way fare on the Providence Line would be $3.00 and that the Joy Line fare would now have to go up from $1.50 to $2.00, so that the big railroad steamers could have a chance of claiming a fair share of the traffic.

In 1904, for the first time since 1900, the railroad placed the *Pilgrim* on the Providence Line with the *Plymouth*. In spite of the efforts of all the king's men and W. and A. Fletcher, the *Connecticut*'s engines were still giving trouble, whereas the *Pilgrim*, after two major overhauls, was now in fairly good operating condition. In addition, while passenger traffic was not expected to increase appreciably, the rerouting of freight, now that the Stonington Line had been discontinued, put a far larger burden on the Providence Line than the *Connecticut* could carry. In fact, during the summer of 1904, the freight agents of the New Haven's marine district complained that the *Plymouth* and, more particularly, the *Pilgrim* (which, while larger, had less cargo space than her running mate) were unable to carry all of the Providence Line freight. Much of the freight had to be sent on to Fall River, where the company ran a large freight steamer every night in addition to the largest freight-carrying passenger steamers on the sound.[15]

The 1904 summer excursion season began with the worst tragedy in the history of American steamboats. On June 15, the excursion steamer *General Slocum*, chartered for the day to a German church on the Lower East Side for a Sunday School picnic, caught fire when approaching Hell Gate, and, before her captain could bring her to shore at North Brother Island, the whole steamer was a mass of flames. Well over a thousand bodies were recovered that day, either from the water or from the smoking ruins of the steamer. Most were small children.

It was fortunate for the Joy Line that the *Tremont* fire took place before rather than after the burning of the *General Slocum*. At the time, the fire on the *Tremont*, occurring as it did at the pier and with the loss of only one human life, attracted relatively little public attention. But following the hideous tragedy of the *General Slocum* fire, the public, understandably, became acutely attuned to the potential danger of a large wooden steamer's burning at sea. (In this connection it is fair to note that in the entire history of navigation on Long Island Sound, no overnight passenger steamer, except the *Lexington* in 1840 and the *Nutmeg State* in 1899, was ever destroyed by fire while underway.)

The summer of 1904, like the summer before, was a particularly warm one, and, in spite of the terrible *General Slocum* tragedy, the excursion business flourished. That year the *Chester W. Chapin* took over the *City of Worcester*'s circuitous Sunday trips to Greenport and Newport. Her running mate, the *City of Lowell*, continued her Sunday excursions up the Hudson, out of New York, and the *Richard Peck* hers to New Haven and back.

Shortly before the 1904 summer excursion season was to start, John Rowland of the Joy Line asked for another conference with the railroad authorities. This time he was granted an appointment not with Percy Todd, his old friend of Cincinnati days, but with George Conner, the railroad's traffic manager. Hat in hand, Rowland once again asked if the Joy Line might run its summer excursions to Cottage City. Much to Rowland's surprise, Conner, after a great deal of pompous talk, finally conceded that it could—with but one minor stipulation: If, during that summer, the Providence Line were to decide to run an excursion from Providence to Cottage City, the Joy Line would not run the *Larchmont* that day. There was very little chance, in any event, that this would happen. The Providence Line did plan a few excursions later in the summer to other places, but at the moment had no plans to run to Cottage City and did not, in any event, plan any excursions on Sundays inasmuch as its steamers sailed on Sunday evenings. In short, the answer was yes. So, through the summer of 1904, the *Larchmont* sailed every Sunday to Cottage City with the usual two-hour stopover. There were no more all-day sails to Montauk and back or trips to look at Indians. Considering how grandly magnanimous the railroad must have felt to have granted the Joy Line the right to run excursions to Cottage City after having so categorically refused it the previous fall, Percy Todd was astounded on returning from a short holiday early in August to find what to him must have seemed a naively tactless and ungrateful letter from Frank Dunbaugh. Dunbaugh asked that the Providence Line cancel all plans for excursions out of Providence in August!

> I understand that your company plans to make several excursions with your boats from Providence during the month of August. If this is the case, considering the comparatively few people who go on excursions, we might just as well forego the idea of running excursions with our boats against your floating palatial palaces. We feel that you have the cities of Bridgeport, New Haven, New London, Fall River, and New Bedford, from which to run excursions, whereas we have only Providence. If you also run excursions from Providence, it seems to us we might just as well not try to run excursions from that city, thus cutting us entirely out of this source of revenue.
>
> If you view this matter as we do, will you not consider it, and arrange to call off any excursions which you may have in contemplation from Providence during the summer months?[16]

One begins to understand why the Joy Line tended to send the diplomatic John Rowland on its missions to the offices of the railroad rather than its feisty president.

Once Todd had recovered from the shock of Dunbaugh's ingratitude, his reply to the letter, while bristling with indignation, was nevertheless reasonably controlled, under the circumstances.

We have advertised excursions from Providence to New London and another one around Block Island, and have not so far advertised any to Cottage City, and possibly will not this summer, feeling that we were doing a very generous act in connection with this matter, thinking we could get our excursion earnings by running to some other point of interest and for this summer if possible not running any excursions to Cottage City and thereby not having to ask Mr. Rowland to keep his agreement to withdraw from the Cottage City excursion business.

In view of our having taken what we supposed was a very broad view of this matter I was quite a little surprised at your asking us to withdraw entirely from Sunday excursions out of Providence, which I assure you we are not willing to do.[17]

On Wednesday, July 27, with the summer now nearly half over, the *Edgemont* finally returned from the shops and took her place on the line. Just the day before an accident to one of Morse's Boston to Bangor boats left the Eastern so short of steamers in midseason that Austin must have had serious second thoughts about having so willingly sold the *Edgemont* to the Joy Line. On the morning of July 26, the still new *City of Rockland*, heading into Penobscot Bay in a fog, struck a ledge and sank up to her Saloon Deck. At first, there was some question whether she could be salvaged. Eventually she was raised and repaired, but she was off the line for the rest of the summer. Meanwhile, the *Ransom B. Fuller* from the Kennebec Line, which was very similar to the *City of Rockland*, went on the Bangor Line with the *City of Bangor* for the rest of that season, and the *Penobscot* had to be taken off the International Line—where she had the *Edgemont's* old run—to fill in on the Kennebec Line. Since Morse now controlled many different lines, he was able to borrow a ship from the Mallory Line that summer, which, as an ocean-type steamer, was structurally better suited to the run than the old wooden-hulled *Penobscot*, though she lacked the sidewheeler's passenger capacity.

Once the *Edgemont* was back in service at the end of July 1904, the times of the Joy Line's daily cliffhangers were pretty well over. The line's two near-sisterships were to run back and forth between New York and Providence, without any major incidents, for another two and a half years, coming off the route only for their annual overhauls. In studying the history of steamboats, one tends to give attention to newspaper accounts of them when they are in trouble, so that one often ends up with the impression that life aboard an overnight steamboat was one of harrowing nights in raging seas or midnight crashes in the fog. There were many such incidents, of course, but for the most part, a trip between New York and Providence aboard the *Larchmont* or the *Edgemont* was a quiet, routine, and often serenely beautiful experience.

During the day, as the steamer sat silently at her pier in lower Manhattan, the interior of the ship, during the morning at least, was the scene of frenetic activity. Sheets and other debris from the night before came flying out of stateroom doors to be placed in piles along the corridors, while the stewards made up each room with clean linen, dusted woodwork, polished brass, and ran sweepers over the miles of carpeting. (There were no electric vacuum cleaners as yet.) When the passengers arrived on board several hours later, the steamer was as neat and sparkling clean each night as she had been when she was built. Below decks the stevedores loaded all of the freight, piece by piece, onto small carts by hand, and wheeled it noisily down the wide freight gangplanks (which were often at steep angles if the tide were high) onto the pier. Later the job was reversed, and the freight which had been delivered to the pier earlier on large horse-drawn wagons was carried back up the gangplank to the freight deck.

At the same time, the enormous amounts of food, alcoholic beverages, and other provisions—as well as hundreds of large blocks of ice to store it in—necessary for the overnight voyage of over two hundred passengers and crewmembers also moved up the freight gangway to be stowed in the room-sized ice box in the hold. (Both the *Larchmont* and the *Edgemont* had their galleys in the hold forward and sent the prepared meals up to the Saloon Deck dining areas via dumbwaiters operated manually with ropes.)

Although the loading of freight often continued right up to sailing time, the work in the passenger quarters was usually completed during the morning, so that the stewards could have a few hours of off-duty time. During the afternoon, the interior of the steamer took on an almost eerie stillness.

By about four in the afternoon, the passengers began to arrive, usually by trolley, for by then the New York subway system was still under construction. Since there were no special walkways on the Joy Line's rather simply constructed pier, the passengers, following the stewards (who doubled as porters before sailing) who met them at the street, made their way as well as they could among the horses and wagons still moving on and off their pier with freight. Crossing the gangplank onto the steamer, the passenger left the noisy bustle of the pier and entered a world of quiet Victorian elegance—albeit a rather subdued elegance on these small Maine coast steamers which lacked the elaborate decor of the Fall River liners—as soon as they stepped onto the Quarter Deck, the area at the stern end of the Main Deck (freight deck) which served as an entrance foyer for passengers. Here, behind a caged window, stood the purser, from whom the passenger secured a key to a stateroom (for a small extra payment, about a dollar), after which the waiting porter led the passenger (or, not unusually, a family) up the brass-plated staircase to the Saloon Deck and along the carpeted corridors, stopping finally before a door which he opened with the big brass key. Within, the staterooms on the Joy Line steamers were simple to the point of austerity, containing an upper and lower berth (the lower being a few inches wider), a wash stand with a pitcher of fresh water, a towel rack, and one small stool. But the stateroom, after all, was only a place to sleep, and that for just one night.

After unpacking and perhaps washing up a bit after traveling through the less savory sections of Manhattan to reach the pier, the passengers were usually anxious to forsake the questionable comforts of the stateroom to see what was happening outside. Standing on the upper deck of the steamer, passengers could watch while the final loads of freight were trundled aboard before dockworkers hauled the freight gangplank onto the pier with a loud crash. While officers began shouting orders both to crewmen and to dockworkers preparatory to departure, the poor unsuspecting passengers would be shocked nearly to stupefaction when the steamer's whistle suddenly sent up three long blasts announcing that it was then five minutes to sailing time. During these last five minutes, one of the stewards was dispatched to walk around the steamer ringing a gong and shouting "All ashore that's going ashore."

At 5:30 the whistle blew again, this time one long blast as a warning to other vessels in the area that the steamer was moving out into the river. Slowly at first, so slowly that one was never sure just when it started, the steamer pulled away from the dock and out into the stream. The East River, into which the Joy Line steamers had to emerge, is not in fact a river. It is a strait through which rush the tides between two large bodies of water. The current sometimes moves at several miles per hour so that it is often difficult, if not actually treacherous, for a small steamer to pull into it. It was to avoid the dangers of the East River that most of the other steamer lines chose to place their piers on the slower moving North River, in spite of the longer route entailed. But the Joy Line, as usual, cut corners by docking at a cheaper pier on the East River, in spite of the dangers involved. Often before the Joy Line boat could gain headway, she would drift backward downstream several hundred feet before getting up enough power to overcome the current and get on course. With the steamer thus virtually out of control for the first few minutes, she was in serious danger if another vessel should appear in this usually crowded channel. Thus, the Joy Line captains had to exercise special caution when pulling out of their pier to be sure no other ships were approaching.

Once underway, however, the passengers found that they had left the noise and heat of the city behind them for the new and serene world of the steamer. Once past the shipyards, factories, and breweries that lined the East River as far as the upper sixties, the steamer began to pass the several large estates along the river on both sides, in the eighties on the Manhattan side and elegant Astoria on the Long Island side, just before taking a sharp turn to starboard and entering the tortuous passages of the upper river known appropriately as Hell Gate. Here the steamer slowed almost to a stop while the pilot studied the currents and tides to ascertain the best approach to the narrow and eddying channel; the steamer gained speed again in order to have sufficient power to buck the rushing waters.

Emerging successfully from Hell Gate, the steamer passed by the estates and colonies of summer cottages along the shores of the Bronx and Whitestone for a few miles and then slowed again for a ninety-degree turn to port at Throgs Neck to leave the East River and enter Long Island Sound. As a rule, here at the narrower west end of the sound, the waters were calm, and passengers could enjoy sitting on the deck at sunset as the steamer passed by City Island to port and, soon after, the lighthouse that guarded Execution Rocks in the center of the sound between New Rochelle and Great Neck. About this time the much larger steamer of the Fall River Line appeared astern, ablaze with lights, gradually overtaking the slower Joy Line steamer, which was left to roll ignominiously in her wake as she paddled past and then gradually disappeared ahead.

By this time, the sky would be getting dark, and the big Fall River liner would eventually appear as nothing more than a few dots of lights on the horizon. Astern would be other lights, for most of the other sound steamers left New York at six, a half hour later than the Joy Line boats, but by Glen Cove or Huntington they would be coming up behind and most of them would probably pass ahead during the course of the night. The exception was the *Old Dominion*, which two nights a week left New York ahead of the *Larchmont* or the *Edgemont* but which was the one steamer they would overtake in the course of the night, always blowing a toot of greeting as they did.

Sitting on the deck in the darkness, one would wonder as the steamer passed various groups of lights along the shore just what cities they were: Greenwich, Stamford, Norwalk, Bridgeport. At least once or twice an hour the steamer would overtake a large schooner carrying, as a rule, lumber or coal, sailing along silently in the night with almost no lights showing except the red and green running lights and a muted lantern (few were then equipped with electric dynamos) shining in the cabin. By the time the steamer passed Stratford Shoals at about 10:00 P.M., most of the passengers were beginning to retire to their cabins.

Most would be asleep when the steamer passed its sistership going the other direction off New London at about two in the morning, or when she moved through the Race shortly afterward and out of Long Island Sound into the open water. Here, on stormy nights the seas could be treacherous, but as a rule the larger waves in Block Island Sound did little more than make the steamer rise and fall a little more seductively. By the time the steamer rounded Point Judith about an hour later and headed past the benign eye of Beaver Tail light into the quieter waters of Narragansett Bay, most of the passengers were still sleeping. The stamers were usually moving up through the west passage of Narragansett Bay past Conanicut and Prudence islands when the skies began to lighten. By dawn, they would be paddling up the Providence River almost to their dock. By this time, the Providence Line steamer (which, if the larger summer passenger steamers were running, would have taken the deeper east passage) was already well ahead and could be seen turning around and backing into Fox Point wharf. At about six, the smaller Joy Line boat moved up the river, reversing her wheels to a stop just abreast of her wharf, and then slowly, very slowly, turning completely around in the middle of the narrow river just below the Fox Point Bridge, so that she could ease into the wharf facing southward, ready for the down trip.

The westbound trip was quite different, partly because Providence was not nearly as busy a port as New York, so that the steamers seemed to pull away from their piers at night with far less fanfare, and also because the steamers left the eastern end somewhat later, by which time freight deliveries had long ceased and the atmosphere on dockside was much more subdued. Sailing into New York the following morning, also at a later hour so that the approach was made in daylight (in summer anyway), the Joy Line steamer was usually only one of a whole parade of sound steamers, for almost all of the nightboats were scheduled to arrive in New York at 7:00 A.M. Thus, as the steamer paddled slowly past Throgs Neck again and into the quiet early morning waters of the upper East River, the early-rising passenger would be treated to an unforgettable sight: strung out ahead or astern would be the *Chester W. Chapin* or the *City of Lowell* steaming down from New London, the big *Plymouth* or *Pilgrim* which would have left Providence an hour or more later than the Joy Line steamer but which would have easily made up the difference during the night, the *City of Brockton* or the *City of Fall River* of the New Bedford Line, the *Richard Peck* coming in from New Haven, and, usually in the lead, the wide-beamed *Priscilla* or *Puritan* of the Fall River Line.

An hour later, the *Larchmont* or *Edgemont* would be tied up at Pier 35, the clattering of carts unloading freight would have begun again, and the passenger, somewhat reluctantly, would have to leave the slightly unreal serenity of the world of the night steamer and pass down the gangplank again to the real world. He would perhaps still be a little befuddled, for one never quite got a full night's sleep aboard a steamer and one could always continue to feel the gentle rise and fall of the deck for several hours even when walking on the concrete solidity of a New York sidewalk.

Late in the summer of 1904, the little steamer *Longfellow*, abandoned to the underwriters by the Clyde Line after her stern had been rammed by the *Herman Winter* and laid up in New York for several months, was purchased by P. M. Cabell of Wilmington, Delaware, who thereupon chartered her to the Dupont Company to carry a load of dynamite from Wilmington to Lake Superior. The old steamer, built as a freight and passenger boat for the Boston-Provincetown route, had shown her mettle by taking winter cruises from Boston to the Bahamas in the 1880s and then making several trips between New York and Puerto Rico when she served as a feeder boat around that island. But the *Longfellow* was beginning to feel her age, and her long layover had obviously weakened her seams. Plying her way northward, the steamer began to leak badly when passing Nantucket Shoals. For the next several hours she tried desperately to reach Provincetown, her old home port, but she never made it. Off Pamet Reef lifesaving station, her crew by then having gotten off safely in lifeboats, the old *Longfellow* slowly filled and went under.

Another change in the allocation of the railroad's steamers resulted indirectly from a minor accident involving the Norwich Line's *City of Lowell* in the fall of 1904. After a foggy night on the sound, the *City of Lowell* was an hour late coming down the East River on the morning of Friday, November 4, when she collided with the ferryboat *Columbia* under the Brooklyn Bridge. When the *City of Lowell* subsequently went for repairs, the *New Hampshire*, now finished with her summer stint on the New Haven Line, was put on the New London run in her place. After she had been on the line for a few weeks, it became apparent to the railroad management that the *New Hampshire*, which was much cheaper to operate than the powerful *City of Lowell*, was more than adequate for the winter traffic on the New London route. She therefore stayed on the line for the rest of the winter, and, in subsequent winters, the *City of Lowell* was generally sent to Newport to lay up, while either the *Maine* or the *New Hampshire* came on the New London route to run with the Chester W. Chapin. By that time also, the new freighter *Boston* (entered service July 1904) had been delivered to the Fall River Line, so that the company could put two of its freighters on the New Bedford Line over the winter, thus releasing the *Maine* for winter relief duty.

The *City of Lowell*'s crash with the *Columbia* is surprising not so much in that it happened as in that it did not happen more often. Night after night, all through the year, a dozen or more steamboats moved up the East River to begin their overnight journeys through the sound to New England. The following morning, soon after dawn, their consorts came down the river from the sound on their way to their New York piers. In those days, the Brooklyn Bridge and the recently completed Williamsburg Bridge were the only bridges across the East River, although two more (the Manhattan and the Queensborough) were under construction. Towns further out on Long Island were only beginning to attract commuters, for the tunnel under the river which now brings the trains of the Long Island Railroad directly into Manhattan had not yet been completed and rail passengers from the island had to get off at Hunt's Point (near the present Queens entrance to the Queens-Midtown Tunnel) and from there take a ferry over to East Thirty-fourth Street. Other than the two bridges, therefore, the only way for commuters to cross the river was by ferryboat, so that both in the evening and in the morning when the night boats were passing through the river, the ferry traffic, all going directly across the steamer lane, was especially heavy. Yet, accidents between the steamers and the New York ferryboats were extraordinarily rare.

Just over a week after the *City of Lowell*'s accident, on Saturday and Sunday, November 12 and 13, New England experienced another wild coastal storm. The *Old Dominion*, sailing out of Boston, encountered such mountainous rollers that she paddled into Provincetown harbor for safety rather than risk her life outside the cape. That same day, Captain Rood on the *Aransas* decided to wait out the storm in Nantucket Sound. But he had a troop of traveling actors aboard whose engagement in Boston opened that evening, and they persuaded him to put in at Woods Hole to let them off so that they could proceed to Boston by train. It was fortunate that the actors had chosen the shallow-draft *Aransas* for their trip, for the *Old Dominion*'s draft would have been too deep to have allowed her to enter the harbor at Woods Hole.

During November, Stevenson Taylor was able to present Charles Mellen with the detailed appraisals of the railroad's various steamship properties that he had been asked to prepare. Thus armed, Mellen called meetings of the various boards of directors of these companies, as well as of the New Haven Railroad itself, to vote to sell each of the companies outright to the railroad at the appraised values. In most cases the board of one company would not have to disband in order for the board of another to assemble, although Mellen was careful to keep the meetings separate so as to insure the strict legality of his moves. Edward Buckland, the only surviving human vestige of the Providence and Stonington Steamship Company, now lost one of his hats, although he remained the Providence counsel for the New Haven Railroad. The ultimate irony was that the meeting of the board which voted to end the corporate existence of the Providence and Stonington

Steamship Company took place aboard a railroad car on the New Haven Railroad.[18]

Now that the New Haven owned each of its steamship properties outright, Mellen assembled them in a single new corporation, owned by but separate from the railroad. Thus, the New England Navigation Company was born on December 10, 1904.[19] At its inception, however, it included only the Providence Line, the Norwich Line, the New Haven Line, the Bridgeport Line, and the New London-Block Island Line. The Old Colony Steamboat Company, which owned both the Fall River Line and the freight line to New Bedford, was not officially voted out of existence and its properties were not brought into the new corporation until July 1905.

The Joy Line's rate agreement with the New Haven was scheduled for its second renewal on October 30. But since the reorganization of the railroad's steamship properties was then in progress and it was therefore not too clear at the time with what legal entity the Joy Line should be renewing the agreement, it was allowed to lapse. However, both parties continued to honor its terms, until the New England Navigation Company came into existence in December and could become the official signatory. Finally, Rowland was able to meet with his more august counterparts early in December and, once a few minor issues had been ironed out, to sign a renewal agreement on December 22.[20] The main innovation in the renewal was that for the year 1905 the Joy Line would again be permitted to drop the New York to Providence winter fares from $1.50, the amount originally agreed upon, to $1.25. As a result, the Joy Line now had three one-way fares in effect for its New York-Providence route. For January, February, and March the fare was now $1.25. For April and May and until the start of the summer season of the Providence Line, and again from October through December, the fare was $1.50. During the period when the Providence Line carried passengers (at $3.00), the Joy Line fare again reverted to $2.00.[21]

The winter of 1904-1905 was again a severe one. Ice began forming in the sound as early as the second week of December, and Captain Burton began taking the Old Dominion to Boston via the outside route fairly regularly to avoid damaging her sidewheels. But Captain Rood's Aransas, whose flat bottom tended to pound badly in a heavy sea, generally held to the sound route whenever possible.

Both the Priscilla and the Puritan were taken off the Fall River Line early that season as the result of mechanical breakdowns. The Priscilla, eastbound on the night of December 10, broke her shaft and had to be towed into New London by the New Hampshire, then running on the New London Line in place of the City of Lowell. Rather than repair the Priscilla's shaft so late in the season, the steamer was simply towed to Newport a few days later for her winter layup and the *Pilgrim* put on in her place. Then, just nine days later, the *Puritan*, also eastbound and at about the same spot (off Watch Hill), broke her rod. This time it was the new Fall River freighter *Boston* which came along to tow her into New London. (As noted in an earlier chapter, Fall River Line steamers seemed always to have the good grace to break down within easy towing distance of New London, where New Haven Railroad trains could be found waiting to take passengers to their destinations.) Soon afterward, the *Puritan* was towed up to Newport to join the *Priscilla* in layup, while the *Plymouth* came on to take her place. Thus, for the first time in many years, both of the winter boats of the Fall River Line were in service before Christmas.

Far more serious that month was the burning of the steamer *Glen Island* of the Starin Line. As mentioned earlier, this steamer had previously been the *City of Richmond* of the Hartford Line, which had burned once before in 1891 but had been rebuilt by Starin as a summer excursion steamer. She had been running frequently, however, in the winter as a relief boat on Starin's New Haven route, which was essentially a freight line but which did occasionally carry a few passengers. The *Glen Island* left New York late Friday evening, December 16. It was a clear night but very cold for that time of year. Shortly after midnight, the steamer was just passing Glen Island off New Rochelle, her regular summer port of call, when a watchman reported that a fire had started in the galley and was already spreading to the freight deck. Captain Charles MacAllister examined the situtation and saw quickly that his steamer was doomed. With the flames spreading rapidly in the cold wind, he ordered his passengers and crew into the lifeboats. Of the thirty-one people aboard the *Glen Island*, only twenty-two made it safely into the lifeboats before being caught in the flames. Seven of the crew and two passengers perished. One of the passengers, an older woman, had made her way safely to the deck and was about to get into a lifeboat when she insisted that she had to return to her stateroom to save some valuables. She was never seen again.[22]

The survivors were in the two lifeboats for nearly an hour before being picked up by the passing tugboat *Bully*. Since the Long Island shore is so close at that point, it is difficult to see why they did not row into shore. In any event, the *Bully* eventually encountered the Starin Line's other boat, the *Erastus Corning*, passing in the opposite direction, and the survivors were transferred to her to be taken back to New York where they arrived early in the morning. The blazing steamer floated on by itself until it sank off the shore of Lattingtown just beyond Glen Cove, Long Island. Her skeletal remains have been reported there recently by local fishermen.

The *Glen Island* was the third New York steamboat lost by fire during the year 1904. The *General Slocum* fire had been by far the most serious, since she was a day steamer carrying well over a thousand passengers and had burned en route. The fire on the *Glen Island*, serving at the time as a freighter and traveling in winter, had been far less costly in human terms. The *Tremont*'s fire, since it took place in dock, was, of course, the least tragic.

At the end of the year 1904, the hulls of the *Tremont* and the *General Slocum* lay side by side next to the partially dismantled *Drew* at Gregory's yards in Perth Amboy.

1905

The winter of 1904 which had set records in New England turned out to be but practice for the winter of 1905. The year began with temperatures dropping well below zero for several days in succession and gale force winds all along the coast. The captain of the *James M. Whitney*, arriving in Boston on January 3, obviously chastened by the elements, reported the worst seas of his career. The Joy Line, beginning to show signs of maturity in its sixth year, kept its steamers in port most of that week and allowed freight to pile up on the piers, and the New England Navigation boats did the same. On January 6, the *Pilgrim*, bound for Fall River, and the *New Hampshire*, then carrying freight to Providence, made one attempt at the run, but both were forced to seek shelter at New London rather than risk venturing outside the Race. On about January 20, the weather began to ease up some, and the steamers were again making regular sailings for about a week. But by January 25, the elements gathered force again for another assault on the sound.

In the darkness of the early morning of January 25, the little freighter *Pequot* (replacing the *Maine* on the Providence Line) churned her way up the west channel into a blinding blizzard. Less than half a mile behind her was the *Larchmont*, though the officers of the two Providence-bound steamers could barely make out the lights of the other through the storm. As he was making his starboard sweep near the end of the channel, Captain Hazard felt the *Pequot* unexpectedly touch ground and come to a stop. As was apparently so easy to do when visibility was poor, he had misjudged the narrow passage by a matter of a few feet and grounded at Warwick Neck, at the very spot where the *Larchmont* had struck just one year and a day before. Steaming up behind, Wilcox understood the *Pequot*'s plight and stopped to throw her a line. But even with the *Larchmont*'s big wheels straining at full throttle, the *Pequot* stayed stuck, so the *Larchmont* proceeded to Providence arriving somewhat later than usual at about 10:00 A.M. Later, after the *Pequot* had slid off by herself on the rising tide and pulled into her pier in Providence, Hazard gratuitously informed reporters that Wilcox had been very lucky that he had been navigating up the bay that morning by following the *Pequot* and that, had the *Pequot* not gone aground first, the *Larchmont* surely would have. Unfortunately, Wilcox's response was not recorded. During the course of the day the storm thickened, and there were no sailings that night on any of the sound lines. The storm continued sporadically for another two weeks during which the steamers stayed in port more often than they sailed, while the accumulation of freight became critical. During February, sailings were again infrequent. The storms subsided, but the cold continued and the sound was frozen solid from Throgs Neck to Execution much of the time.

The *City of Fall River*, coming into New York on February 4 from New Bedford, was trying to break her way through the ice in the upper East River when her bow rose up and then slapped down again not on the ice but on a rock, puncturing her hull. When icy water began seeping in, however, the crew stuffed mattresses into the opening and thus managed to keep the freighter afloat until she reached her pier, at which time two tugs came along and held her up while she unloaded her cargo and then took her across the river to Fletcher's.

During this period of bad weather, the railroad's steamer lines changed their sailing schedules so that all of them left New York together. In this way, the lanes broken through by the first boat, usually the *Plymouth* or the *Pilgrim* of the Fall River Line, could be kept open by the others following astern until they all got through. In addition, if one of the steamers were damaged or caught in the ice, the others would be nearby to provide assistance.

Throughout most of January and February 1905, both the Metropolitan Line freighters and the Joy Line's Boston boats regularly used the outside route when they were able to sail at all. But both the *Aransas* and the *Old Dominion* were forced to give up many trips, not only because of the bad weather but also because of the frequent damages sustained in trying to buck the ice. In mid-February, the *Aransas* was off the run for a few days, having several plates renewed and getting a new starboard propellor. With the regular Boston steamers missing so many trips, back freight began to accumulate and the Joy Line had to send the *Seaboard* through the icy seas to Boston on every occasion that a break in the weather permitted. During February, the line even chartered the *Surprise* again to help get caught up with Boston freight, and the reliable old *Rosalie* was also in service both to Boston and to Providence.

During February, the forty-year-old *Pequot*, her seams strained by nightly battles with the ice, had to be taken off for repairs, and for several weeks the *City of Lowell*, about the only steamer then available, came on with the *Maine*. (Thus, the *City of Lowell* was on the Providence Line replacing the *Pequot*, which was replacing the *New Hampshire*, which was on the New London Line replacing the *City of Lowell*.) It was during her short service as a Providence Line freighter that the *City of Lowell* ran down the second vessel in three months. With her maneuverability hampered by the ice, the *City of Lowell*, outbound off Whitestone on Wednesday, January 15, was forced off course and crashed into the schooner *Oakwoods*. The schooner sank immediately, but her crew was taken safely aboard the *Lowell*. Under the conditions, there was no possible place nearby to dock, so the crew of the unfortunate *Oakwoods*, whether or not they enjoyed it, had a free trip to Providence as the only passengers aboard one of the railroad's finest steamers.

By mid-February, the ice in Long Island Sound had held up the sailings of the steamers for so long that both the railroad lines and the Joy Line felt they could not afford to let their freight accumulate any longer. So between February 18 and February 25, the *Pilgrim* (to Fall River), the *City of Lowell* (to Providence), the *Larchmont*, and the *Edgemont* all made several trips by way of the outside passage around Long Island.[1]

The *Larchmont's* first trip to Providence by way of Sandy Hook and the Atlantic Ocean produced some unexpected excitement aboard that was not, however, related to the unusual route it involved. As the *Larchmont* eased out of her East River pier shortly after five on Saturday evening, February 18, the air was still bitter cold but fortunately the wind was not strong. That night, instead of heading up the river, the steamer headed down under the Brooklyn Bridge and past Staten Island into the open Atlantic. Since they had been built for an ocean run, the Atlantic presented no novelty for either the *Larchmont* or the *Edgemont* which also took the outside route coming down from Providence that night.[2] As the seas were relatively calm, the passengers aboard noticed no difference in the gentle rising and falling of the steamer from what they might have felt on a similar night on the sound. Dawn found the *Larchmont* paddling contentedly past Montauk and heading northward toward Block Island Sound and Narragansett Bay. Again the day was clear but very cold, and she moved up the bay during the morning with good speed, tying up at her Providence wharf shortly before noon. By 12:00 her passengers, already well overdue at their various destinations, were disembarking, and the men who doubled as dining room stewards at mealtimes and room stewards in the morning began making up the staterooms for the Monday sailing as quickly as possible, since their short weekend leaves had already been curtailed by several hours.

Robert Dickerson, who had charge of the row of staterooms on the

Saloon Deck forward alongside the dining area, went into Room 12, one of four opening onto a short passageway off the saloon, yanked a bunched-up blanket from the upper berth, and found himself staring at a dead man. Recovering, he ran down to the Quarter Deck to report the matter to James Harrison, the chief steward, who was then at the gangway taking tickets from passengers leaving the ship. Harrison followed Dickerson to the room, confirmed that the man was dead, and examined the corpse more closely. The body was that of a fairly young man; a small wound in his left cheek showed that he had been shot at close range. Since the man was lying on his side with his arms folded and his eyes closed, it appeared that he had probably been shot in his sleep and had never known it was happening. Dickerson noted also that, while the dead man was in the upper berth, the lower berth had obviously also been occupied during the night. Dickerson next notified Captain Wilcox who came and took a look, touched nothing, and telephoned the Providence police.

With such a large number of passengers boarding the sound steamers every day and remaining only for the short overnight voyage, it was possible for many of them to disembark forever without having been noted or remembered by any of the steamer's personnel. But the police were able to collect enough small bits of information regarding the deceased's overnight voyage on the *Larchmont* to assemble a story of sorts. The young man's name was John Hart. He was single. His home was in Providence, but he had been working for several months in New York, returning home fairly regularly, usually via the Joy Line, to visit his parents. By taking the steamer out of New York on a Saturday evening after work and returning from Providence on Monday night, he could spend two full days at home, missing only one day of work, and be back at his job in lower Manhattan early Tuesday morning.

On the evening of Saturday, February 18, John Hart had boarded the *Larchmont*, apparently alone, shortly before she sailed and had booked a stateroom by himself. The purser, Alden Trickey, remembered selling him the stateroom, because Hart had asked the purser if he knew a cousin of his who worked in the Providence office of the Joy Line. Hart had next been noticed in the steamer's dining area at suppertime both by Moses Thornton, the assistant steward, and by Ernest Krieger, the steward who had waited on him. Although the *Larchmont* sailed soon after five, the dining room did not begin serving until six. According to Krieger, Hart, whom he described as short and stocky in build, had entered the dining room shortly after six, and, as Thornton was then occupied, he had seated Hart himself. When his dinner of steak and french fries was presented to him, Hart indicated to Krieger that he had hurt his hand badly by falling in the steamer's hold (though he did not explain what he had been doing there), handed him a quarter, and asked him to cut his meat for him. Krieger had obliged.

Soon after Hart had been served, Thornton brought a second man to his table. The two men apparently did not know each other, but according to the testimonies of both Thornton and Krieger, they became friendly almost immediately. The second man, according to Krieger, asked Hart if he were familiar with a certain magazine, and when Hart replied that he was, their conversation quickly became intimate. When the two men had finished eating, Krieger collected fifty-five cents (the price of a steak with french fries aboard the *Larchmont* in 1905!) from each. In remembering the amounts collected, Krieger was also able to recall that neither had ordered wine with his dinner. The second man had paid in coin, but Hart had taken a ten dollar bill from his wallet and asked for change, at which time Krieger remembered seeing another ten dollar bill in the wallet.

Thorton later described the second man as fair-haired and clean-shaven as well as somewhat older, slightly taller, and much better dressed than Hart. (Since the man was said to have been wearing a blue polka-dot shirt, a red-and-white striped four-in-hand necktie, and a yellow vest, either Thornton's taste must be questioned or sartorial standards for men have changed a great deal since 1905!)

After dinner, the two men left the dining room together and wandered aft. Some time later, about the time the dining room was closing at eight o'clock, Hart and his new friend reappeared in the forward saloon and walked together into the alcove leading to Hart's stateroom. Thornton clearly remembered seeing them at that time because smoking was not permitted in the dining area, and both men were then smoking cigars.

Purser Trickey also remembered seeing Hart again on two occasions that evening. Shortly before eight, he recalled, Hart had appeared at the door of his office. He simply said, "You look as though you were busy," and then wandered over to the bar on the other side of the Quarter Deck. A minute later, Hart reappeared, handed Trickey a cigar, and left again. Trickey remembered seeing Hart about two hours later sitting on the Quarter Deck, which served as a sort of men's lounge on the smaller steamers. Since several men were then sitting on the Quarter Deck, Trickey could not recall whether Hart had been alone or talking with others. One of the passengers interviewed, Mr. John Breeze, who had occupied the stateroom across the alcove from Hart's, thought he remembered seeing Hart talking with two or three other men during the evening, one of whom he identified as a "Hebrew."

Apparently, the two men had walked aft after dinner and down to the Quarter Deck, where Hart had first greeted Trickey and then purchased three cigars in the bar, one each for himself and his friend, and one for the purser. The two had then retired, cigars in hand, to Hart's stateroom for a time, but later, it seems, returned again to the sociability of the Quarter Deck, at which time Trickey saw Hart for the second time.

The following morning Assistant Steward Thornton and the waiters were back at their stations in the steamer's dining room by six in the morning, at which time the *Larchmont* would still have been well out in the ocean. None of them remembered seeing either Hart or the other man at breakfast that morning. But after breakfast had been served and the tables cleared, Thornton retired to a small room, formerly a stateroom but then used for silver and china storage, to eat his own breakfast. This room, as it happened, opened onto the same small passageway as Hart's stateroom. While he was in there, with the door left open, he saw the man he had seated with Hart the night before come out of Hart's stateroom. Apparently in good spirits, the man called, "Eat 'em up Jack," to Thornton, stepped up to the forward part of the saloon for awhile to look out of the window, and then walked aft. That was the last Thornton saw of him. That was the last anyone saw of him.

Further investigations showed that Hart was twenty-five years old, that he had worked as a stationary engineer in New York, and that he had been shot through the head with a 32 calibre bullet which had entered the left cheek and lodged in the brain. The coroner concluded that the man had been murdered at about two o'clock in the morning, though, strangely, no one seemed to have heard a shot. It appeared fairly evident also that Hart had offered to share his stateroom with his new acquaintance, even taking the narrower upper bunk for himself and letting the other man sleep in the wider lower bunk. But what exactly happened after Hart was seen by Purser Trickey sitting on the Quarter Deck about ten o'clock was never determined.

Since Hart had been murdered somewhere out in the Atlantic Ocean, Providence police were relieved to be able to turn the investigation over to federal authorities. U.S. Marshall Charles C. Newhall of Providence was detailed to handle the investigation. In conducting his inquiries, Newhall encountered unique difficulties in that every possible witness plus the scene of the crime sailed out of the city on Monday night promptly at 5:30 and returned to Providence thereafter only three times a week and then for barely twelve hours before departing again for another two days.

Hart's murder was never solved. Several months later, John Carey, also known as "Jack Irish," the piano player on the *Larchmont*, was accused of the murder and tried in Providence, but there was not enough evidence and Carey was subsequently released. (Later, Carey was convicted of the armed robbery of a jewelry store in Fall River and sentenced to a term in the Massachusetts state prison in Charlestown.) The man Hart met at supper and who apparently later shared his stateroom was never found or identified.[3]

The weather broke briefly toward the end of February but turned cold again on March 4, the day of Theodore Roosevelt's inaugural, and stayed cold for the rest of the month. The Joy Line steamers continued making outside trips, when they could leave their piers at all, through March, but so many trips had to be canceled that whenever the weather did permit sailings, the *Rosalie*, the *Seaboard*, and sometimes the *Surprise* were still kept busy running extra loads of freight to Providence as well as Boston. Both the *Plymouth* and the *Chester W. Chapin* suffered ice damage and had to be taken off their routes. The *Priscilla* came on for the *Plymouth* during March, for the second year in a row, and once again stayed on the route for the rest of the winter. The *City of Lowell* also went back on the New London Line, but only until the *Chapin* was repaired.

Another terrible snowstorm hit New England on Sunday, March 17. The Joy Line steamers, of course, did not sail on Sundays and were spared. But the Winsor Line steamer *Spartan*, on her regular run between Providence and Philadelphia, did sail that afternoon, and four hours later she stranded on the southern end of Block Island. Battered by gale force winds, she was soon a total loss.

Two days later, the weather had improved enough for the recently completed *Providence* to sail under her own power from the shipyard in Quincy to Tietjen and Lang's in Hoboken for interior painting and fitting out. Those on board claimed she reached a speed of twenty knots during the trip, which is unlikely, since the *Providence* was usually rated at about seventeen or eighteen knots. She was not as fast as the *Priscilla* or the *Puritan*, which did make about twenty knots, the *Priscilla* perhaps a little better occasionally. As a winter boat, the *Providence* had not been designed to be as fast as the larger steamers.[4] Eighteen knots was more than enough speed to make the overnight trip from New York to Providence or Fall River in the allotted time, with some to spare.

As soon as the weather began to clear in April, the *Larchmont* went over to Fletcher's to have her boilers rebuilt and her hull resheathed. As a sign of its unwonted prosperity since its treaty with the New Haven Railroad in 1902, the Joy Line again chartered the relatively new and comfortable *Shinnecock* of the Montauk Line to take the *Larchmont*'s place rather than use its own spare steamer, the *City of Key West*, which was now no longer considered to be up to Joy Line standards.[5] In order to arrange this charter, the *Larchmont*'s repairs were scheduled between the time the *Shinnecock* returned from her winter charter in Florida and the start of her summer service on the Montauk Line. Since the *Shinnecock* came with her own captain (Abram Mitchell), Dave Wilcox took a vacation while the *Larchmont* was off the route, though there is no record to show whether he was also reconditioned.

Early in May came the utterly unexpected announcement that the Whitneys had sold the Metropolitan Line to Charles W. Morse.[6] The Whitney family had owned the line since it started running in the 1860s, first in partnership with the Clydes and then, after 1872, by themselves. The line had since then been a one-family operation. Even H. F. Dimock, the New York agent who had been so intransigent in dealing with the Joy Line opposition, was a brother-in-law of the president, H. M. Whitney. Since the line had always been profitable and remarkably free from accidents, no one ever expected that the Whitneys would sell. But the deal, in the typical Morse manner, had apparently been a quick one. The assets of the Metropolitan Line—steamers, wharves, and liquid assets—were then valued at $1.6 million.[7] Morse arrived in H. M. Whitney's office one morning and offered him $3 million for the line. Whitney said yes. The whole interview lasted less than twenty minutes.[8]

No sooner had Morse acquired the Metropolitan Line than he followed this first blow with an annoucement that he was planning to start immediately on the construction of two large and very fast steamers with which he would inaugurate daily overnight passenger service between New York and Boston.[9]

None of this information was received with undiluted glee at Pier 35. At that time, the *Aransas* and the *Old Dominion* were the only steamers providing direct passenger service, such as it was, between New York and Boston. The prospect of having to compete with two modern flyers sailing daily to Boston on a schedule roughly the same as the Joy Line's Providence boats was not an altogether pleasing one.

The Joy Line was still reeling from the news of Morse's purchase of the Metropolitan Line on May 4, when three days later a telephone message informed the Joy Line that the *Aransas* had been sunk off Cape Cod and was a total loss. The *Aransas* sailed from Boston shortly after 5:00 P.M. on Saturday night, May 6. Passing Provincetown at about 10:00, she encountered some fog which became increasingly thicker as she passed southward along the cape. At about 1:30, Pilot C. P. Crockett was heading the steamer to starboard to pass through the Pollock Rip Channel into Nantucket Sound, when through the fog he perceived the lights of a tug also heading into the channel. As he rang the engine room to hold the speed of the *Aransas*, he could also hear the tugboat blowing its whistle to indicate that the *Aransas* should wait for its barges to pass. In time the tug and two barges, each a hundred feet apart, passed ahead of the *Aransas*. Crockett, noting that the tug's whistle had stopped blowing, had just rung to the engine room to pick up speed, when, too late, he saw the lights of a third barge headed straight for his steamer. He swung the wheel to starboard but not in time, and the barge *Glendower* crashed into the port bow, splitting open the hull. The *Aransas* heeled slightly to starboard and then, righting herself again, she began to fill rapidly and go down at the bow.

Captain Rood, awakened by the crash—as nearly everyone else on the ship was—soon appeared in the pilot house and, quickly sensing that his steamer did not have long to live, gave the order to abandon ship. Within minutes, all but one of the thirty-seven passengers (one passenger, Anna Field, was never found) and all of the crew were on the deck, and the lifeboats were in position. The sea that night was mercifully calm, so that the boats were soon loaded and lowered into the water without difficulty. About ten minutes after the crash, by which time most of the passengers were already in lifeboats, the tugboat, the *Patience*, having unhitched its barges and left them to drift, came alongside and took the remaining passengers directly from the deck of the *Aransas*, now nearly at a level with the sea. With many of the passengers and crew aboard, the *Patience* then took the two lifeboats in tow across the dark waters to Vineyard Haven on Martha's Vineyard, about thirty miles away. Then, while the *Patience* hastened back to find her drifting barges, the *Aransas* survivors waited on the pier for the 6:45 sailing of the island steamer *Martha's Vineyard* which took them over to Woods Hole in time to catch the 7:45 train for Boston.

Surprisingly, a majority of the passengers accepted the Joy Line's offer of a free trip to New York on the *Larchmont* from Providence the following night (Monday, May 8), in spite of the fact that most of the clothing and other belongings they had been carrying had gone down with the *Aransas*. The officers of the *Aransas* also went west on the *Larchmont* that night at the request of Charlie Dimon, who wanted a full account of the incident himself before official investigations began.

A few days later, divers sent out to the *Aransas* by the insurance company managed to retrieve the steamer's manifest but decreed that raising the steamer would be impracticable. Government inspectors subsequently pronounced the wreck a menace to shipping and ordered the remains of the *Aransas* blown up.

For some reason the Joy Line made no immediate attempt to replace the *Aransas*, after having found a replacement for the *Tremont* when she burned the year before in a matter of days. There were steamers available at the time. Two retired propellor steamers of the Old Dominion Line, the *Guyandotte* and the *Richmond*, later versions of the Joy Line's *Old Dominion*, for instance, were then laid up in Brooklyn and for sale. The *Guyandotte* was subsequently purchased by the Winsor Line. Renamed the *Cretan*, she went on its Providence-Philadelphia run in place of the *Spartan* which had been wrecked on Block Island in March. With the former owners no longer in control of the Metropolitan Line and with Morse's Boston project in the offing, the New Haven would certainly no longer have any reason to prevent their sale to the Joy Line. Perhaps after Morse's announcements, the Joy Line had decided to wait and see what actually developed in that quarter before spending money for new steamers. The line may even have had doubts by that time about the wisdom of maintaining its Boston service at all. By 1905, the Providence route was definitely making more money for the company, and some of the officers believed that it was actually beginning to carry the Boston service. In any event, Captain Rood and the crew of the *Aransas* were transferred back to the faithful *Seaboard* which took the schedule of the *Aransas* for another year, with the *Rosalie*, generally under Captain Coleman, adding extra service when needed.

Still more troubles were facing the Joy Line's Providence service by the spring of 1905. First, the railroad opened the new season of the Providence Line with the brand new steamer *Providence*. Thirty feet longer than her running mate the *Plymouth*, and nearly as large as the big Fall River steamers *Priscilla* and *Puritan*, the *Providence* was the largest steamer ever to run regularly into that port,* and a great source of pride to the city. With the new *Providence* now running summers to Providence and winters to Fall River with the *Plymouth*, the grand old *Pilgrim*, with her iron hull and coal-hungry walking beam engine, went into retirement and was tied up at Newport, to be used only for emergencies.

The Providence Line's summer service began, as usual, on the first Monday in June, the fifth, with the *Plymouth* sailing from New York and the new *Providence* from her namesake city. On Saturday, June 3, however, Captain Oliver Griffen brought the *Providence* up from Newport two days early so that Providence people could come aboard and see what "their" new steamer looked like. The *Providence* had hardly pulled out of her pier in Newport before she ran hard aground right in Newport Harbor, but, after suffering the embarrassment of being pulled off by the ferry boat *Conanicut*, she collected her pride and sailed on to Providence, her new paint to all appearances unscratched.

Far more threatening to the Joy Line than the railroad's new steamer was the appearance that summer of another low-fare steamship line, the Enterprise Line, or as it was more commonly known, the New Line, between New York and Fall River. This was the first time since the fall of 1902 that the Joy Line had faced any competition in the Narragansett Bay area except from the considerably higher priced lines of the railroad, which clearly appealed to a different sector of the traveling public.

The Enterprise Transportation Company was a reorganization of the earlier company of the same name that had run the *Surprise* (formerly the *City of Fitchburg*) on the Maine coast during the summers of 1903 and 1904. The main organizer of the new line was David Whitcomb of Worcester, who owned most of the stock personally, though other members of his family and some other Worcester investors were also involved. For his New Line to Fall River, Whitcomb had recently acquired the former Maine

---

*Second only to the *Puritan* which made several trips on the Providence Line between 1908 and 1911 but was never regularly assigned to that route.

Central Railroad steamer *Frank Jones*. With her small sidewheels neatly hidden in her deckhousing and her raked single stack, the *Frank Jones* presented a sleeker profile than most of the other Maine boats. She also had a self-advertising name, for *Frank Jones* was the name of a beer then very popular in New England. While not as good a sea boat as the Joy Line steamers, she was smarter-looking underway than either the *Larchmont* or the *Edgemont*, and also considerably more modern. As noted in an earlier chapter, she had been built in 1892 as a replacement for the aging *City of Richmond* (later the *City of Key West* of the Joy Line) on the run from Portland to Rockland, Bar Harbor, and Machiasport, Maine. By 1904, however, the traffic on this route had declined to such a degree that the railroad decided to discontinue the service, replace it with a series of shorter and more direct routes using smaller steamers, and put the handsome *Frank Jones* up for sale.

One reason Whitcomb may have chosen to run the *Frank Jones* on Long Island Sound rather than revive the old route of the *Surprise* was that the railroad probably stipulated in the sale that the steamer not be used for any service on the Maine coast. In any event, Whitcomb obviously saw that the Joy Line's operation to Providence was proving profitable and decided to start a similar service to Fall River competing directly with the great Fall River Line. When we consider the New Haven Railroad's past history in dealing with competition, such a project took more courage than wisdom.

The Enterprise Line started its new operation on Thursday night, June 1, with the *Frank Jones* sailing from Fall River. Thenceforward, the *Frank Jones* sailed from New York on Mondays, Wednesdays, and Fridays, and from Fall River on Tuesdays, Thursdays, and Saturdays. Beginning in mid-July, the former *Surprise*, now rebuilt as a freighter and renamed the *Warren*, provided cargo service from each port on the alternate nights. Somehow, the Enterprise Line managed to lease a dock in Fall River at the foot of Turner Street, very near the Fall River pier. (The Enterprise Line, like the Joy Line before 1902, or any other company competing with the New Haven monopoly, tended to have the support of the local politicians.) Since the Fall River Line was owned by a railroad, which also owned most of the local trolley lines, it had arrangements for trains and trolleys to deliver passengers directly to its pier. But now, Enterprise Line passengers could avail themselves of these same connecting trains and walk a few feet further along the Fall River waterfront to the cheaper Enterprise Line steamer. In New York the Enterprise Line docked at Pier 29, East River, just a few piers south of the Joy Line's Pier 35.

From the start, the Enterprise Line's moves were directed as much at getting business from the Joy Line, which shared the same public, as from the Fall River Line. The Joy Line fare at that time, in accordance with the agreement of 1902, was fixed at $2.00 in the summer. The Enterprise, not restricted by any such agreement, offered a trip on the *Frank Jones* for $1.00. Taking even more direct aim at the Joy Line's following, the Enterprise advertised that a passenger could take a trolley from Providence direct to the Enterprise pier at Fall River for twenty cents, making the combined trolley and steamer fare via the Enterprise Line eighty cents cheaper than the direct route via the Joy Line. Just to make the pill more bitter, the ad went on to point out that the trolley which left downtown Providence at 5:15, just fifteen minutes before the departure of the Joy Line steamer, would get the passenger to Fall River in ample time for the 6:30 sailing of the *Frank Jones*! Realizing at last that the *Larchmont* and the *Edgemont* were faster than the *Tremont* had been, a few days after this provocative ad appeared, the Joy Line announced that its sailng time from Providence had been moved up to 6:30. Neither line said anything about the arrival times in New York.

The directness with which the barbs in the Enterprise Line ads were aimed at the Joy Line should not have come as a surprise, for the New York agent of the Enterprise who conducted much of the actual business of the line was none other than "Captain" George Brady, who had been fired by the Joy Line two years before and by the railroad a year before that.[10]

When the Enterprise Line entered the field, the Joy Line management does not seem to have given any thought to making common cause with an operation similar to its own, though admittedly such a course could have proved suicidal. Instead, they followed the usual human pattern, adopting a haughtily hostile stance and showing every willingness to cooperate with the New England Navigation Company, which might have been their common adversary, in their efforts to stave off the intruder. Soon after the *Frank Jones* began running on the sound, an obviously much concerned John Rowland wrote Percy Todd pleading for permission for theJoy Line to maintain its $1.50 fare through June in the belief that the line could thus force the Enterprise out of business sooner. In this letter, Rowland uses the same military analogies and battlefield clichés that had characterized Todd's remarks about the Joy Line a few years earlier:

> We feel that if we allow Mr. Whitcomb and his people to get a few good months, it will take a long time to convince them that there are not enough more good months in store for them if only they fight long enough; whereas if we never allow them to get a dollar on the right side of the ledger, the fight will be a much shorter one. We know or believe we know his makeup.[11]

Rowland did indeed know the enemy's makeup; he was obviously speaking from the Joy Line's own experience and seems to have been suggesting that had the New Haven acted sooner than it did to get rid of the Joy Line back in the early years (1899-1902), it might have been more successful.

The unexpected appearance of a competing line between New York and Fall River (the only passenger line not actually owned by the railroad itself ever to attempt to compete directly on the New York-Fall River run in the entire history of the Fall River Line) at first caught the railroad management off guard but very soon set off a series of responses at every level of its operation. Some New Haven officials believed that the Joy Line was in some way behind the new Enterprise Line and so informed Mellen, but Percy Todd hastily assured the president that the Joy Line was not connected with the new operation and that the line had in fact (as we have seen) indicated a willingness to cooperate with the railroad in fending off the intruder. Todd's personal view was that C. W. Morse might in some way be behind the Enterprise Line.[12]

Railroad officials now began busily exchanging memos once again with various battle plans. The suggestion that Fall River Line fares be reduced to meet the competition was quickly rejected on the grounds that the prestigious position of the famed Fall River Line should not be compromised. A proposal that the railroad should place a low-fare line of its own on the New York to Fall River route as it had done on the Providence route in 1900-1902 was also rejected with the perfectly logical argument that the New Line to Providence had been an expensive mistake that did not need to be repeated. Finally, at Todd's suggestion, it was agreed that the best tactic, for the time being, would be to grant John Rowland's request and permit the Joy Line, which had little prestige to lose, to reduce its summer fare between New York and Providence from $2.00 to $1.50.[13] Meanwhile, the railroad engaged agents in New York and in Fall River to keep a vigil at the Enterprise Line piers and make daily reports on the number of passengers and the amount (and kind) of freight carried by the line.

Another reason the railroad elected not to open a competing line of its own to Fall River was that it had already inaugurated one new overnight passenger service on the sound that summer which would compete actively with its Fall River Line. For in 1905 the New England Navigation Company had decided, very belatedly it would seem, to yield to the persistent demands of the people of New Bedford, as well as of the summer residents of Cape Cod, Martha's Vineyard, and Nantucket (or, more likely, to the figures in its own projections) and again offer a daily overnight passenger service between New York and New Bedford during the summer months. The former Stonington Line sisterships, *Maine* and *New Hampshire*, were available and assigned to the new service. (Their handsome lines notwithstanding, both the *Maine* and the *New Hampshire*, as noted earlier, were essentially freight steamers with very attractive and spacious but nevertheless limited passenger accommodations, and therefore not altogether satisfactory for a passenger line to a growing summer resort area.) The *Maine*, as we have seen, had run to New Bedford the summer before as a freight boat. The *New Hampshire* had run on the New Haven Line the previous year, replacing the *Chester W. Chapin*. But by 1905 the Navigation Company had realized that the *Richard Peck* alone could handle the passenger traffic to New Haven, and until its new freighter *New Haven* was completed in 1906, it placed the *City of Lawrence* on the line with the *Richard Peck* rather than the *New Hampshire*. For the next fifteen years, until the tragic loss of the *Maine* in 1920, the sisterships *Maine* and *New Hampshire*, generally regarded after the *Priscilla* and the *Puritan* as the most beautiful of the sound steamers, ran to New Bedford in the summer.* With the summer resorts on the cape and on the islands already becoming popular, particularly as a place for summer homes for people from New York, Boston, or even Philadelphia (no proper Philadelphian would ever be seen in the summer on the New Jersey shore), the new route was so immediately popular with passengers, it seemed strange that the railroad had not tapped this vein sooner.

On July 2, the *Larchmont* started her Sunday excursions for the summer. "All Aboard for Cottage City! Just what you've been waiting for," the ads intoned. Although the prestigious Providence Line rarely stooped to joining the excursion trade, on July 4, a Tuesday, the *Providence* deigned to take a run to Block Island and back. It must have been a fast trip, for she was ready to sail for New York that night on schedule, though one must note that there was probably very little freight, if any, to load on the holiday. The following night, on her way back from New York, the brand new *Providence* broke a shaft off Cornfield Light at about 11:30 at night. (Thirty years to the day later, the *Providence* was to break her shaft again in almost the same place.) The *Puritan* of the Fall River Line was ahead and stopped, but Captain Griffen sent a message by wireless that she should proceed, since she was carrying an exceptionally large number of holiday passengers who expected to reach Fall River on schedule, most to make other connections. Instead, he waited for the *City of Taunton* and the *New Hampshire* to come up from astern; these two steamers lashed themselves on either side of the big *Providence* and carried her into New London. On the run just a few weeks and the *Providence* had to be off again for nearly a month. (The *Providence* did not return to the line until August 4.) The old *Pilgrim*, laid up in Newport, got steam up and sailed up to Providence to make the run that evening.

Since the *Larchmont*'s Cottage City trip of July 9 was interrupted by some unexpected rain, she returned to Providence early. For the next two

---

*Early in September each year, the *Maine* and *New Hampshire* were replaced on the New Bedford route by freight steamers, usually at first by the *City of Brockton* and the *City of Fall River*. One of the sisterships went to join the *Chester W. Chapin* on the New London Line for the winter, and the other ran as a freighter to Providence for most of the season, and then later served as the relief boat on the New Haven and Bridgeport lines.

weeks, Providence was visited by another heat wave, and the decks of the *Larchmont* were crowded both Sundays. Arthur Pitts put an ad in the *Journal* that began "Gee Whiz, It's Hot." As with almost all of the Joy Line ads, it went on to say "Courteous Treatment of Our Patrons Our First Consideration."[14] During the heat wave, the *Providence Journal* made one brief entry announcing curtly that John Morrison of 520 Wickenden Street had committed suicide because of the heat wave.[15] No further details were offered. Apparently, we should not take the blessings of air conditioning too lightly. That week the *Larchmont* cleared Providence on Sunday with over six hundred excursionists aboard.

The following weeks were not as successful. On July 23 the trip was canceled because of rain; on July 30 it rained again, but the *Larchmont* took a shortened trip; on August 6 there was fog and again the steamer turned back early; but, according to reports the passengers had a good time anyway. On the same day, the *Plymouth* of the Providence Line took an excursion to New London and back, apparently undeterred by the fog.

The Joy Line's situation was not improved in the fall when the Enterprise Line, after a successful summer season, announced it was starting a daily passenger service. In September, Whitcomb purchased a second steamer, the *Kennebec*, from the Kennebec Line of Morse's Eastern Steamship Company, the same steamer Chapin had chartered to run to Providence with the *Richard Peck* in the fall of 1899. On Saturday, September 22, the *Kennebec* made her first sailing from New York to Fall River, thus inaugurating six-day a week passenger service on the Enterprise Line. (With the *Kennebec* on the line with the *Frank Jones*, the much smaller *Surprise* was now tied up at the Enterprise Line's Fall River pier to be used to carry extra freight when needed or as a spare.) Like her running mate, the *Frank Jones*, the *Kennebec*, a typical Maine coast overnight boat, was similar in size and layout to the Joy Line steamers. But also like the *Frank Jones*, she was both newer and more modern in appearance than the *Larchmont* or the *Edgemont* (though, unlike her running mate, she had the traditional beam engine and large paddle boxes). While the *Kennbec* lacked the lovely sheer lines that made the *Frank Jones* such a beauty underway, she was probably the better boat, for the *Frank Jones* was known to be difficult to handle and inclined to roll badly in even a moderate swell.

Why did Morse sell the *Kennebec* to the Enterprise Line? It would be hard to say that she was no longer needed by the Eastern. She had run all that summer on the Kennebec Line with the *Ransom B. Fuller*, and Morse had no other steamers available at the time to replace her. The following season the *Penobscot*, which was older and less suitable for the Kennebec run, was brought on the line with the *Ransom B. Fuller* and a steamer brought in from one of Morse's other lines to take her place on the International Line. By selling the *Kennebec*, Eastern not only ended up one boat short on the International Line but also without even one steamer available to serve as a spare in the event of another major accident such as the one which had taken the *City of Rockland* out of service the previous season. Since it clearly was not in Eastern's best interests to dispose of the *Kennebec* at that time, one wonders whether the real reason for the sale might not have been that Percy Todd's guess was correct, that the Enterprise was indeed receiving some kind of backing, either moral or financial, from Charles W. Morse.

With or without Morse's support, the Enterprise Line did a good business. The Joy Line and the railroad's New Line had already proved there were plenty of people who wanted to participate in the nation's new passion for travel, but who could not afford the Old World elegance—or perhaps did not always feel at ease with it—which had become the hallmark of the Fall River and Providence lines. And the Joy Line's agreement with the railroad, which obliged the line to hold the fare at $1.50, gave the Enterprise a strong advantage, particularly in the off-season months, for in those days fifty cents still made a great deal of difference to many people. The Enterprise also undercut both the Navigation Company and the Joy Line in its freight rates, and here again the Joy Line was prevented by its agreement from adjusting its rates to meet the competition.

In establishing a new steamship line in competition with one operated by the omnipotent New Haven Railroad, the Enterprise ran into the same difficulties that the Joy Line had encountered six years before. In the ensuing struggle between the Enterprise Line and the railroad, the scenario begins to take on a familiar sound. The New Haven refused to make any through ticketing arrangements with the Enterprise people, and railroad officials located at Grand Central Station in New York noted that agents of the Enterprise Line turned up there every morning to purchase blocks of one hundred Fall River to Boston tickets to sell aboard their steamer that night.[16] In dealing with the Enterprise Line, however, the New Haven went much further than refusing to issue through tickets. Passengers seen disembarking in Fall River from the Enterprise steamer were often physically barred from the platform of the railroad station (admittedly a special spur maintained specifically as a service to the through passengers of the Fall River Line), and, on several occasions, porters carrying Enterprise baggage to the station were treated roughly by thugs hired by the railroad. When Whitcomb took this matter to court, he was joined by the mayor of Fall River, who, like the mayor of Providence a few years earlier, fully supported the low-fare competition operating into his city. The result was a court ruling that the railroad must "cease and desist" from any further physical abuse of Enterprise porters or passengers and must in the future allow them free access to the company's facilities.[17]

In its effort to siphon off some of the Joy Line's Providence freight, the Enterprise resorted, in reverse, to the same tactic the Joy Line had used in 1902: that is, hiring a local line to carry freight between Providence and Fall River. In 1905, the Enterprise concluded an arrangement with the Providence, Newport, and Fall River Steamboat Company, a local freight and excursion operation, to have a steamer meet the Enterprise boat on her arrival in Fall River each morning to transport freight to Providence and to bring freight picked up in Providence back to Fall River in time for the line's evening departure from New York. For this service the Providence, Newport, and Fall River used the freighter *Conoho*, a steamer not dissimilar to the *Rosalie*, which they had purchased from a Chesapeake Bay freight line recently bought out by the Old Bay Line.

The New Haven again used its influence to dissuade the Pennsylvania Railroad from making through arrangements with the Enterprise Line for passengers or freight destined for points south of New York. This time, Whitcomb took the case to the Interstate Commerce Commission, charging the New Haven with unfair business practices. He won the case and the Pennsylvania was obliged to negotiate through shipping arrangements with the Enterprise.[18] The question naturally arises why the Joy Line did not seek a similar solution when faced with the same problem five years earlier. The temper of the times had changed drastically between 1902 and 1905, as it was to change, for instance, between 1968 and 1970 or in other periods when popular movements have pricked the nation's conscience. In the period of more than a generation between the administrations of Abraham Lincoln and William McKinley, the nation had largely accepted the phenomenal growth of big business, as well as the often questionable methods and practices this growth entailed, as synonomous with and necessary to the growth and prosperity of the country itself. The philosophy of laissez-faire, which held that a nation's prosperity depended on its allowing businesses to function and grow freely following the laws of supply and demand and not hamstrung by government regulations, was accepted without much question. This attitude, combined with the vague notions of Social Darwinism then in vogue, meant, in effect, that if a large company, using any methods at its disposal, could force a smaller company to the wall, the nation as a whole, in the long run, would prosper. Thus, in this era the unmourned demise of many smaller oil companies provided the mound on which Standard Oil was built; numerous smaller steel companies sacrificed their independence to Andrew Carnegie's new United States Steel Corporation in 1901, and so forth, including the absorption of the smaller steamer lines on Long Island Sound by the New Haven Railroad's New England Navigation Company. In about 1902, however, American attitudes began to change. This time period was marked by the coal strikes, the arrival in America of large numbers of European intellectuals with socialist sympathies, and the beginnings of the so-called muckraker literature, which attempted to demonstrate to the public that many of the practices of large corporations were not only exploitive of their employees, their customers, and of smaller businesses, but were also often of questionable legality, or, in short, corrupt.

As public opinion in regard to big business tended to shift in this short period, President Theodore Roosevelt, or at least the public side of him, and his administration tended to shift with it. But the only handle available to the federal government in its attempt to control business, and that a small one, was the constitutional clause giving it the right to regulate interstate commerce. Once Roosevelt had been elected to the presidency in his own right in 1904, the Interstate Commerce Commission, which had been in operation since 1887 but whose authority, lacking any administrative support, had until then been negligible, was now empowered to enforce such federal laws as existed regarding interstate commerce. Since a steamship line operating between Massachusetts and New York and seeking the right to transship freight from New York to Pennsylvania came clearly under the heading of interstate commerce, the Enterprise Line was able to apply to agents of a now greatly expanded federal Interstate Commerce Commission, which had not been available to the Joy Line in the period from 1899 to 1902 when it had faced similar difficulties.

In another effort to combat the competition of the Enterprise Line, the Fall River Line adopted the utterly unprecedented and totally uncharacteristic tactic of reducing its own fares to $1.50—the same as the Joy Line fares—for the winter of 1905-1906. The line would not go so far, however, as to sully the decks of its beautiful and elegant *Priscilla* or *Puritan* with passengers paying only $1.50. In addition, the new steamer *Providence* actually had more staterooms and far greater cargo space than the larger *Puritan* and was cheaper to operate, making it impractical as well as unnecessary to keep the larger steamers running until January. Thus, in 1905 the Providence passenger service ended late in September, somewhat earlier than usual, and by mid-October the *Providence* was running on the Fall River Line with the *Priscilla*. Toward the end of November, the *Plymouth* came on for the *Priscilla*, and on December 1 the new low fares went into effect.

With the *Providence* and the *Plymouth*, the Fall River Line now for the first time was operating two steamers built especially for the winter service rather than summer steamers superseded by more modern vessels. Since they were designed for winter service, the *Plymouth* and the *Providence*, while both spacious and elegant, had proportionately somewhat less space devoted to passenger accommodations and more to freight than the summer boats. With these steamers on the line, it was not always necessary to operate a separate freight steamer as well. In any event, the Fall River Line, since the delivery of the *Boston*, now had four freighters. Two were kept for service that winter on the Fall River Line, with the *Boston* for the most part handling the Fall River freight alone on alternate nights and the *City of Fall River* standing by at Newport as a relief boat. The *City of Taunton* and the *City of Brockton* took over the New Bedford run as soon as its passenger service ended the last week of September. Both the *Maine* and the *New Hampshire* spent most of the fall carrying freight to Providence, with the *Pequot* coming on when the *New Hampshire* went to replace the *City of Lowell* on the New London line in January.

Another new steamer line appeared on the sound briefly in the fall of 1905 when a group of Maine businessmen decided to revive the direct freight service between New York and Penobscot River ports as far as Bangor. This service had been started once before in 1898 with the steamer *Pentagoet*, but she had made only a few trips when the little freighter was lost with all hands in November 1898 in the same storm that claimed the *Portland*. The steamer they employed on this service now in 1905 was the *Westover*, a near-sister of the Joy Line's overworked *Seaboard*. (The *Westover* and the *Seaboard* were two of the three surviving freighters built by the Old Bay Line in the 1870s.) The *Westover* left New York on her first voyage to Maine on Saturday, December 2, under the command of none other than Captain D. W. Joy. She was scheduled to make one round trip per week leaving New York every Saturday. On her second trip out of New York on December 9, the little *Westover* ran into a furious gale off Cape Cod, not unlike the one that had earlier engulfed her predecessor at about the same time of the year. In fact, the Nantucket lightship, built to withstand all kinds of weather, foundered during the storm, and it was only minutes before she went down that a rescue boat appeared to take off her crew. The *Westover*, however, survived this first ordeal and made it to the Penobscot several hours late but intact. But on the final leg of her third round trip, while approaching New York in the relatively quiet waters of Long Island Sound, the *Westover* struck on Execution Rock and stove a hole in her hull. Later, she was floated, but she was taking water so fast that she was beached again at nearby Glen Cove on Long Island, near the site where the burning *Glen Island* had sunk just one year earlier. Her Maine owners decided that she was not worth saving, and the second attempt to start a New York to Bangor Line failed after only three trips. It should be almost unnecessary to add that Charlie Dimon later bought the remains of the *Westover* for the Joy Line.

Two announcements late in the summer of 1905 indicated that the Morse takeover signaled a whole new era for the staid Metropolitan Line. The first stated that the old *Glaucus* and *Neptune*, the last of the steamers the Metropolitan had inherited from the Neptune Line of Providence in the 1860s, had been towed from Brooklyn, where they had been laid up for years, to a scrap yard in Massachusetts. The second confirmed that the Metropolitan Line had placed orders with Roach's yard in Chester, Pennsylvania, for two four-hundred-foot, triple-screw steamers for the line's proposed new passenger service between New York and Boston. The announcement also stated that the engines for these new steamers, in order to procure maximum speed, would be of the new turbine type, as yet untried in America, but then being installed in the Cunard Line ships, *Mauretania* and *Lusitania,* then under construction.

As the season ended, therefore, although it had been an unusually profitable one, the prospects for the Joy Line's future, at least on its Boston route, visibly dimmed. As Morse's plans for his new Boston line took shape during the summer of 1905 and the Enterprise Line continued to make deeper inroads into the line's business in the Narragansett Bay area, the Joy Line management began to question seriously whether it should consider basic changes in its operation in order to meet the competition, or even if it would continue to be profitable to stay in business at all.

Once again, as in 1902, the Joy Line gave serious consideration to starting a new line to Philadelphia. Apparently, there were many shippers in New England, with whom the Joy Line was already doing business, who needed to have freight delivered to points south of New York and who had indicated a willingness to patronize the Joy Line if it were able to get it there. The Joy Line was barred by its agreement with the New Haven from accepting any freight in Providence for points beyond New York or from running any steamer lines out of New York to ports other than Providence or Boston. Thus, according to the letter of the agreement, the Joy Line was not permitted to run a line to Philadelphia from either Providence or New York, the two terminals of its Providence boats. But the agreement did not specifically prevent the line from a run between Boston and Philadelphia, and, now that the railroad was no longer on such intimate terms with the Metropolitan Line, it would have far less reason for using other means to prevent it. By disguising the manifests, Providence freight could still be carried to Philadelphia, provided the goods were not perishable, by going first to New York and then to Boston, at a rate lower than the railroad's. And, if Morse's new Boston service were to force the Joy Line to give up its own Boston run, as it probably would, the Joy Line would have an alternate service to which to divert at least some of its previous customers.

During the summer of 1905, Charles Dimon had been dispatched to New Orleans once again to buy another Gulf of Mexico steamer, this time the *Stillwater,* a British-built freighter which had been operating in the gulf for the United Fruit Company. Built in 1883 as the *Stroma,* the *Stillwater* was a steel-hulled steamer, unusual for that era, 195 feet long, about the same size as the *Cocoa,* and only slightly longer than the *Seaboard.* Sometime in

September, she was towed up to New York and taken to Morse's for what promised to be a major job of reconditioning. A few weeks later, the Joy Line announced that the *Stillwater*, as soon as her renovations were completed, would be used to start the new Joy Line service between Boston and Philadelphia, and that the line was in the process of acquiring another steamer, named the *Georgetown*, to join her on this line.[19]

The purchase of the *Georgetown* was a typical Dimon-shaped deal. Like the *Stillwater*, a small British-built freighter, though in her case still under British registry, the *Georgetown* had been sunk in the Delaware River by the American freighter *Friesland*. Raised and towed to Robins' drydock in Brooklyn, she was offered for sale "as is," and that was where Dimon found her.[20]

Meanwhile, the Joy Line's Providence and Boston lines continued operating as usual. As soon as the *Shinnecock's* summer season to Shelter Island ended in mid-September, she was again chartered by the Joy Line, this time in place of the *Edgemont*, which went off for her annual overhaul and for another major reconditioning of her engines. The *Shinnecock* took the *Edgemont's* sailing out of New York on Friday, September 22, the day before the first sailing of the *Kennebec* for the Enterprise Line, and stayed on the Joy Line for exactly one month.

Morse's announcement that he was building steamers for the passenger line to Boston produced an immediate and vehement response from the New Haven Railroad as well. Failing to find a week day in which all could be present, President Mellen summoned the members of the subcommittee on water lines of the railroad's board of directors to a special evening meeting on Friday, September 15, at the Manhattan Hotel (near Grand Central Terminal on Forty-second Street and Madison Avenue). He presented them with a detailed five-point plan for dealing not only with Morse but also with the Enterprise Line and a variety of smaller competitors.[21]

First, Mellen advised the august assembly that the New England Navigation Company should start a line of its own between New York and Boston and begin immediately the construction of three steamers for this line comparable in size and speed to the two new steamers Morse was then building. These steamers, Mellen suggested, should be built at first as freighters, so that if the threat alone sufficed to scare Morse off the field, the steamers could be used on the company's other services. But they should be designed with quick conversion to passenger use in mind, in the event that Morse held out longer and the railroad was forced to compete in kind.[22]

Second, the railroad should proceed with the purchase of the Old Colony Steamboat Company (Fall River Line and New Bedford Line) and complete its integration into the New England Navigation Company.[23]

Third, the New England Navigation Company should inaugurate new freight lines between New York and the cities of the nearby Connecticut south shore to force out the small independent lines operating to these places. Mellen, it would appear, had contracted Morgan's mania for monopoly to such a degree that he could not tolerate even these small steamers, owned by a handful of local merchants, carrying package freight from their home towns of Norwalk, Stamford, or Greenwich to the markets of New York. This "competition" seems to have earned almost as much of Mellen's attention as the threat of a new express passenger service between Boston and New York. As it turned out, however, this was the only one of Mellen's recommendations of that day that the directors failed to approve. After some debate, the suggestion was made that the railroad's Bridgeport steamer add a stop at Stamford. But the railroad's marine superintendent in New York, who was present at the meeting, pointed out that the long channel into Stamford was so narrow that the *Allan Joy*, once in, would be obliged to back out. As such an operation would add at least two hours to her present four-hour run to Bridgeport, it was simply not feasible.[24]

The fourth part of Mellen's program was that the railroad buy the Hartford Line "as soon as it can be had at a reasonable price." The Hartford Line (Hartford and New York Transportation Company) was the only steamship line of any size, other than the Joy Line or the Enterprise Line, running between New York and any port west of Boston, that the railroad did not already own. As it happened, the Hartford Line was for sale. President Charles Goodrich had already expressed the opinion that the line, run as an independent business, could not realize enough profit to make the operation worthwhile. Negotiations began soon after the meeting at the Manhattan Hotel, and the New Haven eventually did purchase the Hartford and New York Transportation Company. The line was never integrated into the New England Navigation Company, however. For reasons that may or perhaps may not become apparent later, the New Haven found it in its interest to keep the Hartford and New York Transportation Company alive as a separate corporate entity, although, like the New England Navigation Company, it was owned outright by the New Haven Railroad.[25]

Mellen's fifth and final proposal was that the railroad buy the Joy Line. After six years, he confessed, the railroad had finally accepted the fact that there was a strong public demand for a cheaper form of steamship travel on Long Island Sound than the well-staffed steamers of the New England Transportation Company could provide. For the company to offer cheaper rates on its prestigious Fall River Line or Providence Line, in Mellen's opinion, would destroy a long-standing reputation for high standards of service and was therefore out of the question. Nor should the railroad continue to waste its resources in projects designed to force out the various competing steamer lines that were bound to appear in the future given the demonstrated demand. The surest solution, Mellen explained to the committee, was for the railroad to go into the low-fare steamship business itself, not merely as a temporary expedient to force out a competitor, as it had with the New Line in Providence a few years before, but as a permanent part of its steamer services, and thus to discourage any future attempts by others to start low-fare lines on the sound. According to Mellen:

> There is a marked demand for a cheaper character of transportation than we furnish by the present service of the New England Navigation Company. The operation of the Joy Line and the new Enterprise Line at Fall River evidence this conclusively, and it would appear to be wise to offer the public not so high character service exclusively that there will be an inducement for others to build up a low-priced business, and, on the strength of the profit made in that, compete for the higher class traffic later.[26]

President Mellen went on to explain to the committee that he did not think it would be necessary, or even particularly wise, for the railroad to set up a whole new low-fare steamship system. The steamers it had operated on the New Line were, for the most part, no longer available, and those that were had proved very expensive to operate in that kind of service. On the other hand, in the Joy Steamship Company, there already existed a functioning low-fare steamship line complete with steamers, crews, wharves, and management facilities. It would be far less expensive and more expedient for the railroad simply to purchase this company and operate it than to attempt to start one of its own. Furthermore, since, as Mellen believed, it would be to the railroad's advantage in public relations to keep its ownership of the low-fare line secret, the public would be less likely to suspect railroad control of a line it had already come to know as an independent operation. What Mellen proposed, in short, was to purchase the Joy Line, preserve its management and its operation intact, use it as a fighting line against the Enterprise competition, and ward off any further competition, but not to publicize the fact that the line was owned by the railroad.[27]

The idea of the New Haven's buying out the Joy Line was not entirely a new one when Mellen presented it to the subcommittee in September. Mellen and Stevenson Taylor had discussed such a proposal as early as March of that year.[28] Taylor had then presented the proposal to Frank Dunbaugh of the Joy Line who was prepared to sell. In fact, Dunbaugh accepted $10,000 on the spot from Taylor in return for an option to buy the Joy Line, in Taylor's name personally, for the price mentioned.[29]

Why was Dunbaugh so willing to sell the Joy Line after working so hard to get the line established, especially now that things were at last going so well? The answer was that things were not going all that well. The line was financially in far better shape than it had been in the fall of 1901, at which time the line was clearly staying in business largely because the owners could not give up at a time when they would all have been financially ruined if they had. By 1905, the Joy Line had become a popular way to travel and had earned a loyal following. And it was making money. But it started as a shoestring operation with very little capital and with old boats, and although circumstances had improved, profits were still marginal (about $60,000 in 1905 according to Dunbaugh's personal estimate), and, as things then stood, probably always would be. It would not take too great a change in the winds of fortune for the company to slip under again and the owners thus lose all they had worked for.

The Joy Line people were also well aware that their present prosperity, not to mention their survival, was a direct product of their rather tenuous rate agreement with the New Haven and that one large sweep of the lion's paw could end the line's existence at any time. In addition, they were genuinely apprehensive about the future of their Boston service. It was doubtful that the *Old Dominion* or the *Seaboard*, both of which were over thirty years old, would have much chance of surviving once Morse's turbine flyers came on. There was a great deal of wisdom in showing a willingness to accept a check for close to a million dollars in place of a steamboat line with a collection of aging steamers and a dubious future.

On April 18, 1905, Frank Dunbaugh, as the majority stockholder of the Joy Line, and Stevenson Taylor, ostensibly acting for himself, signed a document in which Dunbaugh agreed to turn over to Taylor the entire stock of the Joy Steamship Company as soon as he should receive a sum of $925,000.[30] This then was the state of affairs when the *Aransas* sank two weeks later. Given the fact that, as far as Dunbaugh was concerned, the Joy Line had already been sold, it is easier to see why the line made no immediate effort to replace the *Aransas*.

By the time Taylor got back to him with the option, however, Mellen had ascertained that some of the key directors of the railroad were opposed to the purchase of the Joy Line.[31] The matter was, therefore, shelved indefinitely, perhaps to be brought up again when the time seemed ripe. Meanwhile, the Joy Line people, discouraged by the failure of the sale to go through, had turned their attention to acquiring boats to start their service between Boston and Philadelphia. Then, in late August had come Morse's announcement about the proposed Boston line, followed a few weeks later by Mellen's special meeting of the waterlines subcommittee of the New Haven's board of directors. Taking full advantage of the "crisis," Mellen included the purchase of the Joy Line in his five-point plan for dealing with the emergency. Mellen, as usual, had played his cards very carefully, and he won. With the exception of the plan to run small freighters to Greenwich, Stamford, and Norwalk, the board voted overwhelmingly for the other four proposals, including the purchase of the Joy Line.

According to Frank Dunbaugh, Mellen sent for him a few days after this meeting and asked what he would take for the Joy Line. Dunbaugh named a figure of about a million.[32] In arriving at this figure, Dunbaugh placed a value of $200,000 each on the *Larchmont*, the *Edgemont*, and the *Old Dominion* (in each case about three times what the Joy Line had paid for the steamers), $35,000 each for the *Seaboard* and the *City of Key West* (a reasonable though still somewhat inflated, figure), $25,000 for the *Rosalie*, and $250,000 for the line's good will. Mellen told him politely that the figure was too high, and after about an hour's discussion Dunbaugh accepted $775,000 for the line, which represented the $925,000 he had already agreed to in March in his arrangement with Stevenson Taylor minus $150,000 deducted for the *Aransas*.[33]

In a letter reaffirming the agreement with Mellen, Dunbaugh both justified his price and attempted to help Mellen appreciate the value of his acquisition by praising such positive attributes as the various Joy Line steamers possessed:

> The steamer *Rosalie* was built for the purpose of carrying copper . . . and is of her class probably the strongest vessel in these waters.
>
> The S. S. *Old Dominion* has an iron hull, and has always been kept in first-class condition, and is today as staunch and strong a vessel as there is afloat. . . .
>
> The steamers *Larchmont* and *Edgemont* were built to run between Boston and St. Johns, N.B. . . . You will appreciate that in that service they were out in the ocean practically all of the time, exposed to all kinds of weather conditions, and we challenge the world to produce two better steamers of their class.

After going on to describe wharves and other facilities, Dunbaugh ended the letter, and then added as a P.S.: "The *City of Key West* we do not consider a very valuable vessel."[34]

The agreement transferring the Joy Steamship Company to the New Haven Railroad was signed on December 16, 1905. This agreement stipulated that the operation of the Joy Steamship Company would continue as before, that Dunbaugh would stay on as president, that the entire management of the line, in fact, would continue in their present functions, and that the purchase of the Joy Line by the New Haven Railroad was to be kept completely secret from the public.

In short, the Joy Line people were to pocket the $775,000 and then go on running the line just as they had before, but at no personal risk to themselves. To be sure, they were losing their independence, but an independence that had been both precarious and costly, and that, since October 1902, had been pretty much a phantom in any event.

Two other events in December 1905 signaled the end of an era. Early in the month, the name *Allan Joy* was painted out of the nameplates of the railroad's Bridgeport steamer and her new name, *Naugatuck*, painted in their places. Then, on December 7, the Joy Line's steamer *Rosalie* was destroyed by fire. The little *Rosalie*, the ugly old *Rosalie*, the very first steamer purchased by the trio of Dunbaugh, Dimon, and Joy to run from New York to Providence, the little steamer that had served the Joy Line so faithfully since, running to Providence or Boston or on charter whenever called on, running winters through the heaviest storms and thickest ice and always arriving at her destination eventually and with her cargo intact, was gone.

After running all summer and most of the fall to Boston (with the *Old Dominion* and the *Seaboard*), the *Rosalie* had been at Morse's yard (now reopened) in Brooklyn. At about 2:00 A.M. on Friday, December 7, the watch on the United States transport *General McClellen*, lying nearby, saw flames on the freight deck of the *Rosalie*. Several men from the *General McClellen* raced over to the *Rosalie* to awaken the skeleton crew that stayed aboard her. Fortunately, they were all saved, some just in time by jumping into the water, for the fire spread rapidly and in a short time the entire superstructure of the *Rosalie* was in flames. The fire also spread to the *City of Key West*, which was quickly towed to safety. Several other vessels in the yard were also towed into the stream. The city fire boats arrived eventually and fed so much water into the burning vessel that when the fire was finally extinguished, the *Rosalie*'s stern was totally under water. After the fire, the vessel's hull and engines were found to be still in good shape. They were purchased by the H. R. Rowe fishing boat concern operating out of New Haven, and a few months later the remains of the *Rosalie*, rebuilt and repainted, again sailed on Long Island Sound as the fishing steamer *H. R. Rowe and Company*. In this new guise she ran for another sixteen years until she burned again, this time a total loss, in Peconic Bay in 1922.

1906

In 1906, New England had the warmest January in seventy years. After two especially brutal winters during which the sound steamers had either been blown and buffeted by recurrent gales and blizzards on their nightly trips through the sound or forced to fight their way through narrow channels in the ice, this milder winter in 1906, which was free even from the fogs of 1903, was welcome indeed. It was to be a good year for the sound steamer lines in general, for, in spite of the competition from the Enterprise Line, the Fall River, Providence, and Joy lines all carried more passengers in 1906 than in any other year of their histories.

It was a good year financially for the Joy Line people but a strange year as well. They were running a very different sort of business from the one they were used to. The steamers sailed every night well-booked, and the line made more money than ever before. But they were not their steamers, and it was not their money. They were no longer struggling. They were no longer sending their passengers into the sound each night on whatever vessel they could afford to run at the time. They were no longer wondering each day how they were to meet their mounting obligations or whether some unexpected northeast wind would blow them all into financial ruin. They no longer reached anxiously for their morning papers to see if their superannuated steamers were all still afloat and their passengers landed safe and alive at their destinations. The ultimate responsibilities had now passed to others. They were no longer the underdogs, the courageous, if a little naive, small-town businessmen who had come from the pioneer West to challenge the J. P. Morgan-inspired monopoly of the New Haven Railroad. Now they were part of that monopoly. They were its hirelings. They were still at war, but now the war was against others, and they were on the side of the railroad.

The public was not supposed to know that the Joy Line had sold out. But, of course, the public did know. The people of Providence who had been so consistently supportive, who had cheered the underdog even when the Joy Line steamers seemed so prone to run onto rocks or into other vessels, now became suspicious and even hostile. Like all those who had come before, the Joy Line had let them down. Now all passenger and freight rates out of Providence could again be manipulated by the New Haven monopoly. The Enterprise people knew too. Starting in January 1906, their ads began to read, "The only independent line."

How could the public not know? In its operations during 1906, the Joy Line was clearly no longer functioning as an independent company. It was now the "fighting line" of the New Haven Railroad, leaving the Fall River Line and the Providence Line free to maintain their dignity. After 1906, the New Haven quite blatantly used the Joy Line, as it had the New Line between 1900 and 1902 (this time with an only slightly better disguised cover), to undermine its competitors, real or imagined, and force them out of business. Thus, as soon as the Joy Line became part of the New Haven's system, instructions arrived that the line was to expand its services to offer direct competition with those lines then threatening the railroad's monopoly.

Since the railroad had a working agreement with the Winsor Line, then running steamers from both Providence and Boston to Philadelphia, the railroad instructed the Joy Line to drop its proposed Boston-Philadelphia service. Early in 1906, both the *Stillwater* and the *Georgetown*, which the Joy Line had purchased with this new run in mind, were resold without ever having served on the line. Instead, the railroad wanted the Joy Line to improve service on its New York to Boston line, at least until the railroad's own new freighters, then still in the planning stage, were ready to begin operating. The Joy Line was also instructed to start a new low-fare line between New York and Fall River to compete directly with the Enterprise Line, as well as another new service between New York and Bridgeport, Connecticut, to fight off a small new steamer line recently established on that route. No less than seven steamers were added to the Joy Line fleet during the first six months of 1906, for which the railroad, quite casually, made out checks amounting to $560,000.[1]

The first of the Joy Line's new purchases (this one, however, not financed by the railroad) was the *Olympian*, another bargain, which Charlie Dimon traveled all the way to Portland, Oregon, to find. Negotiations for the purchase of the *Olympian* were already well underway when the railroad bought out the Joy Line; Dimon was on the West Coast completing the arrangements when the sale of the line was consummated in December 1905. Since the Joy Line did not wish to alter the terms of the sale agreement Dunbaugh had signed with Stevenson Taylor in April 1905, the *Olympian*, like the other two steamers acquired after that time (the *Stillwater* and the

Georgetown), was not purchased by the Joy Steamship Company, which would thus have made it the property of the New Haven Railroad. It was purchased privately with Frank Dunbaugh and Allan Joy, as partners, owning two-thirds, and Charles Dimon, as an individual, owning one-third.[2]

The *Olympian* was a beautiful ship. With her long graceful lines and her one very tall stack set at a jaunty angle, she somewhat resembled the handsome *Frank Jones* in her general appearance, although, unlike the *Frank Jones*, she had walking beam engine and a large decorated paddlebox. The *Olympian* and her near-sister *Alaskan* had been built in 1883, the same year as the *Tremont*, to run between Tacoma, Washington, and Victoria on Vancouver Island. Constructed on the East Coast, the two had made the long trip around Cape Horn to Puget Sound under their own steam. Both were fast, as they would have to have been to make the daily round trip their schedule called for. The *Olympian* was the faster and was said to have been capable of over eighteen knots, which meant that she could have equaled the speed of most of the Long Island Sound steamers, except the very fastest ones, of course, and far exceeded that of the *Larchmont* and the *Edgemont* or even of the slightly faster Enterprise steamers. At 280 feet overall, the *Olympian* was also somewhat longer than either the Joy Line or the Enterprise boats, but, since her interior tended to reflect the western taste for opulence rather than Maine coast austerity, so much of it was devoted to her famous red plush saloon that she did not carry as many staterooms as the smaller Maine steamers.

Handsome and elegantly furnished as they were, the pair was never successful. Business was not as good as expected, and the fast steamers turned out to be expensive to operate. After only a few seasons on their original run, they were taken down to a route on the Columbia River for awhile but were not popular there either. Following a later and again unsuccessful stint on Puget Sound, the *Alaskan*, en route to San Francisco for an overhaul, was caught in a storm and was lost. After this the *Olympian* was laid up for the most part, seeing only occasional service. Her owners, the Oregon Railroad and Navigation Company, kept her in excellent condition even in layup until, like the prince in the story, Charlie Dimon came along in 1905 to restore her to life.

As long as he was on the West Coast, Dimon decided to do some shopping, and down in San Francisco he came across another bargain in the form of the *Zealandia*, a retired British-built trans-Pacific liner that had once run between San Francisco and Australia. Like the *Olympian*, she had once had a sistership, named predictably the *Australia*, which had also since been lost. Finding the *Zealandia* tied to a pier in the backwaters of San Francisco Bay was roughly like finding a white elephant tied to a tree. But Dimon could never resist a bargain and so he bought her, the official owners again being Dunbaugh, Joy, and Dimon, rather than the Joy Steamship

Company. Nearly 400 feet long, the *Zealandia* was of almost the same length as the new steamers Morse was building for his Boston line, but there the similarity abruptly ended. Built in 1875, she was of the same vintage as the *Old Dominion* and not nearly in such good condition.

Dimon ostensibly bought the *Zealandia* to tow the *Olympian* around to New York. If this had indeed been the only reason, surely he could have picked up a serviceable tugboat for the same price. Then at least he would have had a vessel that could have been put to some use back in New York when he got it there. Besides, the *Olympian* had made the trip around the horn once under her own steam; there was no reason to assume she could not have done it again, and, as things turned out, she would have been far better off if she had.

The *Olympian* was brought down to San Francisco by the tug *Dauntless*, and there her sidewheels were detached from the machinery, so that they would turn freely and not drag in the water, and her stack removed. Thus emasculated, the lovely *Olympian* was taken in tow by the *Zealandia*. On January 31, 1906, the strange procession moved slowly out of the Golden Gate and into the Pacific, just ten weeks ahead of San Francisco's great earthquake.[3] Six weeks later, the pair passed into the Straits of Magellan. They had almost reached the Atlantic when one of the violent storms that are common to the straits blew up unexpectedly and kept the two steamers tossing about for several hours in mammoth waves. When the storm finally subsided, the *Zealandia* and the *Olympian* both anchored for a few days in Possession Bay to give their crews some needed relaxation before proceeding into the Atlantic. While they were there, the storm came up again, quite without warning. With the winds roaring furiously, the *Olympian* broke her anchor chain and was blown up on the beach. When the efforts of the *Zealandia* to pull her off proved unavailing, the officers had to call in a salvage company, which eventually refloated the *Olympian* at a cost equivalent to $15,000. The *Zealandia* soon set sail again with the *Olympian* in tow, but they had been underway only a short time before they were struck by a third flash storm during which the towrope suddenly snapped and the *Olympian*, helpless and without power in the stormy seas, was again blown onto the beach.[4]

This time the problem was far more serious. Possession Bay, like the Bay of Fundy, is subject to extraordinary tides, in this case about 45 feet measured vertically. As it happened, the *Olympian* had been blown onto a long, gradually sloping beach at the height of an exceptionally high equinoxal tide. The salvage company pointed out that the only way to float her again would be to dredge a long channel back to the deep water, a job that would cost in excess of $40,000. The *Olympian* was becoming less of a bargain every day. The *Zealandia* and her crew waited in the straits for nearly a month, hoping that a way could be found to float the *Olympian* less expensively. But finally the *Zealandia* weighed anchor and, leaving her burden there alone on the beach, steamed on to New York alone. Four men, including the retired Captain Jacob Wise, who had come along to oversee the *Olympian* during the voyage, stayed behind for several months to guard the steamer.[5] Her owners considered many ways of refloating the *Olympian* over the next few months. But they no longer controlled the Joy Line, the service for which she had been intended. In the succeeding months, their own position in the company became daily more ambiguous, so that, in the long run, the matter of salvaging their steamer was taken out of their hands. As it turned out, the beautiful *Olympian* was left on the beach in the Straits of Magellan to rot—her remains can still be seen there today—not as a result of a conscious decision, but merely by default.

When questioned in New York about his purchase of the *Olympian*, Dimon, without making any reference to his connection with the Joy Line, professed that he had wanted to use the steamer in the excursion business out of Boston.[6] Since Dimon later did engage in the excursion business, after his Joy Line days, though out of New York, it is possible that he had some thought of purchasing his partners' share of the steamer and starting an independent excursion business, especially as Dimon definitely had not approved of Dunbaugh's selling the line to the New Haven. When she was first purchased, however, it seems certain that she was intended as a third steamer for the Providence route. After the sale of the Joy Line to the New Haven, the line probably planned to use her on its proposed new line to Fall River.

As soon as the sale of the Joy Line to the railroad was completed, Mellen had instructed Dunbaugh to make plans for a line between New York and Fall River, the sole object of which would be to force the Enterprise out of business. Mellen made funds available to purchase steamers and lease wharves for the new service. Early in March, the Joy Line was fortunate in being able to buy the steamer *Tennessee* from the Old Bay Line, by far the best boat the line ever ran and a luxury it would not have been able to afford had it not been permitted to reach into Mellen's apparently ample pockets. The *Tennessee* spent much of her life on steamship lines designed to drive other lines out of business, and, on her first such assignment, she had proved successful in this mission even before she came from the builders. The Old Bay Line* at that time was operating the two smart propellor steamers *Alabama* and *Georgia* on its overnight route between Baltimore and Norfolk. For over fifty-five years, the Old Bay Line had successfully warded off any competition that had appeared on this route, but

---

*Then embarking on a program of expanding and improving its fleet under the direction of the popular "Captain" John R. Sherwood, first vice-president and general manager and then, after 1907, as president.

in 1896, the Chesapeake Line, which until then had been running smaller steamers between Baltimore and West Point, Virginia, with train connections for Richmond, decided to run a competing line between Baltimore and Norfolk. The Bay Line retaliated by starting a line of its own from Baltimore directly to Richmond to outflank the Chesapeake Line's West Point service. On this new run the Bay Line placed its older spare steamer, the sidewheeler, *Virginia*, which, as we have already seen, was later to appear under charter on the Joy Line. At the same time, it placed an order for a brand new steel propellor steamer for the run which appeared a year later as the *Tennessee*. In general appearance, the *Tennessee* was a much smaller and slightly less attractive version of the *Georgia* and *Alabama*, but very narrow and equipped with twin screws to help her navigate the winding passages of the upper James River (which the wider sidewheeler *Old Dominion* was managing without much difficulty at the time).

This tactic did not drive the Chesapeake Line from the Baltimore-Norfolk route, but, before the *Tennessee* was completed, the two lines did reach a mutually satisfactory rate agreement and the Bay Line dropped its Richmond route. When the smart and fast *Tennessee* was delivered, however, the line decided to keep her as the spare steamer and to dispose of the *Virginia*. The *Virginia* then wandered for a number of years on a variety of charters, including the one to the Joy Line in 1901-1902, before starting a whole new career, lasting longer than the one on the Chesapeake, as the St. Lawrence River steamer *Tadousac*. Then, early in January 1906, the Bay Line took possession of a new steamer, also called *Virginia*, which was an almost identical sistership of the much older *Alabama*. With the *Virginia* on the line, the *Georgia* now became the company's spare, so that Captain Sherwood was able to put the *Tennessee* up for sale at the time the Joy Line was looking for a steamer to run on its new line to Fall River with its recently acquired *Olympian*.

When the Joy Line brought the *Tennessee* up from Baltimore, she was still less than ten years old and had rarely been used. She had a steel hull, twin screws, and could cruise easily at eighteen knots, making her by far the fastest steamer ever operated by the Joy Line. The *Tennessee* was also known to be an excellent sea boat. Since she was very narrow, however, her one disadvantage over the older sidewheelers was that her interior accommodations were cramped; she did not have the wide carpeted corridors and open saloons that the broad-beamed sidewheelers could carry between their rows of staterooms. But she was new and clean, and the Joy Line took great pride in her.

Although the *Tennessee* was purchased in March, the new service to Fall River was held up for several months while the line first waited for the arrival of the *Olympian*, then debated whether to salvage her, and scouted around for another steamer to replace her.

Shortly after his return from San Francisco, Dimon, who had been the general manager of the Joy Line since it started and one of the three original partners who had conceived the idea of a low-rate steamer line for Long Island Sound, resigned to become vice-president and general manager of the newly organized Brunswick Steamship Company. As noted, Dimon had not approved of the sale of the line to the New Haven Railroad. Although he was a part-owner of the *Dover*, the *Olympian*, and the *Zealandia*, he did not own any stock in the company itself and had therefore had no part in the decision to sell the line. The Brunswick Steamship Company was an extension of the Atlantic Railway, which had recently undergone a major expansion under the leadership of its president H. M. Atkinson of Atlanta. The railroad brought lumber out of central Georgia to its terminus at Brunswick, and the main function of the steamship line was to carry the lumber to New York, though under Dimon's direction its horizons were somewhat expanded. In addition to the four lumber ships that were soon to be delivered, Dimon had also purchased a passenger steamer, the *Brunswick*, which he proposed to run between New York, Brunswick, and Havana, Cuba. John Rowland, who had been the general passenger agent for the Joy Line, and whose extraordinary competence, as we have seen, made him especially valuable to the line, particularly in the difficult days during the rate negotiations with the New Haven Railroad, followed Dimon to the Brunswick Line shortly afterward.[7]

Although no one could ever really fill his place at the Joy Line, many of Dimon's duties were taken over by Robert L. Noble, who held the title of general superintendent.[8]

During the first week in February 1906, a newspaper announcement stated that the Clyde Line had been acquired "by new interests based in Bath, Maine." When questioned about it, Charles W. Morse said he knew nothing about such a deal, though no one seriously considered the possibility that anyone else in Bath, Maine, was likely to have bought the Clyde Line. The line was one of the largest marine operations along the Atlantic Coast, with steamers running from Boston and New York to Charleston and Jacksonville, as well as between Philadelphia and Norfolk, and on the St. John's River in Florida.[9] So far, Morse's acquisitions had been limited to the Maine coast and the Hudson River. Bringing together the various lines of his native Maine or even the two major night lines on the Hudson River could be made to appear to have advantages to the public. But the purchase of the Clyde Line and then of the Mallory Line (between New York and various ports on the Gulf of Mexico) shortly thereafter made it apparent that Morse had nothing less in mind than a monopoly of Atlantic Coast shipping, with which he could manipulate fares and freight rates to his own profit.

Mellen was summoned to Washington by Theodore Roosevelt to discuss the matter on February 15 (two days before Roosevelt's eldest daughter Alice was to marry Senator Nicholas Longworth, thus becoming a more permanent fixture in Washington than her illustrious father). Mellen—known to be the right-hand man of J. P. Morgan—suavely assured the president that the New Haven Railroad was doing all it could to curb Morse's monopolistic bent! As an example of the railroad's efforts, he cited its proposed new steamer line to Boston, which was intended to improve the services already offered by the railroad to the people of New England.[10] That he could convince the president that Morse's new line to Boston represented monopolistic tendencies while the New Haven's new line to Boston represented improved service, is either a tribute to Mellen's talents or a comment on Roosevelt's intelligence.

Through much of the winter, the *Maine* and the *New Hampshire* again served as the freighters on the Providence Line. With the Joy Line now controlled by the New Haven, it seems difficult to believe that winter passengers to Providence were limited to the *Larchmont* or the *Edgemont*, while the attractive and modern steel propeller steamers *Maine* and *New Hampshire* sailed alongside them on the same route carrying cargo. When the *Maine* was taken off in February to replace the *City of Lowell* on the New London Line, as she had been doing each year during the colder months, the sidewheeler *Nashua* took her place on the Providence Line. This was to be the *Nashua*'s last year of service. On February 21, 1906, the *Pequonnock*, the first of two new steel-hulled propellor freighters being built by the railroad to replace the *Nashua* and the *Pequot*, was launched at Roach's yard in Chester, Pennsylvania.

On Saturday, March 3, the Fall River Line brought the *Pilgrim* up to Fall River from Newport to take the *Plymouth*'s place on the line for the rest of the winter season so that the *Plymouth* could go to Newport for major repairs to her engine. Her engine frame was coming apart and had to be replaced, an operation that necessitated removing the entire engine from the steamer, putting in a new frame, and then replacing the engine again. It was estimated that the *Plymouth* might be out of service about three months and return just about in time to start the summer Providence service. After three weeks in the Newport shops, much of the *Plymouth*'s engine had been dismantled and was lying on the dock on large wooden racks, when at 2:25 A.M. on the morning of Tuesday, March 27, a fire broke out on the laid-up steamer. Before any help could be summoned, the whole superstructure was ablaze and there was little hope of saving her. The line's management requested that the fire department not pour water onto the burning *Plymouth* as the streams of cold water on the red-hot steel could permanently weaken the strength of the hull. Since the wooden superstructure was doomed anyway, it was better, they argued, just to let it burn. Then, at least, there would be some chance of salvaging the hull.

The fire also spread to the *City of Lowell*, which was laid up near the burning *Plymouth*, but a passing tug came by and pulled the *City of Lowell* out into the stream before the fire was out of control.

That very evening the New England Navigation Company almost lost another steamer to fire. The *Richard Peck*, then operating temporarily on the New London Line, was off Faulkner's Island near Guilford, Connecticut, when just before midnight a fire broke out in one of the forward staterooms. The blaze was serious enough for Captain T. Harvey MacDonald to order the passengers onto the deck and the lifeboats swung out into position. But the fire was eventually brought under control, and all the passengers returned to their berths.

Once the ruins of the *Plymouth* had stopped smoldering, the company officials examined the remains and decided that the hull was still in good condition. The engine, too, was intact, since most of it had been out of the steamer during the fire anyway. So they decided to build a new *Plymouth* using the hull and engines of the old one. In designing the new *Plymouth*, J. Howland Gardner, the man who had replaced George Peirce as the company's marine architect, made her interior decor and her stateroom arrangements conform as much as her somewhat smaller size would allow to those of the new *Providence*. Thus, while the two steamers were quite different in exterior appearance (especially since the *Plymouth* was the only Fall River liner with just one stack) after the *Plymouth* was rebuilt, their interior accommodations were very similar, and the railroad had two relatively new and modern steamers for the winter service to Fall River and for the summer Providence Line.

Since the Fall River Line was already planning another new steamer, larger than any it then operated, to run with the *Priscilla* in the summer service to Fall River, one might ask why the line went to the expense of rebuilding the *Plymouth* when it might just as well have kept the *Puritan*, probably the most beautiful of all the sound liners, in service with the *Providence*. As we have previously noted, the Navigation Company had already determined to retire its steamers with the older walking beam type engines. The *Puritan's* engine was particularly expensive to run and, in recent years, had begun to require a great deal of repair. A rebuilt *Plymouth*, with its smaller, more efficient plant, could be operated much more cheaply. Moreover, in Gardner's plans for her reconstruction, the deck arrangements were so efficiently laid out that she would now have almost as many staterooms as the larger *Puritan* and considerably greater cargo space.

When the new *Providence* appeared the year before, it had been expected that the *Pilgrim* would be retired or, at best, maintained only as a spare. But after the burning of the *Plymouth*, the *Pilgrim* was given a reprieve and was back in service with the *Providence* for over a year until the rebuilt *Plymouth* was finished.

With the weather continuing warm through the spring and business better than ever that year, most of the summer operations started early in 1906. Both the *Priscilla* and the *Puritan* were on the Fall River Line by the first of May and the *Providence* and the *Pilgrim* were scheduled to open the summer service to Providence on about May 15, two weeks earlier than usual. But on May 4, after only a few trips, the *Priscilla* developed a problem with her port wheel and was off the route again for nearly two weeks. The *Providence* went back on the Fall River Line in her place, with the result that the *Chester W. Chapin*, replaced on the New London Line for several days by her predecessor the *City of Worcester*, was assigned to join the *Pilgrim* in opening the Providence Line's season.

In the season of 1906, the Enterprise Line steamers also began making stops in each direction at Jamestown, Rhode Island, on Conanicut Island, imitating the Fall River Line's tradition of stopping each way at Newport. This landing was intended only in part as a service to the relatively small population of Conanicut Island. The Enterprise Line was clearly attempting to siphon off some of the Fall River Line's Newport passengers. It would have scheduled its stop at Newport itself had not the railroad been able to prevent the line's getting docking rights there. But the ferry from Newport to Jamestown took just fifteen minutes and cost only a dime. Thus, Newport passengers could still travel to New York on the Enterprise boat for only $1.10 rather than the $3.50 which was the fare that summer on the *Priscilla* or the *Puritan*, if they were willing to leave Newport a few minutes earlier. The New Haven was offered an opportunity of preventing the Enterprise from securing dockage at Jamestown as well,[11] but for some reason did not take advantage of it.

Late in April, the *Shinnecock* arrived back in New York after her winter charter in Florida. As she had the year before, she went almost immediately on the Joy Line, sailing from New York on Monday, May 7, to relieve the *Larchmont* for her spring overhaul.

Early in June 1906, Dunbaugh and Joy must have been somewhat startled when the large hulk of the *Zealandia*, in which they had bought a two-thirds interest, sight unseen, appeared, quite alone, in New York harbor, and made her way to lay up at Morse's where all good Joy Line boats went when they had nothing better to do.[12] Through the summer, marine reporters came up with many interesting theories about the Joy Line's plans for the *Zealandia*, some of them undoubtedly based on thoughts expressed by the owners themselves. One report had her getting ready for the Joy Line's Boston run, though this must have been the least likely possibility.[13] Another more plausible story was that Charles Dimon planned to run her as a cruise ship between New York and Havana.[14] Still another source reported that she was being converted into an army transport. Would that this had been so, but alas, none of these reports was true. What happened to the *Zealandia* was that she sat in layup for another ten years, while her owners paid dock charges and taxes, and she rusted. Finally, even Charlie Dimon got disgusted with the old ship and was prepared to take whatever the scrap yard would offer to get her off his hands. But by this time Frank Dunbaugh had become intrigued by the idea of owning an ocean liner, useless as it was. So, much to his former partner's amusement, Dunbaugh bought Dimon's share and Allan Joy's as well. Now owned by Dunbaugh alone, the *Zealandia* continued to sit, taking up space and getting older until World War I came along. With tonnage of any kind suddenly skyrocketing wildly in value, Dunbaugh sold the old ship to the government at a positively embarrassing profit. Dunbaugh later congratulated himself on his business acumen in outsmarting Dimon. But clearly only luck and a world war saved Dunbaugh from being stuck with a large white elephant.

At about the same time, the Joy Line took possession of a considerably more serviceable vessel, the *Santiago*, which it had recently purchased from the New York and Cuba Mail Line (Ward Line), this time with Mellen's money, to replace the *Seaboard* on the line's Boston run.[15] A propellor steamer built in 1879, she was newer than her running mate by a few years, and at 280 feet overall also slightly longer. She was hopelessly uninteresting in appearance: her straight-sided black iron hull had an unusually high freeboard and relatively little superstructure above it. Nonetheless, she had an enormous cargo-carrying capacity for her size, and once in the service she proved slow enough to maintain the *Old Dominion*'s established schedule. In short, from the time of her first sailing for the Joy Line out of New York on Friday night, June 9, 1906, she proved a suitable running mate for the *Old Dominion*. Captain Richard Holmes and most of the officers from the *Seaboard* now transferred to the *Santiago*, although the *Seaboard*, now commanded by Josiah Kelly, remained in service on the Boston run, carrying freight only, for the rest of the summer.[16]

That same week the Joy Line acquired still another vessel, for, having abandoned any hope of refloating the *Olympian*, the line had decided to purchase another steamer to run with the *Tennessee* to Fall River. The steamer it finally found was the *Martinique*, which had been the Joy Line's first passenger boat in 1900.[17] By 1906, she was proving too small for the rapidly growing Miami-Key West-Havana traffic, so at the end of that season the P. and O. Line had decided to sell her. She was also really too small to serve either as a suitable running mate for the *Tennessee* or as much of a challenge to the *Kennebec* or the *Frank Jones* of the Enterprise Line. Thus, while the Joy Line had felt fortunate when it had been able to charter the *Martinique* in 1900, it did not now find her very satisfactory. But she was the best the line could find on such short notice and was brought on as a temporary expedient until a better steamer could be located. The *Martinique* left Miami soon after her season there ended and arrived in New York during the last week of June. With no time for painting or refitting, she was placed almost immediately on the line, since the service was already scheduled to start with the sailing of the *Tennessee* out of New York for Fall River on Saturday night, June 30.

Some weeks earlier, Frank Dunbaugh and Allan Joy had booked passage to Fall River aboard the *Frank Jones*, partly to get a closer look at what the competition had to offer but mainly to see about acquiring dock property in Fall River. This search was made much easier than similar ones several years earlier now that the powerful New Haven Railroad was backing them and not using its considerable influence to frustrate their efforts. Dunbaugh and Joy first made a bid to lease the wharf of the Providence, Newport, and Fall River Steamboat Company, which had recently given up its passenger service, but the city of Fall River offered objections to their use of that pier, possibly in an effort to protect the locally popular Enterprise Line. Finally, on May 10, the Joy Line obtained a one-year lease on a pier previously used by the Winsor Line located at the foot of Center Street,[18] near the Fall River Line's pier and therefore convenient to the railroad, in an area now filled in to provide parking for visitors to the battleship *Massachusetts*.

Ads in the local newspaper that appeared a few days before the service began told the people of Fall River that the *Tennessee* and the *Martinique* would sail between New York and Fall River six nights a week. The fare was $1.00, the same as the fare on the Enterprise Line and fifty cents less than the Joy Line's fare to Providence, which the railroad allowed the line to keep at $1.50 for the second summer in a row.

Since the twin-screw *Tennessee* was a much smarter and much newer steamer than any of the other steamers then on the Joy Line, it was fitting that her captain should be David Wilcox, who had been the captain of the *Rosalie* on her first trip for the Joy Line seven years before and had since remained the senior captain of the line. The *Tennessee's* first pilot was Foster Gray, who had been first pilot on the *Rosalie*. Wilcox's place as captain of the *Larchmont* was awarded to the youngest man ever to serve as master of a Long Island Sound night boat, the twenty-five-year-old George William McVay. Fellow officers were unanimous in their belief, however, that in spite of his youth, McVay was an excellent choice for the position and a thoroughly capable mariner. Born in Bangor, Maine, he began his Long Island Sound career as a bow watchman on Chapin's Narragansett Bay Line at the age of nineteen, serving on both the *Richard Peck* and the *Chester W. Chapin*. He then worked his way up very rapidly, serving the railroad first on the New Line steamers *Massachusetts* and *Rhode Island* and later on the Fall River Line steamers *City of Fall River* and *Plymouth* before transferring to the Joy Line as a pilot when he got his master's papers in 1902 at the age of twenty-three. His first Joy Line assignment was as a pilot on the *City of Key West* under Captain Jacob Wise. Later, he served under both Wise and Olweiler on the *Tremont* and under Olweiler on the *Edgemont*, before being transferred to Wilcox's *Larchmont*. McVay had distinguished himself in February 1904 when, as the pilot on duty aboard the *Tremont* the morning she burned in New York, he had walked through the blazing steamer making sure that everyone on board was awake, and he himself was the last to leave.

Apparently, the Joy Line had been a bit optimistic in placing the *Martinique* in service so soon after her arrival from the South. One round trip sufficed to show that she was not ready for service, and on her return to New York she was taken off for repairs, not to return to the line before early August. In the meantime, the *Tennessee* was left alone on the run making sailings three nights a week from each port. When the *Martinique* finally reappeared on the line, she had been extensively overhauled, had several new state-rooms added, and sported a brand new name on her bow: *Kentucky*. Her master was Captain E. C. Rood, who had commanded the *Aransas* when she went down. For the rest of that summer, the *Kentucky* left New York on Monday, Wednesday, and Friday evenings and sailed to Fall River in company with the *Priscilla* and the *Frank Jones*, while on the same evenings the *Puritan*, the *Kennebec*, and the *Tennessee* came down from Fall River.

As soon as the Joy Line began its new low-fare service to Fall River, the Enterprise countered with an announcement that it had plans already drawn up for four new propellor steamers. Two, which were to be turbine driven, would replace the *Frank Jones* and the *Kennebec* on the present Fall River run. The second pair, which were to be powered with the more conventional triple expansion engines, would be used to inaugurate a new Enterprise Line service between New York and Providence.[19] Once again, one detects the voice of Charles W. Morse behind these announcements, although Morse's involvement in the Enterprise operation was never proved.

The very day after the Joy Line opened its new service to Fall River, the line also inaugurated a second new service between New York and Bridgeport, Connecticut, another route on which Mellen had seen the specter of competition. The "competition" in Bridgeport, which was known as the Merchants Line, was provided by three local businessmen with an accumulated capital of $16,000 (about one-sixth the capital the Joy Line had started with). They chartered a boat about the size of the *Rosalie* to carry freight for Bridgeport shippers at a rate admittedly well below that charged on the railroad-owned line. The boat they had chartered was the *Conoho*.[20] The Enterprise Line had found that the amount of cargo picked up in Providence was not sufficient to continue paying the Providence, Newport, and Fall River, to carry it for them every day, and so the company had now chartered the *Conoho* to the Merchants Line. Given the small amount of capital available to the new company and its chances of survival against the competition already offered by the railroad's line, the service was probably scheduled for a fairly short life from the start, without Mellen making any special effort to hasten its demise. But it was not the nature of the New Haven to let a competitor die in peace, and, even before the Merchants Line actually began operating on March 5, 1905, Mellen had already instructed the Joy Line to get ready to operate a line to Bridgeport.

Early in the year, the Joy Line once again dipped into the New Haven's till and gave yet another venerable steamer a reprieve from the scrap yards. This one was the *Richard Borden*, also from the Providence, Newport, and Fall River Steamboat Company.[21] She was an odd-looking craft, having been built as a double-ender like a ferry boat, so that she would be able to run in and out of the narrow channel at Bristol without turning around. A sidewheeler, 225 feet long, or about the same length as the *Allan Joy* or the *City of Key West*, and very broad with a walking beam engine, she had been built in 1874 and placed on the Providence to Fall River run. By 1900, however, by which time the *Richard Borden* had been plying this route nearly every day for over a quarter of a century, trolleys were taking passengers from Providence to Fall River in less than half the time. The line therefore gave up its passenger service, and the *Richard Borden* found her way to that half-way home for aging steamboats, the Joy Line. After a few trial excursion trips to Bridgeport as the *Richard Borden*, the Joy Line sent her over to Morse's where she joined the *Tennessee*, which had been acquired at about the same time, for an extensive rebuilding and overhaul, from which she emerged in June renamed the *Fairfield*.*[22]

In past years the *Allan Joy*, now the *Naugatuck*, had run on the Bridgeport Line alone during the winter months, leaving New York at 3:00 P.M. and arriving in Bridgeport after what must have been a fairly leisurely trip at 8:00 P.M. Returning, she left Bridgeport at midnight and got to New York by 6:00 A.M. But, since her freight capacity was limited, when the railroad took over the line in 1904, it usually ran the *City of Lawrence* in the winter. In the spring, however, when the two-boat schedule started and the day boat

---

*While Morse in this period was naming his new steamers after various members of his interlocking directorates, the New Haven was naming its new ones for the towns they served, first with the *Providence*, which came out in 1905, and later with the renaming of the *Allan Joy*, the *William G. Payne*, and now the *Richard Borden* as the *Naugatuck*, the *Bridgeport*, and the *Fairfield*, respectively. Some consideration was given at the time to renaming the *Chester W. Chapin* the *City of New London*, which not only would have honored the port she ran to but would also have better conformed with the name of her running mate the *City of Lowell*, and to renaming the *Richard Peck* the *City of New Haven* as well. But the citizens of the towns the New Haven so intended to honor took such pride in their steamers' names as they had come to know them that they complained bitterly when they heard of the proposal, and the plan was dropped.

took much of the freight, the *Naugatuck* was back leaving Bridgeport at midnight but now departing from New York at 11:00 A.M. and making the return trip by day. The *Bridgeport* made a round trip from Bridgeport by day, leaving there at 8:00 A.M. and New York at 3:00 P.M. on the return schedule that the *City of Lawrence* had in the winter. On Sundays, when little if any freight was moved, the *Bridgeport* adjusted her schedule for the excursion trade by moving her departure from Bridgeport up to 9:00 A.M. and from New York to 5:00 P.M.

The new Merchants Line's schedule followed fairly closely the winter schedule of the *City of Lawrence*, though one hour later, leaving New York six days a week at 4:00 P.M. and Bridgeport at 1:00 A.M.

The Joy Line's new line to Bridgeport (which now made the third line between New York and that city), unlike its new Fall River service, was preceded by a great deal of publicity. The *Fairfield* was to be a day steamer with a round-trip schedule similar to the *Bridgeport*'s, though leaving Bridgeport one hour later, at 9:00 A.M. on weekdays. On Sundays, the *Fairfield* was to leave Bridgeport earlier, at 7:30 in the morning, so that on her arrival in New York, she could go on to Coney Island and back, both to provide additional pleasure for the Bridgeport passengers who wanted to stay aboard and to take on extra excursionists in New York, before departing again for Bridgeport at 4:00 P.M. The one-way fare on the *Fairfield* was forty cents—a whole dime less than that of the Bridgeport Line—and for the round trip, seventy-five cents.

The Joy Line operation to Bridgeport was kept completely separate from the regular Bridgeport Line and was managed entirely by the Joy Line organization. The public was not to know that the Joy Line was also owned by the railroad. Bridgeport Line officials were instructed merely to work out a reasonable apportionment of freight with the Joy Line.[23] The arrangement in Bridgeport was to be similar to that in Providence and now also in Fall River: through freight and most bulk freight were to be routed via the Bridgeport Line, whose two piers were on the west bank of the Pequonnock River near the railroad station. Local freight and most package freight were to go to the Joy Line, whose pier was on the east side of the river, at the end of Main Street and extending to Pembroke Street, nearer most local manufacturers. (The Merchants Line dock was at the foot of Nichols Street, on the same side of the river as the Joy Line pier but further up the Yellow Mill Channel.) In order to compete with the Merchants Line, or any future lines that might be established (the Norwalk freight line was then also considering extending its route to Bridgeport), the Joy Line rates were much lower than the Bridgeport Line's, though, as in Providence, the differentials were agreed to in advance. In the process of working out these agreements, Charles A. Dart of Bridgeport left the employ of the railroad to become the auditor of the Joy Line.

The first trip of the *Fairfield* was out of Bridgeport on July 1, the day after the *Tennessee*'s first sailing to Fall River. Since it was a Sunday, the first trip included the excursion to Coney Island. After this much-publicized beginning, the New Haven very quickly came to realize that the Joy Line's cheap boat to Bridgeport was having the same effect that the New Line had in Providence six years before: it was taking more business away from its own line than from the competitor's. After only one more Sunday excursion, the *Fairfield* suddenly ceased to be a day boat and became a night freighter operating on a schedule like that of the *Naugatuck* and the Merchants Line's boat, departing from New York at 4:00 P.M. and from Bridgeport at 1:00 A.M.

The repairs to the thirty-year-old *Fairfield* had taken so long that, by the time the Joy Line to Bridgeport got started, it was no longer really needed. By July, the Merchants Line had just about decided to give up the struggle on its own accord, although the Joy Line may be credited with the *coup de grace*. The *Conoho* had proved too slow for the service and had been returned to her owners in June. (The Enterprise Line had also complained a year earlier that the *Conoho* was unable to make the run from Fall River to Providence and back in time to meet the evening sailing; the line had even considered establishing a freight stop at Bristol to shorten her route.) The Merchants Line next chartered the *Meteor* from the Long Island Railroad, a small freighter that had once run with the *Conoho* on Chesapeake Bay, but this charter was of short duration. Next the *Lizzie Henderson*, a very small boat from the Wright and Cobb Lighterage Company, made a few trips until the Merchants Line managed to charter the *Plain Mary*, another Narragansett Bay steamer. But the owners could not afford to maintain this charter for more than a few weeks, and the *Plain Mary* was soon replaced by the *Lorraine*, another lighter, leased from the Downing Transportation Company of Brooklyn. By the time the *Lorraine* came on in July, one of the three men who had originally organized the Merchants Line had already backed out, and the remaining two had come to understand that they would soon be forced to give up. When the *Lorraine* developed engine problems early in August, the Merchants Line first chartered the *John M. Worth* for one round trip and then asked the Joy Line to accept all of the line's contractual obligations for the future. The Merchants Line, of course, believed that it was dealing with a fellow low-rate competitor and not with a surreptitious agent of the New Haven Railroad. With the departure of the *John M. Worth* from Bridgeport at 1:00 A.M. on August 3 the Merchants Line ceased to exist.

In spite of the demise of the Merchants Line, the New Haven kept the Joy Line to Bridgeport running, although later under a different name, until the 1930s. One reason was to discourage future low-rate competition. Another was that the New Haven realized the value of having two sets of rates to serve the needs of different kinds of shippers, but obviously it could not post two separate rate schedules for the same line.

With the addition of two new routes out of New York and the purchase of a larger steamer for its Boston run, the Joy Line had, in the course of a few weeks, outgrown the north side of Pier 27, East River,* which had served it since the spring of 1900. In June, therefore, the railroad-financed Joy Line took a ten-year lease on Pier 28 as well, both sides, and from this time the Boston steamers had Pier 27 to themselves. The *Larchmont* and *Edgemont* for Providence, the *Tennessee* and *Kentucky* for Fall River, and the *Fairfield* for Bridgeport all departed from Pier 28.

During the summer of 1906, the New England Navigation Company again ran its usual Sunday excursions: the *City of Lowell* up the Hudson, the *Richard Peck* her special Sunday sailings from New York to New Haven and back, and the *Chester W. Chapin* her roundabout route from New London to Greenport and Newport. As she had the previous summer, the *New Hampshire* again made regular Sunday trips from New Bedford to Providence and back with stops each way at Newport. In 1906, the Enterprise Line also got into the excursion business with the *Frank Jones* out of New York taking excursionists up the sound to nowhere and back without stopping, while the *Kennebec* at the other end now inaugurated a weekly Sunday trip from Fall River to Providence and back.

In July, the Joy Line again arranged its sailings so that the *Larchmont* would lay over in Providence on Sundays, and in 1906, she was again carrying throngs of overheated Rhode Islanders down Narragansett Bay and over to Martha's Vineyard. After several Sunday trips to Cottage City, on July 22, the *Larchmont* tried something new—a trip to New London and back. The New England Navigation Company, which in the past had shown only disdain for the Sunday excursion business, now saw from the Joy Line's proceeds that there was a considerable profit to be made from these trips. It therefore decided to send one of its big Providence Line boats out on Sunday excursions. Since the Providence Line had a sailing out of New York on Saturday nights but not out of Providence, both of its steamers were in Providence on Sundays, but only one of them needed to be ready for the Sunday night sailing. Not wishing to impinge on the business the Joy Line had built on its Cottage City run, the Providence Line was looking for some other destination that would appeal to Sunday excursionists. Since the New Haven Railroad already had a dock in New London, which the *Chester W. Chapin* did not occupy on Sundays, it decided to try an excursion from Providence to New London and back. But first it asked the Joy Line to run

*The Joy Line had not moved from the pier it leased in 1900. During the period under discussion, many of the East River piers were rebuilt, necessitating a general renumbering. Thus, the Joy Line's Pier 35, East River, now became Pier 27, East River.

the *Larchmont* to New London instead of Cottage City for a few trips to see if the route would prove popular enough to place a larger steamer on the run. After the *Larchmont's* second trip to New London on July 29, the New England decided that the route would indeed serve its purpose. The following week, August 5, the big iron wheels of the *Pilgrim* thrashed down Narragansett Bay on the first of what was expected to be a regular weekly excursion of the Providence Line.

Although the excursion to New London was successful and repeated often thereafter, the trip the following week was not to be made by the *Pilgrim*. That Sunday night, August 5, the *Puritan*, coming up from New York, broke her shaft when passing New London, again near the spot where Fall River steamers tended to break down. The *Providence* was sailing out of Providence that night and, having passed the inbound *Pilgrim* just north of Newport and tooted greetings, three hours later she came across the disabled *Puritan* wallowing in the sound. Throwing her a line, the *Providence* towed the *Puritan* into New London and then proceeded, somewhat late, to New York.

On Monday the *Pilgrim*, which was supposed to sail from Providence that night, paddled instead down to Fall River to take the place of the *Puritan*. Thus, the Fall River Line had a sailing on Monday night, but the rearrangement of steamers caused a great deal of confusion and not a little anger when three hundred passengers turned up at Fox Point wharf in Providence that evening prepared to go to New York and found no boat. The most logical replacement for the *Pilgrim* on the Providence Line would have been the *Connecticut*. But she was then in Stonington, and it would have taken several days to get steam up and have her ready for the run. Since the smaller *Rhode Island* was at Newport, which was closer, the company gave instructions for the *Rhode Island* to go up to Providence that Monday. The crew spent most of the day trying to get steam up only to discover that, since the *Rhode Island* had not been in service for some time,* her boilers were in very poor condition. They finally got the *Rhode Island* moving, but she did not turn up in Providence until 10:00 P.M. for a 7:45 sailing. About an hour later, when the over three hundred tired and now rather angry passengers had been ushered aboard and assigned to staterooms (on a steamboat considerably smaller than the one they expected to sail on), the engineer informed the captain that the *Rhode Island* was simply not in condition to sail that night. The passengers were then ordered off again and

---

*The *Rhode Island* had not been in regular operation since the demise of the New Line in 1902 and had not even been used in relief service after the suspension of passenger service to Stonington in the fall of 1903 had released the *Maine* and *New Hampshire* for winter relief duty. With the *Plymouth* and the *Puritan* both out of commission in midsummer 1906, however, the railroad lines were facing a serious shortage of large steamers for the first time since 1902.

delivered to the Providence railroad station sometime after midnight, by now thoroughly irritated.

The following day, the *Chester W. Chapin* was transferred to the Providence Line (for the second time that season) at New York while the *City of Worcester* deadheaded down from Stonington to take her place on the New London Line. The company naturally preferred to have the new *Providence* on the Fall River Line rather than the *Pilgrim*. Thus, the following Sunday, after the *Providence*'s Saturday night layover synchronized her schedule with the *Pilgrim*'s, the two changed places, the *Providence* sailing down to Fall River and the *Pilgrim* up to take the Sunday night sailing from Providence. The *Chester W. Chapin*, which arrived in Providence on Sunday morning, therefore, took the Sunday excursion that day to New London.

The *Puritan* was back on the line fairly soon, sailing out of New York on Sunday, August 19, and, with somewhat less confusion this time, all of the various steamers were shifted back to their regular routes. The following Sunday, August 25, the *Pilgrim* again made the excursion to New London. The *Larchmont*, however, tried a different route that day: this time she sailed from Providence to New Bedford and back, the reverse of the trip the *New Hampshire* made the same day. Then the following week, September 2, she again ran to Cottage City, a trip the Joy Line advertised as "the last of the season." It was also to be the last for the *Larchmont*.

The fine weather that had characterized the year 1906 lasted well into September and then broke abruptly when on September 16 a hurricane that lasted for three days swept the New England coast. It was soon calm again, and New England enjoyed a long Indian Summer.

Passenger service on both the New Bedford Line and the Providence Line was discontinued at the end of September, and the *Maine* and the *New Hampshire* again transferred to freight service on the Providence Line. Early in October, the repairs to the hull and engines of the burned-out *Plymouth* had been completed, and work was starting on the superstructure. Still, the yard estimated that it would be another year before the *Plymouth* could be back in service. Thus, the *Pilgrim*, so recently retired, was now to run another full winter on the Fall River Line. The *Providence*, which, as we have previously noted, had more staterooms and more cargo capacity than the larger *Puritan*, came on the Fall River Line with the *Priscilla* early in October. From this time, it became the practice of the Fall River Line, even after the arrival of the *Commonwealth* in 1908, to run the *Providence* and the *Priscilla* through the autumn months. That season the *Priscilla* again stayed on the route until some time in January before the *Pilgrim* came on to relieve her.

On the Joy Line, the *Larchmont* under Captain McVay and the *Edgemont* under Captain Olweiler continued to run to Providence. That fall, however, the *Kentucky* rather than the *Shinnecock* filled in when the *Edgemont* went for her end-of-season overhaul, leaving the *Tennessee* to run temporarily on an alternate night schedule to Fall River. Aside from this two-week break, the *Tennessee* and the *Kentucky* still provided the Joy Line's Fall River service, and, while Captain Wilcox continued to command the *Tennessee*, during the fall Foster Gray, who had served as first pilot under Wilcox since the first sailing of the *Rosalie*, replaced E. C. Rood as master of the *Kentucky*. Since the Joy Line to Bridgeport turned out, soon after it started, to be an overnight freight line rather than a passenger-carrying day line as had originally been intended, the cantankerous sidewheeler *Fairfield* was not really suited to the service. So the *Seaboard*, which had been running as a third boat on the Boston route all summer, came on for the *Fairfield* in September and remained on the railroad's second line to Bridgeport (with one break), a route for which she was far better adapted than an outside run to Boston, for another twenty-five years.

Now that the Joy Line had a low-rate steamer line direct to Fall River, in the fall of 1906 the Enterprise Line decided to counter with a line of its own to Providence. Ironically, the steamer it bought for this new service was the *St. Croix*, the former running mate of the *Larchmont* and *Edgemont* this case. In any event, it made her much narrower than the sidewheelers of and *Edgemont* in Maine, she was a very different type of steamer. A wooden-hulled propellor boat, similar to the *Manhattan* and the *Cottage City* of the New York and Portland Line, she had a modified ocean-type design. That is to say, she had a minimal guardrail, so that her Main Deck was a continuation of her hull with no overhang. This design was intended to make her more seaworthy, although contemporary accounts question its success in this case. In any event, it made her much narrower than the sidewheelers of the line. Hence, while the *St. Croix* was of about the same length as the other two steamers, she had a somewhat smaller passenger and cargo capacity. (The *St. Croix* had 90 staterooms, the *Edgemont* 106, and the *Larchmont* 107.)

The Joy Line had been aware for some time, even before its own Fall River service started, that the Enterprise was planning to run to Providence. As early as May, Dunbaugh wrote to Charles Mellen informing him that the Enterprise people had been inquiring about dock property in Providence.[24] In October, Dunbaugh wrote Mellen again with the news that the Enterprise was seeking to lease a dock in Providence then held by his former partner Charles L. Dimon.[25] But the dock ultimately obtained in Providence by the Enterprise was the Clyde Line dock, one later used by the Colonial Line, which was located directly ahead of the Joy Line's landing. Since the Clyde Line was then part of the Morse combine, one is again led to suspect that at least a working arrangement existed between Morse and Whitcomb. The fact that the *St. Croix* was one of Morse's steamers and that the

Enterprise had obtained it with a very low down payment and generous terms tends to substantiate this suspicion.

On November 3, the powerful new steamer *Governor Cobb** of the International Line arrived in New York from her builders on the Delaware and, after a brief stay, raced on up the sound and around the cape to Boston in fifteen hours at an average speed of eighteen knots. With this new steamer soon to be ready to go into commission, the International Line was now prepared to part with the small wooden-hulled *St. Croix* which sailed down to New York a few days later to start her new career as a New York to Providence night boat for the Enterprise Line.

Her first trip for the Enterprise Line was from New York on Monday, November 12, hardly a propitious time of year to start a new steamship line on the sound, after which she sailed every Monday, Wednesday, and Friday from New York and on alternate nights from Providence. Taking advantage of the fact that neither the Joy Line nor the Providence Line's winter freight boats ran on Sunday nights, the *St. Croix* arranged her sailings from Providence on Sundays rather than Saturdays. Since she was somewhat faster than the *Larchmont* or the *Edgemont*, the *St. Croix* was able to schedule her departure from Providence at 7:45, the same hour as the summer Providence Line steamers. This time, however, the Joy Line accepted reality and did not attempt to adjust its schedule. While the *St. Croix* provided passenger service only on alternate nights, the Enterprise also had the faithful old *Warren* (formerly the *City of Fitchburg* and *Surprise*), on the Providence run, carrying freight only on opposite nights.

The Enterprise fare to Providence was the same as to Fall River: $1.00. Encountering no resistance this time from the railroad, the Joy Line quickly dropped its fare to a dollar also for the winter of 1906-1907. It was like the old days with the New Line** again, except that this time someone else was paying the bills.

Soon after the Enterprise Line started its service to Providence, there were new rumors that the line had been taken over by the Morse interests. It was known that Morse had talked with Whitcomb on Thursday, November 15, and one report stated definitely that he had offered to pay Whitcomb an even million for the Enterprise operation.[26] R. W. Miller, who had now

---

*Launched in April 1906, the *Governor Cobb* was the first American steamer with a turbine engine. The *Mauretania* of the Cunard Line, the first large trans-Atlantic turbine steamer, was not launched until October 1906.

**The Enterprise Line, although officially named the Enterprise Transportation Company, was also known popularly at the time as the New Line, the same name the railroad had used for its low-fare line in 1900-1902. In fact, "New Line" was painted prominently on the bows of the Enterprise steamers. Here we have tended to refer to the line as the Enterprise Line in the hope of avoiding confusion.

replaced Percy Todd as vice-president and general manager of the railroad's marine operation, wrote Mellen that he did not see how Morse could have been "such a fool."[27] In any event, both parties quickly denied the rumor. Calvin Austin lunched with Stevenson Taylor the day before Thanksgiving and assured him that the Morse people had not purchased the Enterprise.[28] A few days later, David Whitcomb also issued a denial that he had sold his line. The Enterprise did expand its original capitalization considerably at this time, however, in order to start the new Providence service. What probably happened, therefore, was that Morse made a substantial investment in the Enterprise company, possibly even buying controlling interest (which could still have allowed him to deny that he had bought the line), while leaving Whitcomb as manager. In short, it seems likely that, while the Enterprise remained independent of any of Morse's other marine properties, it probably now played a role for Morse similar to the one the Joy Line played for the New Haven. Whatever the actual relationship, Morse still held mortgages for a large part of the value of both the *Kennebec* and the *St. Croix*.[29]

One result of the new competition with the Enterprise Line was that, when the time came for the rate agreement between the railroad interests and the Joy Line to be renewed for the fourth time in the fall of 1906, both parties now decided to suspend it. One might be surprised that any rate agreement at all was necessary between two subsidiaries of the same company. But one must remember that the railroad was still maintaining the position that its ownership of the Joy Steamship Line was a secret, though from whom, since it was freely discussed in the public newspapers of the time, it is not clear. With the appearance of the Enterprise Line, and particularly its new service to Providence, and given the fact that the Enterprise people were free to set their passenger and freight rates wherever they chose, the New Haven authorities concluded that, in the interest of competition, it was wisest that the Joy Line have the same freedom. The man designated to go to the Joy Line offices and make the final arrangements for removing the controls on the Joy Line's freight rates was none other than Robert Haskins, the former Metropolitan Line official who had once been so adamant in refusing to deal with the Joy Line. After the Whitneys sold the Metropolitan Line to Morse, Haskins had called upon his old friend Percy Todd for a job and was now the general freight agent for the New England Navigation company.

With the agreement now abrogated, Joy Line fares dropped to seventy-five cents, one way, to either Fall River or Providence during the winter of 1906-1907. This was twenty-five cents below the Enterprise fares and far lower than the Joy Line fares had been since its rate war with the New Line ended in 1902. The difference this time was that the railroad absorbed the operating deficit.

The year 1906 was not only one of the most profitable in the history of Long Island Sound steamboats, but also one of the most exciting, with two low-fare steamer lines competing with the older established lines then running to Providence and Fall River and even to Bridgeport, albeit in each case one of the competing lines—namely, the Joy Line—was secretly operated by the same parent company as the established line. But as the year closed there were already indications that the nature of steamship travel on Long Island Sound was changing, that the days had passed when the grand old wooden or iron-hulled sidewheelers, their wheels enclosed in huge colorful paddle-boxes and their iron walking beams pounding rhythmically above, would be seen each night churning their way up the sound. One of the clearest signs of the new era was an event in Chester, Pennsylvania, on the first day of December, a bright cool Saturday afternoon, when C. W. Morse's new 400-foot turbine steamer *Yale*, soon to inaugurate the Metropolitan's New York to Boston passenger service, slid gracefully down the ways at Roach's yard. That night, the 250-foot Joy Line steamer *Old Dominion*, now nearly thirty-five years old, paddled out of Pier 27, her big iron wheels thrashing as hard as they could against the rushing East River currents in hope of getting up enough speed to get the steamer through Hell Gate under her own power before starting her leisurely twenty-four hour voyage through the sound and around the cape to Boston. Not even the most enthusiastic publicity agent could have been blind to the fact that by 1906 the *Old Dominion* was an anachronism, one that could not long survive the bright light of reality once the *Yale* and the *Harvard* were in operation. With the established lines providing fast new steel-hulled steamers, with many new and overdue safety regulations coming into effect after the burning of the *General Slocum* and even more regulations eight years later with the sinking of the *Titanic*, and with better pay and working conditions for seamen not far in the offing, the days when a small company could run outdated steamers at low fares were clearly numbered.

1907

The second year that the Joy Line operated under railroad ownership probably saw more drastic changes and frenetic activity than any other year in the history of Long Island Sound steamboat history. By now it was clear that the express passenger and freight service between New York and Boston was only one step in Charles W. Morse's plan to create a vast shipping monopoly along the Atlantic Seaboard. Since such a monopoly would overlap and compete with the transportation monopoly in southern New England, which now was almost fully realized by the New Haven Railroad, as well as the monopoly of North-South shipping by rail then being assembled by J. Pierpont Morgan, the New Haven's most influential director, and since this new New York-Boston service was aimed directly at the market served by the New Haven's own steamer lines, all of the considerable power of the New Haven and its many subsidiaries were being marshalled for a war to the death with Charles W. Morse. During the year 1907, practically every independent steamship line remaining on the Atlantic Coast was bought up by either Mellen or Morse in a series of moves by each to check the other's ability to expand into a particular area. In this fast and unpredictable battle between giants, so small a pawn as the Joy Line counted for little. It could be moved about the board or removed altogether in reponse to the iron-clad whims of Mellen or Morse.

With three lines running to Providence, three lines to Fall River, and two new express lines planned for Boston, the position of the Joy Line became daily more precarious. By now, railroad officials were becoming increasingly certain that, one way or another, the Enterprise Line was being operated in the interests of the Morse empire. Should this line, as appeared to be the case, have Morse money available with which to build the large modern turbine steamers it had promised to run from New York to Fall River, the terminus of the railroad's principal steamer line, it could become an even more serious threat than Morse's Boston line. Thus, one of Mellen's prime objectives in 1907 was to force the Enterprise out of business. The acquisition of the Joy Line and the addition of a Joy Line service to Fall River had not been successful. Against such competition as the *Tennessee* and the *Kentucky* had provided, the Enterprise had managed not only to hold on but also to continue to thrive. Keeping his moves secret, even from Dunbaugh and Joy, Mellen had already decided to discontinue the Joy Line to Fall River—perhaps even to phase out the Joy Line operation altogether—and substitute a far more formidable competitive line on the Fall River run.[1]

In line with Mellen's proposals to the marine subcommittee of the railroad in 1905, the New Haven had set up a whole new marine subsidiary, the United States Transportation Company. (When a few months later the New Haven Railroad also purchased the Hartford and New York Transportation Company, the railroad then controlled four separate marine subsidiaries: the New England Navigation Company, which operated most of the sound lines, the new United States Transportation Company, the Hartford and New York Transportation Company, and the Joy Steamship Company.) The United States Transportation Company was to be an umbrella corporation for any low-rate services that Mellen might create in the future.[2] Thus, neither the name nor the reputation of the New England Navigation Company needed to be sullied by association with second-class steamship operations. One day in August 1906, Mellen asked Stevenson Taylor to become the president of this new organization:

> I was in the offices of Mr. Mellen consulting about some other matters, and he turned to me one day and said to this effect: "I have made up my mind that we have got to have a cheap line, because we cannot reduce our rates on our first-class lines; but there is a cheap business to be transported out of New York to Fall River and I want to have another corporation formed to carry out that business. I want you to take it if you will. You can take any of our boats . . . and you will manage that company as though it was your own, and you will be under no criticism from anybody any more than you would if it were your own."[3]

Taylor was by now thoroughly familiar with the railroad's available marine properties, having recently made a complete appraisal of them. For the new steamer line to Fall River he chose the former Providence and Stonington Line steamers *Connecticut* and *Rhode Island*, which were rescued from retirement in Stonington during January 1907, brought down to New York, and tied up to a pier at Fifteenth Street on the North River to see what needed to be done to them to make them serviceable. As it turned out, it was a great deal, especially in the case of the *Connecticut*.

In another move in the Morse-Mellen war, the New Haven had beaten Morse to one of the most lucrative steamer lines on the coast, the Maine Steamship Company's New York to Portland Line, which was then operating the fast ocean-type steamers *North Star* and *Horatio Hall* and the smaller wooden-hulled *Manhattan*. The New Haven bought the line late in 1906; on January 3, 1907, the operation of the Portland Line was formally taken over by Stevenson Taylor's newly created United States Transportation Company. With its acquisition of the Portland Line, the New Haven had not only added a profitable piece of property, but it had also invaded the heart of Morse territory.

Through January 1907, the weather was mild, as it had been the year before, and the steamer lines continued to be busy through the holiday season. The *Priscilla* stayed on the Fall River Line with the *Providence* through the first week of January before being relieved for the winter by the *Pilgrim*. The *City of Lowell* also remained longer than usual on the New London route; it was February 11 before the *Maine* came to take her place. The three sidewheel freighters of the Fall River Line were all on different routes that winter. The *City of Taunton* stayed on the Fall River Line with the *Boston*; the *City of Brockton* was again on the New Bedford Line but that year was running with the recently completed *Pequonnock*; while the *City of Fall River* was on the Providence Line, first with the *Maine*, and then, after the *Maine* went to the Norwich Line on February 11, with the *New Hampshire*. The Joy Line's four lines on the sound also managed to operate without unplanned interruptions throughout January; either the *Old Dominion* or the *Santiago* sailed every other day from Boston and New York, and the *Larchmont* and *Edgemont*, sailing six nights a week between New York and Providence, kept well booked in spite of the competition that winter from their former running mate, the *St. Croix*. The *Tennessee* and the *Kentucky*, on the other hand, running to the city that already supported the great Fall River Line as well as a low-rate line that had won the support of the local citizens, were not carrying enough passengers or freight to have been considered profitable had the operation not been subsidized by the railroad. In contrast, the *Seaboard*'s service to Bridgeport was very profitable, and she sailed with her cargo deck well loaded on almost every trip.

The Enterprise Line was apparently doing well enough to be able to have the *Frank Jones* completely refurbished during the winter of 1907. On January 24 she was taken off the line and sent down to New London to have some major work done, including having her Main Deck rebuilt to give her greater cargo capacity, a sign that the line was not having trouble finding freight customers. While she was there, she also had her entire interior repainted, her mattresses rebuilt or replaced, and new carpeting laid in her staterooms and saloons. During the overhaul of the *Frank Jones*, the daily freight service to Providence was temporarily suspended; the *St. Croix* ran alone to Providence three nights a week while the *Warren* went to run opposite the *Kennebec*, carrying freight and occasionally a few passengers to Fall River.

Late in January, occupying as prominent a place as marine news could find amid the daily details of the trial of Harry K. Thaw for the murder of his wife's lover, the famed architect Stanford White, which began on January 22, one could also find reports of two steamship launchings in Pennsylvania. One was that of the *Massachusetts*, the first of the New Haven's fast Boston freighters, launched on Tuesday, January 29, at Cramp's yard in Philadelphia with the full panoply of champagne, speeches by dignitaries, bunting, toasts, dinners, and more speeches by more dignitaries that typified steamship launchings in the early years of the century. The following day, an even more impressive spectacle was staged a few miles away when Morse's *Harvard* was launched at Roach's yard in Chester down the Delaware. (The *Harvard's* sistership, the *Yale*, had been launched there a month earlier.)

Eight days later, on Thursday, February 7, Charles W. Morse, using the same blitzkreig method that he had used successfully in acquiring many smaller operations, without any advance warning, offered the New Haven Railroad a flat $20 million for all of its marine properties.[4] It took the cool Mr. Mellen no more than a few seconds to recover, and his first inclination was to accept the offer. In the first place, Mellen was in possession of the careful and expert appraisal of all of the railroad's marine properties prepared three years earlier by Stevenson Taylor in anticipation of their purchase by the newly formed subsidiary, the New England Navigation Company. Mellen therefore knew that even the most liberal evaluation of the railroad's marine properties fell far short of $20 million. This money, used to pay off bonds and other debts or to develop other areas of the railroad's vast empire, would, in Mellen's opinion, eventually earn far more for the company than the continued operation of the New England Navigation Company. In addition, Mellen was beginning to be somewhat concerned over the Roosevelt administration's threats to crack down on trusts and monopolies, and he felt that unloading the marginally profitable steamship holdings might save the railroad some embarrassing antitrust probes in the future. But Mellen had to discuss the offer with the New Haven's directors before giving Morse an answer.[5]

The fair weather which had lasted through January broke on February 1 when it suddenly turned very cold; on Saturday, February 2, a chilly fog settled over the sound. That night the little freighter *Warren* remained tied up at her pier in Fall River for some time in anticipation that the fog would lift. When it appeared that it would not, Captain Brown finally sounded his departing whistle, and at about 10:30 the *Warren* slipped slowly into the icy mist headed for New York. He made his way down Mount Hope Bay and past Newport. Then at about 1:00 A.M., there was a loud crunching noise and the *Warren* stopped; she had fetched up on the Dumplings, a menacing group of rocks at the southern tip of Conanicut Island.

The next morning, Sunday, February 3, the tugs *Solicitor* and *Roger Williams* went out to the *Warren* to help her get off but did not have any success. The Jamestown ferry also came alongside to take off the *Warren's* freight and thus lighten the load, but still she did not come off. On Monday, the two tugs, pulling at the steamer with full force, were finally successful. The *Warren* was in bad shape and had to be off the line for several weeks, leaving the Enterprise Line temporarily with only one steamer on each line: the *Kennebec* to Fall River and the *St. Croix* to Providence.

The *Warren* came off the rocks just in time. On the night of Monday, February 4, it started to snow, and during the night a strong wind began to gather which turned into a forty-mile-an-hour gale. Block Island, less protected than most weather stations but more reflective of conditions on the sound, reported winds up to sixty miles per hour. That night the *Larchmont*, sailing west, was several hours late arriving in New York. Both the *Edgemont* and the *Maine*, bound east, put into New Haven when they encountered the height of the storm. The *St. Croix* continued on to Providence but arrived coated in ice. The *Edgemont* left New Haven at 10:00 the following morning and finally made it into Providence by about 4:00 Tuesday afternoon, but the *Maine* did not show up until after dark and was thus not able to reload and sail before midnight. By the time the storm subsided, over twelve inches of snow had fallen.

By Sunday, February 10, the blizzard was over and the skies were clear again, but the cold temperatures, hovering near zero, were to remain for another two weeks. That morning the *Larchmont* arrived in Providence only an hour behind schedule. Since the *Larchmont* did not sail on Sunday nights, Captain McVay, who was married and lived in Providence, and any of his crew who were not on watch, were able to go to their homes overnight and to enjoy a much deserved rest. By the time the *Larchmont* docked that morning, the *Maine* was already tied up at Fox Point wharf ahead. She had just completed her last trip on the line for the season. That day she sailed down to New London to go on the Norwich Line for the *City of Lowell*, and on Monday morning the *New Hampshire* came up from Newport to take her place.

As the *Larchmont* prepared to sail again the next night, her officers were relieved that the heavy weather seemed to have abated, though the cold was numbing and a pretty stiff wind was coming up. With horses and trolleys both slowed by the snow still in the streets, not much freight was delivered that day and the *Larchmont* was traveling with about half her usual load. But the passenger bookings that night were unusually large for that time of year. The Enterprise Line did not have a sailing on Monday nights, and many people tended to go to New York at the beginning of the week.

Passengers began arriving at the pier from about 4:00 P.M. on, most by trolley, carrying their own bags. A few arrived in horse-drawn cabs, whose usual clatter on the cobblestones was muted by the snow, giving the pier a quieter air at sailing time than usual.

Among those arriving on the Joy Line pier that night were Samuel Paul and his wife Rose with their two teenaged daughters Pauline and Matilda, all in a particularly festive mood. Their son, Philip, who had gone to New York to work, was to be married on Saturday in Brooklyn, and the whole family was on its way to the wedding. Benjamin Winiker, from Vienna, had been in America for four months seeking work, but he had given up and was now taking the *Larchmont* to New York, where he would board a liner and return to his wife and four children in Austria. Handsome twenty-four-year-old James McLeod and his pretty wife Jennie, twenty-three, newlyweds, were moving from Providence to Kearny, New Jersey, Jennie's home town, where Jimmy had recently found a job working in an iron foundry. Gawky blond Millard Franklin, aged seventeen, boarded the steamer all alone at about 5:00 P.M., looking nonchalant, since he was used to traveling by himself. Billed as the boy Houdini, he had an act in which he extricated himself, like the master, from manacles, locked boxes, and the like. He was on his way to an engagement in Trenton. His mother in Pawtucket was so accustomed to her son's traveling that she did not even remember he was planning to take the *Larchmont* that night until she noticed he was not at home that evening.

Young Jacob Michaelson and Sadie Michaelson boarded the steamer together and had some difficulty explaining to purser Oscar Young (Trickey had decided to leave the *Larchmont* a few days before) that they wanted separate staterooms. In spite of the fact that they had the same last name, and in spite of the fact that many observers could not help noticing they were very much in love, they were not married. They were first cousins and were planning to be married in ten days. From Beaumont, New Jersey, they had been visiting relatives in Boston. Twenty-two-year-old Frank Riley from Providence took the *Larchmont* that night to New York where he wanted to visit a married sister. All that day, both his mother and his fiancee Emma Dube had tried to persuade him that it was not safe to take a steamer in such cold weather, but he had not let them change his plans.

Sadie Golub, a nineteen-year-old girl who looked even younger, was also traveling alone, although her brother Solomon had come down from Boston to see that she got on the boat safely. Sadie was rushing to New York to help a married sister whose baby had unexpectedly become very ill. Blond, baby-faced Claude Reed appeared on the Quarter Deck dressed in a blue suit, black tie, long overcoat, and derby hat. He had been working for some time as a fireman in Providence, but now, at thirty-two, he had become a salesman for the Melrose Jewelry Company and was based in New York, where he was returning, after a two-day visit with his family, on the same steamer that had brought him. Henry Apple, who was from Pawtucket but now lived on Block Island, was going to New York the hard way. He had taken the little steamer *George W. Danielson* up from the island that afternoon to catch the sailing of the *Larchmont*, and, more than any of his fellow passengers, he knew how cold it was going to be out there that night. Oliver Janvier, a twenty-one year old from Providence, was on his way to New York to find work.

Millard Franklin and Sadie Golub were not the only teenagers traveling alone that night. Also aboard was Fred Hiergesell, aged sixteen, who had run away from his parents' home in Brooklyn six months before, found his way to New England, supported himself with a variety of odd jobs, and was now on his way back for his first visit with his parents.

Cavalier Francesco Spatalo, arriving at the pier with a great deal of baggage and wrapped in a heavy overcoat, a musician of some renown in his native city of Palermo, Sicily, had been persuaded by relatives to bring his talents to America. With snow gathering on his large handlebar moustaches, he explained that America was too cold for him and that after two miserable months in Boston, he was taking the *Larchmont* to New York where he would catch a boat back to sunny Sicily. Stamping snow from his boots as he walked up the gangway, David Fox, a man in his forties, from Bridgetown, New Jersey, elected not to engage a stateroom for a dollar, but instead inquired about free berths and was directed to the men's cabin in the hold down the narrow stairway leading from the Quarter Deck.

Porters carried the baggage of Mrs. Anna Jensen, a Swedish-born woman who was the wife of a Providence greenhouse proprietor, to her stateroom on the Saloon Deck aft. With Mrs. Jensen and sharing her stateroom was her nineteen-year-old daughter, Louise. Listed as Louise Jensen, she was actually Mrs. Hans Vigo de Thestrup. Just over a year earlier, while a student in a music school in Boston, Louise had been secretly married to de Thestrup, an employee of her father's. When she graduated from the school in June, the couple informed the Jensens of the marriage, and a few days later Louise went to her parents' home to pick up her belongings. That was the last time her husband had seen her. After several months of keeping their daughter at their home by persuasion, the Jensens had decided to take her away from New England altogether. Jensen put his greenhouse up for sale and was planning to remain in Providence until a purchaser appeared, while his wife and daughter left the city on the *Larchmont*, presumably on their way to Mrs. Jensen's home in Sweden or perhaps her husband's home in Denmark.

The Jensens were not the only Scandinavians aboard the *Larchmont*, however. Among the passengers were six young Salvation Army members, two men and four women, all from Worcester, Massachusetts, and all of Scandinavian descent, on their way to a congress of the Eastern Scandinavian Corps of the Salvation Army about to be held in New York.

At 6:00 P.M., one half-hour before sailing time, just at the hour when most of the passengers were arriving at the dock and boarding the steamer, snow suddenly began to come down quite heavily, giving some alarm to the men in the pilot house who had just been through a week of sailing through blizzards. Young Captain McVay, believing the snowfall might not last, delayed the sailing of the steamer until visibility was more certain.

One person at least was pleased by this decision. Fred Elsbree, a Providence businessman, had important matters to attend to in New York on Tuesday and had booked passage on the Fall River Line that night. Because of the snow, the trolley he took to the Fox Point railroad station, where passengers boarded the boat train to Fall River, was fifteen minutes late, and he was informed by the conductor that he would not be able to make the train. On hearing this, Elsbree jumped off the trolley at Point Street, realizing that since he had to be in New York in the morning, he would have to settle for the Joy Line. As it was already past 6:30 P.M. when he ran up the *Larchmont*'s gangplank, he was glad that McVay had decided to delay the sailing.

At about 6:45, as the captain had predicted, the snow stopped, and, in a surprisingly short time the sky was again clear enough to show stars. At 6:55 Captain McVay blew the whistle three times to announce the *Larchmont*'s departure. Just then another trolley trundled past the pier. It had come all the way from Woonsocket and was several minutes late. Out bound Joseph Foncier of Woonsocket who walked as fast as he could through the snow with all his baggage toward the Joy Line dock. Unfortunately, his wife and daughter, who followed him out of the trolley, were not able to move so fast. When Foncier reached the steamer, there was still time to board, but in another minute, the cry to "Cast Off" rent the chilly air. Two men on the pier pulled back the gangplank with a loud clatter, just as Mrs. Foncier and her daughter were coming onto the pier, their long skirts already wet from the snow. Disappointed, the three Fonciers took another trolley back to Woonsocket.

By the time the *Larchmont* pulled away from her pier at 7:00, it was completely dark, so that all that could be seen of the steamer from the shore was a row of bright lights as she paddled slowly down the Providence

River. When the *Larchmont* left her dock, all of the pilot house staff were together in the wheelhouse: Captain McVay, the two pilots, John Anson and George Wyman, and the quartermasters John Staples and John Moreland. Both Anson and Wyman had been chosen especially by Captain McVay when he first took command of the *Larchmont*. Until then Anson had been second pilot on the *Edgemont*, and Wyman had been hired by the line at McVay's request. Both were young single men. Wyman, who was twenty-eight, lived with his parents in Taunton; Anson, thirty-two, lived alone in Providence but was to be married in a few weeks. Soon after the steamer's departure Wyman and Moreland, whose watch was to begin at 2:00 A.M., retired to their rooms, while Anson took the middle window for the first half of the trip and Staples stood at the wheel. McVay also remained in the pilot house for another hour and then began a tour of the steamer.

The dining room opened for service as soon as the *Larchmont* left the dock. All of the sound steamer lines chose to serve dinner, usually in a totally enclosed room, during the only part of the trip when the scenery was interesting. But tonight, with the steamer's thermometer registering four degrees above zero, no one thought of standing on the deck, except the bow watchman, a Norwegian named Tom, whose tour of duty was, incredibly, the entire length of the voyage. In the well-heated dining area, no one thought much about the cold weather outside, in spite of the rising and falling of the deck as the *Larchmont* began to buck the seas kicked up by the increasing winds. With the rapid turnover of employees at the lower levels characteristic of the Joy Line, none of the dining room waiters whom we encountered at the time of the murder of John Hart just two years earlier was still employed there. But Jamie Harrison, the thirty-seven-year-old Scottish steward, was still at his post. After three nights away, Jamie was looking forward to getting home to Brooklyn, where his wife was in a hospital.

Sitting on the Quarter Deck soon after sailing, young Oliver Janvier got into conversation with an Indian who was in a traveling "Wild West" show but had taken a few days off to visit his wife and two chidren at their home in New Jersey. The Indian had planned to stay up all night rather than spend the money for a stateroom, but Janvier insisted that he take the other bunk in his stateroom.

After dinner the young Salvation Army group gave a concert in the after part of the Main Saloon, singing hymns to the accompaniment of an accordian for over an hour, while the steamer paddled down the west channel with Conanicut Island to port, past Beaver Tail light, and out into the open sea. While the passengers listened to the concert in the saloon, some with pleasure, others whether they wanted to or not, Captain McVay sat for some time on the Quarter Deck below talking with Jamie Harrison and

Oscar Young. Soon after 10:00, however, as he felt the *Larchmont* begin to roll and pitch in the sea, he excused himself and, after a check through the passenger quarters to assure himself that all was well, returned to the dark silence of the pilot house. Here everything was also in order. John Anson stood at the center window, silent as usual. In spite of the cold wind blowing, the window was open several inches at the top, both to allow Anson to hear any calls from the bow watchman and to keep the window from frosting over. A quick scanning of the horizon showed McVay that his steamer was on course. They had just passed Block Island, and Montauk light could be seen in the distance to port while Watch Hill light appeared to be about four miles ahead to starboard. McVay saw one New York-bound steamer way ahead and fast disappearing. It was probably the *Tennessee* which had emerged from the east channel as the *Larchmont* was passing Beaver Tail but, being the faster by far, had pulled way ahead by the time they reached Point Judith. Since the Joy Line steamers left early, the other New York boats were still too far astern to be visible.

McVay chatted with Staples for awhile, and then at 10:30 he disappeared down the three or four steps to his private cabin just aft of the pilot house to attend to some paper work. At about that time, Pilot Anson began to pick out the lights of an approaching schooner almost directly ahead. She was showing both red and green lights, but as the red port light was the more prominent, Anson assumed that the two vessels would be passing fairly close but safely port to port. As the *Larchmont* and the schooner got closer together, however, the schooner's green light began showing more often. Anson, becoming somewhat concerned now, ordered Staples to "port the wheel." Since the *Larchmont* was an older steamer which steered by hand, turning the big wheel to port meant turning the steamer to starboard, thus giving the schooner more space for a port to port passing. But big steamers responded slowly to changes in course, the *Larchmont* more slowly than most, especially with the forty-mile wind blowing out of the Northeast, so that the prow of the steamer did not begin to nose northward for an agonizingly long several seconds. Meanwhile, the same wind was bringing the schooner closer at a much faster rate than Anson had anticipated. Then when the schooner was no more than a few hundred feet away and still moving at a very fast pace, it seemed actually to turn toward the *Larchmont*. Anson shouted to Staples to "port the wheel; port the wheel!" and signaled to the schooner by blowing the whistle four times rapidly, the danger signal.

McVay, hearing the whistle, bounded into the pilot house. Seeing the schooner now just a few feet off the port bow he yelled, "John Anson, what have you done?" Anson did not respond; he just stood there staring at the schooner through his binoculars. Then came the crash. The schooner rammed into the port side of the *Larchmont* just forward of the paddlebox and then, as both vessels were still moving, scraped her prow along the full length of the *Larchmont*'s port side and disappeared around the stern.

The captain ran out to the rail and looked over to find that the side of his ship had been shattered. He then hurried back to the pilot house to see how to get her beached as quickly as possible. But the engines had stopped. By that time, George Wyman, the second pilot, had appeared, and McVay sent him and Staples to the engine room to see if the *Larchmont* was taking water and whether Chief Engineer William Gay could get the engines moving. They had not been gone more than a few seconds before McVay realized the answer to the first question. He could see himself that the steamer was going down fast. But only slowly did McVay begin to comprehend the full horror of what had happened. The *Larchmont*'s hold was divided by three thick wooden bulkheads into four separate compartments: the crew's quarters forward, the fire room, the engine room, and the men's free berths aft. If any one of these compartments flooded, the other three would hold long enough to beach the steamer or to get the passengers off safely, as had been the case when she had been hit in Boston harbor in 1902. But, as it happened, the schooner had struck right at the midships bulkhead, so that the fireroom flooded immediately and water soon rushed into the engine room as well. Soon after the strain also opened the planks of the hull by the men's cabin which also started to fill, so that, within seconds after she was struck, the *Larchmont* began to go down at the stern.

The crash had cut off the steamer's dynamo, so that passengers seeking escape found themselves suddenly in total darkness. It also severed the main steam pipe, cutting off the engines and releasing great clouds of scalding steam through the darkened steamer. Most of the 128 people aboard the *Larchmont* stood no chance of escaping. The men in the fireroom were swamped as soon as the crash occurred. The men's free berth cabin flooded in the first five minutes, and most of the occupants were trapped and drowned. David Fox was awakened by the crash, and by the time he jumped from his berth, his feet were already in two feet of water and he saw the seas pouring in through cracks opening up on the sides. Running for the narrow stairway leading to the Quarter Deck, he found it completely blocked by men who were literally fighting with each other to get through. Quickly seeking another exit, he spotted a vent in the ceiling, and, squeezing his way through with great effort, he found himself somewhere on the Quarter Deck, by which time the water was almost up to the guards in the stern and the struggle in the cabin below was nearly over.

Passengers awakened by the crash and running out of their staterooms found the completely dark saloon crowded with screaming, frightened people, most of whom were soon overcome by the gushes of scalding steam rising from below in which no one could continue breathing for more than a few seconds. Anyone who had slept through the crash or whose stateroom doors had become jammed had no chance of staying alive once the steam began to seep in.

A minute or two after the crash, after receiving no answer at all to his signals to the engine room, McVay realized there was no hope of beaching the steamer. He therefore gave orders for all of the crew to go immediately to the lifeboats to which they were assigned and prepare to abandon ship. Staples returned to the pilot house soon after he left. His eyes were watering, and he was unable to speak for several seconds. He had not gotten anywhere near the engine room and had nearly been overcome by steam. Wyman did not return and was never seen again. Next, the young captain left the pilot house to check the exact condition of the steamer himself and to assist in guiding the passengers to the lifeboats. But he got no further than the port paddlebox, in the searing wind, before he realized that the *Larchmont* was sinking much faster than he had thought possible. In the bow water was already up to the Saloon Deck. McVay's only thought now was to get the lifeboats launched as quickly as possible before they, too, went down with the steamer. He shouted to his officers to hurry with their boats and to whatever passengers he saw to get into them. Since there was so little time, the boats had to be lowered immediately whether or not they were full; once in the water they could pick up passengers. With the wind howling furiously and the decks of the steamer already partially hidden in gushing steam, the captain was aware that he did not see many passengers about, but he did not yet realize how many had been overcome by steam. When only twelve people, mostly crewmembers, appeared in his own boat, he assumed that the bulk of the passengers had congregated on the port side away from the freezing wind. With little time for thought, he decided to lower his boat as fast as he could before it was swamped and to row around to the leeward side and load passengers there. Just as his boat was about to go down, Captain McVay hopped across the dome to inspect the Chief Engineer's boat, which was nearly full, and gave orders for it to be lowered. That was to be the last anyone was to see it. The captain then ran back to his own boat, by which time the steamer was so far down that the lifeboat needed be lowered only a few feet.

Harris Feldman, a strong man who had once been in a wreck while serving in the Russian Navy on the Black Sea, quickly saw the seriousness of the situation and, with his wife Bertha, ran from his stateroom to the deck and forced his way up the stern stairway. By the time he reached the lifeboats on the Hurricane Deck aft, the *Larchmont* was so far down in the stern that one lifeboat, already launched, was almost level with the deck. Feldman helped his wife into the boat, but it had soon drifted too far away for him to jump himself. His wife, refusing to leave without him, jumped out of the boat again and would have drowned had not a wave literally washed her back onto the deck of the steamer. By that time, the lifeboat had pulled away, and the Feldmans had no choice but to climb up on top of one of the two rows of outside staterooms, each sitting separate from the rest of the superstructure, one over each paddlebox, which had been added sometime after the steamer was built. Once there, on the highest part of the steamer, they found the perch already occupied by several other passengers including David Fox; Samuel Lacombe, who had left his cabin in nothing but his underwear and was now freezing with the temperature at about zero and the wind off the sea at forty miles an hour; Richard Hall, one of the *Larchmont*'s waiters; and Anton Razukiewitz, who sat silently, since he spoke no English and, like everyone else, was thoroughly frightened, though he managed a smile and did respond when Harry Feldman addressed him in Polish.

Sadie Golub, all alone in her stateroom, was awakened by the crash and ran out of her stateroom in her nightgown, grabbing a short jacket as she left. In the corridor crowded with confused people, she became too petrified even to yell. She somehow made her way to the Hurricane Deck and started to get into a lifeboat but was shoved out of the way by a large man in uniform whom she took to be the captain. She, too, using all her strength, climbed to the top of the small row of staterooms on the port side. These few people, ultimately sixteen of them, who found their way to the top of the row of staterooms on the Hurricane Deck were fortunate. The ship was going down fast, and the Hurricane Deck itself was soon awash. Of the few passengers who were able to make their way out of the steaming corridor to the outside, most lost their footing on the icy deck or were washed overboard by the waves that came crashing in unrelenting succession over the still exposed upper part of the steamer. A young boy of about twelve tried to shimmy up the forward mast, but his fingers were too cold to hold on, and, as he fell, a rush of water swept across the deck and carried him away.

Oliver Janvier got up when he heard the crash and calmly took time to dress, even fastening his collar and tying his tie. When he saw the confusion in the saloon, he returned to his stateroom to assist his Indian friend, but the latter only fought him off angrily when he tried to help him into a life preserver. Young Oliver, therefore, left him to fend for himself, and he headed for the upper deck. Miraculously, he made it to the after part of the Hurricane Deck, which by then was nearly on a level with the sea, and found an unoccupied lifeboat sitting there. The tarpaulin covering was frozen solid, which was why no one had tried to use it, but Janvier simply jumped on it until it cracked open and took a seat, waiting for an officer to come along and lower it. But none came. Soon he was joined by several other men, and they decided the best thing was to sit there until the steamer went under and hope that their little boat would just float off.

She did just that. . . . Pretty soon the steamer went down with a rush and nearly sucked in our boat, but she kept afloat and we got clear. We saw a couple of men hanging onto planks with their fingers half frozen. They cried out "Save us," and I took a piece of tackle and hauled one of them in. We got the second in the same way. By and by two more men came floating by on pieces of wreckage and we swung them on in the same way. They were the steward, James Harrison, and a colored porter. I didn't learn his name.

We were floating around looking for people we might pick up and I saw a woman who was partially under a piece of wreckage. I wanted to reach out for her, but just then the other fellows in the boat got scared and took to the oars. They wouldn't listen to my demands that they save the woman, and she hung there before our eyes crying out to save her. Every little while the piece of wreckage would dip in under a wave and she would be swamped. Then she would come up and again shout out to us to save her. But the men at the oars would not do it and they pulled away and let her drown or freeze.[6]

Captain McVay's boat was lowered on the starboard or windward side before the steamer went under, with twelve aboard including Quartermaster Staples and Purser Young. Before the boat pulled away, Captain McVay shouted out for any passengers standing on the deck to get into the boat, but no one appeared. By this time, the decks themselves were so enshrouded in steam that the men in the boat could not tell whether there was anyone on the deck. Then, after cutting a piece of tackle that had become tangled, they took the oars and prepared to row around to the leeward where more of the passengers were huddled trying to escape the stinging cold wind. Try as they would, they could not bring the boat back against the wind once they had crossed the *Larchmont*'s bow. While they were still trying to tug at the oars, they saw the *Larchmont* give up, and, still on a fairly even keel, sink below the water. As she went down, McVay turned his head and buried his face in his hands. She was his first ship.

In a short while the steamer was gone, and the twelve men were alone in the sea, with the wind howling and the waves high and the air so cold that no one exposed to it could expect to live long. The other boats had all drifted away before the *Larchmont* went down, and none of the men in the captain's boat ever saw any of the other boats afterward. For awhile they tried to row to Watch Hill, Rhode Island, which was not too far distant. But still the boat refused to move at all against the wind, and the small band had no choice but to drift with the wind to the southeast, hoping to land on Block Island, for, if they did not, there was no land before they reached the open sea. Soon after the *Larchmont* went down, the Enterprise steamer *Kennebec* steamed by no more than a mile away, followed by the big Fall River Line steamer *Providence*. Their brightly lighted decks spoke of passengers warm within and the air of calm and security in their pilot houses that had been taken for granted on the *Larchmont* less than an hour before.

The men in the lifeboat started to pull toward the passing steamers, but McVay reminded them that it would be of no use, that they were wasting needed energy. The *New Hampshire*, which left Providence about an hour later than the *Larchmont*, must also have passed by at about the same time, but as her passenger decks were not lighted, she might not have been visible from the water level.

Aware that in this cold anyone could drift into unconsciousness and then meet a quick death by freezing, McVay ordered everyone on his boat to keep moving at all times and to take turns at the oars. As the cold was severe, some resented the orders, but those who understood helped the captain keep everyone aboard in constant motion. Soon after they started drifting southward, however, there was a sudden scream in the darkness, and a man fell into the bottom of the boat covered with blood. One of the seamen, a Russian who spoke no English and who was therefore unable to explain his condition, had been badly scalded by the steam. Now in the freezing wind, with the ice-cold spray breaking over him, the pain was more than he could bear and he slit his throat.

As the *Larchmont* was going under, the row of staterooms on the Hurricane Deck wrenched free and remained afloat with sixteen people on it. Though more fortunate than most, it was only with extreme difficulty that even these people were allowed to hang on to life. The deck of the small improvised raft was cold and slick with ice, while powerful waves threatened continuously to push its occupants off into the water. Of the sixteen people huddled on the deck, six managed to survive. After they had been drifting about an hour, Harris Feldman, the man who had served in the Russian Navy, noticed his wife beginning to slip into that stupor which is the first signal that a person is freezing to death and from which one usually never awakes. Struggling to keep from losing his balance and being washed overboard, he grabbed her, shook her as vehemently as he could, and even hit her in the face, finally bringing her back into consciousness. Soon after he noticed also that little Sadie Golub, with her arms wrapped tightly around a man who was already dead, had relapsed into silence, and both Feldman and Lacombe, himself in severe pain from the cold, worked on her until she, too, showed signs of consciousness. From that time on Feldman and Lacombe, as well as David Fox, Anton Razukiewitz, and Richard Hall, all worked to keep the two women, as well as each other, alive. Nine others on the floating deckhouse either froze during the night or were washed overboard.

As the lifeboats were being loaded, Fred Hiergesell, the sixteen-year-old-runaway, had jumped into one of those which drifted away from the *Larchmont* almost immediately after it had been lowered. During the freezing night that followed, the boy watched while one after another of his companions succumbed to the cold until, finally, he found himself alone in a lifeboat with several frozen corpses. Twenty-one-year-old Oliver Janvier had a similar experience. Those young men sharing his boat who had refused to pick up the drowning woman all died during the night. One of them, a barber by trade apparently, unable to stand the pain in his freezing hands and feet, took out a razor and slit his throat, the second suicide among the survivors. Eventually, Steward Harrison and the unnamed porter also died. Janvier, who kept himself alive by continually stamping his feet, although they were under a foot of freezing water, was the only one of the ten in the boat who survived.

The winds were cold, but they were also kind for they blew the small boats right to the shore of Block Island which was about seven miles from the scene of the wreck. Just after dawn, at about 6:30 in the morning, the first boat to wash ashore was the one containing six frozen bodies and young Fred Hiergesell who had finally slipped into unconsciousness. A Block Island farmer saw the boat come to rest on a reef not far from shore and waded out to it. Finding Hiergesell still alive, he carried him ashore and took him to the lighthouse about a half mile away. Soon after, Captain McVay's boat, having floated on the sea in the freezing cold for nearly eight hours, also came to rest at Sandy Point on Block Island, and local farmers helped the six men who were still alive to the same lighthouse. All of them, including Captain McVay and Purser Young, fell unconscious almost as soon as they entered the warm front room of the keeper's house. They were carried upstairs to bedrooms and left to rest.

All that day dead bodies continued to wash up on the beach at Block Island, most encased in several inches of ice. The local citizens set up a watch and took turns patrolling the windy beaches. At 10:30 A.M., the boat containing ten dead bodies and young Oliver Janvier, only barely alive, was the last to be found. All of the others disappered. The Block Island fishermen, who had decided that the wind was too cold and the seas too rough to go out that day (it was also Lincoln's birthday, a school holiday), went to their boats as soon as they heard of the tragedy to comb the seas for survivors. At 11:00 A.M. the fishing schooner *Elsie*, under Captain Smith, came across the floating Hurricane Deck, with seven of its sixteen occupants still alive, though it was obvious that they could not have lived much longer. All owed their lives to the previous experience and the untiring efforts of Harris Feldman in those twelve hours that they had floated in the cold of Block Island Sound.

Captain Dodge of the fishing schooner *Clara E.* came across a life raft with seven dead bodies aboard. Dodge said he saw several other bodies floating singly but did not take time to stop for all of them. Another fishing schooner came into port with the frozen corpse of Harry Apple, the Block Island resident who had left the island just twenty-four hours before to catch the *Larchmont* for New York.

The first news of the wreck on the mainland was from the crew of the schooner, who came ashore on a Rhode Island beach several hours before the *Larchmont* survivors reached Block Island. The schooner involved was the *Harry S. Knowlton*, a three-master 128 feet long, which was running a heavy load of coal from Perth Amboy, New Jersey, to Everett, Massachusetts. She had left Perth Amboy on Sunday, February 10, but had been held up several hours by the ice off City Island. By Monday, February 11, however, she was underway again, and, with a strong northeast wind blowing all day, she made excellent time up the sound until encountering the *Larchmont* at about 10:40 P.M. Captain Frank Haley of the Knowlton and his mate Frank Govant had a slightly different story from the one told by Quartermaster Staples, who was the only surviving witness of the events from the *Larchmont's* pilot house. (John Anson, the only person who really knew what happened, had not been seen since the crash and had probably gone down with the ship.) Staples asserted that the approaching *Harry S. Knowlton* had been showing her red light for the most part indicating an intention of passing port to port, but that she had gone out of control at the last minute, blown off her course by an unexpected shift in the wind, and had luffed right into the *Larchmont* without warning. In his version McVay, who admitted that he had not been in the pilot house at the time, followed Staples' story. But Haley insisted that from the time he had sighted the *Larchmont*, he had seen only her green starboard light, suggesting that she would pass to the south of him, starboard to starboard, but that, at the last minute, the steamer had veered northward, right across his bow, leaving him little choice but to ram into her.[7]

It is possible that both stories were partly true, especially since, as those who have ever held the tiller of a sailboat can attest, it is very hard to hold a vessel under sail on a straight course in a strong wind, and a sailing vessel viewed at different times may appear to be changing its course. Another possible explanation derives from a rumor circulated much later and attributed to one of the sailors on the *Harry S. Knowlton*, that the schooner's crew at the time of the accident had lashed the wheel and all had gone below to get warm but had fabricated the other story later.

In any event, after the accident, the *Harry S. Knowlton* continued to drift northward toward the Rhode Island shore. Seeing that she was taking water, however, Captain Haley ordered his men into the small boat and the *Knowlton* was allowed to drift. The small boat, which, unlike the *Larchmont's*, was light enough to row against the wind, struck on the Rhode Island shore at about 1:15 in the morning, by sheerest chance right at the Qunonchontaug Life Saving Station, where the crew received warm food and clothing and were otherwise cared for. The following morning, Haley telephoned the Scott Wrecking Company in New London asking them to try to salvage the *Harry S. Knowlton*. A Scott tugboat later found the *Knowlton* nearby on a sand bar about a mile from shore, still intact but breaking up so rapidly that the tug's crew found it impossible to save either the schooner or her cargo.

Haley's call to the wrecking company on Tuesday morning was the first news anyone of the mainland had of the disaster.[8] Robert Noble, arriving in the Joy Line's New York office shortly after 8:00 A.M. on Tuesday, was surprised to see that the *Tennessee* had docked but that the *Larchmont* was not yet even in sight. Then a call from Block Island informed him of the accident. Still, no one in the Joy Line office had any idea just what had happened or any sense of the extent of the tragedy. During the day, the two cables to Block Island were operating badly because of the high winds, so that no one was able to get any more specific news for several hours. Noble called Arthur Pitts in Providence and told him to do what he could for the survivors. He also telephoned Foster Gray, the captain of the *Kentucky*, which had docked in Fall River that morning, and told him to find as many doctors and nurses as he could in Fall River, as well as ample medical supplies, and sail as soon as possible for Block Island, canceling his sailing for New York that night. At this early hour, he still had no idea how few of the passengers that had sailed on the *Larchmont* the night before had any need of doctors or medical supplies.

Gray had the *Kentucky* ready about noon and sailed her first to the scene of the accident, in the naive belief that he might find survivors there. He then proceeded to Block Island, coming to anchor near the lighthouse at Sandy Point, where the boats had come ashore. Rowing toward the beach from the *Kentucky*, Captain Gray was curious when he noticed what appeared to be large blocks of ice laid out along the beach. What he had seen were more than thirty human bodies, each encased in as much as six or seven inches of ice. "It was the most horrible thing I ever saw," he told reporters.[9] Only gradually did Gray realize that the *Kentucky*'s errand of mercy was virtually useless, that the tragedy had been far worse than anyone could ever have imagined. Of the 128 people who had sailed on the *Larchmont* from Providence the night before, only nineteen were still alive and of these some were hanging on uncertainly.

Gray attempted to find out details from George McVay, but after a few incoherent sentences, McVay fell unconscious again. Gray also tried to talk to Oscar Young, but the purser proved to be delirious and unable to give sensible answers. The local cornoner, Dr. J. C. Champlin, explained to Gray that the bodies had to be examined, that he would not be able to release them until the following day, and that the *Kentucky*, therefore, would have to remain at Block Island overnight. During Tuesday afternoon, eighteen of the nineteen survivors were placed in the *Kentucky*'s lifeboats and taken out to the steamer where they could have comfortable beds and proper medical attention. It is hard to imagine how difficult it must have been for these people to get into lifeboats again, even for so short a journey, only a few hours after their ordeal. One survivor, young Sadie Golub, refused to go to the *Kentucky*, literally screaming with hysteria at the thought of being taken on another steamer. Mr. and Mrs. Milliken, farmers on Block Island, agreed to take Sadie into their home and care for her until she was able to travel again.[10]

During the day on Wednesday, the boats of the Block Island fishing fleet continued to bring in bodies, twenty-two in all by the end of the day. Captain Sanchez of the schooner *Theresa* brought in the body of a man described at the time as the third *Larchmont* suicide. He was a black man, and he was found floating in a life preserver with a deep knife wound near his heart. Captain Sanchez, himself a black man from the Caribbean, said he could tell from the man's features that he was also a Carib. He insisted that a man of his race would not have committed suicide, especially to avoid danger or pain, and that the wound must have been inflicted by his crew's boat hook while fishing the body out of the water.[11] Considering that the man's two hands, locked in rigor mortis, were firmly gripping the life preserver, it would have been impossible for him to have killed himself with a knife. And considering that a great deal of blood had spilled on the man's clothing, it was equally impossible for the wound to have been inflicted several hours after he had frozen to death. No one seems to have mentioned the third and most likely possibility, although Captain Sanchez certainly must have guessed it: that the black man had been murdered when he tried to get into a lifeboat.

During the morning of Wednesday, February 13, the bodies of the dead (except that of Harry Apple who, as a Block Island resident, was to be buried there) were loaded onto the freight deck of the *Kentucky*. With Dr. Champlin aboard, the boat sailed from Block Island at about 3:00 P.M. for Providence. With so many curious spectators standing on the Joy Line pier (which was empty since the *Larchmont* would have been sailing again that Wednesday evening), the authorities decided to dock the *Kentucky* at the railroad's Fox Point pier instead when she arrived at about 7:00 P.M. Several doctors were waiting there from the Rhode Island Hospital in Providence which had also sent horse-drawn carriages to the pier to transport the survivors to the hospital.

Thomas Monahan's mortuary in Providence donated its facilities to the Joy Line. Since there was not enough room in the mortuary itself, several large wooden boxes, in which coffins had been delivered, were set up along the walls of Monahan's carriage house next door. On this makeshift platform, the thirty or so bodies so far recovered were laid out. Among those either laid out there in the mortuary or claimed by the sea were Mrs. Jensen and the daughter she was trying to take away from her husband; the young newlyweds, Jim and Jenny McLeod; lanky Millard Franklin, the boy Houdini; Sam and Rose Paul and their two daughters, who never made it to their son's wedding; Fred Elsbree, who wanted to take the Fall River Line but was five minutes too late and therefore did not keep his appointment in New York; Jacob and Sadie Michaelson, who were to have been married in a few days; Benjamin Winiker, of Austria, and Francesco Spatalo, the musician from Palermo, neither of whom would ever go back to Europe; Claude Reed, the jewelry salesman in his new blue suit; Frank Riley, whose girlfriend had pleaded with him not to make the trip that night because it was too cold at sea; and many, many others.

Although most of the survivors eventually recovered, James Vann, one of the porters who had come ashore in McVay's boat and who had appeared to be recovering, contracted pneumonia on Thursday and died within a few hours. Samuel Lacombe, one of the two men to whom Sadie Golub owed her life, died the same evening from the effects of exposure, thus reducing the number of survivors to seventeen.

Two days later, one reporter found David Fox, Harry Feldman, and Anton Razukiewitz sharing a hospital room and apparently in good shape. Fox and Feldman were engaged in heated but good-natured arguments about what had really happened on the night of February 11, while Razukiewitz looked on silently, only occasionally injecting a remark in Polish.

During the next several days, the newspapers printed many lurid accounts of the *Larchmont* disaster which presented a most unfavorable picture of the *Larchmont*'s crew. On Sunday, February 17, many sermons were delivered in local churches in which various divines who had never been to sea spoke eloquently and authoritatively on the morality of managing a steamboat in an emergency. Sixteen-year-old Fred Hiergesell gave an interview to the press, printed under the caption "Captain McVay accused of cowardice." Hiergesell described how the captain had been the first to leave the sinking steamer and how he had sailed away without taking any passengers in his boat.[12] Given McVay's decision to get boats into the water before they were completely lost to use, and the subsequent impossibility of bringing his boat around to the leeward side, it is easy to see how the young passenger might have perceived the situation as he did. It was also difficult to make a very emphatic denial, although the printed testimony of James McFarland, a waiter who left in the captain's boat, praised the captain and showed that he had done all he could in the face of the hostile elements to save his passengers.[13] Sadie Golub also told how the captain had shoved her aside and not allowed her to enter his boat.[14] But to a young girl, or indeed to almost any unseasoned passenger, especially under these circumstances, any officer she encountered, as far as she was concerned, would be the "captain." Considering that she described the "captain" as a large man, it is unlikely that she had seen McVay who was slight of build. As shown by the testimonies of several survivors, there can be no doubt, however, that some of the officers of the *Larchmont* had not done all they could to save the lives of the passengers, but, as so few of them lived through the ordeal in any event (ten of the nineteen survivors were crewmembers), very little of the whole story of the night of February 11, 1907, can ever be known. The accusations of cowardice, however unsubstantiated, appeared daily in the local papers and took a heavy toll on George McVay. His promising career as a young steamship master never recovered from this terrible tragedy for which he could not be held personally responsible.

The Joy Line accepted Staples' version of the accident and forthwith sued the owners of the *Harry S. Knowlton*, claiming that the schooner had been incompetently manned and had changed course without warning and rammed the *Larchmont*. The owners of the *Harry S. Knowlton*, on the other hand, accepted Haley's story and countersued the Joy Line, on the grounds that the *Larchmont*, without warning, had cut across the *Knowlton*'s bow. With such conflicting testimony, plus McVay's candid statement that, since he had not been in the pilot house at the time, he could not honestly attempt to reconstruct what had happened, and the added confusion caused by the absence of Anson, the only man on the *Larchmont* who did know, the court of inquiry had some difficulty reaching a conclusion. In the end it rendered the only decision possible by finding the *Larchmont* at fault, since, whatever the circumstances, the ship under sail had the right of way over the steam-powered vessel. Pilot Anson, they announced, should have allowed the *Knowlton* more room to pass.[15]

This quite justifiable decision was somewhat mitigated by the court's further statement: "To the conditions of weather on this occasion, thermometer at zero and fierce gale blowing, and the almost instantaneous sinking of the steamer, was due the inability to get all the boats overboard."[16]

The final verdict on Captain McVay was that his conduct under the circumstances was "neither commendable nor censurable." McVay was deeply hurt by this verdict, believing that he had done all he could in the short time allowed. He might have remembered, however, that three years earlier the captain of the *General Slocum*, who similarly had not been responsible for the fire and had done all he could to save his passengers in the short time allowed, had been sentenced to ten years in prison.

With the court decision against the *Larchmont*, the owners of the *Harry S. Knowlton* won their suit for damages against the Joy Line. But, according to marine law at the time, the liability of the owners of a vessel involved in an accident was limited to the value of the vessel. Since the *Larchmont* was declared a total loss and all that was recovered from her was one lifeboat worth $40.00, a piece of cargo evaluated at $8.12, and $55.00 in cash that the purser grabbed from the steamer's safe, Judge Adams of the admiralty branch of the U.S. District Court ruled that the extent of the Joy Line's liability for all losses incurred in the sinking of the *Larchmont*, including that of over a hundred lives, was $103.12.[17]

Whatever happened on the night of February 11, 1907, on those two vessels, it is possible many years later to say that to some extent the Joy Line itself must be held largely to blame. In the three years between February 1904 and February 1907, the Joy Line had lost four steamers: two had sunk as a result of accidents at sea and two had burned. The *Rosalie* had burned in layup. But only luck prevented the sinking of the *Aransas* or the burning of the *Tremont* from resulting in human disasters as devastating as the sinking of the *Larchmont*. Any steamer line must expect a share of accidents. But when a line loses four of the six ships it is operating in a three-year period, there would seem to be room for questioning. None of the officers of the Joy Line were steamboat men, and by their own admission they understood little about running steamboats. They ran the line as a business and followed the rules they had learned in the horse-trading West. The Joy Line was operated as cheaply as it possibly could be. The steamers were clean, but they were dated and they carried only minimal equipment. While the New England Navigation Company may have been charging its passengers top dollar to travel on its steamboats, it also provided them with steamers to travel on that were equipped with every modern safety device then known. Its steamers, with few exceptions, had iron or steel double hulls divided into watertight compartments; its lifeboats were equipped with the latest designs for safe and fast lowering; and by 1907 all steamers carried wireless radios.

The New England Navigation boats were also manned by experienced mariners. The Joy Line's practice was to hire either raw youths who had only recently received their papers or men past retirement age who were glad to get a job, and to pay them about two-thirds the salary that was paid on the other sound lines. The young officers on the Joy Line steamers were competent, reliable, and intelligent men, unusually so according to many accounts. But, as anyone over forty can attest, it takes a great deal of experience before a person understands the extent to which Murphy's Law really operates. Pilot Anson probably had every reason to believe that, if all went as it should, the *Larchmont* would have passed the *Harry S. Knowlton* quite close but cleared her nevertheless. In the course of the inquiries, a tugboat captain appeared who claimed that on the same evening, the *Larchmont*, coming down Narragansett Bay, had cleared his barges by what he considered a dangerous margin.[18] The unexpected may take place only one time in a thousand. But when an officer is responsible for the lives of over one hundred other human beings, one time is too many. The sound is wide. The two vessels need not have been so close in the first place that a mistake could have become a disaster.

During the inquiry which followed, Captain Wilcox of the *Tennessee* testified that he remembered passing "some steamer" that evening when leaving Narragansett Bay and that it "might have been the *Larchmont*."[19] Might have been the *Larchmont*? Wilcox had commanded the *Larchmont* for four years and surely must have recognized her at sea, even if she appeared as nothing more that a string of moving lights on the horizon. What Wilcox was avoiding was that he should not have sailed past the *Larchmont* so cavalierly on a night like that. If two steamers of the New England Navigation Company were operating on similar schedules, such as the Providence Line and the New Bedford Line did, for instance, their commanders were instructed to sail within sight of each other throughout the voyage, in the event of an emergency. It seems inexcusable that over a hundred human beings should have been allowed to perish in a freezing sea while another steamer of the same line and operating on the same schedule was steaming safely along so far ahead that its officers did not even notice the lights of the *Larchmont* suddenly disappear.

It also came up at the inquiry that the Joy Line did not keep a list of its passengers,[20] which steamers on routes exceeding one hundred miles were required by law to do. The line regularly kept a list of those who had engaged staterooms, but with the class of people who usually chose the Joy Line, this list accounted for only about half of the passengers aboard. Those who took berths in the free cabins or slept on the decks, as many did in the warmer weather, were merely required to show a ticket as they disembarked in the morning. Even more surprising was the revelation that the Joy Line did not even have an exact list of the crewmembers on its steamers. Lists of the officers were maintained at the New York offices, for payroll purposes. But, according to Noble, the seamen, the firemen, and the waiters changed so often that it was impracticable for the line to keep up-to-date lists. Only the pursers on each steamer, who were responsible for paying the people at this level, actually kept a list of their names.[21]

Toward the end of the week following the *Larchmont* disaster, Solomon Golub came down from Boston to Newport to take the *George Danielson* over to Block Island and to bring his sister home. His older sister's baby, whom Sadie was going to New York to take care of, had died. When he arrived on the island, he found that his sister was not yet well enough to make the trip home, but the Millikens gave him another room in their home and made him welcome there until Sadie finally consented to return to Boston with him, going as far as Newport by boat.[22]

In Brooklyn, Philip Paul, whose mother, father, and two younger sisters had all perished on the *Larchmont* while en route to his wedding, decided to go through with his marriage, since many of his bride's relatives had traveled some distance to attend. But immediately after the ceremony he took a train to Providence to attend to the bodies of his parents and sisters.

Since Charles Mellen was at that time already uncertain about the future of the Joy Line, except for definite plans to discontinue the Fall River service as soon as the *Rhode Island* and the *Connecticut* were ready to start the new line, he did not now encourage the Joy Line to replace the *Larchmont*. For the next several months the *Edgemont* ran to Providence alone three nights a week, and the *Kentucky* ran to Fall River alone the same three nights. On the opposite nights, Captain Wilcox and the *Tennessee* maintained an extraordinarily difficult route, sailing from New York to Fall River, discharging passengers and freight there and taking on Fall River freight, then leaving at about 10:00 A.M. for Providence and arriving some time after noon, taking on freight and passengers there, and sailing from Providence to New York in the evening.

Within a week or two after the loss of the *Larchmont*, the marine world wearied of reading about the tragedy and again turned its interest to the continuing battle between the two giants of the marine world. On Saturday, February 9, two days before the *Larchmont* disaster, Mellen had called a special meeting of the New Haven's board of directors, which, apparently acting on Morgan's advice, had voted to reject Morse's offer of $20 million for the railroad's marine properties. On Tuesday, February 14, Mellen reluctantly informed Morse of their decision, although in later private correspondence Mellen indicated that he believed the board had made a mistake.[23]

Morse consoled himself that day by purchasing the New York and Cuba Mail Line (Ward Line). A few days later, he announced that, beginning that fall, his fast turbine steamers *Harvard* and *Yale* would run to Havana during the winter season, cutting the time for that run in half.[24] One week later the New Haven countered by acquiring the Winsor Line which ran steamers from both Providence and Boston to Philadelphia.[25] That same day Morse purchased the New York and Porto Rico Line.[26] One month after that, the New Haven bought the very profitable Merchants and Miners Line, which ran passenger and freight steamers on several routes along the Atlantic Seaboard, turning the Winsor Line operation over to Merchants and Miners' management in the process.[27]

Morse meanwhile continued his program of adding new steel steamers to his Eastern Steamship fleet. The fast turbine steamer *Governor Cobb*, which had been delivered in late 1906, had now finished fitting out and had begun service on the *Larchmont*'s old route about the time the *Larchmont* sank. The *Yale* and the *Harvard*, as we have already noted, were launched in December and January, respectively. Then on February 23, yet another new turbine vessel, the sleek *Camden*, was launched at Bath for the Boston-Bangor Line. Less than an hour after the *Camden* left the ways, work started in the same cradle on her sistership, the *Belfast*. These two steamers were being designed to be fast, faster than the *Governor Cobb* as it turned out, though not nearly as fast as the *Harvard* and *Yale*. With the *Camden* and *Belfast* on the line, it was going to be possible for the first time to maintain daily service between Boston and Bangor with only two steamers.

It was assumed that the *Camden* would be ready for service by June and that she would join the *City of Rockland* on the run, replacing the older *City of Bangor*, which would then be transferred to the Kennebec River

Line to run with the *Ransom B. Fuller*. The *Penobscot*, now no longer needed on either the International or the Kennebec lines, was put up for sale. Since this steamer, whose sale to the Joy Line had been blocked by the New Haven in 1902, would have been a good running mate for the *Edgemont*, the Joy Line made arrangements to purchase her as soon as she became available. Morse, then still trying to remain on friendly terms with the New Haven in the hope that the board might reconsider his offer, made no objections to the sale.[28]

Negotiations for the purchase of the *Penobscot* by the Joy Line were almost complete, when, on the evening of April 10, 1907, the steamer *City of Troy* of the Citizens Line between New York and Troy, also owned by Morse, caught fire off Yonkers on one of her first trips of the season and burned to the water line. Since the line's other steamer, the *Saratoga*, had been sunk in a collision the previous fall, the Troy Line was now left with no steamers at all. Arrangements had already been made to run the *Dean Richmond*, the spare boat of Morse's Peoples Line to Albany, in the *Saratoga*'s place for the 1907 season. But now with a second steamer needed, the Eastern canceled the arrangements to sell the *Penobscot* to the Joy Line so that she would be available to run to Troy.[29]

After Morse had withheld the *Penobscot* from the Joy Line in April, the Citizens Line did not use her to replace the *City of Troy* after all. Late in June, the Montauk Line unexpectedly announced that traffic on the Greenport-Shelter Island route had declined markedly in recent years and that for the 1907 season it would run the *Shinnecock* alone for three round trips a week. The older *Greenport* (formerly the *Star of the East* and *Sagadahoc*) which they had acquired from the Kennebec Line in 1902, they now sold to the Citizens Line to run to Troy with the *Dean Richmond*.[30] In finding replacements for its two steamers lost within a few months of each other, the Troy Line had acquired two of the oldest hulls in service on the East Coast, for both the *Dean Richmond* and the *Greenport* had been built in 1866. One of the few that was older was the *Ulster* of the Saugerties Line which had been running under charter to Troy before the arrival of the *Greenport*.

When the New Haven had so bluntly refused the offer of $20 million for its marine properties, Mellen decided to placate Morse by letting him purchase the Boston service of the Joy Line. Why Mellen chose to break the New Haven's policy of never selling anything by parting with this one small piece of property is not clear. Perhaps it was a joke. If so, it is also not clear whether Morse was a party to the joke or the butt of it. Why would he want to buy the Boston Joy Line? He already owned the Metropolitan Line, and, with five large express steamers then building to run between New York and Boston, he must have realized that the days of the *Old Dominion* and the *Santiago* were already numbered. In any event, Morse did not buy the line to add it to his empire; he bought it only to kill it off and end at least that much of the competition with his Metropolitan Line.

The Joy Line people met secretly with Charles W. Morse and Calvin Austin on March 29 to arrange the sale. Morse began the negotiations by suggesting that the Boston Joy Line simply go out of business. "This," Dunbaugh said, "I declined to do, stating to Mr. Morse that in my judgment it would put our company in a position that did not appeal to me, and that while we were willing to say that we had sold to Mr. Morse, . . . we were not willing to go before the public as quitters." In the end, Dunbaugh made Morse cough up $350,000 (a figure suggested to him previously by Charles Mellen) for the Boston Joy Line, which then consisted of two very slow steamers both over thirty years old.[31]

Since the purchase of the Joy Line by the New Haven had still not become public, the sale of the Joy Line's Boston service as well as Morse's plans to discontinue it apparently came as a complete surprise to the people of Boston who had come to regard the Joy Line fondly as a curiosity. Contemporary reports are quite confused as to who sold what to whom and at whose command the service was suspended. Even the official announcement was made in a cloak-and-dagger manner. As the *Old Dominion* was about to sail from Boston at 5:00 P.M. on Sunday, April 7, a man from Morse's offices handed Captain Burton a sealed envelope with instructions not to open it until the *Old Dominion* was well out to sea. A similar performance took place aboard the *Santiago* as she was preparing to leave Pier 27 in New York. The contents of these envelopes informed Captains Burton and Holmes that the line had been sold to Morse and that the trip they were taking would be the last.[32]

Meanwhile, both the Joy Line and the Enterprise Line were still operating with curtailed schedules to Providence and Fall River as a result of a shortage of steamers. The Joy Line continued to divide its two routes among three steamers, while the Enterprise Line, with both the *Frank Jones* and the *Warren* out for repairs, had only the *St. Croix* running to Providence and the *Kennebec* to Fall River, each on an alternate night schedule. The Joy Line was also still operating its daily freight service to Bridgeport with the *Seaboard*.

Through the spring of 1907, plans were also maturing for the New Haven's new low-rate line to Fall River under the aegis of the United States Transportation Company which was to be known as the Neptune Line, reviving an old name in Narragansett Bay. At the outset, the New Haven made nearly a million dollars available to Stevenson Taylor to start the new line and then "sold" them the steamer *Connecticut* for $375,000 and the steamer *Rhode Island* for $275,000. Taylor himself had placed these values on the steamers in 1904 when he appraised the assets of the Providence and Stonington Line for the railroad. In addition, the repair bills for the two steamers came to $190,956 for the *Connecticut* (including $108,000 for new boilers alone, more than the Joy Line had ever spent to buy a whole steamer) and $85,872 for the *Rhode Island*.[33] The *Connecticut*, which had spent nearly a year being reconditioned in 1901-1902, now five years later took almost a year to get ready for her new service on the Neptune Line. For the price that was paid and the time it took to repair the steamers, the Neptune Line, it would seem, could have completed two fair-sized new steel steamers.

Next, Taylor ran into some difficulty finding a suitable pier in New York. Unable to lease a pier in the downtown area near the garment manufacturers where most of the Fall River freight would be headed, he had to settle for Pier 84, North River, at the foot of West Forty-fourth Street.[34] The fact that this location made the Neptune Line more convenient to passengers than either the Joy Line or the Enterprise Line, both located near the Brooklyn Bridge, does not appear in any of Taylor's correspondence on the subject.

Eventually, the steamers were ready. The Neptune Line began operations on Saturday evening, June 1, 1907, with the *Connecticut*, as beautiful as ever and looking as though she had never caused anyone a care in her life, sailing from New York under Captain Fred Whiting and the handsome and dependable *Rhode Island* commanded by Captain Frank Avery sailing from Fall River. Although the Joy Line's Fall River service was slated to cease operations as soon as the Neptune Line started, the *Kentucky* and the *Tennessee*, in an effort to preserve the fiction that an independent Joy Line had been driven from the route by a new competitor, remained on the run for another week, with the *Tennessee* continuing the triangular New York-Fall River-Providence route she had followed since February.

The *Connecticut* and the *Rhode Island* were not the only additions to the already crowded New York to Fall River route that week. Through the winter the Fall River Line had been running, in addition to its large passenger and freight steamers *Providence* and *Pilgrim*, the good-sized freighters *Boston* and *City of Taunton*. Then, early in June the *Massachusetts*, the first of the three fast freighters designed for the New Haven's new Boston line, came fresh from her builders looking very smart and ready for work. What to do with her? What else? She was assigned to the freight run to Fall River running opposite the *Boston*. She made her first trip under Captain Milton I. Brightman on Monday night, June 3, and immediately gave proof that she would be a match for Morse's new steamers by clipping through the sound between New York and Fall River in 7 hours and 48 minutes, almost one hour less than the previous record set by the *Puritan* about twelve years earlier.[35]

Wednesday, June 5, Friday, June 7, and Sunday, June 9, 1907, must have set records for tonnage arriving in Fall River from New York on one day.

On each of these three mornings, the procession of steamers sailing into Mount Hope Bay and tying up at Fall River included the *Priscilla*, the largest passenger steamer on the sound, the *Massachusetts*, the largest freight steamer on the sound, plus the *Rhode Island*, the *Frank Jones*, and the *Tennessee*. All but one of these five vessels were owned by the New Haven Railroad.

A few hours after her arrival in Fall River on Sunday morning, June 9, the *Tennessee* blew her whistle and sailed again for Providence, as she had been doing for the past four months. This time, however, she was never to return, for with that sailing the Joy Line's Fall River service was to be discontinued, just three weeks short of one year after it started. The following night, the Joy Line reinstituted regular daily sailings on the Providence route for the first time since the loss of the *Larchmont*, with the *Tennessee* under Captain Wilcox and the *Edgemont* under Captain Olweiler. From this time (except for several weeks filling in on the Neptune Line later that year), the *Tennessee* remained on the Providence run of the Joy Line (known in 1914 as the Bay State Line) for another twenty-four years.

During the summer months of 1907, both the Neptune Line and the Fall River Line scheduled sailings seven days a week, the *Connecticut* usually running the same nights as the *Puritan* and the *Rhode Island* with the *Priscilla*. The Enterprise Line, however, stuck to its six-night-a-week schedule. A prospective passenger had a wide range of prices to choose from: the Enterprise boat, leaving Fall River at 6:30, cost $1.00; the Neptune steamer left at 7:00 and also coast $1.00, but on the Fall River Line, which left at 7:40, the price was $3.00 for the trip to New York.

The *Priscilla* and the *Puritan* had again started their seasons early in 1907, the *Puritan* coming on with the *Providence* in the first week of April (replacing the *Pilgrim*) and the *Priscilla* joining her about two weeks later. With the new Fall River liner, as yet unnamed, already under construction, it was understood that this was to be the last season for the graceful *Puritan*. Since the rebuilt *Plymouth* was not yet finished, the *Pilgrim* also joined the *Providence* once again in opening the Providence Line the first week in June for what would also be her last season. At the same time, the *Maine* and the *New Hampshire* started the third season of their passenger service to New Bedford. The *City of Lowell*, for some reason, was out for major repairs through June and part of July, during which time the *City of Worcester* ran to New London with the *Chester W. Chapin*.

Although the moves and countermoves of Mellen and Morse dominated events in Long Island Sound steamboating, the center of attention nationally in the summer of 1907 was the exposition at Jamestown, Virginia, commemorating the three hundredth anniversary of the first English settlement on this continent. Expositions in America always attract optimists who predict great profits for all concerned, in spite of statistics showing that most expositions lose money. In 1907, many of them were not only pre-pared to believe that half of America would feel compelled to travel to Jamestown that summer, but they also seemed certain that most of them would want to arrive there on a steamboat. The Norfolk and Washington Line, while keeping two of its three steamers on the regular night run, placed its largest steamer, the *Newport News,* plus another steamer, the *Jamestown,* a day boat built especially for that summer's business, on a day run, with connections at Old Point Comfort for Jamestown. From Balti-more the Old Bay Line ran a similar service with the *Georgia,* its spare boat, and the Chesapeake Line with the *Atlanta.* The Ericcson Line, which normally operated both a night line and a day line between Philadelphia and Bal-timore, via the Delaware and Chesapeake Canal, seems to have had the most rose-colored view of the situation when it put its fast day boat, the *Penn,* on a day route between Philadelphia and Jamestown, a trip that took seventeen hours traveling at top speed and that, understandably, attracted few passengers.

Another operator planned a second overnight line between Washington and Norfolk to accommodate the expected increased traffic and began nego-tiations for the purchase of the retired New Haven Railroad steamers *City of Worcester* and *C. H. Northam* (the only surviving sound steamer with boilers on the guards) for the route.[36] The new line, however, failed to materialize, and the two steamers remained at their piers in Stonington. The former Bridgeport steamer, *Rosedale,* did make it down to the James River, however, and ran excursions between Norfolk and the exposition. The Troy steamer, *Saratoga,* raised and hastily reconditioned after sinking in the fall of 1906, also served the exposition as a floating hotel. Even C. W. Morse was attracted to the potential business and at one time con-sidered postponing the inauguration of the Boston service so that the *Yale* and *Harvard* could run between New York and Jamestown for the summer of 1907.

Morse eventually abandoned this plan, as well as the one to run to Havana—which was just as well, for only one of his two steamers was ready for the 1907 season. The *Yale* came from the builders late in June, but as Morse did not want to start the Boston service until both steamers were ready, he put the *Yale* in service on the International Line that summer running with the *Calvin Austin* (a route covered not many years before by the *Larchmont* and *Edgemont*), while the new *Governor Cobb* spent her first summer running with the *Governor Dingley* (in place of the *Bay State*) on the Boston to Portland run.

On July 9, the *Bunker Hill,* the second of the New Haven's big freighters, also arrived in New York. Since Mellen was not anxious to start the Boston service before Morse started his, both the *Bunker Hill* and the *Massachu-setts* spent the summer of 1907 as the regular freight steamers on the Fall

River Line. When the third of the trio, the *Old Colony*, the only turbine-driven steamer of the three, arrived in August, she made several unscheduled freight trips to Providence but was not put into any regular service until the Boston line started in the fall. On July 11, two days after the arrival of the *Bunker Hill*, the Navigation Company's smaller freighter *New Haven* also arrived from the builders. The expectation was that the *New Haven* and her sistership, the *Pequonnock*, which had been delivered the previous summer, would run as extra freighters on the New Haven Line and the Bridgeport Line in the summer and run together to Providence in the winter. This would allow the *Maine* and the *New Hampshire* to resume their dignity as passenger steamers, one to run through the winter on the Norwich Line with the *Chester W. Chapin* and the other now available as a general relief boat, primarily on the New Haven and Bridgeport lines.

The year from June 1907 to June 1908 saw the arrival of many new steamers on the sound. But by the same token it was the last year of operation for many favorites. Early in July, the versatile and dependable old *City of Lawrence*, serving that summer as a day boat between New London and Fisher's Island, ran up on Black Rock at the entrance to New London harbor in a fog and was a total loss. Also in July, the *C. H. Northam*, after several years of inactivity, was finally towed to Boston for scrapping. The arrival of the *Pequonnock* and the *New Haven* meant retirement for the former Providence and Stonington Line freighters *Nashua* and *Pequot*, which went to lay up at Stonington and were not used again. As already noted, this was to be the *Puritan's* last season, although she did serve irregularly both on the Fall River Line and on the Providence Line for a few more years. On the other hand, when the rebuilt *Plymouth* resumed her place on the Providence Line in early August, the *Pilgrim* was taken off, this time permanently, and rarely saw service again before being scrapped in New London in 1915. Since, as the astute reader may already have guessed, the Neptune Line was destined for a very short life, 1907 was also the last season for both the *Connecticut* and the *Rhode Island*. Nor should we neglect to mention the disappearance of the *Larchmont* from the lists earlier in the same year.

Late in July, the *Tennessee* got another chance to run to Fall River when the *Rhode Island* had to come off the run for several weeks as the result of an accident for which she was not at all to blame since she was at the time sitting peacefully in her pier at Fall River. On Friday morning, July 26, the *Frank Jones* sailed into Fall River quite late for some reason, by which tme it was already bright daylight, and, as usual, pulled up to the end of her pier preparing to back into it. Somehow a signal was misinterpreted in the engine room, and instead of backing, the *Frank Jones* suddenly lurched forward right into the *Rhode Island*, which had arrived some time earlier and was tied up at the next pier. The *Frank Jones* was not seriously damaged beyond a slightly blunted bow, but the *Rhode Island* was out of service for nearly two weeks, during which the *Tennessee* was "borrowed" from the Joy Line to run on the Neptune Line with the *Connecticut*—an oddly matched pair. The *Kentucky*, which had been laid up at Morse's since the Joy Line's Fall River service ended, was brought out to run to Providence with the *Edgemont*.

During her brief stay on the Neptune Line, the *Tennessee* was involved in an accident which, had circumstances been slightly different, could have been as serious as that of the *Larchmont*. Steaming toward New York with a full passenger list, (it was midsummer and the *Tennessee* had about half the capacity of the *Rhode Island* which she was replacing) the *Tennessee* was trying to hold to her schedule in spite of a thick fog that had settled on the sound during the night. At 4:00 A.M., she was just off Stratford Shoals when the three-masted schooner *Mironus* suddenly appeared directly ahead of her. There was no way to avoid a collision, and the *Tennessee* crashed into the starboard side of the schooner, which sank almost immediately, taking four of her crew of six with her to the bottom. The other two men, one of whom was her skipper, Captain Belatty, jumped to safety, but Belatty, surprisingly, was not a swimmer, and he began shouting for help. Two of the *Tennessee*'s passengers, Joseph Kenny and Michael Coffin, thereupon leapt into the water and supported Belatty until the *Tennessee*'s crew could lower a boat and pick them up. The *Tennessee* waited at the scene for several hours while men in her lifeboats combed the area for the four missing men. While she was there, the *Maine*, coming down from New Bedford, pulled alongside and took the *Tennessee*'s passengers to New York. Finally, later in the morning, the search was abandoned and the *Tennessee* continued her trip.[37]

With the considerable amount of advance publicity for the two proposed new lines to Boston and the many articles then appearing on the Cunard Line's new liners *Mauretania* and *Lusitania*, which were also expected to start running in the fall, an unusual degree of interest was generated in the subject of speed. We have already seen that in July the *Massachusetts* beat the previous record for the run to Fall River by more than an hour. That summer, after she was joined by her sistership *Bunker Hill*, the two vied with each other for new records on the run. During August, C. W. Morse "borrowed" the new triple-screw turbine steamer *Camden* from his own Bangor Line to take a group of two hundred visiting Texas businessmen and their families on a cruise from Boston to New York and back. On her return trip the *Camden* steamed from New York to Boston around the cape in just fifteen hours, better by over an hour than the previous record for the run set by the *Governor Cobb* on her way from her builders to Boston a few months earlier.[38]

It was mid-September and the summer season was well over before the

Fletcher yards in Hoboken finished working on the *Harvard* and Morse was able at last to start running his speedy new steamers to Boston. The passenger service of the Metropolitan Line was finally inaugurated on Monday night, September 16, with the *Harvard* sailing from New York and the *Yale* from Boston. The steamers left both ports at 5:00 each night and arrived at the other end of the route at 8:00 the following morning, thus taking passengers directly from New York to Boston by water in almost the same time that it would take them to travel via the Fall River Line with its rail connections, which had been the most popular route between the two cities for over sixty years. In service both the *Harvard* and the *Yale* proved they could tear up the sound at speeds up to twenty-three knots, making them not only the fastest steamers on the sound but also the fastest vessels flying the American flag. Even the Cunard Line's new turbine liner *Lusitania*, then the fastest ship in the world, which arrived in New York on her maiden voyage on Friday, September 13, just three days before the *Harvard* made hers, clocked only a little over twenty-five knots in breaking the transatlantic record. The fastest run between New York and Boston that year was made by the *Yale* in fourteen hours, one hour less than the *Camden*'s record of a few weeks before.[39]

On Saturday, September 21, at the end of the same week in which the sleek *Harvard* and *Yale* had started running to Boston, Morse's Peoples Line (the Albany night boat) launched its new *Princeton* (later known as the *Berkshire*), a steamer even larger than the Fall River Line's *Priscilla*, as a running mate for the line's four-year-old *C. W. Morse*. By September 1907, Charles W. Morse had, in only six years, reached a pinnacle of success in the maritime world rarely equaled by one man.

No sooner had Morse created his highly successful shipping empire embracing many of the most profitable steamship lines on the Atlantic Coast than the base of that empire suddenly began to crumble. When Morse first made his enormous profits in the ice business, he had used these profits to buy sufficient interest in several banks to give himself considerable influence in their operations. He had then used the services of these banks to create his shipping empire, persuading, or sometimes one might say ordering, their officers to direct a good deal more of the bank's assets than was financially advisable toward the purchase of the very heavily watered stocks of Morse's various steamship companies. No one had been very much the wiser until the unexpected financial flutter which hit the nation in October 1907 forced one of the Morse banks to close. An investigation into the affairs of this bank showed that its investments in Morse's shipping interests had not only been inadvisable, but very likely also constituted criminal misuse of the bank's funds. Operating as it did on watered stocks, on bonds and bank loans on which it could no longer make interest payments, Morse's Consolidated Steamship Company quickly collapsed, while Morse himself suddenly decided it was time for him and his wife to absorb the culture of Europe.

The stockholders of the various steamship lines within the Morse empire were, for the most part, able to pull their separate companies out of the collapsing conglomerate and to function independently again. The Hudson Navigation Company, for instance, the new Morse company which now operated both the Albany and Troy night lines, became an independent concern in good financial condition.[40] There was even enough capital to continue the construction of the two steamers needed for the Troy Line, but work was halted for several years on the new *Princeton* of the Albany Line, which, as the *Berkshire*, was not completed until 1913.

The various coastal lines running south of New York reorganized their corporate structures, once they had extricated themselves from Morse's Consolidated Steamship Company, and survived. Even the Eastern Steamship Company, with Morse's associate Calvin Austin still firmly at the helm, managed to pull through intact, though work on its new steamer *Belfast* was held up for more than a year until the company's finances were somewhat better stabilized.[41] The Metropolitan Line, however, which had just taken delivery of two very expensive steamers, was caught with far greater debts than it could possibly pay, and, though it continued to run the popular new *Harvard* and *Yale* through the fall, the future of the line was at best uncertain.

In October, Charles Mellen was informed, though he undoubtedly could have figured it out for himself by that time, that the Metropolitan Line could be purchased very cheaply if the New Haven was interested.[42] A few years earlier, the New Haven might have been very interested. But Mellen was now treading carefully, lest one move too many invite a federal investigation into the railroad's affairs and possibly an antitrust order to give up all of its valuable marine properties. The same caution also made him wary of becoming involved, even remotely, with the probes into Morse's finances which were obviously then in the offing. Furthermore, the New Haven's objective at this time was not to acquire a steamship line between New York and Boston but to try to prevent one from existing at all to divert traffic from the Fall River Line, which represented a major investment for the railroad. Mellen therefore decided to let the Metropolitan Line fall into whatever hands it might and to continue to oppose it with the railroad's own line to Boston. Thus, not only would the Metropolitan be forced out of business but also anyone else would be discouraged from attempting to run a line to Boston in the future.[43]

When Morse's financial difficulties first surfaced in October, Mellen decided to postpone the inauguration of the railroad's freight line to Boston for a time, although the three steamers ordered for the route had been ready since summer. Eventually, however, he announced that the service would start operating early in 1908 under the name of the Boston Merchants Line.

Meanwhile, the Navigation Company again placed its winter boats on the Fall River Line very early that year. With the large Neptune liners also running to Fall River, there was little need to keep the *Priscilla* and the *Puritan* in service after the summer season. Thus, the *Plymouth* and *Providence*, both essentially new steamers, came on the line soon after the Providence passenger service was suspended at the end of October, though that year the Fall River Line maintained its regular off-season fares. At the same time, the *Bunker Hill* and the *Massachusetts* also came off the Fall River route and the *Boston* and *City of Taunton* once again became the regular freight boats to Fall River. That same week the Fall River Line's new steamer, now officially named the *Commonwealth* (and thus the first Fall River Line passenger steamer since the *Bristol* of 1867 to have a name not starting with "P"), was launched to the accompaniment of the usual speeches and ceremonies at Cramp's yard in Chester, Pennsylvania. That year the *Pequonnock* and the *New Haven* ran as the winter freight boats on the Providence Line for the first time, while the *City of Brockton* and the *City of Fall River* carried freight to New Bedford.

During the fall, the *Connecticut* once again developed engine trouble. Her new boilers, which had been installed in the spring at a cost exceeding $100,000, had somehow taken to admitting salt water, causing a film to form on the interior walls. The steamer, which by then had run a total of five months since her $200,000 reconditioning, was taken off the line, theoretically for repairs to her boilers. Actually, the *Connecticut* was never to turn her wheels again. The *Kentucky*, under Captain Frank Burton, the last commander of the *Old Dominion*, returned to the Joy Line's Providence route with the *Edgemont*, while Dave Wilcox's *Tennessee* took the *Connecticut*'s place running with the *Rhode Island* on the Neptune Line.

Early in October, the Enterprise Line unexpectedly announced that it was giving up its one-year-old service to Providence. The *Frank Jones* had been involved in an accident on the morning of September 26 while coming down the East River and had been off the Fall River route for several days. During this time, the *St. Croix* had followed in reverse the same roundabout route that the *Tennessee* had taken in the months after the loss of the *Larchmont*, sailing every other night from New York to Providence, then taking freight down to Fall River during the following day, and sailing that night as the Enterprise Line steamer out of Fall River. After about a week, the *Frank Jones* was back in service but soon developed new problems and had to be taken off again. A few days later came the announcement that, rather than have the *Frank Jones* repaired, the Enterprise Line was discontinuing its Providence line and placing the *St. Croix* on the Fall River route with the *Kennebec*.

Soon it became clear why the *Frank Jones* was not being repaired. In

November, it was announced that the Enterprise Line had been forced into receivership by the financial panic in October and would have to suspend its operations altogether. With the sailing of the *Kennebec* from Fall River on the evening of Friday, November 14, the Enterprise Line went out of business.

When David Whitcomb was asked subsequently whether he had been ruined personally in the failure of the Enterprise Line, he answered candidly that, although he had managed the line to the end, neither he nor any member of his family had been financially involved in the line for some time. Whitcomb's statement plus the line's declaration of bankruptcy only a few weeks after Morse's financial failure finally made it clear that, in spite of the lack of any specific evidence, the Enterprise had been controlled, however indirectly, by Charles W. Morse. Thus, it turned out that, although the public did not know it, for nearly two years both of the competing low-fare lines running to Providence and Fall River, the Joy Line and the Enterprise Line, had merely been the pawns of the two warring giants.

The New Haven Railroad could now relax. All competition into Narragansett Bay had ended, and even the Metropolitan's Boston line was in serious difficulty. But the Enterprise Line had ultimately failed as a result of internal problems, and not from any of the railroad's various efforts to force the line out. Thus, in the long run, the literally millions of dollars spent by the railroad to run the Enterprise's small steamers from the sound, the purchase of the Joy Line, the addition of two steamers for a Joy Line service to Fall River, and finally the inauguration of the Neptune Line and the expensive reconditioning of the *Connecticut* and the *Rhode Island*, had all been unnecessary. The Enterprise Line would have failed as it did had the New Haven done nothing at all.

With the Enterprise Line at last out of the way, the New Haven no longer had any need to maintain either the Joy Line to Providence or the Neptune Line to Fall River. Mellen did not dare discontinue the Neptune Line immediately, for he did not wish to make it more obvious than it already was that the line had been created solely to force the Enterprise out of business and was thus clearly in violation of the Sherman Anti-Trust Law which the federal government had recently begun to invoke. In line with his proposals to the New Haven's board of directors just two years earlier, however, he intended to continue operating the Joy Line's low-fare service to Providence as a relatively innocuous deterrent to any future entrepreneurs who might dare to contest the New Haven's monopoly of steamboat routes on Long Island Sound.

A few days after the Enterprise Line suspended service, the *Kennebec* was purchased for the Joy Line.[44] With the Enterprise now no longer operating, it was not necessary to maintain such a large steamer as the *Rhode Island* on the Neptune Line. In late November, the *Rhode Island* came off the route and, like the *Connecticut*, never operated again as a passenger steamer. The *Kennebec* now began running on the Neptune Line with the *Tennessee*, while the *Edgemont* and the *Kentucky* continued to run on the Joy Line to Providence.

Although the Joy Line to Providence, later known as the Bay State Line, was to continue operating until 1931, the Joy Steamship Company, founded in 1899 by Dimon, Joy, and Dunbaugh and purchased by the New Haven Railroad in 1905, ceased to exist as a corporate entity on October 31, 1907, shortly before the collapse of the Enterprise Line. Charles Mellen, as we have seen, was becoming increasingly concerned over the New Haven Railroad's vulnerability to charges of violating federal antitrust laws. In his efforts to circumvent such charges, he had transferred most of the railroad's marine properties into the hands of a separate company, the New England Navigation Company, which happened to have the same stockholders and most of the same directors as the railroad. We have also noted that in creating the Neptune Line to compete both with the railroad itself and with the rail-owned Fall River Line (as well as, for one week, the rail-owned Joy Line to Fall River), he had set up still another separate company, the United States Transportation Company. On paper at least, this company was owned almost entirely by Stevenson Taylor acting as trustee for other investors, who were again the stockholders of the New Haven Railroad, although not so labeled.

Thus, with both the New England Navigation Company and the United States Transportation Company, sufficient corporate distance was preserved to protect the railroad from antitrust action for the time being. But federal investigators were beginning to ask embarrassing questions about the Joy Steamship Company, which was not a separate company, but which was owned outright by the railroad itself. In June, when the Neptune Line started running to Fall River, Mellen had placed the management, but not the ownership, of the Joy Line's two remaining services (New York to Providence and New York to Bridgeport) under the general supervision of Stevenson Taylor's United States Transportation Company. Further federal investigations that summer caused Mellen some concern. Accordingly, at his recommendation, the board of directors of the New Haven voted on October 30 to end the corporate existence of the Joy Steamship Company altogether and to sell its assets outright to the United States Transportation Company.

Whereas, the ownership of this company of securities of the Joy Steamship Co. amounting to $1,019,756.26 is being questioned by the Federal authorities, and,

Whereas, it is desirable that this company should be relieved from this position, therefore,

> Resolved, That the President be authorized to arrange the sale of the Joy
> Steamship Company in such manner as he may deem best so as to eliminate
> its control by this company.[45]

Mellen's concern is clear in his letter to a New Haven Railroad lawyer a
few days later asking that the liquidation of the Joy Steamship Company be
arranged with all possible dispatch:

> It seems to me under all advice given that it is wise we discontinue further
> interest in the Joy Steamship Company, and to that end I would like to have it
> arranged . . . that the personal property of the Joy Steamship Company,
> including its leasehold, be sold to the United States Transportation Company,
> and that the Joy Steamship Company be liquidated. . . . It seems to me it is
> very important that no time be lost in carrying the above into effect.[46]

The Providence service of the Joy Line was to continue to operate under
the same name but under the authority of the United States Transportation
Company. The Joy Line's Bridgeport service was also to be transferred to
the United States Transportation Company but to operate now as the
Bridgeport Merchants Line (taking the name of the small company it had
originally been designed to eliminate). Stevenson Taylor was dispatched to
Pier 27 to inform Allan Joy and Frank Dunbaugh that the Joy Steamship
Company had been dissolved and that they would no longer be associated
with the new operation. According to Taylor, they accepted this decision,
asking only that they be granted time to inform all of the employees of the
line personally, both in the offices and on the steamers, of the change.[47]

On October 31, 1907, the Joy Steamship Line was sold by the New Haven
Railroad, its owners, to the United States Transportation Company for
$1,019,756.26.[48] This figure was considerably higher than the amount paid
for the line when it was purchased in 1905. But the railroad had added
considerably to the capital worth of the company in its two years of ownership. The figure was the appraised value of the company *after* the sale of
the Boston Joy Line and its two steamers to Morse. With the purchase of the
Joy Line, the United States Transportation Company received the dock
properties in Providence, the leases on the docks in New York, and the seven
steamers *Tennessee, Kentucky, Edgemont, City of Key West, Seaboard,
Fairfield,* and *Kennebec.*

The day after the official demise of the Joy Steamship Company as a
legal entity, the line's outgoing president received an uncharacteristically
warm note from Mellen:

> My dear Mr. Dunbaugh: . . . . In closing our business relations let me express
> my very great regret that events have so shaped themselves it had become

necessary to sever the very pleasant relationship that has existed during the past two years.

I have appreciated more than I can well express the service you have been to us and shall always be interested if at any time I can reciprocate.

It is not at all impossible we shall have an opportunity to again enjoy an intimate relationship just as has just terminated. In case I have any occasion to use a man in such a way, I shall turn to you first of all my acquaintances.

Wish you the greatest prosperity, and hoping the time may come when I can in some measure contribute again to the same, I remain,

Yours very sincerely,
(signed) C. S. Mellen[49]

Once Dunbaugh and Joy had settled their affairs and moved out of the offices at Pier 27, their place was taken by Robert C. Scholz, the recently hired manager of the United States Transportation Company, although Robert S. Noble was retained as general superintendent. Stevenson Taylor was the titular president, but he was rarely concerned personally with the operation of the steamers. During this period of transition, Taylor and his wife were traveling in Europe, though not, one would assume, in company with the Morses.

With the Neptune Line now operating only two relatively small steamers and the Joy Line reduced to its Providence and Bridgeport lines, the Neptune Line pier at Forty-fourth Street on the North River was given up and its operations moved to the Joy Line's Pier 28, East River. Since the Portland Line pier was also in the vicinity, all of the operations of the United States Transportation Company (the Neptune Line to Fall River, the Joy Line to Providence, the Maine Steamship Company to Portland, and the Merchants Line to Bridgeport) were now concentrated in one area along the East River.

Late in the year an announcement appeared, buried in the marine columns of the local papers, stating that the former Joy Line steamer *Old Dominion* had been sold to the Luckenbach Towing and Transportation Company to be converted into a barge.

Epilogue

By the time the year 1908 began, the New Haven Railroad had once again successfully eliminated all steamship competition from the waters of Long Island Sound except Morse's Metropolitan Line to Boston, which now, following the failure of the Morse-controlled National Bank of North America the previous October, seemed destined to disappear as well. Mellen nevertheless held to his original plans, and the new Merchants Line to Boston began operations on Saturday, January 4, with the big freighter *Bunker Hill* sailing from New York and her sistership *Massachusetts* sailing from Boston. The scheduled time for the run was twenty hours, although these fast freighters could have made much better time with one steamer leaving each port three times a week. For the time being, only two steamers were placed in this service, with the *Old Colony* held in reserve, though in the fall of 1908 the *Old Colony* joined her sisters on the line to begin a daily service. Meanwhile, the Metropolitan Line continued operating its three freighters, passenger service with the *Yale* and *Harvard* having been suspended during the winter months, though revenues on this line dropped off markedly as soon as the Merchants Line operation began.

In January 1908, both the Joy Line to Providence, operating the *Edgemont* and the *Kentucky*, and the Neptune Line to Fall River, operating the *Tennessee* and the *Kennebec*, were still running under the auspices of the United States Transportation Company, which also managed the Portland Line. Although the New Haven planned to continue the Joy Line to Providence indefinitely as a permanent deterrent to potential competitors, the Neptune Line was to be phased out as soon as contractual obligations had been met. Meanwhile, the *Frank Jones* sat at Morse's yard in Brooklyn, waiting to be sold to anyone willing to pick up her $60,000 repair bill, while the *Fairfield*, the *City of Key West*, and the big iron *Zealandia* were also laid up nearby. Later in the year, both the *Fairfield* and the *City of Key West* were sold for scrap and towed to Gregory's bone yard in Perth Amboy, New Jersey. The *St. Croix*, which the Enterprise Line had not fully paid for, was reclaimed by the Eastern Steamship Company, her former owners, who then resold her a year later to the Northern Pacific Steamship Company to run between Seattle and Alaska. She left New York for the West Coast under her own power on January 30, 1909, and arrived there safely about two months later. The *Warren*, evicted from her Enterprise pier in Fall River, had been run aground up-river from Fall River and still sat there, leaning precariously to one side and looking forlorn. On February 17, she was purchased at auction by W. J. Dunn of Boston and towed away to be scrapped.

On the unused side of the Neptune dock* sat the old *Rhode Island* also looking somewhat shopworn in spite of the extensive renovations of less than a year earlier. Later in February, the *Connecticut* was towed up to Fall River from New York by the new freighter *Pequonnock*, on her regular run to Providence. The ever-optimistic Fall River *Herald*, having become accustomed to the procession of liners steaming daily into its city during the previous summer, reported happily that the *Connecticut* had been brought back to Fall River to be fitted out for the Neptune Line's coming summer season.[1] But alas, the *Connecticut*'s next trip, two years later, was to be to the bone yard at Noank, Connecticut, at the end of a tow rope. A few weeks later, the Fall River *Herald* had also announced that the Neptune Line needed newer and larger steamers and would probably purchase the *Yale* and the *Harvard*![2]

The Neptune did indeed get different steamers very soon after, but they were not the *Yale* and the *Harvard*. On January 25, the line announced that it was discontinuing passenger service for the winter and that "due notice of resumption will be given." Of course, there was never any need for such notice. The *Tennessee* and the *Kennebec* now went to run on the Joy Line to Providence, alternating with the *Edgemont*. At the same time, the Merchants Line to Bridgeport, having successfully completed its mission of killing off competition there, was discontinued, though only temporarily, as it turned out. The *Seaboard*, now under Captain Burton, the former commander of the *Old Dominion*, was placed on the Neptune Line with the *Kentucky*, under Captain Frank Avery, to carry freight to Fall River.

During March 1908, with the federal investigation of Morse's financial dealings underway and monopolies in general coming increasingly under

---

*With the Neptune Line runing one former Joy Line steamer and one former Enterprise Line steamer and using the former Joy Line dock, which was more convenient to the railroad than its own, Fall River travelers must have been getting somewhat confused.

government scrutiny, Charles S. Mellen suddenly announced even further changes in the structure of the railroad's marine holdings. In the shuffle which followed, the recently conceived United States Transportation Company was liquidated and its properties sold to the New Haven Railroad's third marine subsidiary, the Hartford and New York Transportation Company, which now took over the management of the Portland Line, the Joy Line, and the Neptune Line, as well as of its own Hartford Line. Stevenson Taylor, the former president of the United States Transportation Company, now devoted his full time, as he had probably done all along, to his two other jobs as engineering consultant to the New England Navigation Company and as vice-president of the Quintard Iron Works. Robert Scholz, the former general manager of the United States Transportation Company, also disappeared from the roster at this time, and Robert J. Noble, who had succeeded Charles Dimon as general manager of the Joy Line, now became the general manager of the entire Hartford and New York Transportation Company's newly expanded operations.

Soon after the transfer, the *Seaboard* was taken off the Neptune Line and laid up at the Joy Line dock in New York, leaving the *Kentucky* to carry freight to Fall River alone on alternate nights, largely to fulfill contractual obligations of both the Joy Line and the Neptune Line. When the Neptune Line finally ceased operations altogether in May 1908, also just short of one year after it started, Stevenson Taylor announced that the line had been forced to quit as a result of the panic of October 1907. In a sense, of course, he was quite correct. Since the Neptune Line had existed only to put the Enterprise Line out of business and the Enterprise had been forced by the panic to close down, the financial crisis had indeed, if somewhat indirectly, been responsible for the demise of the Neptune Line.

During March 1908, the investigations of Morse's dealings with the National Bank of North America, which had been going on since the bank's failure in October, were completed, and Morse was now formally charged with fraudulently falsifying the records of the bank and of misusing the money of its depositors. While waiting for his case to come to trial in November, he continued running his business as usual.

Spring came early in 1908, and by April the summer steamer services were beginning to operate. By mid-April, the *Priscilla* and *Puritan* were back on the Fall River Line. A few weeks later on Monday, May 11, the *Yale* and *Harvard* began their first full summer running to Boston, as though nothing whatever were wrong, and immediately enjoyed a success beyond all expectations. The days, not too long past, when the *Old Dominion's* twenty-four hour run was the only passenger route to Boston by sea, were now quite forgotten. In spite of the competition from the Merchants Line, the Metropolitan continued to run two of its freighters, the *James S. Whitney* and the *H. S. Whitney*, in conjunction with the *Harvard* and *Yale*. The

H. M. Whitney, however, went aground near Hell Gate in a fog one morning and was out of commission for several months. The former Joy liner *Santiago* was brought out of layup to go on the Metropolitan's Boston run for several trips until the *H. F. Dimock* could be made ready to take the *H. M. Whitney's* place on the line. Early in June, the *Plymouth* and the *Providence* started the summer service of the Providence Line, and two weeks later, when the *Maine* and *New Hampshire* began running to New Bedford, the railroad's summer steamer operations were in full operation.

That summer the New England Navigation Company experimented, for the only time in its history, with a special cruise line, using the steamer *City of Worcester*. For several weeks in July, cruise passengers could sail on the *City of Worcester* from New York any Tuesday, Thursday, or Saturday at 2:00 P.M. for a trip up the sound during the late afternoon and early evening. The steamer arrived at Newport, Rhode Island, sometime during the night. Early the next morning, passengers were treated to a tour of the magnificent "cottages" of Newport's wealthy summer residents. Then, at about 1:00 P.M., the *City of Worcester* would sail again for Block Island, where passengers could spend a quiet bucolic afternoon before sailing again for New York late that evening. The experiment was not successful, however, and after a few weeks it was discontinued.

That summer the former Enterprise Line steamer *Frank Jones* was purchased to run with the former Troy steamer *Saratoga* on a new low-fare line between New York and Albany. The captain of the *Frank Jones* on this run was George Cobb, formerly master of the *St. Croix* when she ran to Providence for the Enterprise Line. The New York manager for the line was none other than "Captain" George Brady, who was now working for the fifth different steamship company in a period of ten years. This line, like both the Joy Line and the Enterprise Line on the sound, did a great deal of business, but, with the fare it was charging ($1.00, New York to Albany), it made very little money.

On July 1, 1908, the new *Commonwealth*, the largest steamer ever to operate on Long Island Sound, took her place on the Fall River Line. Longer than the *Priscilla* by sixteen feet and far more modern in design, she was never her equal in beauty or popularity. The beautiful *Puritan*, the last walking beam steamer in regular operation on any of the railroad's overnight lines, now became a spare. After three years during which she saw limited service, she was laid up in Stonington in 1911 and finally scrapped in 1915.

In the fall of 1908, a group of Bridgeport merchants made still another attempt to start an independent freight line to their city, known as the New York and Bridgeport Transportation Company. The New Haven lost no time in reviving its own low-fare Merchants Line to Bridgeport, rescuing the Joy Line steamer *Seaboard* to run once again in this service, and the new line soon gave up. To discourage any future possibility of competition in

Bridgeport, the New Haven continued to operate the Merchants Line with the *Seaboard*, under the auspices of the Hartford and New York Transportation Company, until 1920. In that year, the New England Steamship Company discontinued its own passenger service to Bridgeport and replaced the passenger and freight steamers *Bridgeport* and *Naugatuck* (ex-*Allan Joy*) with the Fall River Line's sidewheel freighter *City of Brockton*, whose cargo capacity was sufficient to make a second freight line redundant.

When the summer season of 1908 ended, most of the sound services had pretty much returned to normal. Both the Enterprise Line and the Neptune Line were gone, leaving the Fall River Line steamers *Plymouth* and *Providence* to run alone on that route through the winter, although the *Plymouth* experienced some mechanical difficulties that season (as she was to do frequently after her rebuilding) and was replaced on several occasions by either the *Priscilla* or the *Puritan*. The Joy Line continued as the only passenger line into Providence with the new *Pequonnock* and *New Haven* now the winter freighters to Providence for the New England Navigation Company. The New England's three freighters still ran daily to Boston through the winter of 1908-1909 as did the older Metropolitan Line freighters, once the *Yale* and *Harvard* finished their season, in spite of the line's financial difficulties.

One casualty that year was the new opposition line operating the *Saratoga* and *Frank Jones* between New York and Albany, which was forced to declare bankruptcy in December at the end of its first season.

In November 1908, C. W. Morse finally came up for trial before a federal court. He was found guilty as charged and sentenced to fifteen years in a federal prison. Pending an appeal, however, he was maintained at the Tombs Prison in New York. From his cell there only a few blocks from Wall Street or from the Metropolitan Line pier, he continued to conduct business as though it were an office until he was released on bail in March 1909. Meanwhile, a group of Boston businessmen, under the aegis of the brokerage firm of Hayden, Stone, and Company, gathered enough resources to rescue the Eastern Steamship Company from Morse's crumbling Consolidated Steamship Company. Following a brief period in receivership, the trustees managed to satisfy the creditors with partial payments and to emerge again as an independent corporation under the presidency of Calvin Austin, who somehow came through the entire mess unscathed. Although it was not generally known at the time, it was later revealed, to the surprise of no one, that in the course of these negotiations, a fair amount of the now inexpensive stock of the reorganized Eastern Steamship Company was purchased by the New England Navigation Company, backed in turn by the New Haven Railroad.

As one of its first acts, the revived company ordered construction on the liner *Belfast* to start again and announced that the new steamer would be ready to join her sister *Camden* on the Bangor Line in time for the 1909 season. During the summer of 1908, while the Penobscot River docks were being strengthened in anticipation of the new steamers, the sidewheelers *City of Rockland* and *City of Bangor* had returned to the line, while the new *Camden* had joined the *Calvin Austin* and the *Governor Cobb* on the International Line (as the *Yale* had done the year before) for one season. At the same time, the Citizens Line between New York and Troy, which, with the Peoples Line to Albany, had extricated itself from Morse's combine, announced that its new steamers *Trojan* and *Rensselaer* would also be ready to operate in the 1909 season. On the assumption that no hitches would develop before their delivery, the aging *Dean Richmond* was sent to Gregory's bone yard in Perth Amboy in April to be broken up and the *Greenport* (ex-*Sagadahoc*) laid up at Cornwall.

Shortly after midnight on the morning of March 10, 1909, the Portland Line steamer *Horatio Hall*, steaming around Cape Cod bound for New York in a heavy fog was suddenly rammed broadside by the Metropolitan Line's freighter *H. F. Dimock* on her way up toward Boston. The accident took place near Pollock Rip at almost the same spot where the Joy Liner *Aransas* had been lost four years earlier. The *Horatio Hall*, badly damaged, sank in a short time, but the *H. F. Dimock*, which was not in sinking condition, kept her nose wedged in the *Horatio Hall*'s side until all passengers and crew had been transferred safely to her bow. As the *Horatio Hall*'s upper decks remained above water for several hours, Captain Jewell and some of his crew elected to stay aboard her. Once the *Hall*'s passengers were aboard, the *H. F. Dimock*, now beginning to take water herself, headed for land and was beached on the sandy shore of Cape Cod.

Meanwhile, the Merchants Line steamer *Massachusetts*, racing toward the accident in the same fog, went hard aground off Martha's Vineyard. Then the following day, the *Boston*, sent out from Fall River to take cargo from the stranded *Massachusetts*, also went aground trying to approach her, so that within a few hours four different steamers had been put out of commission. When the weather cleared several days later, the *Massachusetts*, the *Boston*, and the *H. F. Dimock* were refloated and towed to Boston or Newport for repairs. The *Horatio Hall*, however, slipped into deep water during a subsequent storm and was declared unsalvageable.

With the loss of the *Horatio Hall*, one of its two regular steamers, the Portland Line of the Hartford and New York Transportation Company was caught with only the *North Star* and the much smaller *Manhattan* available for the coming summer season. In the emergency, the company decided to "borrow" a steamer it had recently acquired for its other line, the Joy Line. This was the *Georgia* which the Joy Line had just bought from the Old Bay Line on Chesapeake Bay. Many, including John Sherwood, the Bay Line's president, considered the *Georgia* to be the most beautiful steamer ever to operate on Chesapeake Bay. It had been built in 1887, and since 1906, when the *Virginia* arrived on the line and the *Tennessee* was sold to the Joy Line, it had served as the spare boat of the line. But when the Bay Line's new *Florida*, a sistership of the *Virginia*, arrived in late 1908, the *Georgia* was offered for sale and in early 1909 was purchased by the Joy Line to run with the *Tennessee*.

Although somewhat older than the *Tennessee*, the *Georgia*, at 280 feet overall, was considerably larger and far more elegantly furnished, since she had been built for the Old Bay Line's regular Baltimore to Norfolk service, while the *Tennessee* had been intended for a supplementary service on the narrow James River. When new, the *Georgia*, one of the first propellor steamers in her class, was very modern. She was built several years before the first propellor steamer of that size appeared on the sound, and her design had helped set the pattern for steamers of this type. On the bay, the *Georgia* had staterooms only on her Saloon Deck, her Gallery Deck being open save for the pilot house and a few rooms for officers. But when the Joy Line purchased her in early 1909, instead of bringing her north to her new service on Long Island Sound immediately, it sent her to a shipyard in Baltimore to have forty-six new staterooms added on the Gallery Deck, which now extended almost all the way to the stern. Surprisingly, the addition did not significantly detract from the *Georgia*'s beautiful lines.

Just as the Joy Line was looking forward to the use of this fine steamer, which was far larger and more elegant than anything it had operated in its days as a struggling independent line, Noble announced that she would be needed on the company's Portland run for the summer of 1909. Captain Jewell, formerly of the *Horatio Hall*, brought the *Georgia* up from Baltimore, arriving in New York on June 12, 1909, the day that the new Queensborough Bridge was opened across the East River. While the *Georgia* now spent her first summer running to Portland, the sidewheeler *Edgemont* was given another season on the Joy Line's Providence run, her sixth.

In spite of the heavy liens on its steamers and its president's impending trial for fraud, the Metropolitan Line ran the *Yale* and the *Harvard* to Boston again in 1909 with great success. Generally, all of the lines of the New England Navigation Company ran that summer pretty much as they had the year before. There were some exceptions. When the *City of Lowell* was out for repairs for several weeks in August, the *Puritan* was brought out of layup to run to Providence with the *Providence*, while the *Plymouth* went to join the *Maine* on the New Bedford run, so that the *New Hampshire* could take the *City of Lowell*'s place running with the *Chester W. Chapin* to New London.

On about July 1, 1909, the Central Vermont Railway brought out two new freighters, the *New York* and the *New London*, sisterships, for its New London run, releasing the older but very similar *Mohawk* and *Mohegan*, which the New Haven Railroad had been running for them, for other uses. From this time the *Mohawk* and *Mohegan* tended to be the regular winter freighters on the Providence Line, and the *Pequonnock* and the *New Haven* on the New Bedford Line.

Later that month, a new low-rate line to Albany called the Manhattan Line purchased the *Frank Jones* and the *Saratoga*, which had been laid up awaiting buyers since December 1908. This new line, which had no connections with the low-rate line that had run these steamers the previous summer, was more successful and managed to stay in business for several seasons before the established Peoples Line finally forced it out by starting a low-rate line of its own, a method that had not proved successful for the New Haven Railroad, either in Providence or Fall River. The Manhattan Line later lost the *Frank Jones* and the *Saratoga* to its creditors. For most of its history, it operated the former Enterprise Line steamer *Kennebec*, purchased from the Joy Line (leaving only the *Tennessee* and the *Edgemont* on the Joy Line in 1909), and the *Penobscot* (which had run under charter on the Joy Line during the summer of 1901), purchased from the Eastern Steamship Company.

In September 1909, the city of New York staged another of its mammoth marine parades. This one was in conjunction with the Hudson-Fulton celebration, commemorating both the discovery of New York and the invention of the steamboat. A variety of spectaculars, of which the marine parade was only one, were staged throughout the city. Both the New England Navigation Company and the Hartford and New York Transportation Company contributed steamers to the event, the latter sending the *North Star*, the *Georgia*, the *Tennessee*, and the *Middletown* (of the Hartford Line) out with spectators, while the Fall River Line's *Providence* played an important role in the parade itself as an example of a modern steamboat.

By October, the various steamer lines ended their summer services, and the Portland Line, now able to operate with one large steamer (the *North Star*), returned the *Georgia* to the Joy Line. From this time until the line was permanently discontinued in 1931, the *Georgia* and the *Tennessee*, both very handsome small propellor steamers, although not very evenly matched, made up the Joy Line (later the Bay State Line) between New York and Providence. One of the smaller steamers of the Hartford Line, usually the *Hartford*, came on as a relief for long periods during the winter.

In November, Morse's appeal finally came to trial. Again he was convicted on all counts, and again a federal judge sentenced him to fifteen years in the federal penitentiary at Atlanta, Georgia. Once again resorting to fraud, however, he managed to secure a pardon after serving less than two years.

In the weeks before Morse's new trial, the other owners of the Metropolitan Line anticipated correctly that, in the event of conviction, the attachments on the *Yale* and *Harvard* would almost certainly be enforced and the steamers taken over by their creditors. They therefore wished to disassociate themselves legally and financially from Morse's ownership of the steamers and to sell them as quickly and as profitably as possible. They realized that by selling them they stood a better chance of saving at least some of their investment than they would by trying to run them, thus risking repossession. With considerable assistance from the obliging lawyers of the New Haven Railroad, the stockholders formed a separate company in the fall of 1909 called the Metropolitan Steamship Company of New Jersey, to which they sold the *Yale* and the *Harvard* during their winter layup. Meanwhile, to operate these steamers (under charter) another company was formed, the Metropolitan Steamship Company of Maine. This organization was also free of associations with the earlier Metropolitan Line, although Morse still managed, at least until he left for prison in January, to serve as its president.

In the fall of 1909, the new Seattle owners of the *St. Croix* chartered her over the winter to run, for the second time in her life, on a low-fare line competing with an established line, this time on the Pacific Coast between San Francisco and San Pedro, California. The *St. Croix* had made only a few trips in this service when she caught fire at sea eighteen miles north of Santa Monica and was soon consumed by flames, though not before all 160 of her passengers and crew left the burning steamer in lifeboats. Representatives of the Seattle company, arriving in New York almost immediately after the disaster to seek a replacement in time for the following season, purchased the inactive Joy Line steamer *Kentucky*, which, though much smaller than the *St. Croix*, was apparently the most suitable steamer they could find. In the process of refitting the *Kentucky* for her new assignment, the owners created a new hatch for loading from a boom at the bow, in a style characteristic of Puget Sound steamers. In the process, her Saloon Deck stateroom housing was cut back several feet further aft. The *Kentucky* cleared New York on January 17, 1910, and two days later ran into one of the most severe storms the Atlantic had seen for several years. Even the Cunarder *Lusitania* arrived nearly twenty-four hours late with part of her bridge stove in. As soon as the raging seas began pouring into her newly built hatch, the little *Kentucky*, which had frequently made the trip down the Atlantic to Florida and back in safety, filled rapidly and sank. Fortunately, the Mallory liner *Alamo* came along in time to take off her crew.

Undaunted at having lost two steamers in so short a time, the West Coast owners returned to the Hartford and New York Transportation Company to purchase still another steamer for their line. By this time, the company's Portland Line was expecting the delivery of its new steamer *North Land*, which had been ordered to replace the recently lost *Horatio Hall* and was therefore disposed to make the *Manhattan* available in time for summer service on the West Coast. No sooner had the sale been negotiated than the *Manhattan* caught fire while approaching Portland on the morning of March 7, 1910, less than two months after the sinking of the *Kentucky*. Although the steamer made port and all aboard were safely disembarked, the handsome little *Manhattan* was soon a total loss. The Fall River Line's freighter *Boston* filled in briefly on the Portland Line until the *North Star*, then in winter layup, was readied to take over the run.

Now that Morse was safely in jail in Atlanta, and the *Yale* and *Harvard* had been sold to another company of the same name in which the New Haven held a significant amount of stock, the railroad no longer found any need to run three very expensive competing steamers to Boston. Therefore, on March 19, 1910, with no apologies whatever to the city to which it had made such lavish promises of service two years earlier, the railroad quietly discontinued the Merchants Line to Boston, just as it had discontinued the Neptune Line to Fall River only weeks after the demise of the Enterprise Line. The smaller Metropolitan Line freighters continued carrying freight to Boston as they had for years, until the *Yale* and *Harvard* began their season in the spring.

Although the New Haven Railroad now had every reason to believe that with its two steamship corporations, it had again assured itself of a monopoly of Long Island Sound steamship traffic, in the spring of 1910, it once again found itself faced with a low-fare competing line to Providence, one which was to prove far more tenacious than any it had dealt with previously. After two unsuccessful years of seeking new business opportunities in Colorado, Frank Dunbaugh, one of the former promoters of the Joy Line, was back in New York. This time he had no partners, and he was ready to start a new steamboat line between New York and Providence to be known as the Colonial Line. This time Dunbaugh, who had been thoroughly shaken by the *Larchmont* disaster, did not want any part of a cheaply run line. His steamers were to be small and their accommodations modest, but they were to be well run by experienced crews, and the captains were to make a safe arrival in port, at whatever hour, their first consideration. His first steamers were the small (265 foot overall) propellor steamers *Norfolk* and *Washington*, purchased from the line that ran between those two cities. As the *Concord* and *Lexington* of the Colonial Line, they were to run nightly between New York and Providence for another quarter of a century, longer by several years than any other steamers ever employed on that run.

The iron-hulled steamers *Concord* and *Lexington* were two of the smartest looking small steamers ever built, far handsomer than any steamer that ever ran on the Joy Line, with the possible exception of the *Allan Joy* or the *Virginia*, both of which had also hailed from Chesapeake Bay. They were also about the smallest steamers anywhere to carry a full deck of staterooms on the Gallery Deck. They had originally been designed with a half-gallery, like the *Maine* and the *New Hampshire*, but their gallery decks had been extended and many staterooms added when they had been rebuilt in 1900.

These steamers, however attractive, were not entirely suited to the Providence run. They were exceptional in having an enormous number of staterooms for their size (about 120), more than the *New Hampshire* or the *Richard Peck*, both of which were much larger steamers. But, built to run primarily on the Potomac River, their narrow construction gave them very limited cargo space. As with most of the bay steamers, designed for a run in an essentially segregated society, the free dormitories on the *Concord* and *Lexington* were inadequate for the demands of Long Island Sound. Thus, the Colonial Line converted its dining rooms, which, as usual, were located in the hold below the Quarter Deck, into dormitory space. Copying the Maine coast system with which it had become familiar on the Joy Line boats, the Colonial Line created a small but very attractive dining area on the Saloon Deck forward.

Compared with the other sound steamers, the *Concord* and *Lexington*, which cruised at about fifteen knots, were not particularly fast, but they were fast enough to cover the route on schedule, barring unforeseen delays, and considerably faster than most of the earlier Joy Line steamers had been, though not as fast as either the *Tennessee* or the *Georgia*. In spite of their limitations, these very handsome steamers were popular with the line, since they were easy to maintain and inexpensive to operate.

In Providence, the Colonial Line obtained the former Clyde Line dock along Water Street (between the Joy Line wharf under the Point Street Bridge and the New England Steamship Company's piers at Fox Point). The dock had once been used by the little freighter *Longfellow* but more recently by the Enterprise boats.

In starting his new line, Dunbaugh had no difficulty luring many former Joy Line employees away from their jobs with the Hartford and New York Transportation Company. Arthur Pitts, for instance, became the Providence agent of the line and remained in that post until World War II caused the closing down of the Colonial Line's service (in March 1942 after thirty-two years). Since Atkinson's railroad empire in Georgia had recently collapsed and with it Charles Dimon's Brunswick Line, Dunbaugh was fortunate in securing John Rowland once again as his freight and passenger agent in New York. The first captain of the *Lexington* was Foster Gray, who had been a pilot on the first trip of the *Rosalie* in 1899 and later captain of the *Kentucky*. The first captain of the *Concord*, when she made her maiden voyage for the Colonial Line out of New York on May 18, 1910, was, of course, Captain David Wilcox. Wilcox, now a very old man, stayed with the new line only a year, largely as a favor to Dunbaugh. His place as master of the *Concord* was taken by George Cobb, former captain of the rival Enterprise Line steamer *St. Croix* when she ran to Providence. Cobb was to remain captain of the *Concord* well into the 1930s, and when he retired he was succeeded by George Olweiler, who had commanded both the *Tremont* and the *Edgemont*, and who remained with the *Concord* until she was scrapped in 1936.

On May 23, 1910, just five days after the first trip of the *Concord*, the *Yale* and *Harvard*, recently converted to oil burners, began their last season on the sound, during which they were still owned by the Metropolitan Steamship Company of New Jersey but operated under charter by the Metropolitan Steamship Company of Maine. At the end of that season, the *Yale* and the *Harvard* were sold for service on the Pacific Coast. Late in October, almost as soon as their season was over, these two fast and strikingly attractive steamers departed under their own steam for the West Coast where they entered a long and very popular service between San Francisco and Los Angeles (later extended to San Diego). Both steamers later sailed to Europe during World War I and served as troop carriers in the English Channel but returned to California as soon as the war was over. The *Harvard* was later lost by going aground, apparently needlessly, off Cape Arguello on May 30, 1931. The *Yale* continued on the run until it was discontinued in 1936 during the Depression. After serving in various capacities through yet another world war, she was scrapped in 1948, at which time she was still one of the fastest ships under American registry.

With the *Yale* and *Harvard* off the Boston run, the New Haven Railroad now graciously agreed to take over the Metropolitan Line operation and to convert its freight steamers *Massachusetts* and *Bunker Hill* to passenger vessels for this service. During the winter, all three freighters, the *Massachusetts*, the *Bunker Hill*, and the *Old Colony*, were converted into passenger steamers. For the operation of the line to Boston in 1911, the New England Navigation Company "sold" the three steamers to the Maine Steamship Company, itself a subsidiary of the Hartford and New York Transportation Company (operators of the Joy Line), which then converted them with money borrowed from the New England Navigation Company and operated them under the name of the Metropolitan Line. Through this transaction, the Maine Steamship Company now owned the converted *Old Colony*, which was not needed on the Metropolitan Line. It therefore operated her between 1911 and 1917 on its own increasingly popular Portland Line with the *North Star* and the new *North Land*.

At the end of the 1911 season, a whole new organization was worked out for the Eastern Steamship Company. The original corporation was dissolved altogether, and a new Eastern Steamship Company formed, with Calvin Austin still president. The company now included all of the lines that had been part of the former Eastern Steamship Company (International Line,

Bangor Line, Kennebec Line, and Portland Line), as well as the Maine Steamship Company (New York-Portland) and the Metropolitan Steamship Company. In return for turning over the lucrative Maine Steamship Company to the new Eastern Steamship Company, as well as its considerable interest in the Metropolitan Line, the New Haven received about one-third of the stock of the Eastern, which it later sold back to the other stockholders to avoid antitrust action in 1912.

With the Maine Steamship Company now removed from its collection, the Hartford and New York Transportation Company consisted only of the Hartford Line, the Merchants Line to Bridgeport (to 1920), and the Joy Line to Providence.

The new Eastern Steamship Company, although well managed, was overcapitalized and unable to maintain its interest payments. As a result, it was obliged to raise cash by selling its three large liners, as well as three of the Metropolitan Line freighters, to the government during World War I, all at very good prices but at the cost of severely curtailing its services. For the next several years, the Metropolitan Line got along as well as it could with the smaller *Belfast, Camden, North Land*, and *Calvin Austin* taking turns covering the New York to Boston route, while older and smaller steamers ran on their Maine coast runs. Finally, in 1924, by which time the opening of the Cape Cod Canal had considerably shortened the route, the company brought out the new liners *Boston* and *New York*, steamers even larger than the *Harvard, Yale, Bunker Hill, Massachusetts*, or *Old Colony*, though not nearly as fast.

After the arrival of the *Commonwealth* in 1908 and the inauguration of the Colonial Line in 1910, the operations of the various Long Island Sound steamer lines remained relatively the same for another quarter century, aside from the addition of the *Boston* and the *New York* in 1924. This in itself was a signal of impending decline. With the increasing popularity of automotive transportation, both passenger and freight traffic via Long Island Sound began a very steady decline after about 1913. The decline was slow and did not bring an end to the sound services for many years, but it was sufficient to discourage further expansion such as the addition of new services or the construction of new steamers at the rate that had been typical in the thirty years between 1880 and 1910.

From 1908 when the *Commonwealth* arrived until 1937 when the Fall River Line stopped running, a period of nearly thirty years, the *Commonwealth* and the *Priscilla* continued to run regularly on the line every summer and the *Providence* and the *Plymouth* in the winter. As time progressed, the season for the smaller boats became progressively longer each year.

At the beginning of the 1912 season, a landmark of sorts was passed, at least insofar as this book is concerned, when the Hartford and New York Transportation Company stopped using the name Joy Line for its New York to Providence route and renamed it the Bay State Line. One might wonder why the name Bay State, the nickname for the state of Massachusetts, should be used for a steamer line running to Rhode Island. The fact is that the former Joy Line had not ever, even under railroad ownership, had a through ticketing arrangement between New York and Boston with the New Haven Railroad. The railroad had arranged the ticketing for its low-fare line to Providence via a railroad-owned trolley line named the Bay State Line running between Providence and Boston. Since the name of this line was well known by New York-bound passengers starting from Boston, it was also used as the name of the connecting steamer line. Thus, in 1912 the name Joy Line was painted out of the bows of the steamers *Georgia* and *Tennessee* and painted out of the signs over the piers in Providence and in New York.

In 1916, the Hartford and New York Transportation Company sold the *Edgemont*, which was now thirty-four years old, to parties in Philadelphia. When the line upgraded its service with the addition of the smart iron-hulled propellor steamer *Georgia* in 1910, it also tended to use the Hartford Line's propellor steamers as relief boats in the winter. Thus, the older wooden sidewheeler *Edgemont* saw very little service at all, although she once filled in on the New London to Block Island line for a short period when the steamer *Block Island* was out of commission.

Her new owners were the Philadelphia, Lewes, Cape May and Wildwood Transportation Company, a recently organized concern, of which the mayor of Cape May was the president, designed to promote the summer excursion trade to southern New Jersey. Beginning in late July 1916, the *Edgemont*, now renamed the *Cape May*, left Philadelphia every Tuesday, Thursday, and Saturday at 6:00 P.M., stopped briefly at Chester, and then during the night sailed down Delaware Bay. She arrived at Lewes, Delaware, at some unspecified but apparently very early hour in the morning, and then crossed over to Cape May, New Jersey, arriving there at 7:00 A.M.

The project was not successful and was not repeated the following season. In 1917, by which time the United States was at war, the *Cape May* (formerly the *State of Maine* and the *Edgemont*) was chartered to serve as a boarding house for workers employed at the Merchant Shipbuilding Company in Bristol, Pennsylvania. By the spring of 1918, she was back in layup in Philadelphia, where, after nearly a year of neglect, she filled and sank at her pier. Later raised, she sat at the pier for several more years, unpainted, unattended, and slowly rotting, until on September 24, 1925, her superstructure was set afire so that her engines could be salvaged for scrap metal.

At the end of the 1918 season, the New England Steamship Company (as the New Haven's marine subsidiary was now named) canceled its summer service to Providence, claiming it was no longer profitable. By that time, the Providence Line had been running every summer for forty-one years, since it had been inaugurated in 1877 with the *Rhode Island* and the then brand-new *Massachusetts*. Providence continued to be served by the smaller steamers of the Colonial Line and the Bay State Line, which ran throughout the year. The Providence Line itself also continued as an all-year freight service operating now, for the most part, the freighters *Mohawk* and *Mohegan*.

The following year, the *Plymouth* and the *Providence* joined the larger *Commonwealth* and *Priscilla* to reinstate a four-boat service on the Fall River Line for the first time since 1897. This arrangement was continued for only nine seasons, however, and beginning in 1928 the *Commonwealth* and the *Priscilla* again ran alone to Fall River in the summer.

The loss of the beautiful steamer *Maine*, which was forced onto Execution Rocks by fast-flowing ice on February 4, 1920, precipitated a series of changes in the operation of the New England Steamship Company's lines. Passenger service on both the New Haven Line and the Bridgeport Line had been dwindling rapidly in recent years. It was discontinued on the New Haven Line in the spring of 1920, soon after the sinking of the *Maine*, and on the Bridgeport Line in December, the passenger steamers on these lines being replaced by freighters. The Bridgeport day liner *Bridgeport* was sold and became the Hudson River excursion steamer *Highlander*, while the *Naugatuck*, converted to a freighter, was kept on the line but rarely used, as the line had many larger freighters available, usually the *City of Brockton*, for this service. Later, the *Naugatuck* was sold to the Sound Steamship Lines, an excursion boat company, which ran her for many years between Providence and Block Island. The *Richard Peck*, which had been running regularly to New Haven since 1892, except for the brief period in 1900-1901 when the New Haven Line had been extended to Providence, now went on the New London Line where she ran at first with the *Chester W. Chapin*, the steamer that had been built as her running mate, but with which she had not been paired since 1904. The *City of Lowell*, which rarely ran in the winter anyway, was then transferred to the summer service of the New Bedford Line with the *New Hampshire*, replacing the lost *Maine*.

While business on most of the other lines continued its slow decline through the 1920s, traffic to the summer resorts of Cape Cod and the islands of Martha's Vineyard and Nantucket via New Bedford was picking up. Accordingly, by 1922, the *New Hampshire* was transferred to the New London Line to run with the *Richard Peck*, while the larger *Chester W. Chapin* now came on the New Bedford Line with the *City of Lowell* for several seasons. During the 1920s, as previously noted, the *Pequonnock* and the *New Haven* were generally the winter boats on the New Bedford Line.

In 1928, however, the New England decided to revive the Providence Line as an all-year passenger and freight line with the *Chester W. Chapin* and the *City of Lowell*, smaller and more economical steamers than had been used on this line before it was discontinued in 1918. These steamers were reboilered for the new service, the *City of Lowell* in 1928 and the *Chester W. Chapin* in 1929. Both emerged as one-stackers, which was very becoming to them, and, in the case of the *Chester W. Chapin*, a distinct improvement over her former two-stacked profile.

At the same time, with the steadily declining traffic no longer supporting four steamers on the Fall River Line and with passenger business on the New Bedford Line continuing to increase, the company ended its four-boat service to Fall River after the 1927 season. In the summer of 1928 it placed the large Fall River winter boats *Providence* and *Plymouth* on the summer New Bedford Line in place of the *Chester W. Chapin* and the *City of Lowell*.

The Colonial Line, hard hit by the addition of the new line to Providence operating steamers far superior to its now aging *Concord* and *Lexington*, countered by chartering the steamer *State of Virginia* from the Old Bay Line for the summer season of 1929. The *State of Virginia*, a 330-foot steamer built in 1923, was far more modern than any of the New England Steamship Company's boats, for by now even the great Fall River Line steamers were beginning to show their age. Certainly it was far superior to the two boats of the rival Providence Line. (The *Chester W. Chapin* was now thirty years old and her running mate, the *City of Lowell*, five years older.) By running its spare steamer *Cambridge* to Providence with the *State of Virginia*, the Colonial Line was also able to start its own daily summer service to New Bedford with the steamers *Concord* and *Lexington*.

The following summer, the Colonial Line planned to repeat this pattern, but in 1930 the *State of Virginia* was not available. The Bay Line had chartered one of its other new steamers, the *President Warfield* (later famous as the *Exodus* which carried Jewish immigrants from France to Palestine in the face of opposition from British warships in 1948), to run as an extra steamer on the Eastern Steamship's New York to Boston line that summer. Instead, the Colonial Line secured the much older but very attractive *Southland*, a later and larger version of the *Concord* and *Lexington*, also from the Norfolk and Washington Line, to run with the *Cambridge* to Providence, while the *Concord* and *Lexington* again ran to New Bedford.

By 1930, the Depression was hastening the decline of passenger traffic on the sound steamer lines, a decline that had been apparent for a decade. That winter the New Haven Railroad, understandably, no longer considered it profitable to run two steamer lines to Providence. The *Georgia* of the Bay State Line, in spite of her unflagging beauty, was by now the oldest passenger steamer running on the sound. Late in the season of 1930, she developed serious mechanical problems, and, rather than spend the money to repair her, the line had borrowed first the *New Hampshire* from the New London Line and then the *Middletown* from the Hartford Line, to run with the *Tennessee*. Finally, in January 1931, the Bay State Line ceased operations altogether and the last vestige of the Joy Line—except as its spirit lived on in the Colonial Line—ceased to exist. The following October, at the end of the summer season, the Hartford Line was also discontinued, and the Hartford and New York Transportation Company was dissolved.

The beautiful *Georgia* was sold to become a floating anchorage for yachts in New Haven harbor; she was poorly maintained and large signs were painted on her sides. Finally, in 1937, the new owners mercifully sent her to be scrapped. The *Tennessee*, still in excellent shape, remained tied up at the Joy Line dock in Providence throughout the Depression years until she was sold in 1935 to become the Boston-based excursion steamer *Romance*. The following season, in September, when picking her way into Boston harbor during a dense fog, she was hit and sunk by the outgoing Eastern Steamship liner *New York*.

For the summer season of 1931, the Colonial Line was able to charter both the *President Warfield* and the *Southland*. Thus, for the first time it ran two fairly large and modern steamers to Providence, steamers that clearly outclassed the older *City of Lowell* and *Chester W. Chapin*. The *Concord* and *Lexington* ran to New Bedford again that year, but it was to be their last season on that run. By 1931, the Depression had hit the country in force. Not only did passenger traffic reach new lows, but also the collapse of many of New England's once-prosperous industries was reducing freight shipments to a fraction of what they had been at the beginning of the century. In 1932, the Colonial Line decided not to charter any steamers for its Providence Line; instead, it discontinued its summer passenger service to New Bedford and kept the smaller steamers *Concord* and *Lexington* running to Providence throughout the year. The New England also curtailed service on its New Bedford Line that year by keeping the older *Plymouth* (whose machinery was now becoming increasingly cantankerous) laid up over the summer and by running only the *Providence*. The previous season the New England had also curtailed service on its New London Line. From this time it ran only the steamer *New Hampshire*, which left New York for New London in the morning and returned on an overnight schedule late the same evening. The *Richard Peck* meanwhile was kept in reserve as a relief steamer for both the New London Line and the Providence Line.

In spite of the Depression, the Colonial Line again chartered the large steamer *State of Virginia* for the summer of 1934 and also the somewhat smaller *Yorktown* from the Chesapeake Line. The *Yorktown* was not an unqualified success, however. Although she had been built in 1928 and was practically a new boat, she was nevertheless very old fashioned and not a significant improvement over the line's own steamers. The line did not revive its New Bedford service that summer, and the *Concord* and *Lexington* were merely laid up.

On the night of January 2, 1935, the Colonial Line steamer *Lexington*, bound up the East River shortly after leaving her pier, was struck amidships by the freighter *Jane Christensen* under the Manhattan Bridge and sank in ten minutes. Although four of the crew lost their lives, all passsengers were saved. This was the only serious accident involving a Colonial Line steamer in its thirty-two years of operation, a distinct difference from the appalling record of the same management's Joy Line in the first decade of the century. For another year the line was served by the *Concord* and the spare steamer *Cambridge*, although the *State of Virginia* was again chartered to run with the *Concord* during the summer of 1935.

At the end of the 1935 season, the New England Steamship Company, which by then had given up its freight services to New Haven and Bridgeport, decided to discontinue its passenger and freight line to New London as well. The last trip of the *New Hampshire* in November marked the end of steamboat service to New London after more than a hundred years.

That same fall, the venerable Boston to Bangor line in Maine also succumbed to the combined forces of the automobile and the Depression, and its fast turbine-driven sisterships, *Belfast* and *Camden*, once the pride of Charles W. Morse, were offered for sale. A few months later, in the spring of 1936, they were purchased by the Colonial Line, whose steamers *Concord* and *Lexington* had long been too small and too old for the service, and which, with the loss of the *Lexington*, was now desperately in need of new steamers. After considerable refurbishing, these fast and still very trim (though hardly new) steamers began running between New York and Providence for the Colonial Line as the *Arrow* and the *Comet*. The captain of the *Comet* was William Pendleton, who had served many years as master of the *Lexington*, while George Olweiler, the former Joy Line captain, commanded the *Arrow*.

With its new steamers, the Colonial Line was in a far better position in these Depression years than the New England Steamship Company. The *Arrow* and the *Comet* were about the same size as the Providence Line's older *City of Lowell* and *Chester W. Chapin* but, as was typical of Maine coast steamers, had much larger passenger capacities and less cargo space. Most important, they were inexpensive to operate; their very efficient turbine engines ran on oil fuel (in those days still relatively cheap) and required comparatively small crews, so that even with a small number of passengers, they could operate at a profit. The Fall River Line, on the other hand, had to maintain not two but four large sidewheelers for its operation, all of them requiring large crews and all of them, but especially the giant *Commonwealth*, far more expensive to run than the turbine steamers.

Thus, it was almost impossible for the Fall River Line to operate at a profit unless its steamers were heavily booked on a fairly regular basis, which in those days they were not. Although the summer business was still active, at least on weekends, it did not generate enough profits to pay for the maintenance of four large and aging steamers twelve months of the year.

In the spring of 1937, the New England Steamship Company reluctantly ended service on both its Providence Line and its summer line to New Bedford but announced that the Fall River Line, the only overnight line still maintained by the railroad, would continue to operate. That same spring, the Fall River Line faced a crisis when the Coast Guard demanded that the line make a great many expensive alterations to the *Priscilla*. Since she was now forty-three years old, the company debated whether it would pay to spend so much money to meet the Coast Guard's demands and seriously considered retiring the aging queen that season. Several alternate suggestions were presented. The most probable plan was to run the *Commonwealth* and the *Providence* in the summer and the *Providence* and the *Plymouth* in the winter. But since the *Commonwealth*, which ran well booked for a short two-month season in the summer, rarely earned enough for her own maintenance, the line also considered retiring both the *Commonwealth* and the *Priscilla*, running the *Plymouth* and *Providence* all year and maintaining the *Chester W. Chapin* as a spare. Some thought was also given to running the smaller *City of Lowell* and *Chester W. Chapin*, both of which were good freight carriers but short on passenger accommodations, all year on the Fall River Line. This plan was not seriously contemplated inasmuch as the *City of Lowell*, which was as old as the *Priscilla*, was not in very good condition and was also fairly expensive to operate.

The company eventually decided to repair the *Priscilla*, and by the end of June the big sidewheelers *Commonwealth* and *Priscilla* were running to Fall River as usual. Then, on July 12, 1937, only a few weeks after the new season started, crews on the *Commonwealth* and *Priscilla* staged a sit-down strike and refused to allow the steamers to sail. Officials of the line began negotiations with the union, assuming that a settlement could be reached and that the steamers would soon be sailing again. But the trustees of the New Haven Railroad decreed otherwise and, after briefly reviewing the situation, announced that they were closing down the Fall River Line.

This decision meant the sudden and utterly unexpected end of one of America's oldest steamboat lines. To anyone familiar with the steamships of Long Island Sound, it was almost impossible to believe that there would no longer be a Fall River Line. With this decision, the New Haven Railroad, which thirty years earlier had been buying up steamship lines with apparent abandon, was no longer in the overnight steamship business at all. The *Arrow* and the *Comet* of the Colonial Line, operated by the former management of the Joy Line, were now the only overnight steamers running between New York and Narragansett Bay.

During the spring of 1937, the railroad had disposed of its two former New London Line steamers. The *New Hampshire*, which had been tied up at the company's New London wharf for two years, was towed to Baltimore for scrapping. But the *Richard Peck*, already forty-five years old, began a career as an excursion steamer for the Meseck Line operating out of New York, usually to Playland and Bridgeport (although in 1941 the Meseck Line ran the *Richard Peck* to her original port—New Haven—for one season). By late July, the giant *Commonwealth* still lay at the pier in Fall River from which she had been preparing to sail when the strike began. The *Priscilla* was towed from New York to the company's Fox Point wharf in Providence, and the *City of Lowell*, which had been tied up there when the Providence Line stopped running a few weeks earlier, was moved to another railroad pier at right angles to it. Both the *Providence* and the *Plymouth* were tied up at Newport where they had been in summer layup, as was the *Chester W. Chapin*.

In the fall of 1937, the four sidewheelers of the Fall River Line, the *Commonwealth, Priscilla, Providence,* and *Plymouth*, were sold at auction and together brought $88,000. Through that winter, they were towed one by one to Baltimore where they were all reduced to scrap.

By the spring of 1938, the Colonial Line no longer considered that its spare steamer *Cambridge* measured up to the new standards it had achieved with its steamers *Arrow* and *Comet*. It was therefore reluctant to put her on the line again when the larger steamers went for their annual spring overhaul. Instead, the Colonial Line chartered the *Richard Peck* from the Meseck Line, which ran first with the *Comet* and then with the *Arrow* during April 1938. Meanwhile, the line arranged to purchase the *Chester W. Chapin* from the railroad to replace the *Cambridge* as its spare boat. The fact that the New Haven Railroad would even consider selling one of its best steamers to a competing line gives some indication of the degree to which the Depression had negated the importance of sound steamer lines in the eyes of the railroad.

Although the purchase was not completed in time for the Colonial Line to use the *Chester W. Chapin* as a relief boat that spring, it took possession of the steamer in May. One month later, the line placed the *Chester W. Chapin*, now renamed the *Meteor*, on a revived three-night-a-week summer service between New York and New Bedford. This arrangement proved very popular and was continued for four seasons until World War II brought an end to the Colonial Line. In general, as soon as her summer run to New Bedford had ended, the *Meteor* would run for several weeks to Providence in place of the *Arrow* or the *Comet*, since freight was always heaviest in the fall and the *Meteor* had about twice the cargo capacity of the *Arrow* or the *Comet*. Then in the spring, the *Meteor* again ran to Providence for several weeks when the *Arrow* and *Comet* went for their annual overhauls, before beginning her own New Bedford run late in June.

With the arrival of the *Meteor* on the line, the *Cambridge*, which had never been much appreciated, although she had always been a dependable steamer if not very attractive, was sold to the Sound Steamship Company, the excursion boat operator which also owned the *Naugatuck* (ex-*Allan Joy*). For a few seasons the *Cambridge*, considerably rebuilt with many state-rooms removed to create more open space, replaced the *Naugatuck* on the Providence-Block Island run. During the war, however, the *Cambridge* was requisitioned by the government for service in South America, and the *Naugatuck* was back on the Block Island run for several seasons.

The *Arrow* and the *Comet* continued running to Providence, quite profitably in spite of the times, and the *Meteor* to New Bedford in the summer, through the season of 1941. Then, in December of that year, the United States entered World War II. Shortly before the attack on Pearl Harbor, the Navy had run a mesh net across the entrance to Narragansett Bay to prevent German submarines, then active off our coasts, from coming into the bay. As this net was never opened until dawn, the Colonial Line had to make considerable modifications in its schedules. For a period of three months, the steamer in New York had to postpone its sailing to about 9:00 P.M. so that it would not arrive at Newport before daylight, while the steamer departing from Providence could not leave its pier until nearly 5:00 A.M., just at dawn, and did not arrive in New York, therefore, until about 3:00 P.M.

This inconvenient schedule was not to last for long. In March 1942, the government requisitioned all three of the Colonial Line's steamers, and the operation of overnight passenger steamships on Long Island Sound ended forever. The *Arrow* and the *Comet*, completely rebuilt so that their identification as overnight passenger carriers was lost, were sent to carry supplies among the Hawaiian Islands. The *Meteor* was employed for awhile ferrying troops around New York harbor, but was then lent first to the Old Bay Line on Chesapeake Bay and later to the Norfolk and Washington Line, both of which had lost most of their regular steamers to the war.

The *Meteor*'s former consort, the *Richard Peck*, was also requisitioned by the government and sent to Newfoundland as a barracks ship. In 1943, she was brought down to Norfolk, Virginia, renamed the *Elisha Lee*, and put on the line between Norfolk and Cape Charles where she was to replace the newer steamers of this line which had also been taken by the government. Although on her arrival the *Elisha Lee* was regarded as an antiquated old tub which they had been obliged to use in the emergency, her officers were soon forced to admit that the former *Richard Peck*, now over fifty year. old, was the fastest and most maneuverable steamer that had ever served on this run. In the two years between 1943 and 1945, the two former Long Island Sound running mates, the *Elisha Lee* (ex-*Richard Peck*), running on the Norfolk to Cape Charles Line, and the *Meteor* (ex-*Chester W. Chapin*), now running on the Norfolk and Washington Line, frequently passed each other coming in or out of Norfolk in the early evening or the morning.

None of the overnight steamers returned to Long Island Sound after the war. The *Arrow*, while being towed along the West Coast in October 1945, broke loose in a storm and went aground, a total loss, on the coast of Oregon. The *Comet* was sold to the Chinese and ran for several years on the Yangtse River before being scrapped sometime in the early 1950s. The *Meteor*, after finishing her service on Chesapeake Bay, was laid up for a time with thousands of other postwar surplus ships in the James River but was finally scrapped in 1948. Her former running mate, the *City of Lowell*, which also served the Army during the war, was scrapped at about the same time. The *Cambridge* was taken to the Amazon River during the war and ran there until she was lost by grounding in 1950.

Rather ironically, the last two Long Island Sound night boats to survive were the *Elisha Lee* (ex-*Richard Peck*) and the *Naugatuck* (ex-*Allan Joy*). The *Naugatuck* had begun her life on the Norfolk-Cape Charles route where the *Richard Peck* finished hers. The two had served on the rival Joy Line and Narragansett Bay Line in 1899. Both had later been part of the New Haven Railroad's fleet, and for many years the *Richard Peck* had been the single passenger vessel running to New Haven at the same time that the *Naugatuck* had been the single passenger vessel serving nearby Bridgeport. The *Richard Peck*, which, as the *Elisha Lee*, was popular on the Cape Charles route and still looked smart in spite of her age, remained on that run until she was condemned by the Coast Guard at the end of the 1954 season and was subsequently broken up. The *Naugatuck* continued running to Block Island until replaced in 1948. She then ran on various excursion routes around New York and served rather ignominiously for awhile as a general work boat around New York harbor for the Lackawanna Railroad before being laid up at Perth Amboy for some time in the early 1950s. When she was finally scrapped in 1956, this former Joy Line steamer was the last of the Long Island Sound night boats to survive.*

---

*The *Naushon*, built as a day boat for the railroad-owned New Bedford, Martha's Vineyard, and Nantucket Steamboat Company in 1929, did carry several staterooms and between 1929 and 1931 frequently served as a relief night boat on the New London Line. She survived as the excursion steamer *John A. Meseck* operating out of New York and later out of Baltimore as late as the 1960s, but was not in the strictest sense a nightboat. The *Iroquois*, which was built for the Clyde Line's New York to Miami service, and which was running as the Turkish cruise ship *Ankara* as late as 1975, might count as a Long Island Sound steamer since she ran one summer on the New York to Portland Line, but she was an ocean-type steamer and also would not qualify in the sense here intended as a "night boat."

50a. Courtsy of Frank E. Claes

50b. Courtesy of the Steamship Historical Society Collection, University of Baltimore Library

50. The (a) *Frank Jones* and the (b) *Kennebec*, both former Maine coast steamers, ran on the Enterprise Line's new low-rate service between New York and Fall River from 1905 to 1907.

51. Courtesy of the Mariners' Museum of Newport News, Va.

51. Deck scene aboard the Enterprise Line's steamer *Frank Jones*.

52. Courtesy of the Steamship Historical Society Collection, University of Baltimore Library

52. The Puget Sound steamer *Alaskan* (pictured here), a near sistership of the ill-fated *Olympian*, purchased by the Joy Line in 1906.

53. The *Olympian* (pictured here), minus her stack, being towed through the Golden Gate by the *Zealandia*.

54. The trans-Pacific liner *Zealandia* (pictured here), which the Joy Line purchased to tow the *Olympian* around the horn to New York.

55. The *Olympian*, beached and abandoned in the Straits of Magellan.

56. *Courtesy of the Steamship Historical Society Collection, University of Baltimore Library*

56. The Narragansett Bay steamer *Richard Borden* (later renamed *Fairfield*) was acquired in 1906 by the Joy Line to start a new service between New York and Bridgeport, Connecticut.

57a. Courtesy of the Peabody Museum, Salem, Mass.

57b. *Courtesy of the Steamship Historical Society Collection, University of Baltimore Library*
57. In 1906 the Joy Line began a new service between New York and Fall River with
the steamers (a) *Tennessee* and (b) *Kentucky*, formerly the *Lincoln* and *Martinique*.

318

58. The *Santiago* (pictured here), formerly of the Ward Line's New York to Cuba service, was purchased in 1906 by the Joy Line to run between New York and Boston with the *Old Dominion*.

59. A view of the *Santiago* in Cuban waters.

60. Courtesy of the Mariners' Museum of Newport News, Va.

60. The *Westover*, formerly the *Dover* of the Old Bay Line, was purchased by C. L. Dimon in 1906 for the Joy Line but she never actually saw service on the Joy Line.

61. Courtesy of the Steamship Historical Society Collection, University of Baltimore Library

61. When the Joy Line began running to Fall River, the Enterprise Line countered by starting a new service to Providence with the *St. Croix* (pictured here), acquired from the International Line (Boston-St. John, New Brunswick), and the *Warren*.

62. *Courtesy of William B. Taylor*

62. On February 11, 1907, the Joy Line steamer *Larchmont* (pictured here) was rammed just forward of the port paddlebox by the schooner *Harry Knowlton* and sank with a large loss of life.

63. The schooner *Harry Knowlton*, beached near Watch Hill, Rhode Island, after ramming the *Larchmont*.

64. Courtesy of John Cobb

64. The officers of the Joy Line steamer *Larchmont* photographed a few months before the tragic accident took the lives of most of them. Front row (left to right): First Asst. Engineer Hess, Mate John Kannaly, First Pilot John Anson, Captain George McVay, Second Pilot George Wyman, an unnamed Ast. Purser, possibly Oscar Young. Back row: Quartermaster Hanson and Quartermaster Wing (both of whom had left the *Larchmont* by the time of the accident), Third Asst. Engineer Herrick Nelson, Boatswain Andrew, Chief Engineer Robert Gay, Bow Watchman Christopher Anderson, Purser Alden Trickey (no longer with the *Larchmont* at the time of the accident), an unnamed Saloon Watchman, and Chief Steward Jamie Harrison.

65. Courtesy of the Steamship Historical Society Collection, University of Baltimore Library

65. Following the loss of the *Larchmont*, the *Tennessee* (here pictured at the Joy Line's Providence dock) took a triangular route for several weeks, running from New York to Fall River, then up to Providence, and from Providence to New York. When the Joy Line gave up its Fall River service later in 1907, the *Tennessee* was transferred to the Providence route, running with the *Edgemont*.

66a. Courtesy of the Steamship Historical Society Collection, University of Baltimore Library

66b. Courtesy of the Steamship Historical Society Collection, University of Baltimore Library

66. For the season of 1907 the New Haven Railroad started still another low-fare line between New York and Fall River, called the Neptune Line, with the still handsome former Providence Line steamers (a) *Rhode Island* and (b) *Connecticut*.

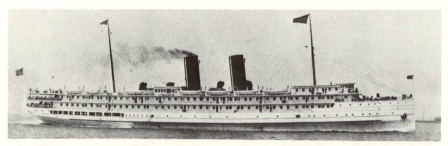

67. The Joy Line's lumbering *Old Dominion* and *Santiago* were certainly no match for the Metropolitan Line's fast new passenger liners *Yale* (pictured here) and *Harvard*, which began running between New York and Boston in the fall of 1907.

68. Courtesy of the Steamship Historical Society Collection, University of Baltimore Library

68. When Charles W. Morse began running the *Yale* and *Harvard* to Boston, the New Haven Railroad countered by bringing out three large and speedy freighters to run between New York and Boston: the *Massachusetts*, the *Bunker Hill* (pictured here), and the *Old Colony*. All three were later converted to passenger steamers.

69. Courtesy of the Steamship Historical Society Collection, University of Baltimore Library

69. The Providence Line steamer *Plymouth*, which burned in March 1906, had a slightly different appearance after she was rebuilt in 1907.

70. *Courtesy of the Mariners' Museum of Newport News, Va.*

70. When the Joy Line abandoned all of its services except the one to Providence in 1907, some of its already antiquated steamers were sent to the boneyard. Here the *City of Key West* and the *Fairfield* are pictured at Gregory's yard in Perth Amboy, New Jersey, alongside the burned-out bones of the *Tremont*.

71. With the arrival of the *Commonwealth* on the Fall River Line in 1908, the beautiful *Puritan*, here shown steaming out of Newport toward Fall River, was withdrawn from regular service.

72. The Fall River Line's *Commonwealth* of 1908 was the largest, and also the last, steamer to be built for overnight services on Long Island Sound.

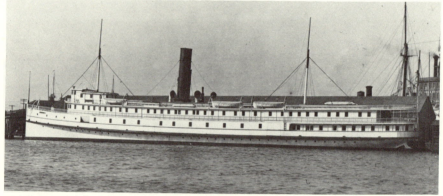

73. Courtesy of the Mariners' Museum of Newport News, Va.

73. The *Georgia*, acquired from the Old Bay Line in 1909, was the last steamer purchased for the Joy Line. The subsequent addition of a full tier of staterooms on the Gallery Deck did not detract from the *Georgia*'s graceful lines.

74a. *Courtesy of the Steamship Historical Society Collection, University of Baltimore Library*

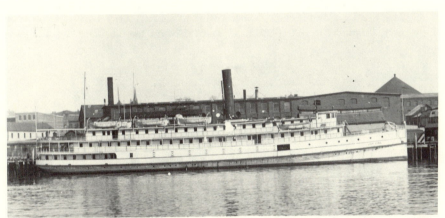

74b. *Courtesy of the Steamship Historical Society Collection, University of Baltimore Library*

74. The steamers (a) *Georgia* and (b) *Tennessee* ran together on the New York to Providence route of the Joy Line (known after 1914 as the Bay State Line) for twenty-one years, from 1910 until the line was discontinued in 1931.

75. *Courtesy of John Lockhead*

75. The Joy Line's faithful *Seaboard* ran as a freighter between New York and Bridgeport, Connecticut until 1920. Later she was converted into a tanker, as shown here.

76. *Courtesy of the Steamship Historical Society Collection, University of Baltimore Library*

76. The *Naugatuck* (formerly the Joy Line steamer *Allan Joy*) served as the night boat of the Bridgeport Line until that line was discontinued in 1920. Later, she had several of her staterooms removed and was used as an excursion steamer. Here she is shown at her dock in Providence when she was running on the Providence to Block Island route. When she went to the scrapyard in 1956, she was the last surviving Long Island Sound overnight steamer.

Appendix

A. THE JOY LINE

1. Allan Joy (a. Cape Charles; c. Naugatuck)

Steel screw freighter
Tonnage: 1,113 gross; 655 net
Dimensions: 220.7 x 37.2 x 14.0
Horsepower: 1,000
1898: Built for New York, Philadelphia, and Norfolk Railroad and named
   Cape Charles (Norfolk-Cape Charles Ferry)
1899: Burned; sold to Joy Line; renamed *Allan Joy*
1899: Sold to Bridgeport Line
1905: Renamed *Naugatuck*
1905-1920: On Bridgeport route of New England Steamship Company
1920-1953: Used on various excursion routes (largely Providence-Block Island)
1956: Scrapped

2. Aransas

Iron screw passenger and freight steamer
Tonnage: 1,156 gross; 678 net
Dimensions: 241.0 x 35.5 x 16.5
Horsepower: 650
1877: Built for Morgan Line (Gulf of Mexico)
1904: Sold to Joy Line
1905: Sunk off Cape Cod

3. *City of Key West (a. City of Richmond)*

Wood sidewheel passenger and freight steamer
Tonnage: 939 gross; 600 net
Dimensions: 227.5 x 30.6 x 10.0
Horsepower: 900
1865: Built for James River service and named *City of Richmond*
1866-1892: Ran Portland to Machiasport, Maine
1898-1902: Ran Miami-Key West for Florida East Coast Steamship Company
          and Peninsular and Occidental Steamship Company
1902-1908: Joy Line
1908: Sold for scrap

4. *Cocoa (a. Cuba; b. Argonauta; d. M. F. Plant; e. Yukon)*

Iron screw passenger and freight steamer
Tonnage: 1,241 gross
Dimensions: 205.4 x 36 x 25
Built Spanish
1898: Captured by Americans in Spanish-American War
1898-1903: Operated as *Cocoa* by Florida East Coast Steamship Company
          and Peninsular and Occidental Steamship Company
1902: Chartered to Joy Line
1903-1911: On various Atlantic Coast services as *M. F. Plant*; later *Yukon*
1911: Sold to Pacific Alaska Navigation Company and renamed *Alaska*
1913: Wrecked and lost off Alaskan coast

5. *Dover (a. Westover)*

Iron screw freighter
Tonnage: 617 gross; 397 net
Dimensions: 165.0 x 28.0 x 12.0
Horsepower: 400
1873: Built for Baltimore Steam Packet Company (Old Bay Line) as *Westover*
1897-1901: Served on Great Lakes
1901-1906: Served as freighter on Atlantic Coast
1906: Acquired by C. L. Dimon for use on Joy Line and renamed *Dover*
1906-1912: Again on Atlantic coastwise service
1912: Stranded in St. Johns River, Florida; abandoned and scrapped

6. *Edgemont (a. State of Maine; c. Cape May)*

Wood sidewheel passenger and freight steamer
Tonnage: 1,409 gross; 818 net
Dimensions: 241.0 x 37.1 x 14.6
Horsepower: 1,200
1882: Built for International Steamship Company (Boston-St. John) as
     State of Maine

1904: Sold to Joy Line; renamed *Edgemont*

1915: Sold for service Philadelphia-Cape May (served only one season); renamed *Cape May*

1916-1924: Laid up

1924: Scrapped

7. *Fairfield (a. Richard Borden)*

Wood sidewheel passenger and freight day steamer

Tonnage: 892 gross; 673 net

Dimensions: 203.0 x 33.0 x 10.0

Horsepower: 1,200

1874: Built for Providence, Newport, and Fall River service as *Richard Borden*

1906: Sold to Joy Line and renamed *Fairfield*

1908: Scrapped

8. *Georgia*

Iron screw passenger and freight steamer

Tonnage: 1,749 gross; 1,188 net

Dimensions: 280.0 x 40.0 x 15.0

Horsepower: 1,950

1887: Built for Baltimore Steam Packet Company (Old Bay Line)

1909: Sold to Joy Line (then part of Hartford and New York Transportation Co.)

1931: Sold to become floating yacht anchorage in New Haven, Connecticut

1937: Scrapped

9. *Kennebec (cf. Kennebec of Enterprise Line)*

10. *Kentucky (cf. Lincoln)*

11. *Larchmont (a. Cumberland)*

Wood sidewheel passenger and freight steamer

Tonnage: 1,605 gross; 896 net

Dimensions: 252.2 x 37.0 x 14.8

Horsepower: 1,000

1885: Built for International Steamship Company (Boston-St. John) as *Cumberland*

1902: Sunk in Boston harbor; sold to Joy Line; renamed *Larchmont*

1907: Sunk in collision with schooner *Harry S. Knowlton*

12. *Lincoln (b. Martinique; c. Kentucky)*

Wood screw passenger and freight steamer

Tonnage: 996 gross; 532 net

Dimensions: 203.4 x 37.9 x 12.6

Horsepower: 1,600
1897: Built for Kennebec Steamship Company as *Lincoln*
1900: Chartered to Joy Line
1910-1906: Operated Miami-Key West-Havana by Peninsular and Occidental
   Steamship Company; renamed *Martinique*
1906-1910: Operated on Joy Line as *Kentucky*
1910: Sold for service on West Coast; foundered en route

13. Newburgh (b. Nantasket)

Iron screw passenger and freight steamer
Tonnage: 1,033 gross; 741 net
Dimensions: 200.0 x 32.0 x 11.0
Horsepower: 1,000
1886: Built for Homer Ramsdell Transportation Company (New York-
   Newburgh)
1900: Short charter to Joy Line
1932: Sold for excursion service in Boston harbor; renamed *Nantasket*

14. Old Dominion

Iron sidewheel passenger and freight steamer
Tonnage: 2,222 gross; 1775 net
Dimensions: 255.5 x 42.5 x 20.9
Horsepower: 2,250
1872: Built for Old Dominion Steamship Company (New York-Norfolk-
   Richmond)
1899: Sold to Joy Line
1909: Sold to E. F. Luckenbach; reduced to a barge
1937: Scrapped

15. Penobscot (b. Mohawk)

Wood sidewheel passenger and freight steamer
Tonnage: 1,414 gross; 1,244 net
Dimensions: 255.0 x 38.0 x 13.0
Horsepower: 1,200
1882: Built for Boston and Bangor Steamship Company (after 1902 part
   of Eastern Steamship Company)
1901: Chartered to Joy Line
1911-1915: Manhattan Navigation Company, New York-Albany
1912: Renamed *Mohawk*
1917: Converted to five-masted schooner
1918: Disappeared at sea

16. Rosalie (a. City of Bridgeport; c. H. C. Rowe and Co.)

Wood screw freight steamer
Tonnage: 500 gross; 340 net

Dimensions: 144.8 x 28.4 x 10.0

Horsepower: 500

1886: Built as freighter for Bridgeport Steamboat Company as *City of Bridgeport*

1899: Sold to Joy Line; renamed *Rosalie*

1900-1902: Chartered to Old Dominion Line for James River service

1902-1905: Spare steamer of Joy Line

1905: Burned in layup in Brooklyn, December

1906: Sold to H. C. Rowe and Company of New Haven and converted to fishing steamer; renamed *H. C. Rowe and Co.*

1922: Burned in Peconic Bay and abandoned

17. *Santiago*

Iron screw passenger and freight steamer

Tonnage: 2,358 gross; 1,695 net

Dimensions: 269.0 x 39.1 x 22.4

Horsepower: 1,376

1879: Built for New York and Cuba Mail Steamship Company (Ward Line)

1906: Sold to Joy Line

1907: Sold to Mallory Line

18. *Seaboard*

Iron screw freighter (passenger accommodations added later)

Tonnage: 662 gross; 563 net

Dimensions: 184.5 x 28.7 x 12.3

Horsepower: 693

1874: Built for Baltimore Steam Packet Company (Old Bay Line)

1898-1900: Used in various Atlantic Coast services

1900-1908: Served on Joy Line

1908-1931: Continued in service with Hartford and New York Transportation Company (successor to Joy Line), on the Merchants Line freight service, New York-Bridgeport

1934: Rebuilt and dieselized as coastwise tanker

19. *Shinnecock (b. Empire State; Town of Hull)*

Steel sidewheel passenger and freight steamer

Tonnage: 1,205 gross; 706 net

Dimensions: 260.0 x 35.0 x 14.3

Horsepower: 1,600

1896: Built for Montauk Steamboat Company

1900-1907: Chartered at various times to the Joy Line

1922: Converted for excursion and ferry service; later renamed *Empire State* and *Town of Hull*

1944: Damaged by hurricane; later abandoned and scrapped

20. Surprise (a. City of Fitchburg; c. Warren)

Wood screw passenger and freight steamer
Tonnage: 821 gross; 433 net
Dimensions: 188.0 x 33.4 x 13.5
1874: Built for New Bedford Line and named *City of Fitchburg* (taken over
    that year by Old Colony Steamboat Company); operated New York-
    New Bedford
1899: Burned
1900: Sold and rebuilt for freight service on the coast of Maine, subsequently
    renamed *Surprise*
1904: Served under charter to Joy Line in February
1905-1907: Spare steamer of Enterprise Line on Long Island Sound, renamed
    Warren
1907: Abandoned and later scrapped

21. Tennessee (b. Romance)

Steel screw passenger steamer
Tonnage: 1,240 gross; 743 net
Dimensions: 245.0 x 38 x 15.8
Horsepower: 2,100
1898: Built for Baltimore Steam Packet Company (Old Bay Line)
1906: Sold to Joy Line
1906-1931: Ran on Joy Line (later Bay State Line), first New York-Fall
    River, then 1907-1931, New York-Providence
1935: Sold to Charles Ellis; converted to excursion steamer; renamed
    Romance; operated out of Boston
1936: Rammed and sunk in Boston harbor by Eastern Steamship liner *New
    York* on September 9

22. Tremont

Wood sidewheel passenger and freight steamer
Tonnage: 1,427 gross; 1,023 net
Dimensions: 260.0 x 37.0 x 12.3
1883: Built for Boston-Portland service
1901: Sold to Joy Line
1901-1904: Joy Line: New York-Providence service
1904: Burned at pier in New York, February 7

23. Virginia (b. Tadousac)

Iron sidewheel passenger and freight steamer
Tonnage: 990 gross; 665 net
Dimensions: 251.0 x 34.7 x 7.9
Horsepower: 800

1879: Built for Baltimore Steam Packet Company (Old Bay Line)

1900: Sold to Joseph Wainwright; later transferred to a variety of short-term owners

1901: Operated under charter on Cape May, New Jersey-Lewes, Delaware route

1901-1902: Chartered to Joy Line

1903: Sold to Richelieu and Ontario Navigation Company for service on St. Lawrence River

1905: Renamed *Tadousac*

1927: Scrapped

B. NARRAGANSETT BAY LINE

1. Chester W. Chapin (b. Meteor)

Steel screw passenger and freight steamer

Tonnage: 2,868 gross; 1,822 net

Dimensions: 312.0 x 64.0 (o.a.) x 16.9

Horsepower: 4,200

1899: Built for New Haven Steamboat Company's Narragansett Bay Line for New York to Providence service

1900: Sold with rest of fleet to New Haven Railroad; placed on New Haven Line

1904-1923: Ran on various lines of the New Haven Railroad's New England Steamship Company, but primarily New York to New London

1923-1927: On summer New York-New Beford line

1928-1937: On all-year New York to Providence line

1938: Sold to Colonial Navigation Company; renamed *Meteor*

1938-1941: Served as spare boat on Colonial Line's Providence service and ran regularly in summer New York-New Bedford

1942: Requisitioned by War Shipping Board

1944-1945: Used under loan by Old Bay Line and by Norfolk and Washington Line on Chesapeake Bay

1948: Scrapped

2. C. H. Northam

Wood sidewheel passenger and freight steamer

Tonnage: 1,436 gross; 1,179 net

Dimensions: 312.0 x 44.0 x 10.0

1873: Built for New Haven Line

1899: Served occasionally on New Haven Line's New York-Providence line

1907: Scrapped

3. Richard Peck (b. Elisha Lee)

Steel screw passenger and freight steamer

Tonnage: 2,906 gross; 1,819 net

Dimensions: 303.3 x 48.0 x 17.8
Horsepower: 2,906
1892: Built for New Haven Line
1899-1900: On New Haven Line's New York-Providence service (Narragansett Bay Line)
1900: Sold with rest of fleet to New Haven Railroad
1900-1920: Served on various lines of New Haven Railroad (marine properties later known as New England Steamship Company) but primarily on New York-New Haven Line
1920-1931: New London Line of New England Steamship Company
1931-1937: Relief steamer of New England Steamship Company
1937-1941: On Meseck Line (excursion steamer line out of New York) primarily on New York-Rye Beach-Bridgeport service
1942-1943: Barracks ship in Newfoundland
1943-1954: Operated by Pennsylvania Railroad on ferry route between Norfolk and Cape Charles; renamed *Elisha Lee*
1954: Scrapped

C. ENTERPRISE LINE

1. Frank Jones (b. Fenimore)

Wood sidewheel passenger and freight steamer
Tonnage: 1,634 gross; 1,078 net
Dimensions: 253.2 x 36.3 x 13.8
Horsepower: 1,200
1892: Built for service on Maine coast: Portland-Machiasport
1905: Sold to Enterprise Transportation Company
1905-1907: Served on Enterprise Line, New York-Fall River
1908: New Hudson Line: New York-Albany
1909-1910: Manhattan Line: New York-Albany
1911-1915: Capital City Line: New York-Albany
1915: Renamed *Fenimore*
1915-1918: Laid up
1918 (April): Chartered to U.S. Navy
1918 (June): Burned in James River, Virginia, a total loss

2. Kennebec (b. Iroquois)

Wood sidewheel passenger and freight steamer
Tonnage: 1,652 gross; 1,271 net
Dimensions: 256.0 x 37.6 x 13.1
Horsepower: 1,400
1889: Built for Kennebec Steamship Company (Boston-Kennebec River); after 1902 part of Eastern Steamship Company
1905: Sold to Enterprise Transportation Company
1905-1907: Enterprise Line: New York-Fall River

1907: Sold to Joy Line (part of United States Transportation Company; later part of Hartford and New York Transportation Company)

1910: Sold to McAllister Brothers

1911-1915: Chartered (later sold) to Manhattan Navigation Company, New York-Albany

1912: Renamed *Iroquois*

1915-1918: Laid up

1918-1919: Carried supplies for U.S. Navy around port of Norfolk, Virginia (temporarily renamed *Iro*)

1919-1924: Laid up in Elizabeth River, Virginia

1924 (approximately): Abandoned and burned

3. St. Croix

Wood screw passenger and freight steamer

Tonnage: 1,993 gross; 1,064 net

Dimensions: 240.7 x 40.4 x 25.9

Horsepower: 2,700

1895: Built for International Steamship Company, Boston-St. John; after 1902 part of Eastern Steamship Company

1906-1907: Enterprise Line, mostly New York-Providence

1907: Reclaimed by Eastern Steamship Company

1908: Sold to Northern Pacific Steamship Company (Seattle-Alaska)

1909: Made trip west; ran briefly on Seattle-Alaska run; chartered for winter run between San Francisco and Los Angeles; burned, a total loss

4. Warren: cf. Surprise, Joy Line

NOTES

PROLOGUE

1. Gordon Newell, *Pacific Steamboats* (New York: Bonanza Books, 1958), p. 80.

2. William Leonhard Taylor, *Productive Monopoly* (Providence, R.I.: Brown University Press, 1970), pp. 131-41.

3. Ibid., pp. 34-40.

1890s

1. J. Howland Gardner, published advance copy of a paper delivered at the annual meeting of the Society of Naval Architects and Marine Engineers, November 11 and 12, 1943.

1899

1. Donald C. Ringwald, *Hudson River Day Line* (Berkeley, Calif.: Howell-North Books, 1965), p. 93.

2. *Providence Board of Trade Journal*, 11, 4 (April 1899), pp. 55-56.

3. Ibid.

4. *Providence Journal*, May 2, 1899, p. 1.

5. Ibid.

6. Ibid.

7. *Marine Journal*, June 17, 1899, p. 2.

8. *Providence Journal*, June 9, 1899, p. 1.

9. *Marine Journal*, July 1, 1899, p. 2.

10. Ibid., June 24, 1899, p. 4.

11. Ibid., July 13, 1899, p. 4.

12. *Nautical Gazette*, January 11, 1900, p. 3.

1900

1. *Nautical Gazette*, February 2, 1905, p. 83.
2. Ibid., April 18, 1907, p. 345.
3. Ibid., February 2, 1905, p. 83.
4. *Marine Journal*, July 8, 1899, p. 2.
5. *Nautical Gazette*, January 25, 1900, p. 8.
6. Ibid., February 8, 1900.
7. *Marine Journal*, February 10, 1900, p. 2; *Nautical Gazette*, February 22, 1900, p. 8.
8. *Providence Journal*, March 26, 1900, p. 8.
9. *Nautical Gazette*, March 22, 1900, p. 3.
10. *Providence Journal*, March 28, 1900, pp. 1, 9.
11. *Marine Journal*, March 31, 1900, p. 2.
12. Ibid.
13. *Nautical Gazette*, April 12, 1900, p. 8.
14. *Providence Journal*, April 21, 1900, pp. 1-3.
15. Ibid.
16. Ibid.
17. Ibid.
18. *Marine Journal*, March 10, 1900, p. 2.
19. Ibid., May 12, 1900, p. 2.
20. *Nautical Gazette*, May 3, 1900, p. 8.
21. Interstate Commerce Commission, Docket 6469, *Application of the New York, New Haven, and Hartford Railroad Company for Permission to Continue Certain Service by Water after July 1, 1914*, 26 vols., Record Group 134, National Archives, Vol. 8., Exhibit 42: Letter from John M. Hall, Vice-President of the New Haven Railroad, to J. M. Williams, Freight Traffic Manager, Marine Division, New Haven Railroad, May 28, 1900.
22. *Marine Journal*, June 23, 1900, p. 2.
23. ICC, Docket 6469: Letter from John M. Hall to Edward G. Buckland, Agent and General Counsel for the New Haven Railroad in Providence, Rhode Island, July 11, 1900.
24. *Providence Board of Trade Journal*, 12, 6 (July 1900), p. 308.
25. *Marine Journal*, August 25, 1900, p. 2.
26. *Nautical Gazette*, August 30, 1900, p. 8.
27. *Marine Journal*, August 25, 1900, p. 2.
28. ICC, Docket 6469: Letter from Robert Haskins, General Freight Agent, Metropolitan Steamship Company, to Percy Todd, Vice-President, New Haven Railroad, July 25, 1901.
29. *Marine Journal*, June 30, 1900, p. 3.
30. Ibid., October 13, 1900, p. 2.
31. *Nautical Gazette*, October 18, 1900, p. 13.
32. Ibid., October 4, 1900, p. 8.
33. Ibid., November 1, 1900, p. 10; June 18, 1901, p. 11.
34. *Providence Journal*, November 2, 1900, p. 3.

35. ICC, Docket 6469: Letter from John M. Hall, President of the New Haven Railroad, to Charles F. Booker, Member of the Board of Directors, New Haven Railroad, n.d.

1901

1. *Marine Journal*, February 2, 1901, p. 2.
2. Ibid., February 9, 1901, p. 2.
3. *Providence Journal*, February 15, 1901, p. 1.
4. *Marine Journal*, January 19, 1901, p. 2; March 2, 1901, p. 2.
5. *Providence Journal*, April 5, 1901, pp. 1ff.
6. Ibid.
7. Ibid.
8. Ibid.
9. Ibid., April 8, 1901, pp. 1ff.
10. Ibid.
11. Ibid., April 5, 1901, p. 10.
12. Ibid., May 1, 1901, p. 1.
13. *Nautical Gazette*, May 30, 1901, p. 10.
14. Ibid.
15. Francis B.C. Bradlee, *Some Account of Steam Navigation in New England* (Salem, Mass.: The Essex Institute, 1920), p. 104; John M. Richardson, *Steamboat Lore of the Penobscot* (Augusta, Me.: *Kennebec Journal* Print Shop, 1941), p. 16.
16. *Nautical Gazette*, June 18, 1901, p. 11.
17. Ibid., July 4, 1901, p. 11; *Marine Journal*, July 13, 1901, p. 2; Taylor, *Productive Monopoly*, p. 159.
18. *Marine Journal*, July 13, 1901, p. 2.
19. Ibid.
20. *Providence Journal*, July 18, 1901, pp. 1ff.
21. Ibid.
22. Ibid.
23. Ibid.
24. ICC, Docket 6469: Letter from Robert Haskins to Percy Todd, July 25, 1901; Letter from Percy Todd to Robert Haskins, September 19, 1901.
25. Ibid.
26. Ibid.
27. *Marine Journal*, August 3, 1901, p. 2.
28. Ibid.
29. ICC, Docket 6469: Letter from Robert Haskins to Percy Todd, July 23, 1901.
30. Ibid., Letter from Robert Haskins to Percy Todd, August 17, 1901.
31. Ibid.
32. Ibid., Letter from Robert Haskins to Percy Todd, July 23, 1901.
33. *Nautical Gazette*, August 29, 1901, p. 11.
34. Ibid., October 24, 1901, p. 11.
35. Ibid., November 14, 1901, p. 11.
36. ICC, Docket 6469: Letter from Robert Haskins to Percy Todd, July 25, 1901.

37. Ibid., Letter from John M. Hall to Percy Todd, July 24, 1901.

38. Ibid., Letter from Robert Haskins to Percy Todd, August 4, 1901.

39. Ibid., Letter from S. M. Prevost, Third Vice-President of the Pennsylvania Railroad to Percy Todd, October 24, 1901.

40. Ibid., Letter from Percy Todd to S. M. Prevost, October 29, 1901.

1902

1. *Nautical Gazette*, January 16, 1902, p. 14.

2. ICC, Docket 6469: Copy of Telegram from M. Rosenbaum to Max Strauss, January 7, 1902.

3. Ibid.

4. Ibid., Letter from Percy Todd to Max Strauss, January 10, 1902.

5. Ibid.

6. Ibid., Letter from Percy Todd to Max Strauss, January 11, 1902.

7. *Nautical Gazette*, February 20, 1902, p. 3.

8. *Marine Journal*, February 1, 1902, p. 2.

9. *Nautical Gazette*, January 14, 1902, p. 15.

10. ICC, Docket 6469: Letter from Percy Todd to F. S. Holbrook, General Freight Agent, New Haven Railroad, December 28, 1901.

11. Ibid., Telegram from Percy Todd to W. B. Thomas of the American Sugar Refining Company, August 5, 1902.

12. Ibid., Telegram from W. B. Thomas to Percy Todd, August 8, 1902.

13. Ibid., Letter from Robert Haskins to Percy Todd, August 20, 1902.

14. Ibid., Letter from W. B. Thomas to Percy Todd, August 21, 1902.

15. Ibid., Letter from Robert Haskins to Percy Todd, August 20, 1902; Telegram from Percy Todd to Robert Haskins, August 21, 1902; Letter from Percy Todd to J. M. Williams, August 21, 1902; Letter from J. M. Williams to Percy Todd, August 23, 1902.

16. Ibid., Letter from Robert Haskins to Percy Todd, August 4, 1902; Letter from Percy Todd to J. M. Williams, August 7, 1902.

17. Taylor, *Productive Monopoly*, p. 160.

18. ICC, Docket 6469: Letter from J. N. King, Jr. (no title given) to I. W. Marshall, Superintendent of Old Colony docks, Newport, Rhode Island, March 12, 1902.

19. Ibid.

20. Ibid., Letter from J. C. Whitney, Second Vice-President, Merchants and Miners Transportation Company, to Percy Todd, July 21, 1902.

21. Ibid.

22. Richardson, *Steamboat Lore of the Penobscot*, p. 31.

23. *Marine Journal*, June 28, 1902, p. 3.

24. Ibid., June 7, 1902, p. 2.

25. *Nautical Gazette*, June 19, 1902, p. 12; ICC, Docket 6469: Letter from Percy Todd to O. H. Taylor, General Passenger Agent, Marine District, New Haven Railroad, n.d.

26. *Nautical Gazette*, July 3, 1902, p. 2; *Providence Journal*, June 28, 1902, p. 1.

27. *Providence Journal*, July 2, 1902, pp. 1-2.

28. Ibid.

29. Ibid.

30. *Marine Journal*, July 26, 1902, p. 2.

31. Ibid., July 12, 1902, p. 2.

32. *Nautical Gazette*, July 10, 1902, p. 8.

33. Ibid., July 24, 1902, p. 8.

34. Ibid., August 14, 1902, p. 10.

35. Ibid., October 2, 1902, p. 12.

36. *Marine Journal*, August 9, 1902, p. 2; ICC, Docket 6469: Letter from C. S. Cavette, Freight Agent in New York, Marine Division, New Haven Railroad, to F. S. Holbrook, n.d.

37. Ibid.

38. *Marine Journal*, August 30, 1902, p. 2.

39. *Nautical Gazette*, August 14, 1902, p. 10.

40. *Marine Journal*, March 15, 1902, p. 2.

41. *Providence Evening Bulletin*, October 11, 1902, p. 1.

42. ICC, Docket 6469: Telegram from Percy Todd to G. L. Conner, General Passenger Agent, Marine Division, New Haven Railroad, October 8, 1902.

43. Ibid., Letter from John M. Hall to Percy Todd, August 9, 1902.

44. Ibid., Letter from Percy Todd to John M. Hall, August 8, 1902.

45. Ibid.

46. Ibid.

47. Ibid.

48. Ibid., Copy of telegram from John M. Hall to Percy Todd, August 9, 1902; Letter from Percy Todd to John M. Hall, August 12, 1902.

49. Ibid., Letter from John M. Hall to Percy Todd, August 9, 1902.

50. Ibid., Letter from Percy Todd to John M. Hall, August 12, 1902.

51. Ibid.

52. Ibid., Letter from J. M. Williams to Percy Todd, August 15, 1902.

53. Taylor, *Productive Monopoly*, p. 161.

54. ICC, Docket 6469, 8, A, 40.

55. Ibid., 6, 5198, Testimony of Adrian Boole, March 13, 1916.

56. Ibid.

57. Taylor, *Productive Monopoly*, p. 162.

1903

1. *Nautical Gazette*, January 22, 1903, p. 8.

2. *Marine Journal*, February 28, 1903, p. 3.

3. *Nautical Gazette*, February 19, 1903, p. 8.

4. Ibid., June 25, 1903, p. 15.

5. *Marine Journal*, August 22, 1903, p. 6.

6. *Nautical Gazette*, August 6, 1903, p. 8.

7. Ibid., November 5, 1903, p. 311; *Marine Journal*, December 26, 1903, p. 4.

8. ICC, Docket 6469: Letter from Percy Todd to Frank Dunbaugh, December 1, 1903.

9. Ibid., Letter from Frank Dunbaugh to Percy Todd, October 20, 1903.

10. Ibid.

11. Ibid., Letter from Percy Todd to Frank Dunbaugh, December 1, 1903.

12. *Marine Journal*, December 12, 1903, p. 5.

13. John L. Weller, *The New Haven Railroad* (New York: Hastings House, 1969), pp. 45-50.

1904

1. *Nautical Gazette*, January 21, 1904, p. 2.

2. Ibid.

3. ICC, Docket 6469: *General Agreement* between the New Haven Railroad and the Joy Steamship Company, October 18, 1902. Cf. Appendix.

4. *Providence Journal*, February 17, 1904, p. 11.

5. *Marine Journal*, April 23, 1904, p. 7.

6. Ibid., March 26, 1904, p. 3.

7. *Nautical Gazette*, April 21, 1904, p. 2.

8. *Marine Journal*, February 6, 1904, p. 2; Taylor, *Productive Monopoly*, p. 169.

9. Taylor, *Productive Monopoly*, p. 169.

10. ICC, Docket 6469, 9, Report of meeting among Percy Todd, J. W. Miller, new General Manager, Marine District, New Haven Railroad, and F. S. Holbrook, in Todd's office, April 4, 1904.

11. Ibid.

12. *Marine Journal*, May 14, 1904, p. 7.

13. ICC, Docket 6469, 9, Letter from Percy Todd to J. W. Miller, May 4, 1904.

14. Ibid., Letter from J. W. Miller to Percy Todd, May 6, 1904.

15. Ibid., Special File, A-22, Letter from F. S. Holbrook to Percy Todd, December 24, 1904.

16. Ibid., 8, Letter from Frank Dunbaugh to Percy Todd, August 12, 1904.

17. Ibid., Letter from Percy Todd to Frank Dunbaugh, August 14, 1904.

18. Ibid., Stockholders' Report, New Haven Railroad, December 22, 1904; *Marine Journal*, December 17, 1904, p. 7; Taylor, *Productive Monopoly*, pp. 167-68.

19. Taylor, *Productive Monopoly*, p. 168; *Marine Journal*, December 17, 1904, p. 7.

20. ICC, Docket 6469: Letter from Percy Todd to Charles S. Mellen, President, New Haven Railroad, December 22, 1904; Letter from Percy Todd to Frank Dunbaugh, December 22, 1904.

21. Ibid., Letter from George L. Conner, Passenger Traffic Manager, New England Navigation Company, to Percy Todd, January 3, 1905.

22. *Marine Journal*, December 24, 1904, p. 2.

1905

1. *Nautical Gazette*, February 23, 1905, p. 154; March 2, 1905, p. 171.

2. Eldredge Collection, The Mariners Museum, Newport News, Virginia.

3. The story of the murder of John Hart as is assembled here has been culled largely from the pages of the *Providence Journal*, the *Providence Evening Bulletin*, the *Fall River Herald*, or the *Boston Globe* for the period of several weeks following

the murder. FBI files on this case were also consulted, but they contained no additional information.

4. Private conversation with Albert Haas, one-time Marine Superintendent, New England Steamship Company.

5. ICC, Docket 6469: Letter from Frank Dunbaugh to Charles S. Mellen, November 23, 1905.

6. *Nautical Gazette*, May 4, 1905, p. 346; May 18, 1905, p. 374.

7. *Marine Journal*, May 6, 1905, p. 2.

8. *Nautical Gazette*, May 18, 1905, p. 374.

9. Ibid.

10. ICC, Docket 6469: Letter from Percy Todd to Charles S. Mellen, May 29, 1905.

11. Ibid., 9, Letter from John Rowland to Percy Todd, June 2, 1905.

12. Ibid., 8, Letter from Percy Todd to Charles S. Mellen, June 14, 1905.

13. Ibid.

14. *Providence Journal*, July 9, 1905, p. 11.

15. Ibid., July 19, 1905, p. 2.

16. Taylor, *Productive Monopoly*, p. 170.

17. *Boston Daily Globe*, February 16, 1906, p. 1.

18. Taylor, *Productive Monopoly*, p. 172.

19. *Nautical Gazette*, October 12, 1905, p. 269.

20. *Marine Journal*, October 7, 1905, p. 7.

21. ICC, Docket 6469: Report of a meeting of the Subcommittee on Waterlines of the Board of Directors of the New Haven Railroad, September 15, 1905.

22. Ibid.

23. Ibid.

24. Ibid.

25. Ibid.

26. Ibid.

27. Ibid.

28. Ibid., Excerpts from Exhibit, ICC No. 11, Docket No. 6469: Financial Transactions of the New York, New Haven, and Hartford Railroad Company. Printed as Senate Document No. 543, 63rd Cong., 2d Sess., pp. 1448-81. Letter from Charles S. Mellen to Stevenson Taylor, March 25, 1905.

29. Ibid., Receipt presented to Stevenson Taylor and signed by Frank Dunbaugh, April 18, 1905.

30. Ibid.

31. Ibid., Letter from Charles S. Mellen to Stevenson Taylor, March 25, 1905.

32. Ibid., Letter from Frank Dunbaugh to Charles S. Mellen, November 23, 1905.

33. Ibid.

34. Ibid.

1906

1. Taylor, *Productive Monopoly*, p. 171.

2. ICC, Docket 6469, 8, Letter from Stevenson Taylor to Charles S. Mellen, October 20, 1906.

3. *Marine Journal*, February 10, 1906, p. 7.

4. Ibid., May 5, 1906, p. 7.

5. Ibid.

6. *Nautical Gazette*, March 22, 1906, p. 20.

7. Ibid., April 19, 1906, p. 292.

8. Ibid.

9. Ibid., February 15, 1906, p. 122; *Marine Journal*, February 17, 1906, p. 3.

10. *Boston Daily Globe*, February 21, 1906, p. 1.

11. ICC, Docket 6469: Letter from George L. Conner to Charles S. Mellen, January 2, 1906.

12. *Nautical Gazette*, April 19, 1906, p. 292.

13. *Marine Journal*, June 9, 1906, p. 7.

14. *Nautical Gazette*, September 27, 1906, p. 222.

15. Ibid., June 14, 1906, p. 437.

16. Ibid., p. 438.

17. Ibid., July 12, 1906, p. 33; *Fall River Daily Herald*, July 7, 1906, p. 7.

18. ICC, Docket 6469, *Report to Stockholders of the United States Transportation Company*, October 21, 1907, p. 6.

19. Roger Williams McAdam, *Commonwealth* (New York: Steven Daye Press, 1959), p. 44.

20. *Marine Journal*, March 10, 1906, p. 7.

21. *Nautical Gazette*, August 9, 1906, p. 104.

22. Ibid., May 24, 1906, p. 362.

23. ICC, Docket 6469: Letter from Frank Dunbaugh to Charles S. Mellen, May 26, 1906.

24. Ibid.

25. Ibid., Letter from Frank Dunbaugh to H. A. Fabian, Assistant to Charles S. Mellen, October 10, 1906.

26. Letter from R. W. Miller to Charles S. Mellen, December 1, 1906.

27. Ibid.

28. Ibid.

29. Ibid.

1907

1. ICC, Docket 6469, 8, Exhibit 6: Excerpt of evidence given by Stevenson Taylor before the Interstate Commerce Commission, April 30, 1914.

2. Ibid.

3. Ibid.

4. *Nautical Gazette*, February 7, 1907, p. 177; *Marine Journal*, February 9, 1907, p. 7.

5. Taylor, *Productive Monopoly*, p. 187; Weller, *The New Haven Railroad*, p. 84.

6. *Fall River Herald*, February 14, 1907, p. 2.

7. *Nautical Gazette*, February 14, 1907, p. 190.

8. *Providence Journal*, February 13, 1907, p. 1.

9. Ibid., p. 6.

10. Ibid., February 18, 1907, p. 2.

11. *Fall River Herald*, February 14, 1907, p. 2.

12. Ibid.

13. *Providence Journal*, February 15, 1907, p. 6.

14. Ibid., p. 1.

15. *Marine Journal*, April 27, 1907, p. 3.

16. Ibid.

17. *Nautical Gazette*, March 21, 1907, p. 277.

18. *Providence Journal*, February 14, 1907, p. 2.

19. Ibid., February 13, 1907, p. 4.

20. Ibid.

21. Ibid.

22. Ibid., February 18, 1907, p. 2.

23. *Marine Journal*, February 16, 1907, p. 3; *Nautical Gazette*, February 21, 1907, p. 214.

24. *Marine Journal*, March 16, 1907, p. 3.

25. Ibid., March 23, 1907, p. 7; *Providence Journal*, March 5, 1907, p. 1.

26. *Marine Journal*, February 23, 1907, p. 7.

27. *Providence Journal*, March 24, 1907, p. 11.

28. *Marine Journal*, March 16, 1907, p. 7.

29. *Nautical Gazette*, April 11, 1907, p. 329.

30. Ibid., July 4, 1907, p. 16.

31. ICC, Docket 6469: *Financial Transactions of the New York, New Haven, and Hartford Railroad Company*, Letter from Frank Dunbaugh to Charles S. Mellen, March 29, 1907.

32. *Marine Journal*, April 13, 1907, p. 7; *Nautical Gazette*, April 11, 1907, p. 328.

33. ICC, Docket 6469, 8, *Steamboat Properties Now Controled by the Hartford and New York Transportation Company*, pp. 17-19.

34. Ibid., *Report to the Stockholders of the United States Transportation Company*, October 21, 1907, p. 1.

35. *Marine Journal*, June 15, 1907, p. 8.

36. Ibid., March 16, 1907, p. 7; *Nautical Gazette*, January 3, 1907, p. 89; ibid., February 28, 1907, p. 230.

37. *Fall River Herald*, August 14, 1907, p. 11.

38. *Marine Journal*, June 29, 1907, p. 7.

39. *Nautical Gazette*, July 4, 1907, p. 3.

40. *Marine Journal*, November 9, 1907, p. 3.

41. Ibid., November 30, 1907, p. 6.

42. *Nautical Gazette*, October 31, 1907, p. 296.

43. Ibid.

44. ICC, Docket 6469: Letter from Stevenson Taylor to Charles S. Mellen, November 24, 1907.

45. Ibid., *Steamboat Properties Now Controled by the Hartford and New York Transportation Company*, pp. 39-40.

46. Ibid., Letter from Charles S. Mellen to Edward D. Robbins, counsel for the New Haven Railroad, September 30, 1907.

47. Ibid., Letter from Stevenson Taylor to Charles S. Mellen, October 10, 1907.
48. Ibid., Letter from Frank Dunbaugh to Charles S. Mellen, October 31, 1907.
49. Ibid., Letter from Charles S. Mellen to Frank Dunbaugh, November 1, 1907.

EPILOGUE

1. Fall River *Herald*, March 26, 1908, p. 4.
2. Ibid., January 24, 1908, p. 2.

BIBLIOGRAPHICAL COMMENT

For an overall picture of steamboating on Long Island Sound, or indeed of steam-boating in general, even after many decades, there are still only two standard works: John H. Morrison, *History of American Steam Navigation* (New York: Stephen Daye Press, 1958), which first appeared in 1903, and Fred Erving Dayton, *Steamboat Days* (New York: Frederick A. Stokes Company, 1925). As Morrison's account ends in 1903, it provides little specific information on the era of the Joy Line, while Dayton's work on the Providence night boats of the period is sketchy and, unfor-tunately, largely inaccurate. Of the four books on Long Island Sound steamboating by Roger Williams McAdam, *The Old Fall River Line* (New York: Stephen Daye Press, 1937 and 1955), *Salts of the Sound* (New York: Stephen Daye Press, 1939 and 1957), *Priscilla of Fall River* (New York: Stephen Daye Press, 1947 and 1956), and *Commonwealth* (New York: Stephen Daye Press, 1959), all are excitingly evocative and abound in information otherwise hard to find, but only the last, *Commonwealth*, is chronologically organized. Another reliable standard work, Francis B. C. Bradlee, *Some Account of Steam Navigation in New England* (Salem, Mass.: The Essex Institute, 1920) deals almost exclusively with steamer lines operating north out of Boston and is therefore a valuable source of information about the steamers brought to Long Island Sound from various Maine coast routes, as is also John M. Richardson, *Steamboat Lore of the Penobscot* (Augusta, Me.: *Kennebec Journal* Print Shop, 1941).

A more recent work, William Leonhard Taylor, *A Productive Monopoly* (Provi-dence, R.I.: Brown University Press, 1970), is especially valuable. Taylor uses his extensive and thorough research into many previously unexplored sources to present new material and new perspectives on Long Island Sound steamboating. Donald C. Ringwald, *Hudson River Day Line* (Berkeley, Calif.: Howell-North, 1965), another more recent study, is now a valuable addition to Morrison and Dayton for material on Hudson River steamboating. Perhaps more importantly, it also provides a model of careful research and interesting narrative which all marine historians might profitably follow and which this author gratefully acknowledges.

Among the periodical materials, an excellent overall study of steamboating on the sound, as well as a wealth of valuable specific information about the steamers of the period in question, is to be found in J. Howland Gardner, "The Development of Steam Navigation on Long Island Sound," No. H-16, *Proceedings* of the Society of Naval Architects and Marine Engineers. Similar material, though less up to date, can be found in Leander N. Lovell, "American Sound and River Steamboats," *Cassier's Magazine*, 12, 4 (August 1897). All of the material regarding the later operations of the sound steamers on Hudson River lines comes from Donald C. Ringwald, "Opposition Night Lines on the Hudson 1908-1915," *Steamboat Bill*, 36, 3, No. 151 (Fall 1979).

The *Nautical Gazette* and the *Marine Journal*, two weekly marine journals published in New York during this era, carry informative articles with details about the construction and specifications of the steamers, as well as regular bulletins on such matters as minor accidents, changes in service, or maintenance. For operation information, assignments of steamers to routes, arrival times, or stories about events aboard the steamers, by far the best sources, however unreliable, are the marine columns of the daily newspapers of the New England ports served by the steamer lines. For this study, the *Providence Journal*, the *Providence Evening Bulletin*, the *Boston Daily Globe*, and the *Fall River Herald* were most frequently consulted.

INDEX

Page numbers in italic indicate photographs.

ABOUT THE AUTHOR

EDWIN L. DUNBAUGH is Professor of History at Hofstra University in Hempstead, New York. He is the author of several books and articles.

Recent Titles in
Contributions in Economics and Economic History
Series Editor: Robert Sobel